SO-BAI-095

Making Oscar
WILDE

Praise for Making Oscar Wilde

'You may not think there is new stuff to learn about Oscar Wilde, but there is—as this book proves. Michèle Mendelssohn has succeeded in throwing new light on Wilde's remarkable American lecture tour. Thoroughly researched and beautifully written, this is a valuable addition to Wildean scholarship.'

Gyles Brandreth, President of the Oscar Wilde Society
and author of *The Oscar Wilde Murder Mysteries*

'*Making Oscar Wilde* is a fresh, exciting, and illuminating study of the construction of celebrity and reputation... The story of St. Oscar will never be the same.'

Elaine Showalter, Professor Emerita of English at Princeton
University and Fellow of the Royal Society of Literature

'An original, meticulously-researched, and beautifully-paced account of how a modern writer invented himself, and was invented, as an international artist-celebrity.'

Declan Kiberd, Professor of Irish Studies at the University
of Notre Dame and author of *Ulysses and Us*

'One of the most devastating, complex, and presently political literary biographies I've ever read.'

Eileen Myles, poet and author of *Chelsea Girls*

'Vividly written, consistently illuminating, and lavishly illustrated, this book is full of surprises, above all in showing how Wilde's Irishness played into the story of race relations in post-Civil War America.'

Michael Gorra, author of *Portrait of a Novel: Henry James
and the Making of an American Masterpiece*

'A scholastic triumph, this highly original book rewrites the story of Oscar's tour of America with new, vivid detail, from fresh, unmined sources. Mendelssohn not only offers us a surprising view of Oscar through the lens of nineteenth-century America, but refocuses the young Wilde for a new generation.'

Franny Moyle, author of *Constance: The Tragic and Scandalous
Life of Mrs Oscar Wilde*

Making Oscar
WILDE

MICHÈLE MENDELSSOHN

OXFORD
UNIVERSITY PRESS

OXFORD
UNIVERSITY PRESS

Great Clarendon Street, Oxford, OX2 6DP,
United Kingdom

Oxford University Press is a department of the University of Oxford.
It furthers the University's objective of excellence in research, scholarship,
and education by publishing worldwide. Oxford is a registered trade mark of
Oxford University Press in the UK and in certain other countries

First Edition published in 2018

Impression: 1

Published in the United States of America by Oxford University Press
198 Madison Avenue, New York, NY 10016, United States of America

British Library Cataloguing in Publication Data
Data available

Library of Congress Control Number: 2017953070

ISBN 978–0–19–880236–5

Printed in Great Britain by
Clays Ltd, St Ives plc

PART THREE, 1883–1900

List of Plates

There is for every man some one scene, some one adventure, some one picture that is the image of his secret life, for wisdom first speaks in images.

– W. B. Yeats

Prologue

What's the Matter with Oscar Wilde?

This book tells the story of a local Irish eccentric called Oscar who became an international celebrity called Wilde. Today, he is one of English literature's most famous authors. Known around the world as Saint Oscar, he is the beloved patron saint of all things witty, decadent, and over the top. With every passing year, his stature seems to grow. But his spectacular career and tragic life didn't just happen. They were made possible by a series of unusual events and unique circumstances that determined his fate and afterlife. Wilde was not born a dramatic genius. Yet he eventually became one through a curious process that began when he visited the United States in 1882. It was the Age of Barnum, an era that rewarded the big, the bold, and the blustering. It was here that Wilde's remarkable rise was set in motion. Like a fairy tale in which a young nobody becomes a somebody, the transformative events of 1882 would divide his life sharply into Before and After. How this happened has long been hidden from history, but new evidence now makes it possible to reveal how Oscar became Wilde.

For a long time, I didn't doubt the legend of Saint Oscar. When I first visited his archives, I was interested in the genius he put into his writings, not his life. What I saw didn't immediately suggest that I should change my focus, but it knocked me sideways and, eventually, it knocked me off course and steered me towards writing this biography. History can be like a jack-in-the box: sometimes it shocks us by intruding on the present and demanding that we re-examine the past we think we know.

It was at the William Andrews Clark Memorial Library, in Los Angeles, that I first laid eyes on the big colour poster titled 'THE AESTHETIC CRAZE' that was to become my obsession in the years that followed. The poster featured Wilde, but not as the man I knew. For starters, he didn't look Irish at all. He was brown-skinned and thick-lipped and had spiky Afro hair. On either side of him, there were two black women. They turned towards him as if drawn by some bizarre mix of sex appeal and scorn, love, and hate. The thin one wore a lovey-dovey look, while the fat one didn't seem to think much of the uppity dandy in her midst. Wilde was a polarizing figure, that much was obvious, yet the caption beneath the drawing hinted at darker ideas and murkier feelings (see Plate 1). It reads:

What's de matter wid de Nigga?
Why Oscar you's gone wild!

The racist gag felt obsolete, like a joke of the you-had-to-be-there variety. Who was the butt supposed to be? Wilde, or the women, or all three? The trio appeared stuck in a shoddy plantation scene that defeated, or at least challenged, the dream of 'going wild,' whatever it was. I suspected there was more to this than a pun on Wilde's name, but what was it, exactly? According to the tiny black lettering at the bottom of the cartoon, Currier and Ives, the venerable New York lithographers, had dreamed up this weird scenario in 1882.

The poster impressed me, but I didn't know what to make of it, so I moved on to another folder of material. No sooner did I open it than six more unfamiliar Oscars stared back at me (see Plate 2). These were six cards small enough to fit into my palm. On each one Oscar had a different ethnicity: he was Irish, Chinese, French, German, black, and, finally, a white American. Like the big Currier and Ives poster, the cards were dated 1882.

Was the year significant?, I wondered.

Was there a pattern here?

And what did these ethnic groups have to do with Wilde anyway?

The six little faces stared back at me like pieces of a puzzle I couldn't solve. How they fit together was a mystery that couldn't easily be explained away. Stumped, I slid the six cards back into their sleeve, handed them back to the librarian, and called it a day.

Years passed, but I couldn't unsee those alternative Oscars. They fascinated me.

What was the matter with Oscar Wilde?
What was the matter with these images?
Whose lives were they really about?
What mattered to the people who made them?
And, most of all, why did this happen?

These questions evolved into a quest to solve the mystery of Wilde's identity. I eventually discovered the answers in libraries and in the collections of private individuals. I found them by digging through rare books, reading unpublished letters, and examining priceless manuscripts. But I also found many answers tucked away in vast online archives and in algorithm-driven databases.

None of this digital treasure trove was available to previous biographers, and it revealed a side of Wilde that nobody had suspected. For over a century, Saint Oscar's secret life lay buried in these unexamined artefacts, hidden from sight and scattered in sprawling repositories located all over the world. Without today's resources, it would have been almost impossible to excavate this forgotten history and bring it to light. The book you are holding in your hands could not have been written before now. Technology's great leap forward has propelled scholarly research into the digital future. The Golden Age of the Archive has arrived.

'The historian of the future, when he sits down to wrestle with the great events of this epoch, is going to have his hands full,' the *New York Tribune* confidently predicted in the spring of 1882.[1] The year was to extinguish some of the age's brightest luminaries, including the naturalist Charles Darwin and the Italian politician Giuseppe Garibaldi, the philosopher Ralph Waldo Emerson, the novelist Anthony Trollope, and the poets Henry Wadsworth Longfellow and Dante Gabriel Rossetti. Yet those twelve months also gave life to the men and women who would help to make the twentieth century properly modern. It saw the births of Virginia Woolf and James Joyce, Igor Stravinsky, the suffragette Sylvia Pankhurst, the painters Georges Braque and Edward Hopper, the psychoanalyst Melanie Klein, and the Hollywood movie pioneer Samuel Goldwyn.

For the United States and Britain, 1882 was electrifying—quite literally. Thomas Edison inaugurated the world's first commercial electric
power plant and, in East London, Britain's first electric tram trundled
down the line. Meanwhile, in the Strand, the newly equipped Savoy
Theatre, the first public building in the world lit entirely by electricity,
reopened with the year's hottest ticket, Gilbert and Sullivan's *Patience;
or, Bunthorne's Bride*.

All this novelty marked a jump towards modernity, yet other events
signalled a longing to preserve the status quo or even go back in time.
The United States's new immigration policies reflected this Zeitgeist.
The 1882 Chinese Exclusion Act shut the door on skilled and unskilled
labourers from China.[2] The same year, another Immigration Act
empowered authorities to deny entry to 'any convict, lunatic, idiot, or
any person unable to take care of himself or herself without becoming
a public charge.'[3] Regardless of such policies, the huddled masses
would continue to land at America's door. The influx of Chinese, Irish,
Jews, and Italians had already begun to change the face of America.
Soon, that fact would also change the face of Oscar Wilde.

Wilde could never have imagined how the year 1882 would transform him and deform his image, or how much it would influence the
rest of his life. Fresh lectures, revealing costumes, non-stop interviews,
tantalizing soundbites, egregious flattery, and dubious politicking—
there was almost no showman's trick that wouldn't be rolled out when
he visited the United States that year.

Making Oscar Wilde tells two stories. One is a revisionist history of
Wilde's early life and rise to fame. You'll see up close the moments
where everything fell to pieces as well as how he put them back
together in a new way, making himself into a modern celebrity in the
process. But as big as Wilde's ambitions were, he was a cog in the
wheels of an even greater machine. So this book's second story is an
intimate history of two of the century's most powerful globalizing
mechanisms—America's ethnic melting pot and Britain's imperial
enterprise. As we shall see, this rigging could grant failures a second
chance, turn whites into blacks, and transform impoverished Irishmen
into wealthy slaveholders who sent their sons to Harvard. Wilde's place
in this system fluctuated dramatically from high to low as he moved
from being part of Ireland and England's elite to being regarded as part
of humanity's dregs in the United States. Nineteenth-century America's
ethnic hierarchies put Irishmen and blacks together at the bottom, a

precarious social position that would make things uncomfortable for Wilde. Instead of the upward mobility he had expected, his sudden social downfall surprised him and forced him to grapple with the New World's values. As he mastered them, he rediscovered his Irishness and his masculinity, and transformed himself into a star.

Wilde fashioned myths around himself and also had myths imposed upon him by others. He benefited from the assistance of story-makers, only a few of whom were household names. This biography brings out of the shadows the men and women whose lives touched his—showmen like P. T. Barnum, Colonel William F. Morse, Colonel Jack Haverly, and Charles Frohman; enemies like the journalist Archibald Forbes and the abolitionist Colonel Thomas Wentworth Higginson; allies like Walt Whitman, Dion Boucicault, Julia Ward Howe, and the editor William Henry Hurlbert. Even the President of the Confederacy, Jefferson Davis, contributed in his way. Each one of this cast was a foil to Wilde, and each contributed to make Wilde's image more vivid.

Intelligence, single-mindedness, and relentless optimism in the face of adversity enabled his early successes in the 1880s. These qualities were to be essential to him again after his imprisonment in 1895 for gross indecency—the bookend to the fairy tale that had begun in 1882. Wilde's unmaking was swift and grim. It was a Cinderella story in reverse: he was stripped of his possessions, publicly humiliated, estranged from his wife and two young sons, imprisoned, and forced to carry out menial tasks and hard labour for two years. Grisly anonymity became essential. He became prisoner C.3.3 and then, after his release, took the name Sebastian Melmoth. He would never recover. His name would be blacked out of acquaintances' diaries and deleted from friends' memoirs.[4] Wilde elided the details of his downfall by saying 'what I suffered then, and still suffer, is not for pen to write or paper to record.'[5] The name he had made for himself had become taboo. But that was still to come. For now he was still at the very beginning, and he was just a clever young man from Ireland on his way to an adventure.

PART ONE
1854–1881

Remember that you've got on your side
the most wonderful thing in the world—
youth! There is nothing like youth…
Youth is the Lord of Life.
Youth has a kingdom waiting for it.

– *A Woman of No Importance*

Chapter 1

Turning Points

From his family, Oscar Wilde inherited two gifts: a love of adventure and a talent for reinvention. The Wildes were a prominent land-owning Ascendancy family and so, by definition, part of the Irish upper classes. Ireland's Protestant Ascendancy had effectively been created by the 1703 'Act to prevent the further growth of Popery.' It was the first of several Penal Laws targeting Irish Catholics that the Irish Parliament passed while it was under British control. By the end of the eighteenth century, the Ascendancy was established.

It was around this time that Oscar's paternal great-great-grandfather, a merchant in eighteenth-century Durham, England, sent his son to Ireland in search of a better life. Ralph Wilde settled in County Roscommon and married up, choosing Margaret O'Flynn for his wife, a girl from a high-ranking Gaelic family. So began the Wilde family's upward rise. One of their sons won the Berkeley Gold Medal at Trinity College Dublin (a prize Oscar would also win, in 1874). Another of their sons became a distinguished physician. This was Thomas Wills Wilde, Oscar's grandfather, who continued the family's ascent by taking the wealthy Miss Emily Fynn of County Galway for his bride. Their Saxon–Celt union was a felicitous one. It yielded a son who was to surpass his father's eminence as a medical authority and who would become Surgeon Oculist to the Queen in Ireland. This was Dr William Robert Wills Wilde, Oscar's father. Unsurprisingly given his genealogy, Oscar's father believed his family's own racial mix to be superior to all others. 'I think there cannot be a better one than that of the Saxon with the Celt,' he said in an address to the British Association.[1]

Born in 1815, by the age of 22 the dark, handsome Dr Wilde was an able physician beloved of his patients (see Plate 3). Although he had never been out of Ireland, he had his English ancestor's love of adventure. As soon as he graduated from medical school, he took a position as personal physician to an invalid gentleman. For nine months they travelled together on a 130-ton yacht 'bending our course wherever climate and curiosity attracted us,' he wrote in his memoir.[2] Their ambitious globetrotting is summarized by the breathless title of the book Dr Wilde wrote en route, *Narrative of a Voyage to Madeira, Teneriffe, and Along the Shores of the Mediterranean Including a Visit to Algiers, Egypt, Palestine, Tyre, Rhodes, Telmessus, Cyprus, and Greece with Observations on the Present State and Prospects of Egypt and Palestine, and on the Climate, Natural History, and Antiquities of the Countries Visited*. Those he met along the way often assumed that, being an Irishman, he must also be a Roman Catholic. He accepted their warm welcome and omitted to inform them that the Wildes were, in fact, Protestants.[3]

At Tenerife, Dr Wilde climbed 1,300 feet up the volcano while smoking a cigar and drinking brandy, then descended into the crater.[4] These exploits earned him a reputation as a daring explorer. On his return, he compared notes with his friend, the eminent naturalist Alexander von Humboldt.[5] By then, Dr Wilde had sold the *Narrative* to a publisher for a healthy £250. Two editions quickly sold out and soon he was receiving invitations to lecture on topics ranging from folklore to mummies and chimp anatomy.[6]

Irish society celebrated him. It would have been easy for him to capitalize on this and become a public lecturer. Instead, he chose to return to medicine and to specialize in diseases of the ear and throat, pursuing his medical studies in London, Berlin, Vienna, and Heidelberg. When he came back to Dublin, his first year of practice as a specialist was lucrative and successful. His excellent reputation soon earned him an appointment as Medical Census Commissioner, a position he held from the 1840s until 1871. During this period he was responsible for cataloguing Ireland's most tragic famines and epidemics. Troubled by the plight of his impoverished countrymen, he established a hospital where they could receive treatment for ophthalmic and aural diseases at no cost. His talents extended beyond medicine. He published highly regarded antiquarian, literary, ethnological, and geographical research, alongside a study of Swift, then out of favour among his countrymen. He was knighted in 1864. 'Whatever you have to do, do it with all your might,' was his motto. Tirelessly energetic, industrious, cosmopolitan, and proudly Irish, Sir William was equal parts scientist, adventurer, and literary artist. He was a true polymath.

Despite his demanding schedule, he also found time to father three illegitimate children before he married Oscar's mother, Jane Francesca Agnes Elgee, in 1851. 'Marriages,' she wrote, 'where life glides on in graceful calm without a discord or the crash of opposing temper, are rare and exceptional.'[7] She gave him three children: William in 1852, Oscar Fingal O'Flahertie Wills in 1854, and, in 1857, a daughter named Isola who would die of fever before her tenth birthday.

Oscar's mother was unconventional, bold, and intellectual: a good match for his father (see Plate 4). She was born in Dublin to a respected Protestant Irish family. Her father disappeared to India soon after her birth, leaving baby Jane's mother to scratch out a life by renting mouldy Dublin rooms.[8] Regardless, young Jane pretended she was descended from Dante and so adopted the name 'Speranza.' Though most put her date of birth at 1821, she was always vague about it—just as her younger son would be about his. During her pregnancy with Oscar she was certain that her baby would be a girl, so she dressed him in girls' clothes until he was about 10 years old (see Plate 5).[9] Speranza's unusual outlook influenced her approach to motherhood in other ways, too. She treated her two boys like little gentlemen, and from an early age encouraged Willie and Oscar to sit at the dinner table with adults and partake in the conversations.[10]

In 1864, Speranza published her own *Poems*, sending her literary progeny into the world with a patriotic dedication to her two sons: 'I made them indeed, speak plain the word COUNTRY. I taught them, no doubt, that a country's a thing men should die for at need!'[11]

That same year, Oscar moved from the family home in Dublin (presumably, leaving behind his dresses) to board at Portora Royal School, set high on a hill a hundred miles away. In the classrooms of Portora, one of Ireland's best schools, Oscar stood out because of his tremendous memory, advanced reading skills, and prodigious intellect. His first surviving letter was written to his 'Darling Mama' on his father's monogrammed stationery, and confirms him as a serious-minded 13-year-old, who requested the *National Review*, and politely enquired after his mother's publisher.[12] Yet this precocious young man was also a boy at heart. In the same letter, he babbled cheerfully about a regatta, a game of cricket, and a luxurious hamper of grapes, pears, and blancmange sent by his father.

Women who married men of genius, Speranza believed, should be smiling angels who gave up their lives 'with sublime self-immolation.'[13] Yet she herself was anything but self-effacing. 'Jane has some heart,' her uncle thought, 'but the love of self is the prominent feature of her character.'[14] She despaired of women's political invisibility and declared that they needed to be trained to be self-reliant and assertive if they were to have nobler, freer, and more dignified lives.[15] What seemed like vanity to her uncle may look more like self-confidence today. Although Speranza dressed in an old-fashioned way, she had some rather avant-garde ideas about men and women. At the time, a woman's reputation was thought to be as fragile as a glass bauble. Such conventions didn't matter much to Speranza, who had survived the private scandal of being caught *in flagrante* with a married man before she herself had married Oscar's father.[16] Men, Speranza said, should have 'courteous manners and splendid sins.'[17] Her husband's unfaithfulness had confirmed what she already believed: marriage was no impediment to flirtation.

In her turbulent youth, Speranza was much moved by the Great Famine of 1845–9, which claimed the lives of more than three-quarters of a million people. Since the start of the century, there had been fourteen famines. Irish peasant life was precarious and relied upon the potato for its staple food. When fungus destroyed the crop in 1845, returned with full force in 1846, and struck again in 1848–9, the starvation and disease were overwhelming. The British response to the crisis was delayed and widely thought to be negligent. Eventually measures were taken to distribute food and coordinate public works and price controls. The Famine marked a crisis point that transformed the nation, galvanizing change and propelling modifications in agriculture, economics, and, ultimately, politics. The calamity also led to massive emigration and demographic decline. By the early twentieth century, Ireland's population was half what it had been in the early 1840s.

The nineteenth-century flow of Irish to America was not limited to peasants or Catholics. Many from the Ascendancy went too. Oscar's maternal and paternal relations were among the earliest. On his father's side, there had been Richard Henry Wilde, a distant relation who had emigrated to the American South at a young age, risen to the rank of United States Congressman, and, eventually, owned slaves and a Florida sugarcane plantation.[18] Speranza's eldest brother, John Kingsbury Elgee, emigrated to the United States as a young man and spent the rest of his life there, using his inheritance to buy a vast Louisiana plantation and a workforce of slaves. He rarely figures in Wilde biographies, yet he was to play a small but meaningful role in helping his nephew, Oscar, gain credibility in the New World.

As well as increasing emigration, the Great Famine exacerbated Anglophobia in Ireland. The Young Ireland movement, which Wilde's mother enthusiastically joined, romanticized heroism and violence against the English oppressor. 'The long pending war with England has actually commenced,' she announced on 22 July 1848.[19] 'Oh! for a hundred thousand muskets glittering brightly in the light of heaven.'[20] Young Irelanders congregated around *The Nation* newspaper and many of its propagandists were friends of the Wilde family. Out of necessity, they wrote in English. *Dublin University Magazine*, where Wilde would place some of his first pieces, was associated with Young Ireland's ideology.[21]

Young Ireland's influence was largely rhetorical, despite its proponents' arguments for cultural and linguistic nationalism. The Famine tested Young Irelanders' romantic and nationalistic declarations. Though Wilde's father was sympathetic to the cause, he declared himself a Unionist when pressed. Fuelled by martial and republican rhetoric, Young Ireland's extremist faction concocted a conspiracy theory and accused Westminster of causing mass death by neglect. The movement was crystallized less in religious than in racial terms, as a struggle against foreign domination, with Thomas Osborne Davis, its unofficial leader, piecing together a dubious picture of Celtic racial superiority alongside the virtuous contributions of 'Norman blood and Westminster values.'[22] This racial story was to play its part in the anti-Irish response to Wilde in America.

In the autumn of 1871, just before his seventeenth birthday, Oscar began a three-year classics course at Trinity College Dublin, a bastion of Anglicanism and a verdant imitation of Oxford and Cambridge's older colleges.[23] By all accounts he was academically successful at Trinity but socially unremarkable. His bearing was partly to blame. Standing six feet four inches tall, his frame still seemed too small for his puppy-fat body, and he sometimes had trouble controlling his ungainly movements. His incongruous features—a smooth face, mild blue eyes, and a graceful nose sloping down to voluptuous lips—looked as though they were borrowed from a female relation. His college rooms were dirty and topsy-turvy. His classmates thought him clever but mopey. He rarely had guests.

Despite his ability to cause a stir later in life, Wilde's years at Trinity seem to have been full of study, not controversy. But those who thought him gifted only with brains, not brawn, were swiftly taught not to underestimate his physical strength.[24] When a classmate sneered at one of his poems, Wilde's face fired with hatred, and before long he had beaten his critic in a fistfight. Throughout his life, Wilde's extraordinary muscular might came as a surprise to those who encountered him. Some years later, an American put it best. 'That fellow is some art guy,' the cowboy said, 'but he can drink any two of us under the table and afterwards carry us home two at a time.'[25] Wilde left Trinity with the Berkeley Gold Medal for Greek and a reputation as an excellent classics scholar. This opened the way to Oxford, where he arrived the day after his twentieth birthday, to begin his second university career.

'The two great turning-points in my life were when my father sent me to Oxford, and when society sent me to prison,' Wilde said when he looked back on his life.[26] By then he had become the toast of English society, and he did not wish to remember how uncertain his fate had once been, nor did he mention that Oxford was to be an encore more than a beginning. At Oxford, he chose to read Greats, a famously challenging combination of Graeco-Roman literature, philosophy, and ancient history. Greats was the only course of study at Oxford, Wilde said, 'where one can be, *simultaneously*, brilliant and unreasonable, speculative and well-informed, creative as well as critical, and write with all the passion of youth about the truths which belong to the august serenity of old age.'[27] In choosing this course, he was choosing to return to the classical subjects that had already earned him a distinction at Ireland's leading university. Wilde rarely spoke of the head start he had on his English peers. It was a minor omission, but an advantageous one. Though Oxford proved crucial for him, his academic performances were rehearsed before he arrived in England, and this allowed him to focus on developing his personality, his poetry, and an artistic philosophy.

In autumn 1874, he was one of sixteen new students entering Magdalen College. Across the university, there were nearly four hundred freshmen that term. This was where he would make his mark socially, adopting a personal style that would later ink him indelibly into English cultural life. A fifteenth-century masterpiece of honeyed stone, Magdalen is one of the most beautiful Oxford colleges, and here, in a picturesque setting on the banks of the Cherwell, Wilde was determined to make a social splash. In some circles he became known as 'a personality.'[28] Wilde's golden reputation was enhanced by the glow of a College scholarship. The rumours that he had already scooped 'medals and things' as a sensitive scholar of Greek poetry also helped.[29]

Oxford made a fast and permanent impression on him, and he was only too glad to sit at the feet of the nineteenth century's most significant thinkers. He squeezed in to hear the Slade Professor of Art, John Ruskin, whose lectures were filled to capacity. They were thrilling events, and Ruskin's aesthetics deeply impressed Wilde. A. E. Housman, then an undergraduate, drew a vibrant portrait of the man in action. 'This afternoon Ruskin gave us a great outburst against modern times,' Housman wrote.[30] To make a point about the changing English landscape, Ruskin put a sheet of glass over an 1832 Turner painting of Leicester at sunset. As he lectured, decrying the noxious effects of industrialization on the town, he grabbed a paintbrush and amended the painting accordingly, much to the delight of his spectators. With a few strokes of his brush, the pretty stepping-stones of *Leicester Abbey, Leicestershire* were replaced with an iron bridge, and the water that flowed beneath it turned indigo blue by a local factory's noxious effluent. Then, by adding another brushstroke, the water curdled with soap. The fields beyond were set aflame. Their scarlet tongues lapped at the billowing clouds of smoke overtaking Turner's sky. This done, Ruskin dramatically threw down his brush, turned to face the audience, and received a thunderous ovation.[31]

To undergraduates like Wilde, Ruskin and the absent-minded, reclusive essayist Walter Pater were local celebrities whose intellectual reputations brought éclat to their education. Oxford dons' quirks were legendary and part of university lore. Pater had once stopped High Street traffic for the pleasure of stroking a cat. On one occasion, Ruskin was seen ambling through the streets with an arm draped on the shoulder of Prince Leopold, Queen Victoria's youngest son. The Slade Professor was so absorbed in their conversation that his black lecturer's gown drooped then fell off his shoulders, but he continued unaware, the gown trailing behind him and gathering a dusty grey cloud as he walked along with his royal student. Artistic, good-looking, and a follower of fashion, the mustachioed Prince Leopold captured the eye of many, including the Dean of Christ Church's daughter, Alice Liddell, the inspiration for Lewis Carroll's *Alice in Wonderland*.[32]

Although Wilde had to compete for attention with these local stars, he made an impressive start and swiftly gained an intellectual standing among the undergraduates. With the benefit of three years' university training already, he was more widely read, mature, and mentally prepared than those around him. Nevertheless, he liked to give the impression of precocity and was coy when asked his age, which he would sometimes casually reduce by as much as four years. To keep up the appearance that he was one of the cleverest men in Oxford, he was rarely seen working. He secreted himself away to study, the better to pose as if his brilliance came effortlessly. *Sprezzatura*—the dashing nonchalance that was taken as a mark of his genius—came at the expense of hard swotting. Being exceptional took practice.

What most set Wilde apart was his Irishness. 'You ought to hear him talk!' his English friends told the students who had not yet met him.[33] One of Wilde's chums, William Ward, fondly remembered his allure. 'There was something foreign to us, and inconsequential, in his modes of thought,' Ward said, 'just as there was a suspicion of a brogue in his pronunciation, and an unfamiliar turn in his phrasing. His qualities were not ordinary and we, his intimate friends, did not judge him by the ordinary standards.'[34] Those who talked with him found his 'extraordinary conversational abilities' added extra sparkle to his 'attractive personality,' as David Hunter-Blair noted.[35] George Macmillan, an old Etonian who travelled with Wilde during the holidays, called him 'aesthetic to the last degree,' passionate about sallow colours and William Morris wallpaper, and 'capable of talking a good deal of nonsense thereupon, but for all that a very sensible, well-informed and charming man.'[36]

For all his prominence as an Irishman in Oxford, Wilde conformed outwardly to the manners of the English gentlemen around him by adopting their modes of dress and, eventually, diction. He delighted in aristocratic society, and enjoyed mingling with the sons of the great. 'Oxford gave him the opportunity, which Dublin would never have done, of coming to the front' of English society, one of his fellow Magdalen scholars observed.[37] 'The friends he made there were of great use to him afterwards.'

Wilde didn't forget his family or Ireland, though he put the Irish Sea between them and himself. In his first term, he translated into a poem an excerpt from *The Clouds*, Aristophanes' satire of sophistry and social aspiration, and published it in *Dublin University Magazine*, where 'Chorus of Cloud-Maidens' became his first publication. Though he placed it in an Irish periodical and signed himself 'Oscar O'F. Wills Wilde,' he subscribed the poem 'Magdalen College, Oxford' to subtly indicate his new cultural cachet.[38] Although he wanted to be English, he had no wish not to be Irish. Shrewdly, he chose to be both.

Despite his friends' fascination with his brogue, it progressively disappeared. 'I wish I had a good Irish accent,' he said in later life, regretting the loss and explaining that 'my Irish accent was one of the many things I forgot at Oxford.'[39] Though he did not forget his roots, he certainly overlooked them from time to time. Rather than acknowledging that he came from the heart of Georgian Dublin, he posed as a country gentleman born with a deerstalker on his head and a rifle in his hand. In letters, he rhapsodized about Ireland's 'wild mountainous country, close to the Atlantic and teeming with sport of all kinds.'[40] In the summer of 1876, when he was 22, he told William Ward that he was enjoying himself by fishing 'heaps of sea-trout' and killing 'a lot of hares.' He was accompanied on that expedition by Frank Miles, an artist with whom he would later share a house in London. Miles had never fired a gun in his life. 'I hope to make him land a salmon and kill a brace of grouse,' Wilde said.[41] The hunting trip was memorable for other pursuits, as well. He gushed about his first sweetheart, the '*exquisitely pretty*' grey-eyed Florence Balcombe.[42] She was 'just seventeen with the *most perfectly beautiful face I ever saw*.'

Styling himself a playboy and hunter, he gave the impression that he had no time for writing. 'I have been too much *occupied with rod and gun for the handling of the quill* (neat and Pope-like?)' he declared, with an interrogatory turn that showed that he rarely stopped thinking about literary matters.[43] His allusion hints at the poet Alexander Pope's gun-obsessed squire, who likes hunting more than he loves his mistress. The dominant note in these early letters is often confessional self-satire. Oscar-as-squire was a playful, camp affectation.

For Oxford's Victorian undergraduates, university life and educational demands seldom interfered with social engagements. 'Englishmen,' wrote one Oxford don, 'hardly regard the University as a place of learning and education; they dwell persistently on the social advantages of the place, and send their sons here to "make friends."'[44] This suited many of the tutors, who were not overly concerned with the education of undergraduates. Even when tutorials took place, some dons took more interest in filling themselves from tankards than in filling their charges with knowledge. Many dons saw their students as a distraction from their own pursuits. Sometimes undergraduates would arrive for a tutorial to be greeted only by a closed door pinned with a flimsy note on which a flimsier excuse was hastily scrawled. One winter, for instance, a student discovered that his tutorial had been cancelled at the last minute. 'Gone skating,' the message explained.[45] The icy Cherwell obviously had more appeal than teaching.

Wilde didn't care for the activities that fascinated other students: sport, games, politics, and music left him cold. A college cartoon captured his feelings about 'Aesthetics v. Athletics' by showing him horrified, in an awkwardly angular pose amid a field of rushing athletes (see Plate 6). Wilde preferred to hold court behind closed doors, in his college rooms. As a raconteur, he restricted himself to the private audiences of suppers, salons, and tutorials, where he could dominate conversations. Some of his peers resentfully described him as 'a clever talker of the monopolist type,' but from these modest social ventures he gained an outsize reputation that went towards satisfying his life's aim of attracting fame.

Despite these ambitions, he did not seek out large groups and vigorous public debates, nor did he distinguish himself as an orator. While his contemporary, Herbert Henry Asquith, was making his mark as President of the Oxford Union, the resonantly panelled debating chamber was not Wilde's haunt. The Union was effectively Oxford's school for public speaking, the place to learn how to become a polished orator who could hold forth on almost any topic. The tradition of Union Presidents going into politics was already firmly established, and Asquith would become Prime Minister during the First World War.[46] Union speeches, like those given in Parliament, were expected to sound spontaneous even when they were carefully composed and intensely rehearsed.[47] At the Union, how much a smooth talker actually knew about a subject mattered little because the students who interrupted him with corrections were inevitably booed and hissed into silence. Style, not substance, was paramount.

By then Wilde already cared deeply about style. He was no wallflower, but he was still a scholar at heart. His preference for speaking off-the-cuff at intimate get-togethers originated in the Dublin salons of his childhood. His Oxford gatherings were academic versions of the dimly lit evenings hosted by his mother, a consummate performer whose everyday attire sometimes resembled fancy dress. In her at-homes, she staged herself by matching her magniloquence with head-dresses, Celtic jewellery, and vermillion dresses. Majestic and eccentric, Speranza cut a remarkable figure.

All her flamboyance and self-dramatization were an inspiration for her son. At Magdalen, Wilde showed himself off by hosting cosy soirées with music, tobacco, and gin-and-whisky cocktails. The College help was hard pressed to keep up with the delicate refinement his soirées demanded. 'I bought Venetian glass when I was at college, and for the first term my servant broke one glass every day, and a decanter on Sunday,' Wilde said, 'but I persevered in buying them, and during the succeeding terms of my whole stay at college he did not break a single piece.'[48] Unlike his grimy student digs in Dublin, Wilde's rooms in Magdalen became an exotic setting for these parties. With decorations of blue-and-white china, artistic bibelots, statuettes and photos of the Pope and Cardinal Manning, the effect was eccentric and—crucially for a young man determined to impress—memorable. 'Things of beauty,' Wilde scrawled in the commonplace book he then kept, 'come in a scheme of the noblest education.'[49]

With larger-than-life parents like Sir William and Speranza, Wilde had a lot to live up to. His greatest fear was that he would be a flop. The saddest word, to his ears, was 'Failure!' Wilde's family had given him a terrific start. Both his mother and father were embedded in Ireland's recent history. Yet Wilde's own plans were far from definite. On a questionnaire asking 'What is your aim in life?,' the 23-year-old responded in lazy, looping handwriting with a vague wish for 'success: fame or even notoriety.'[50]

Chapter 2

Do You Find the World Very Hollow?

At Oxford, Wilde took his first steps towards fame, gaining a reputation that spread beyond the student body to a few of the professors. A Balliol College don described him as 'a brilliantly clever scholar, who had strangely good taste in art and in humanity.'[1] When it came to clothes and grooming, however, Wilde wasn't quite so gifted. As an undergraduate, he didn't yet know how to dress with finesse, but he knew how to get noticed, and that was what mattered. The 1875 *Oxford and Cambridge Undergraduate's Journal* satirized him as the outlandishly dressed aesthete O'Flighty (a play on O'Flahertie, his unambiguously Irish middle name) and poked fun at his garish clothes and uncombed hair. His mother enjoyed signalling her Irishness by wearing head-to-toe green, and she may have been responsible for teaching young O'Flahertie to love loud shirts, such as the scarlet and lilac coloured ones he sported as a teenager.[2] Not for him the subtleties of English menswear with its preference for muted tones. In his second year at Oxford, in the spring of 1876, he posed for a photographer with his Magdalen chum William Ward (see Plate 7). Both wore tweeds and derby hats, but while William sported a sober dark check, Oscar selected a large broken pattern overlaid in lighter contrasting colours. He looked more like a try-hard than a sophisticate. In later years, he became adept at dressing with a lighter touch; a green carnation in his buttonhole would become all the fashion he needed.

'From Spring Days to Winter,' the second poem Wilde published, told of springtime love, but it was in the warmer months of 1876 that Wilde's affections blossomed once again.[3] That summer, William Ward's mother and two sisters visited him in Oxford, and Wilde became infatuated with Miss Gertrude Ward. The splendid June weather was ideal for the ladies' visit. Naturally, William's sisters wanted to meet his best friend, Oscar. The gentlemen took the Miss Wards around the colleges. Together they rode on horseback to the nearby village of Radley for tea and lawn tennis, and Wilde entertained them at a private dinner at Magdalen. On another occasion the ladies joined a dozen Magdalen men and their relatives on a picnic visit to the grounds of Blenheim Palace.

The ladies were not disappointed by Wilde's talk, or by his fantastic adaptations of classic menswear, which made him look like an Englishman reflected in an Irishman's funhouse mirror. 'He never looked well-dressed; he looked "dressed up," ' an acquaintance noted.[4] After spending a few days in Wilde's company the younger sister, Florence, had made up her mind about him. She had decided he was a foolish, pretentious fellow. Meanwhile, her older sister, Gertrude, seemed to be falling for Oscar. Florence's diary captures marvellous vignettes of life at Oxford, including Wilde's spirited but inept flirtation with her sister. A thoughtful observer of the world, Florence preferred to watch and listen when, she felt, 'I had not got much to talk about.'[5] She spoke her mind in her private journal, however, detailing her sister's fibs or a friend's 'abominable' cheating at croquet, and sharply judging those she deemed conceited or dull. The perceptive 17-year-old Florence watched as Oscar jostled his way to her sister's side whenever possible—at dinner, on a dray wagonette, in a hayfield, during the picnic at Blenheim—and made copious notes.[6] Florence called Oscar a 'shocking' horseman and observed that whenever he tried to impress Gertrude with his manoeuvres he almost always fell off.[7] She thought Oscar and Gertrude's romantic billing and cooing was terribly silly (she called them 'spoony'), and she got a kick out of eavesdropping on their conversations.

Her sniggering was not as subtle as she believed. One day, Wilde turned his attention to her. *Florence*, he asked, *do you find the world very hollow?*[8] His question might have been intended to stop her fun, but it sounded deliciously strange to her, which is probably why she wrote it down. In a few years' time, Gilbert and Sullivan's aesthetic spoof, *Patience*, would be full of faux-intellectual posing such as this. Wilde was assumed to be the model for Bunthorne, the poet who is the show's butt.

'I am pleased with thee,' Bunthorne tells a pretty girl, 'you are not hollow. *Are* you?'[9] The title of the conceited poet's signature piece was none other than 'Oh, Hollow! Hollow! Hollow!' When Bunthorne declaims the poem, lady aesthetes swoon with delight as if he has cast a spell over them. They think the poem is a masterpiece, but Patience, the simple maiden, has the courage to speak what everyone else in the audience is already thinking. 'Well,' she says, 'it seems to me to be nonsense.' The jig was up: Bunthorne became a byword for those who were full of themselves. Gilbert and Sullivan wouldn't have seen Florence's diary, but they shared her low opinion of Wildean types. Indeed, the convoluted poem they wrote for Bunthorne is actually a lavatorial joke about nature's call. 'Oh, Hollow! Hollow! Hollow!' is an elaborate description of laxatives.

On a warm June evening during her Oxford visit, Florence Ward was strolling near Christ Church, hoping to catch a glimpse of His Royal Highness Prince Leopold, a student of the college. He didn't appear, but Florence wasn't disappointed because she saw another student whose fame rivalled the Prince's. 'Saw Christian Cole (Coal?) also (the nigger),' she scribbled in her diary that night, immortalizing the name of one of the university's first black African students.[10]

It was exciting to see this student celebrity in the flesh. Although she had certainly never seen a black Oxford student, she had probably seen other blacks before. The port city of Bristol, where Florence lived, had been the second largest centre of the slave trade in the eighteenth century, and still had a significant black British population.[11] Outside of London, Liverpool, and Bristol, white Victorians rarely met blacks. Although Florence was more worldly than most, her notetaking evidences the bogus racial notions then in circulation, and shows how fascinated whites were by dark-skinned people. For instance, she had recently transcribed the Bishop of Ely's ghost story about a young black servant who haunted his mistress's London home after she hit him for speaking out of turn. 'It is a known fact,' the Bishop declared, 'that although negroes have such tremendously thick skulls that they can bear almost any blow on their heads, yet the slightest blow, comparatively speaking, on their chests will kill them.'[12]

On 21 June 1876, three days after she had first seen Christian Cole, Florence went to Commemoration, the annual celebration of the university's founders and benefactors. This was more than another occasion for pomp and circumstance: it was an opportunity for Oxford to flaunt its ties to national and imperial powers. Honorary degrees were given to the returning Governor General of India, to Sir Salar Jung (the Prime Minister of Hyderabad), to Lord John Manners (an MP in Disraeli's Conservative cabinet), and to the explorer Verney Lovett Cameron (the first European to make an east–west journey across Africa). The honours awarded to student work aligned with Britain's imperial prerogatives as well: George Smyth Baden-Powell won an essay prize for *The Political and Social Results of the Absorption of Small States by Large*. Later, Powell's younger brother, Robert, would found the Boy Scouts and make it part of his social mission to turn boys into men who bestrode the Empire.

In the Sheldonian Theatre, Florence listened to the students sing 'For he's a jolly good fellow' as a very bored-looking Prince Leopold slouched into view and was awarded an honorary Doctorate of Civil Law.[13] By now Florence was less interested in the Prince than in the dark young man students referred to as 'King Cole.' Though she scanned the Theatre for him, she didn't see him. The weather at Commemoration was withering, and the ceremony tedious and long. Suddenly there was a rumpus in the stalls. Christian Cole had entered the Sheldonian and stood in the middle of the auditorium, where hundreds of eyes fixed on him. The bespectacled 24-year-old was a handsome, serious-looking young man. Born in Africa and descended from a slave, he was the adopted son of the Reverend James Cole of Waterloo, Sierra Leone.[14] He began his studies in 1873, a year ahead of Wilde, and studied on the same course, Greats. Since Greek and Latin classics were at the heart of British public school education, most of Cole's peers had been taught to a very high standard before entering Oxford. In Sierra Leone, Cole had not been nearly so well prepared for this course. In addition, he didn't have many of the material advantages of his peers. To save money, he didn't join a college.[15] He worked throughout his degree to supplement his income, giving music lessons and tutoring candidates for their first BA examination, a test of the work they had done at school.[16] While Wilde preened within Magdalen's golden walls, Cole sought public audiences by giving speeches at the Oxford Union. He was determined, ambitious, and exceptionally brilliant. Whatever disadvantages he faced, Cole showed what he was made of by gaining a degree in Oxford's blue-ribbon subject.

Three cheers for Christian Cole! A great hurrah echoed throughout the hall.[17] The ceremony continued, punctuated by good-humored anarchy, undergraduate antics, and more hurraying.

Three cheers for Mr Disraeli!
For the university rowing crew!
For Captain Webb (who had recently swum the Channel)!
But the crowd was not always in agreement. When someone cried out *For women's rights!*, only a few cheered and a call *For the Slave Circular!* (the debate about the position of fugitive slaves under international law) met with groans.[18]

Florence's eyes were focusing intently on the scene and taking it all in. From her seat in Sir Christopher Wren's elegant Sheldonian Theatre, she had a bird's-eye view of the circular, concentric rows of seats. From the sketch she made of it in her diary, the circles looked like a galactic map of the great and the good with one dark star at its centre, which she labelled 'Christian Coal [*sic*].'[19] From her point of view on the theatre's outermost rim, she could see all the undergraduates, the Liddells of Christ Church, the University Vice-Chancellor, and Sir Salar Jung. To her mind, all of them—even Prince Leopold—seemed to orbit around Cole. Seated in this bastion of the British Empire, Cole appeared to be the centre of gravity.[20] Later, Florence returned to Magdalen's cloisters to have her photograph taken with the students. She posed in the centre of the group while Wilde, dressed in a sober dark suit and bowler hat, hovered on the periphery.

If Wilde was in some respects an exotic outsider at Oxford, Cole's ethnic difference was the more marked. When white Victorians saw people of colour, they often reached for stereotypes or gawped. Even real African kings were ridiculed. In 1879, when British forces invaded Zululand—an independent southern African realm half the size of Ireland—the *Oxford and Cambridge Undergraduate's Journal* portrayed Wilde as 'O'Flighty' sending the 'barbaric' Zulu King Cetewayo two gifts.[21] The first was a few lines of O'Flighty's poetry (quoted directly from Wilde's poem 'Ravenna'). The second gift was a case of eau de cologne and a polite request to ensure his men 'are properly scented before going into action.' Three years later, when the real King of Zululand came to visit Queen Victoria and Prime Minister Gladstone, he was appalled at British behaviour. 'I do not care to be made a show of,' King Cetewayo said of the massive audiences who came to stare. 'If English people have never seen a black man before I am sorry. I am not a wild beast, I did not come here to be looked at.'[22]

But white Victorians could not help themselves, it seems. For most of them, seeing blacks was not a common occurrence and probably exceedingly rare. From the mid-sixteenth century, there were black people in Britain and, by the eighteenth century, there were thousands—an unprecedented level that would remain unsurpassed until after the Second World War.[23] Historians estimate London's black servant population to have been between 10,000 and 30,000 by the end of the eighteenth century.[24] With the abolition of the slave trade in 1807, it became illegal for slaves to accompany their owners to Britain.[25] The 1838 emancipation of slaves throughout the empire gave rise to decades of politicking, appropriation, and conflict. As a result, millions of people of colour became British 'subjects' and it is impossible to say exactly how many black people lived in Victorian Britain because no systematic records were kept.[26]

The few census statistics we have nevertheless paint a striking picture of how rare a Sierra Leonean like Christian Cole was. In England and Wales in 1871 only one person in 225 was foreign-born. That's roughly 0.44 per cent of the population. People from Africa and Egypt counted for less than 0.24 per cent of the foreigners in Britain. Of these 'foreign-born' people few were black, many were ethnically European, and most did not stand out as visible minorities.[27] A decade later, the figures had hardly budged.[28] By 1881, the total population in England and Wales was nearly 26 million, of which only 258 people were born in Africa, like Cole. Of those 258 people, 196 lived in London. The remaining 62 African-born people were sprinkled throughout the rest of England and Wales. Imagine how unlikely it would be to encounter one of them. So how much first-hand experience did the average white Victorian have of black Africans? Probably not much, especially outside of London, Liverpool, and seaports like Bristol, Portsmouth, and Plymouth.[29] Cole was more than a visible minority. He was a statistical blip, an outlier.[30]

As an Irishman at Oxford, Wilde's privileged life as an undergraduate contrasted sharply with Cole's. Despite the competition Oscar faced from more exoticized contemporaries at Oxford, he was creating a scene around himself. He furnished it with paradoxes, witticisms, and nonsenses. By letting his life speak for him, he created a story in which he was inevitably the central character. The story was not to be without misfortune, however. Before the end of Wilde's second year, in the spring of 1876, his father died. Sir William and his son had not been close but had maintained a respectful relationship. Wilde eulogized him in 'Lotus Leaves,' a poem that was a 'herald of my love to Him . . . lying far away | Beyond the reach of human moan.'[31]

A brief but telling testimony of his affection came three decades later, around the time of the anniversary of Sir William's death. Wilde gave his father the credit for launching his first significant self-transformation. For it was his father, Wilde said, who had sent him to Oxford.[32] Transformational departures from Ireland defined nineteenth-century Irish history, but Sir William's gift was a personal one. By sending his son abroad, he gave Oscar a taste of the experience he had had himself when he was a young Irishman venturing out on the high seas. He also showed his son the reputation-making powers of international adventures.

Sir William's death impelled Wilde to make more of his own life. In 1876, as his second undergraduate year came to a close, he vowed his life would not be in vain. Yet the loss of his father struck a serious blow to his beliefs and his confidence. He told his friend William Ward that he felt God had treated his family harshly.[33] It would be impossible, he concluded, to enjoy the First he achieved in his exams that year. 'I have not sufficient faith in Providence to believe it is all for the best,' he said gloomily. The world felt very hollow indeed.

Chapter 3

Astonishing the Dons

Some of Wilde's faith in Providence must have been restored by 1878, his last year as an undergraduate, when he won the university's Newdigate English Verse Prize. The award conferred membership to an elite circle of men. Matthew Arnold, John Ruskin, and John Addington Symonds were among previous winners. They were also among the cultural giants on whose shoulders Wilde hoped to stand, one day. 'I should so like to see the smile on your face now,' his mother wrote from Dublin.[1] The prize was widely publicized in the English-speaking world and especially in Ireland, where Wilde's brother personally delivered the news to the Dublin papers.[2] 'To have snatched the English Verse prize at Oxford is not only a personal distinction,' an Irish friend congratulated him, 'but a triumph for our entire country.'[3]

The Newdigate seemed to write a promissory note to posterity. As well as putting the winner's name in the press, the Newdigate stamped young poets with promise, marking them as the future recipients of 'the more important prizes of life,' as *The Irish Monthly* explained.[4] It proudly headlined its report 'An Irish Winner of the Newdigate' and made much of the 'youthful countryman' from whom 'we have a right to expect much in the future.'

Wilde's winning entry was 'Ravenna,' a 332-line poem celebrating that city's great citizens and its place in recently unified Italy. By a stroke of luck, Wilde had visited Ravenna while touring the Mediterranean the year before the *Oxford University Gazette* announced that the northern Italian city would be the topic of the competition. His inspiration for his poem in heroic couplets sprang 'from the bottom of my heart, red-hot from Ravenna itself.'[5] The city's ancient churches and Christian mosaics fascinated him. His poem makes a mosaic of its own by canonizing an eclectic selection of English poets—Shakespeare, Shelley, Spenser, and Byron, but also Elizabeth Barrett Browning. Critically acclaimed during her lifetime, Barrett Browning's reputation was established long before her death in 1861. Yet her inclusion in this list is a clue to Wilde's nonconformist cast of mind. In 'Ravenna,' he marches warrior poets, chivalric princes, noble sons, glorious knights, and martial lords past the reader in a showy display resembling a masculinity pageant. But in his own life, Wilde reserved the highest place in his personal pantheon for the androgynous poet-heroine of Barrett Browning's epic, *Aurora Leigh*. It was his favourite book and it's easy to see why this tale of an ambitious but unrecognized poet appealed to him. In the most memorable scene, Aurora makes up for being spurned by the literary establishment by seizing her artistic destiny in her own hands and crowning herself poet laureate. Her bold self-making undoubtedly appealed to Wilde, who sent an Oxford friend a copy in which he had marked his favourite passages. 'I look upon it as much the greatest work in our literature,' Wilde said, 'I love it.'[6]

In Italy, Wilde befriended a young American novelist named Julia Constance Fletcher who was to include a disguised version of him in her novel, *Mirage*. The locks of his hair clustered like those of a medieval saint, she wrote. When he talked, he sounded like a gothic manuscript. The words rolled from his lips like those on a medieval saint's speech scroll. 'He spoke with rapidity, with particularly distinct enunciation; he spoke like a man who has made a study of expression. He listened like one accustomed to speak.'[7] Wilde's 1877 Mediterranean circuit also provided the opportunity to commune with Keats, the fair poet whose memory he pledged to keep alive. Further down the Italian coast from Ravenna, on the Mediterranean side, a pilgrimage to Keats's grave at Rome stimulated Wilde to write more poetry and to raise a complaint with the Romantic poet's biographer, Lord Houghton. The medallion profile of Keats's head next to the tomb was '*extremely ugly*,' Wilde thought, because it gave Keats 'thick almost Negro lips and nose.'[8]

In 'Ravenna,' as in many of his early poems, he reimagined his own life through rose-hued spectacles. Despite the pitiful horsemanship Florence Ward had observed, Wilde described himself confidently approaching Ravenna as 'the white road rang beneath my horse's feet.'[9] Thrilled by the sight of the ancient city of Dante and Byron, he 'galloped, racing with the setting sun.' His equestrian alter ego mingled the qualities of a medieval knight errant with those of a pastoral poet who enjoyed wandering through the woods, hoping 'to see some goat-foot Pan make merry minstrelsy amid the reeds! Some Dryad-maid in girlish flight!'[10] Then, mustering all the modesty he could for the finale, he declared that one as young as he ('who scarce has seen some twenty summers') could hardly do justice to the city.[11] This, too, was whimsy: Wilde was 22 years old when he first saw Ravenna.

One of the Oxford friends who had accompanied him to Ravenna in 1877 called him out for his self-mythologizing. David Hunter-Blair remembered a conversation in which he said he had enjoyed 'Ravenna' but added that there was 'a lot of humbug' in it.[12] At that, Wilde protested, defending the poem as a genuine account of his travels. Hunter-Blair would have none of it. He quoted the passage 'I rode at will... The white road rang beneath my horse's feet,' then reminded Wilde that he lived in the nineteenth century—the age of machinery and railways—not in the picturesque Renaissance. 'You went there lounging on the cushions of a stuffy railway carriage,' Hunter-Blair reminded his friend.[13]

Wilde's long tour of Italy at Easter 1877 did more than provide the subject for his prize-winning poem. It also became an excuse to return to Oxford late for the summer term. He wrote cheerfully from Corfu to the Reverend Henry Ramsden Bramley, the University's Dean of Arts, to explain his difficulty. 'My dear Mr. Bramley,' his letter chummily began, before spinning a yarn about how his former tutor from Dublin days, Mr Mahaffy, had met him near Rome and '*insisted* on my going with him to Mykenae and Athens.'[14] Mr Mahaffy's powers of persuasion were so great, Wilde said, that he had given in. 'I am afraid I will not be able to be back at the beginning of term. I hope you will not mind if I miss ten days.' His spring break would, in the way of these things, be useful and instructive. It would enable him to explore Greece, the country whose ancient philosophy had profoundly influenced him from boyhood. When he touched Greek soil, Wilde would pose as a Greek citizen by donning the national costume (see Plate 8). He assured 'dear Mr. Bramley' that 'seeing Greece is really a great education for anyone and will I think benefit me greatly, and Mr. Mahaffy is such a clever man that it is quite as good as going to lectures to be in his society.' Bramley, however, was a conservative who said he was 'in favour of progress, but of progress backward.'[15] On his return to

Oxford, Wilde discovered he had been suspended from the University for the rest of the academic year and fined half of his annual scholarship money. Allowances could be made for brilliance, but not for impudence. This was not to be the last time Oxford rejected him.

London beckoned, sparkling with possibilities. Courtesy of a fast train he could be there in an hour and forty minutes. He promptly had a cello-shaped coat tailor-made and presented himself at the social event of the season: the opening of the Grosvenor Gallery, temple of the aesthetes. The Gallery felt like the inner sanctum of all that was holy to him. Its three scarlet-damasked rooms were stuffed with painting by Millais, Watts, Alma Tadema, Burne-Jones, Tissot, and their contemporaries. Here the undergraduate hobnobbed with Anglo-American elites ranging from the Prince of Wales and the former Prime Minister, William Ewart Gladstone, to the painters James McNeill Whistler and John Millais, and the novelist Henry James. Wilde immortalized the evening in *The Picture of Dorian Gray*, in which the decadent Lord Henry describes the Grosvenor as 'really the only place,' the paradise of art.[16]

Wilde's review of the Grosvenor in *Dublin University Magazine* gloated about the magnificent education he had enjoyed outside Oxford's walls. 'That "Art is long and life is short" is a truth which everyone feels or ought to feel,' he wrote, playing the philosophical sensualist.[17] Then he launched into an account of his activities designed to arouse pangs of jealousy among those who had missed out. 'Yet surely those who were in London last May, and had in one week the opportunities of hearing Rubinstein playing Sonata Impassionata, of seeing Wagner conduct the Spinning Wheel Chorus from the *Flying Dutchman*, and of studying art at the Grosvenor Gallery, have very little to complain of as regards human existence.' He also reported that his time in Greece had enabled him to verify for himself some of the things he had studied in Oxford. 'Boys can still be found as beautiful as the Charmides of Plato,' he wrote, referring to the Socratic dialogue about temperance that deviates into a discussion about a stunningly handsome young man.[18] Back in Oxford, the Brasenose fellow and aesthete Walter Pater read the Grosvenor Gallery review and found in Wilde's first published prose much to admire. 'I hope you will give me an early call on your return to Oxford,' Pater wrote the budding art critic.[19]

Though Wilde made the best of his rustication, it had hurt his pride. Feeling that his peccadilloes might have been overlooked if he had come from a more influential family, especially an English one, he stood on national pride in the pages of the *Dublin University Magazine*. In his review, he tipped his hat to a friend of the family, the nationalist Sir Frederick Burton, 'of whom all Irishmen are so justly proud.' By becoming director of London's National Gallery, Burton had done what Wilde aspired to do: conquered England. Wilde's review concluded with a backhanded compliment to the English. 'This dull land of England, with its short summer, its dreary rains and fogs, its mining districts, and factories, and vile deification of machinery,' had succeeded almost in spite of itself in producing a few great artists, he wrote.[20] With a flourish, he signed himself as a conquering Irishman, Oscar Wilde of Magdalen College, Oxford.

For his final terms of study, Wilde returned to Oxford and recovered his academic footing. The early summer months of 1878 proved exceedingly rewarding. His artistic credentials were burnished by the Newdigate Prize while his intellectual reputation was gilded by a double First in Greats, an outstanding academic result. 'The dons are "astonied" beyond words,' he said, about 'the Bad Boy doing so well in the end!'[21]

'You have got *honour* and *recognition*,' his mother told him.[22] 'This gives you a certainty of success in the future.' And, determined to find her youngest son precocious as well, Speranza praised him for taking the Newdigate 'at the age of only 22.' If only. He was almost 24.

Shortly before Wilde's 1878 graduation, Colonel Thomas Wentworth Higginson arrived in Oxford. 'It is lovely here,' the distinguished American author and Civil War veteran wrote, admiring the 'perfect June weather.'[23] The 54-year-old would be among the listeners when Wilde recited 'Ravenna' as part of the day's Commemoration proceedings on 26 June 1878. Wilde's tutor and travelling companion, Mr Mahaffy, and Wilde's brother were also among the hundreds packed into the theatre. This was to be Wilde's first performance before a large audience. Until then, his only prior experience of public speaking had been occasionally delivering after-dinner remarks.[24]

Colonel Higginson had dedicated his life to humanitarian causes: opposing the fugitive slave law, promoting women's rights and education, supporting religious diversity and immigration, and speaking out against exploitative factory wages. Although he was well-known in the United States because of his accomplishments and his writings, Colonel Higginson learned he wasn't quite so prominent across the Atlantic. When he made it his business to find out what the English thought of Americans, he quickly discovered that they hardly thought of them at all. America seemed to them a 'curious social enigma' that they were content to leave unsolved.[25] Higginson estimated that for every 500 American tourists in England, a single Englishman ventured to the United States. Because so few Englishmen had visited the country, they imagined it as a lonely place that didn't have bishops or even English books.[26] 'But you do not mean that you really like being an American, do you?' one Englishwoman asked him, struggling to conceal her surprise.[27] 'I supposed that you were all Americans because you couldn't help it.' On Colonel Higginson's previous visit to Oxford, six years earlier, he learned that some Oxford dons were no more reliably informed about America or its recent Civil War. At a college dinner, they introduced him as a Confederate officer, an unforgivable mistake since he was a lifelong abolitionist.[28] In fact, he had spent the Civil War leading the Union's first authorized black regiment, a group of nearly 500 soldiers, few of whom were freemen or literate.[29]

Higginson's first-hand experiences with African Americans were of great interest to British intellectuals, including Carlyle, Darwin, and the historian Edward A. Freeman, a fellow of Trinity College, Oxford. Professor Freeman's racial and political theories were as strident as they were untested by real world experience. Brushing aside the events of 1776 and the fact of the American Declaration of Independence, Freeman took as axiomatic the notion that the United States was 'still essentially an English land.'[30] This anachronism became the cornerstone of his controversial theory correlating 'the Irish difficulty' in Britain to 'the negro difficulty' in America.[31] Although it was dressed up as science, this was actually an exercise in racist extrapolation driven by Freeman's private aversion towards the Irish and his near total ignorance about blacks. He would popularize this theory during an 1881–2 lecture tour of the United States. At Boston, Professor Freeman and his wife called on Colonel Higginson. They admitted their astonishment at seeing black women in the city's streets. Excited by the novelty, Mrs Freeman said she was impatient to see a black baby. She would see plenty in Virginia, the couple's next destination, Higginson assured her. 'They had hardly seen even black men before,' Higginson noted with contempt.[32]

Higginson relished such one-upmanship. For all his humanitarianism, he could be terribly competitive and vain, and acquiring celebrity acquaintances was one of his passions. His memoirs are a Who's Who of the Victorian era. Here he is with Darwin, who is laughing at a funny passage Mrs Darwin is reading aloud from Lewis Carroll's *Through the Looking-Glass*, the 1871 sequel to *Alice*.[33] Here he is playing billiards with Herbert Spencer, the sociologist who coined the phrase 'survival of the fittest.' Here he enters the Athenaeum Club smoking room and finds the father of eugenics, Francis Galton. Here he strolls in Hyde Park with Froude and Carlyle.[34] Here you can watch him attempt to suppress his scorn for the 'never exactly interesting or agreeable' Tennyson and his 'crony,' the photographer Margaret Cameron.[35] Here he is alongside Robert Browning, and here again with Matthew Arnold.[36] Yet Higginson also made time for nobodies. When an unknown poet named Emily Dickinson wrote to him in 1862, he took her under his wing. In one of her characteristic pieces, she declared, 'I'm Nobody! Who are you?' Higginson supported her writing for a quarter of a century and, after her death, he was the first to publish her collected work.

Only days before arriving in Oxford, Higginson had been a guest of the Pre-Raphaelites and had spoken appreciatively with 'those who celebrate Morris, Swinburne, Walt Whitman'—the set to which Wilde aspired to belong.[37] He didn't know Wilde yet, but was predisposed to look on a fledgling Irish poet at Oxford as an inherently sympathetic character. They seemed well-suited: they both cared about poetry, Ireland, and young men. Higginson's fascination with masculinity runs through his writings like a bright red thread. In his memoir of army life, he observed his men's bodies in action with a gaze as fond as it was sensual. 'It needs an artist's eye to make a perfect drillmaster,' Higginson explained, as though to justify his lingering looks.[38] If he had been so inclined, Colonel Higginson could have seen Wilde as something of an alter ego. Indeed, the dark-haired winner of the Newdigate looked like a version of the long-haired bohemian Higginson had once been, back in the day, when he was a student at Harvard. As an undergraduate, his artistic tastes were so pronounced that one of his closest friends claimed he suffered from 'the beauty disease.'[39] Contrary to expectations, however, Higginson and Wilde were not destined to be on the same side of history. In a few years, the Colonel would become Wilde's thorniest American critic. And the student who made the biggest impression on him was not the winner of the 1878 Newdigate Prize.

An organ recital announced the start of the Commemoration ceremony. Wilde and Higginson were admitted to the Sheldonian. Black-gowned students, dons, and red-robed honorands processed in swishing gowns—'men only' the Colonel observed.[40] Oxford's pomp and traditions unfurled in a boisterous pageant punctuated by hurrahs. *Three cheers for Disraeli! Three cheers for the British Empire!* With a great rumble, hundreds rose to their feet and sang the national anthem.[41] Honorary degrees were awarded. Reverence to military heroism was paid by Colonel Higginson's host, the Professor of Civil Law James Bryce, a Scotch-Irishman steeped in Celtic tradition who had come to Oxford on a scholarship after a first degree, read Greats, and graduated top of his year.[42]

The excited crowd soon grew overheated and restive. Speakers were taunted. A prize-winning essay *On the Symptoms of Decline in Races* was heard with impatience. The Professor of Poetry was egged on in his Latin oration. 'Couldn't you leave a little out of it, sir?' someone cried out. 'Couldn't you get on a little faster, sir?' another heckled.

Now it was Wilde's turn to submit to the audience's will. Dressed in a sober graduand's gown, he stood up and made his way to the podium. As the winner of the Newdigate, he had to recite 'Ravenna' before the crowd. The June heat seemed to thicken the air. 'A year ago I breathed the Italian air,' he began, declaiming the 332 lines of his poem from memory.[43] A hush settled over the room. 'O how my heart with boyish passion burned,' he continued. Even the boisterous members of the audience listened attentively. They were so impressed by his rote recitation that no one dared interrupt.[44] At the poem's conclusion, Oxford cheered him loudly. It was the culmination of his Oxford career, and a personal triumph.

To the American observer, however, Wilde's recital of 'Ravenna' didn't seem noteworthy. Colonel Higginson was a gifted orator whose talents had been trained at the lectern when he was a schoolmaster, honed at the pulpit as a minister, and burnished on the platform as a speaker at abolitionist and suffrage rallies. He had heard and delivered the most spirited speeches of his generation. His style was modelled on contemporaries like Ralph Waldo Emerson (whose popular lectures were as influential as they were eloquent) and the reformer Theodore Parker (whose flair with words influenced Abraham Lincoln and Martin Luther King, Jr.). In 1878, Wilde's oratorical abilities were still untrained. How to command the attention of thousands of listeners in person or in print, as Wilde's lectures and plays would do later, remained a mystery. For now, he could only work magic on intimate groups: dazzling a tutor one-to-one, charming friends by the fireside, or trilling off a long poem by heart to a home crowd.

Long before Wilde took the stage at Commemoration that day, Colonel Higginson found himself captivated by a striking young man he described as 'a very black youth from Africa' whom he saw conspicuously floating among the cream of English manhood in a BA gown.[45] Christian Cole's darkness and charisma made him a magnet for the Oxford audience's eyes. *Three cheers for Christian Cole!* they had shouted as he entered the theatre.[46] 'King Cole,' a royal name that testified to his celebrity, was the name that Higginson heard the undergraduates call him.[47]

History was repeating itself: two years earlier, at Commemoration, Cole had turned Florence Ward's head and stolen the day. Now, Cole upstaged the other students, aristocrats, dignitaries, and academics once again. He was still a familiar presence in Oxford and had often debated at the Oxford Union that year.[48] After obtaining his degree in 1876, Cole officially became a member of University College, a fairly progressive place by the standards of the day.[49] To win a place here was a coup (Cecil Rhodes, the imperialist who was making his fortune in South African diamond mines, had been refused by the college only a few years earlier). Cole had returned to Sierra Leone and published lectures on education, but was back in England seeking better prospects.[50] He was almost unique: a statistical aberrance in the University's six-hundred-year history.[51] To earn his degree, he had passed the same academic exams as his white peers, but he had also endured tests of his patience by those intrigued by his skin colour. Wilde was special, too, but being an Irishman at Oxford was a less challenging proposition. Besides, there were other Irishmen at Oxford and rabid anti-Irish antipathy like Edward A. Freeman's was not the norm.[52]

As soon as the ceremony ended, Higginson sought out Cole for a tête-à-tête. Both wholeheartedly believed it was vital for whites to recognize blacks as their equals. In the United States, Higginson urged

white Americans to imagine the everyday bravery of the black men
and women who lived alongside them. 'I declare it, as my solemn conviction,' Higginson affirmed in a stirring anti-slavery speech, that 'we
white Anglo-Saxons' must recognize the greater burdens shouldered
by those of African descent and 'must yield the palm of native heroism
to the negro.'[53] Arguing against the prejudice of his contemporaries,
Higginson rejected the view that blacks were inherently inferior.
Instead he pointed to the structural and historical injustices whites had
imposed upon them. How could Americans not see that blacks were
'crushed by social institutions' made by whites? Empathy could be a
step towards acknowledging experiences that too often went unrecognized. Walk a mile in a black man's shoes, he seemed to implore them.
Who was to say, Higginson continued, that behind the so-called heroism of white men there hadn't been some exceptional dark-skinned
soul responsible for even greater acts of bravery? Who was to say that
a single 'swarthy, low-browed, sullen black man' had not been more
heroic than his Anglo-Saxon peers? When Higginson spoke these words,
decades earlier, the hall shook with cheers, his reward for a thought-
experiment that asked his listeners to imagine a possibility just beyond
the limits of their own experience.

Now, as Cole strolled the streets of Oxford, his long black gown
catching the wind and swelling like a balloon, he must have looked
like Higginson's thought-experiment brought to life. Cole made no
secret of his contempt for the colonial mindset. How he smarted at his
mistreatment became apparent the following year when he published
two pamphlets, *What Do Men Say about Negroes?* and *Reflections on the
Zulu War by a Negro, B.A.* In 1879, Britain consolidated its imperial
holdings in Africa as part of its Confederation policy. Cole's *Reflections*
criticized British imperialism and spat at Christian 'charity' towards
so-called 'heathens.'[54]

> Ye white men of England
> Oh tell, tell, I pray,
> If the curse of your land,
> Is not, day after day,
> To increase your possessions
> With reckless delight,
> To subdue many nations,
> And show them your might.

In apocalyptic tones, he warned that whites would not always have the upper hand in Africa. 'Some white men of England,' Cole wrote, 'have always believed they will rule every land: but—they are deceived. They preach always of peace, but revel in war.'[55] Cole addressed the pamphlet from one of London's Inns of Court, the Inner Temple, which had given him the right to practise, so making him Britain's first black barrister. Unfortunately his legal career ended abruptly at the age of 33 when he contracted smallpox during a stay in Zanzibar.

The University librarian, Falconer Madan, who overlapped with Cole at Oxford, did him the service of collecting his writings for the Bodleian, and so memorialized this Oxford student celebrity. But this apparently kind gesture was bungled. On the flyleaf of *What Do Men Say about Negroes?*, Madan scribbled one of the jokes made at Cole's expense. 'Rare pamphlet by "Old King Cole", who is stated to have telegraphed to his African Dominion "I have passed Responsions. Sacrifice 200 of my people," ' the librarian wrote.[56] He left no other indication of Cole's accomplishments. The librarian's feeble joke immortalized a university caricature entitled 'Old King Cole,' after the nursery rhyme. The caricature illustrates how readily black Victorians, no matter how extraordinary or accomplished, were turned into figures of fun. Cole was portrayed as a Christy minstrel, in mortarboard, spectacles, and scholar's gown.[57] With his banjo, striped trousers, and toothy smile, he looks like an entertainer inviting spectators to a singalong (see Plate 9). Another sketch satirized 'King Cole's return Home Sweet Home' by dropping him into an Africanized jamboree with barebreasted women.[58] Although Wilde probably didn't wish to imagine it, his own image would one day intersect with these caricatures.[59] What whites had done to minstrelize Cole would become oddly relevant to Wilde in the United States.

In British towns and villages, Victorians were much more accustomed to seeing blackface minstrel performers than real black people. First introduced from the United States into Britain in the late 1830s, blackface minstrelsy later became associated with E. P. Christy's troupe and soon 'Christy minstrelsy' had become the generic name for blackface spectacles (see Plates 10 and 11). Before and during Wilde's time, it was a standard Victorian entertainment as fit for the folk as for royalty. For instance, it wasn't unusual for the Queen's arrival at Balmoral Castle in Scotland to be celebrated publicly with a 'nigger band,' as she called it, as well as bonfires and dancing.[60]

Alongside civic and professional shows, domestic minstrelsy became common. Do-it-yourself entertainment was the vogue and how-to guides with advice for the aspiring minstrel flourished. 'Nothing gives the amateur such rare opportunities for displaying talent as a negro minstrel performance,' one manual promised.[61] Along with hints on costumes and gestures, such handbooks offered word-for-word scripts of conundrums, riddles, speeches, and sentimental songs that any enthusiast could perform. As for the distinctive make-up, an American specialist shared his professional recipe. 'Take a quantity of corks,' Colonel Jack Haverly advised, 'place them in a tin pail or dish, saturating them with alcohol, then light. Let them burn to a crisp, when burned out, mash them to a powder, mix with water to a thick paste, place the mixture in small tin boxes, and it is ready for use.' Next came Colonel Jack's make-up tips. 'In applying it to your face it is better first to rub the face and hands with cocoa butter,' he counselled. To make your lips look large, you wouldn't need carmine, he promised, if you knew his trick of applying the burnt-cork paste 'about one-half an inch away from the mouth, or more if a larger mouth is wanted.'

It was common for a professional Christy minstrel show's programme to make claims about the authenticity of the characters on stage. Colonel Jack, like his peers in the business, told audiences that what they were seeing was such a faithful replica of real life, it was virtually an ethnological study. Blackface entertainments, programme notes typically claimed, 'are staged and presented in strict keeping with the characteristics of the Negro race, which they are designed to portray.'[62] The recurrence of minstrelsy's stock characters—Sambo, Jim Crow, Tambo, Bones, and others—encouraged the sense of familiarity. Audiences were thus led to believe two spectacular lies: first, that a character like Sambo or Jim Crow was an *accurate* portrayal of a person of colour, and second, that this individual was *representative* of his entire race. Although it's hard to imagine this nonsense succeeding in Britain today, the average white Victorian didn't have access to factual evidence to contradict the insistent rhetoric of operators like Colonel Haverly. With such emphatic reassurances and little first-hand experience to go on, minstrel stereotypes profoundly influenced whites' perceptions of black life. In London, a white aristocrat who disguised himself to experience life as a black man in Britain soon discovered that he would be obliged to walk instead of sitting comfortably in hansoms.[63] When the police allowed him to ride in their carriage, they assumed he would entertain them and so demanded 'a concert all the way.' Blackface minstrelsy's cultural work was insidious and remarkably effective.

Eyewitness observers' insistence on Cole's remarkable presence invites us to look again at Wilde's Oxford. It certainly puts into perspective the legendary student celebrity Wilde is said to have enjoyed: he had his fair share of notoriety, but so did other students.[64] There were many university men who created myths around them and commanded attention because of their specialness. Like Christian Cole's biography, which is omitted from most university histories, the stories of these starry undergraduates are often forgotten or, at best, reduced to thin footnotes.[65]

Sometimes, student days are commemorated after the fact, recalled from obscurity by later success or even philanthropy. This was the case with Wilde and with his contemporary, the diamond magnate Cecil Rhodes. Though a statue of this controversial alumnus now looks down on the comings and goings of Oxford's High Street, Rhodes was not especially influential while a student because he was often called away by business concerns. But on the evening before Commemoration, Wilde and his brother attended the Masonic Ball, as did Rhodes. The 25-year-old had, by then, already discovered thousands of pounds worth of African diamonds and dreamed of controlling and unifying southern Africa. Though Wilde may have known Rhodes—they were both members of the Oxford University freemasons and Rhodes was said to have attended Ruskin's lectures—he never mentioned him.[66]

Rhodes used some of his wealth to endow scholarships that would perpetuate his imperial mission by enabling scholars from selected countries, including the United States, to study at Oxford. When the first African American Rhodes Scholar turned up in Oxford, in 1907, Wilde's name had become legend—but not merely because of his student days, as some have claimed. By Alain Locke's time, there were a few more Irishmen and students of colour at the university. Spry and sophisticated, Locke styled himself as Wilde's spiritual heir. His Oxford degree was not his first—Locke had already done outstanding work at Harvard. Like his hero, he applied to Magdalen, wanted to study Greats, dressed with panache, and was discreetly homosexual.

The most significant way in which Locke modelled himself on Wilde was by imagining Oxford as the place to make himself over. Like Wilde, Locke hoped to become a slightly different person there, a person he described to his mother as 'really cosmopolitan.'[67] That new person, he told her, was going to escape the prejudice Alain Locke had experienced in the United States. 'I'm not going to England as a Negro,' he informed her, 'I will leave the color question in New York.'[68] Oblivious to Locke's hopes and plans, the colour question had designs of its own. It followed him across the Atlantic just as Wilde's brogue came across the Irish Sea to Oxford.

In his first term of study, Locke learned that his wishes were not going to be fulfilled in England. By the early decades of the twentieth century, Oxford attitudes had barely changed since the days of Christian Cole. The university was 'a land of class distinctions,' Locke observed, proving himself a gifted reader of its social exclusions.[69] Locke quickly discovered that British racism worked covertly, not as it did in the United States where Jim Crow laws overtly mandated racial segregation. British exclusion was more discreet but it was still effective. The guiding principle was not to exclude people of colour, but simply not to include them. As a result, five colleges refused Locke before he was finally accepted by Hertford College. His Oxford education taught him to prefer 'persecution even' to the charade called 'race indifference' that he discovered in Britain. Spurred by his Oxford experience Locke later became one of the intellectual leaders of the New Negro movement.

Wilde's career did not immediately bloom after Oxford, and he would have to wait until his 1882 visit to the United States to gain real prominence. There, Colonel Higginson would have plenty to say about him. There, too, dark-skinned people would play a significant part in his public life. But, for now, Oscar Fingal O'Flahertie Wills Wilde, Demy of Magdalen College, Sir Roger Newdigate Prizewinner, holder of a double First in Greats, basked in the glow of his accomplishment. The Sheldonian's audience was far larger than any he had ever spoken before. In the embrace of that circular space built to hold hundreds of listeners, Wilde may have felt that he had found his rightful place. Perhaps that was where his thoughts of becoming a lecturer and academic began to take shape.

One evening among friends, he vowed that he would never be 'a dried-up Oxford don,' yet the idea later became more attractive as the need to find something to do next became more pressing.[70] He decided to apply for an academic fellowship, though his determination was marred by fears that he had not worked hard enough to deserve one. His undergraduate years, he told William Ward, had been spent in mere 'extravagance, trivial talk, utter vacancy of employment.'[71] He despaired at his prospects and predicted he wouldn't win a fellowship. '*I have lost faith in myself.* I am too ridiculously easily led astray. So I have idled and won't get it and will be wretched in consequence.'

Added to fears that his youthful misconduct might not be forgiven, he was feeling increasingly sympathetic towards Roman Catholicism, which was still regarded with suspicion in some quarters of the university. Although in 1871 Oxford had abolished the requirement of conformity to the Church of England, old prejudices died hard.[72] 'You must know,' Wilde told a Catholic friend in later years, 'that I should never, never have won the Newdigate if I had taken the Pope's side against the King's.'[73]

In the event, Wilde's applications for fellowships in classics and archaeology were unsuccessful. He gave vent to his dejection in his poetry, revising happier poems to reflect his melancholy. 'I know but too well that in this, like everything that I do, I have failed,' he said about his poem 'Magdalen Walks,' a description of the college in springtime.[74] When he revised it, he added two gloomy closing stanzas. 'I know that the end is nigh,' he wrote, 'and the joys of a youth long past.'[75] 'With tired eyes I sit and wait the opening of the Future's Mystic Gate,' he fretted in another poem probably completed around the same time.[76] He signed off both poems 'Magdalen College, Oxford,' the name of the mystic gate that would soon close behind him.

What, then, would the gilded Irishman do, now that he must leave Oxford? He would try his fortune as a man without a career, proclaiming the message of art. 'I intend to take up the critic's life,' he told the *Dublin University Magazine* editor.[77] He would become a cosmopolitan, 'a type that was to combine something of the real culture of the scholar with all the grace and distinction and perfect manner of a citizen of the world.'[78] Soon the world was going to teach him what Oxford never could have. Years later, he realized that 'nothing that is worth knowing can be taught.'[79]

Chapter 4

Not Having Set the World Quite on Fire

'You talk a lot about yourself, Oscar,' one of his Oxford friends said, 'and all the things you'd like to achieve. But you never say what you're going to do with your life.'[1] Wilde had gathered his friends around him for a late-night chat. The punch bowl was empty, the tobacco had been smoked, and the lights were turned down low. The conversation was drifting to sober topics.

'What are you going to *do*?' the friend asked.

Wilde turned solemn. There was a long pause.

'What is your real ambition in life?' the friend insisted.

Still, no answer came.

'God knows,' Wilde finally replied. Then, turning serious, he said, 'I'll be a poet, a writer, a dramatist. Somehow or other I'll be famous, and if not famous, I'll be notorious.' Wilde now set about trying all these careers in turn, and a few more besides. After leaving Oxford he moved to London in early 1879. He was not going back to Ireland but was staying on in England 'probably for good,' he said.[2] But what would he do there? His prospects for employment were thin.

It's a great advantage to have done nothing at all, but it's best not to overdo it, would become one of his favourite expressions.[3] The romance of doing nothing would soon be dispelled by the reality of not having an income commensurate to his tastes. On the death of Sir William, in 1876, Speranza and her two sons had discovered that their properties, No. 1 Merrion Square in Dublin and Moytura House in County Mayo, were not owned outright by the Wilde estate, and that the income on the fishing lodge at Connemara and the house at Bray would need to be shared. Financial worry was to be the constant companion of

Speranza's widowhood. For the most part, however, she endeavoured to protect Oscar from such concerns, reminding him that if he managed his share of the properties well, he 'could have £200 a year for ten years.'[4] He was lucky, she told him. 'I do not see that, for so far, your state is one that demands pity,' she said, suggesting he count his blessings that he didn't have to work in a shop or beg for food.[5]

For a young man accustomed to going to the Oxford shops and spending £20 on a Super Fancy Angola Suit and another £16 on Masonic regalia, £200 would not last long.[6] Inured to extravagance as he was, money was to prove a lifelong concern. When it came to managing the Wilde family finances, Speranza took a more pragmatic approach than her profligate sons (Willie, like Oscar, was often in debt). She indulged in extravagant emotions instead. 'If I am to be left in mean pauperism and uncertain chances I see nothing for it but to take prussic acid and so get rid of the whole trouble all at once,' she dramatized when she discovered that she and Willie could not afford to keep Merrion Square and two servants provisioned with food and fires.[7]

A move across the Irish Sea was soon being orchestrated. 'We have done with Dublin,' she announced definitively.[8] Her suggestion that Oscar find lodgings for her and Willie 'next door to you' in London was politely ignored, though the three Wildes briefly lived together at Oscar's until she found other suitable accommodation.[9] By early summer 1879, she and Willie had permanently moved to London where she wasted no time setting up a salon just as genial and peculiar as the one over which she had presided in Dublin. A visitor remembered her looking like a sailing ship caught in the wind: her six-foot frame puffed up by two crinolines, she made her Limerick lace flounces and crimson skirt flutter and toss about violently as she moved.[10] Irish expatriates now made for Speranza's Mayfair rooms. Jesting about Irish emigration to the United States during the Famine, Speranza said her London house was a more popular destination for Irish expats than even New York City.

'We have *genius*. That is something,' she declared, praising what would remain in the family, regardless of their dwindling bank balances.[11] 'Attorneys can't take that away.' How to make genius pay, however, was a matter Wilde was attempting to figure out. A year after graduation, he was unemployed, impatient, and bored. 'Not having set the world quite on fire as yet' was so annoying, he thought.[12]

Between 1878 and 1880, Wilde curried favour among those who might be able to help him, dividing his attention between prominent figures in education and art. At the request of the wicked Cambridge don Oscar Browning, Wilde stalked Paternoster Row behind St Paul's Cathedral, in search of a suitable bible. He also offered his services as a personal shopper with excellent taste in neckties.[13] Speranza suggested he become a private tutor, but instead Wilde asked Browning to help him gain a place as an inspector of schools, a modest occupation gilded by the fact that the august cultural critic Matthew Arnold had once pursued it.[14] When institutional 'Education work' proved impossible to get, Wilde volunteered his erudition to the painter Lawrence Alma-Tadema whom he advised on the Greek writing for his *Sappho and Alcaeus*.[15] Wilde offered his skills as a translator of Greek and an editor of classical plays. He published a poem on England, 'Ave Imperatrix,' whose anti-war send-off he called 'my first attempt at political prophecy.' He reviewed—once for the *Irish Daily News* and twice for the *Athenaeum*.[16]

For all his hustling, he was hardly making a living, let alone making his name. During these precarious years, Wilde enjoyed partaking in a frothier, more effervescent world he called 'Tea and Beauties.'[17] While seeking work, he was also enjoying himself by blowing bubbles at actresses and theatre folk, writing a sonnet for Ellen Terry, translating a poem for Madame Modjeska, and taking dictation from the exquisite Lillie Langtry.[18]

A professional beauty on the rise, Langtry entered London society around the same time that Wilde left Oxford and started looking for a situation for himself. They quickly formed a mutual admiration society. Langtry's good looks were matched by her social ambition. Although she was married to an Irish ship-owner, she was steering a course towards other harbours. Photographs of herself sold publicly, liaisons with royalty, and the birth of an illegitimate daughter by the Prince of Wales made her notorious, if not respectable. She made an accessory of Wilde, using him now as a Latin tutor and then a personal stylist ('I wanted to ask you how I should go to a fancy ball here,' she queried from Plymouth).[19] In return, she appeared as eye candy at his private gatherings. This was fortuitous for Wilde, who advertised this to his guests as a chance to be introduced to the 'beautiful people.'[20] It was all good fun, and formed a colourful spectacle that relieved the grey cloud of frustration hanging over him.

'Wilde was *really* ingenious,' Langtry thought.[21] 'His mannerisms and eccentricities were then but the natural outcome of a young fellow bubbling over with temperament.' There could be no better reinvention of her unseemly past than to create a more splendid future for her. Wilde crowned his friend 'The New Helen' in 1879, and turned her into the era's incarnation of the legendary Greek beauty. 'Thou art Helen, and none other one!' his poem declared.[22] It rebuked wagging tongues by setting its voice against theirs. Wilde recreated Langtry, the woman with a past, as 'Lily without blot or stain!,' a pure goddess who could 'lure the Old World's chivalry.' Langtry declared herself delighted to be 'the inspiration for one of his happiest efforts.' She would have no truck with obstructions to her personal advancement. She endeavoured to crack the glass ceiling by becoming an actress, making her London debut in an 1881 production of *She Stoops to Conquer* and extending her dramatic empire to the United States soon afterwards.

Actors and artists sat at Wilde's dinner table or reclined 'on a red couch like a pallid flame,' as legendary actress Sarah Bernhardt did when they met for tea.[23] Bernhardt left her mark on the wall of Wilde's rented rooms off the Strand by seeing how high she could jump and charcoaling her name near the ceiling.[24] To complement the squiggle, Wilde purchased a crayon sketch of Bernhardt by Whistler.[25] At one of their teas, Bernhardt may have mentioned her plans to lecture in America. Everyone who was anyone was going to the United States, it seemed. At mid-century, promoters had begun to exploit the American public's interest in inspiring, impressive rhetoric and lyceum tours became increasingly popular.[26] There was such a mania for lecturing, one newspaper reported, that 'any Englishman who thinks he has the power to interest an audience for a couple of hours, may very fairly take an opportunity of seeing the United States, and making money at the same time.'[27]

Though Wilde was having fun on the periphery of London's beau monde, professional and financial security continued to elude him. By autumn 1880, he had completed his first play, *Vera; or the Nihilists*, a tragedy set in Russia. For the purposes of Wilde's career, the play's real tragedy was its dialogue. Act One was set in a Moscow garret, where Nihilist conspirators spoke in the Masonic ritual language Wilde had learned at Oxford.

PRESIDENT.   What is the word?
FIRST CONSPIRATOR. Nabat.
PRESIDENT.   The answer?

SECOND CONSPIRATOR. Kalit.
PRESIDENT.   What hour is it?
THIRD CONSPIRATOR. The hour to suffer.[28]

It was a bewildering exchange. Yet Wilde thought that incomprehensibility was a sign of seriousness. He was dogged in his belief that the play's forced constructions were its best feature. The stilted way the characters spoke would make the play really distinctive, he hoped. 'In an acting age perhaps the best test of a good play is that it should not read well,' he informed the Lord Chamberlain's Examiner of Plays, Edward Smyth-Pigott, when he sent him *Vera*.[29] 'I am working at dramatic art because it's *the democratic* art,' Wilde continued. He had other, more pressing motives as well. 'I want fame,' he admitted.[30] *Vera* was unlikely to earn him what he craved. The characters don't speak about tyranny and liberty, they deliver bite-size lectures on it.

Wilde's early dogmas about drama were of his own invention, but they were bolstered by the advice of his friend Hermann Vezin, an established American actor who had made his career in England. Wilde read a draft of *Vera* to Vezin, who probably offered advice on the way the characters should speak. When Wilde's playscript was finished, he sent Vezin a copy with a note. 'Any suggestions about situations or dialogue I should be so glad to get from such an experienced artist as yourself,' he wrote, confiding that playwriting was a craft he hadn't yet mastered.

Today, Vezin's acting style would look grotesquely stilted. Noble but stagy, the American's characters lurched passionately from one scene to the next. On stage, he attacked his lines in an expressive staccato, but to Wilde's ears it sounded like the 'most musical enunciation.'[31] Wilde's appreciation gives us a glimpse into his preference for the artificial and the strange. When Vezin played Iago, for example, he made everything the villain said sound 'symbolic of the leading idea,' Wilde observed appreciatively. Vezin accompanied these audio-cues with big demonstrative gestures illustrating the words. In a fan letter, Wilde said he loved 'the enormous *character* you gave to otherwise trivial *details*,' using italics to imitate the dramatic emphases Vezin usually gave to his speeches.[32] He loved how artificial Vezin made his characters seem, and lavished the actor with praise for making it appear as if it was 'not a conscious effort' to speak and move on stage as nobody actually does in life. Wilde *liked* performances that drew attention to the fact that the characters on the stage were *not* real people, and therefore did not *look* and *sound* like real people. These are important clues to the style he emulated in his early plays and lectures.

There were glaring differences between British and American tastes when it came to acting. At the time, the English theatre was obsessed with realistic costuming and settings, but showed little interest in encouraging actors to deliver their lines in a lifelike manner. Vezin's style was not that unusual.[33] To an experienced American drama critic writing around the same time, Vezin's style seemed 'to lack color and vivacity, humor and irony,' however.[34] Although Henry James acknowledged that Vezin was one of London's best actors, he left no doubt that London standards had nothing on New York or Paris. He ended his review of the moribund English stage by highlighting Helena Modjeska's 'exquisite' Queen of Scots in Schiller's *Mary Stuart*. She 'is the attraction of the hour,' James concluded, 'but it only points the moral of these desultory remarks that the principal ornament of the English stage just now should be a Polish actress performing in a German play.'[35]

Wilde's stilted dialogue in *Vera* was a clue to how green he then was. How would this solemn young playwright one day become the author of society comedies with crowd-pleasing banter so characteristic it would be christened 'Wildean' and gain an adjective all its own? Although Wilde had modelled the passionate heroine of his first play on the foremost actress of the day, Sarah Bernhardt, neither she nor anybody else was interested in playing a suicidal Russian assassin consigned to a dungeon. There were problems with the play's politics, too. Wilde had drawn inspiration from the assassination, earlier in 1881, of Czar Alexander II by nihilists. At a time when the English press was increasingly comparing nihilists and Fenians, this young Irishman's exploration of murder and republicanism would likely be read as linking Irish nationalism and their Land War with an international network of anarchists.[36] This was too political to be politic. Plagued by obscure references, poor plotting, and improbable dialogue, *Vera* would never earn him the fame he craved. 'I have just found out what a difficult craft playwriting is,' he confessed to Vezin.[37] Nobody would fund the staging of *Vera*. The hopes he had pinned on playwriting were dashed.

The conventional view about art, for much of the nineteenth century, was that it should do something for you. Most Victorians expected art to be edifying, enlightening, or useful in one way or another. Aesthetes shunned such dogma. Art, they declared, had no duty other than to be beautiful. It could be valuable in and of itself. Adherents of art for art's sake refused to pander to the demands of moralists and utilitarians, who seemed to them as reprehensible as philistines and barbarians. One of Wilde's heroes, the French poet and novelist Théophile Gautier, had proclaimed these ideas as early as 1834. 'The only things that are really beautiful are those which have no use,' he provocatively declared; 'the most useful place in the house is the lavatory.'[38]

In late nineteenth-century Britain, the idea of art as art for art's sake was nothing short of revolutionary. For the Victorians, it amounted to a whole new way of looking at everything from painting to poetry. Art for art's sake irrevocably transformed the relationship between the public, critics, and artists. By 1878, that shift had become part of one of the century's most famous art trials. It began when the art critic John Ruskin accused the American painter James McNeill Whistler of insulting the public by 'flinging a pot of paint' in its face.[39] During the libel trial that ensued, Whistler persevered with his art for art's sake principles even as his atmospheric nocturnes and impressionistic arrangements were packed into a courtroom and paraded before a puzzled jury. 'Now, Mr. Whistler, do you think that you could make the gentlemen of the jury understand *the merits* of these paintings?' the advocate challenged the painter.[40] Whistler stared him down, surveyed the silent courtroom, and adjusted his spectacles. Accustomed to signing his pictures with a pointy-tailed butterfly, Whistler at last delivered his stinging reply. 'No, I don't think I could.' He believed art's business was to evoke a consciousness of beauty, no more, no less. In the end, Whistler won, albeit by a narrow margin.

By then, Aestheticism had been in the air for several decades. Its prime movers had reached middle age and had recently been satirized as a hoary gang that still thought of themselves as 'the aesthetic young geniuses.'[41] Aestheticism was still loosely tied to the memory of the Pre-Raphaelite Brotherhood that flourished at mid-century. By 1880, however, the movement's brightest lights were fading. William Holman Hunt, Michael and Dante Gabriel Rossetti were in their fifties (Dante would die in 1882). So was Matthew Arnold, the promoter of 'Sweetness and Light' as a shield against Philistinism. John Ruskin had done much to enthuse and direct art criticism, but he was a decade older and now mentally unstable.

These circumstances created a vacuum. There were other aesthetes younger in years, but none of them was likely to lead the movement towards the renewal it so desperately needed. Algernon Swinburne, whose advocacy of art for art's sake had been formative for Wilde, was still in his early forties, but he was also a drunk who needed to be kept away from London's seductions and therefore could not direct the movement. Walter Pater was barely 40, but he had always been a young fogey. His recent reprimand for writing affectionate letters to a student meant that he was unlikely to emerge from his seclusion in leafy North Oxford to take Aestheticism by storm. And William Morris, aged 46, was busy devising socialist utopias and opening a London shop selling wallpapers and rugs.

The crisis was plain: fresh blood was required. While Aestheticism waited for a saviour to step into the breach, a cartoonist named George Du Maurier seized the opportunity to satirize the movement's idiosyncrasies. In the absence of any dissenting voice from the aesthetic side, Du Maurier became the movement's chief chronicler by default.

Du Maurier's pen more or less single-handedly created the general interest in Aestheticism that prevailed in the late 1870s and early 1880s. Since the mid-1860s, the illustrator had been working as *Punch*'s social satirist. He was responsible for a great deal of the prominence Aestheticism enjoyed. His drawings were more than popular, they were a phenomenon. Indeed, they succeeded in bringing a relatively obscure art movement into a wider public's consciousness. Thanks to Du Maurier's lively sketches, the movement's artists became celebrities and its stamping grounds gained prominence. There were downsides to having a caricaturist chronicle the movement, however. Though aesthetes thought of themselves as representatives of taste and culture, Du Maurier saw them as dreamy-eyed eccentrics with outlandish style and tribal behaviours. He portrayed aesthetic men as effeminate, and aesthetic women as asexual anorexics. Aestheticism's detachment from cultural and sexual norms caused Henry James to regard it as 'a queer high-flavoured fruit.'[42] At its most bohemian, he warned, Aestheticism was nothing more than 'zoological sociability.'

Du Maurier gravitated towards the sidelines of fashionable galleries and artists' studios and drew what he saw and heard from there. He had an ear for the ringing phrases that sometimes flew out of people's

mouths, a talent that served him well when he had to write the captions to his drawings. His sketches captured charming creatures and
their flights of fancy. When he sketched the denizens of London's
Grosvenor Gallery, they looked like butterflies fluttering inside the
translucent dome of a glass cloche in which some naturalist happened
to have trapped them so as to note their distinguishing features.
Because of his detailed drawings, even people who would never set
foot in the Grosvenor knew that it was the haunt of aesthetes.

It was because Du Maurier was marginal but knew everybody at
the centre of the art scene that he was able to make a success of
his observational approach. When Du Maurier was a struggling young
artist in 1860s London, he went blind in one eye. He was barely able
to afford to fill his clay pipe with tobacco, but he had the good fortune
that his art school chum, James McNeill Whistler, was by then already
a regular exhibitor at the Royal Academy. The painter had reached such
a 'pinnacle (of fame and notoriety combined) that people can stare at
him from two hemispheres at once,' Du Maurier said.[43] They went
knocking about London together 'as happily as possible, singing and
smoking cigars everywhere.'[44] By the late 1870s, Du Maurier had
achieved professional security. He lived comfortably with his wife and
five children in Hampstead, London's bourgeois suburb. He was by
choice somewhat peripheral to the English capital's art and aristocratic
circles though he haunted them professionally for *Punch* material.

Fatefully for Aestheticism, Du Maurier maintained his acquaintance
with Whistler, whose words his *Punch* cartoons featured alongside those
of the painter's new young friend, Wilde (see Plate 12). Disguised only
by gag pseudonyms, the poet and the painter Maudle and Postlethwaite
disembarked in the pages of *Punch* in 1880.[45] They were trailed by an
entourage of beauties and blue-bloods. That Maudle, Postlethwaite, and
their occasional accomplice, Prigsby, were absurd was obvious to even
the most casual observer. Whether they were really based on Whistler
and Wilde was a point over which there was much debate. Together
they boosted decrepit-seeming Aestheticism, bringing into sharper
focus its intoxication with art-speak and social aspiration. Maudle and
Postlethwaite personified foppery, but they were endearingly funny
and soon they were beloved of British and Americans alike.

In the twinkling of an eye, Maudle and Postlethwaite became a
sensation and their peculiar vernacular caught on. Words like 'utterly
too too' and 'utterly utter' became fashionable. 'These remarkable people

have had a great success in America,' Henry James observed, adding that the duo contributed 'to the curiosity felt in that country on the subject of the English Renascence,' another of the names for Aestheticism.[46]

The *Punch* effect was profound: the Aesthetic Movement suddenly mattered again. *Punch* had such cultural clout that it sprung the door open for Wilde, allowing him to walk straight onto the aesthetic scene. In doing so Du Maurier not only gave Wilde a prominence he didn't have before, but he co-created Wilde's public persona. Like today's semi-famous hangers-on and B-list celebrities who fill out the pages of *Vanity Fair* and *Tatler*, Wilde was until then merely human wallpaper against which the Lillie Langtries shone more brightly. Were it not for Du Maurier, Wilde might have spent many more years on the margins of prominence. Instead, Du Maurier and *Punch* pulled him to the fore-front and drew him larger than he was in life.

This suited Wilde better than it did Whistler, who was two dec-ades older and already famous in his own right. 'Which one of you two invented the other, eh?' the mischievous painter asked when he next saw Wilde and Du Maurier.[47] Wilde's witticisms were a gift to the cartoonist, who usually had to come up with the jokey captions himself.

Whistler was a bully and an egomaniac who only tolerated Wilde's new-found celebrity so long as it didn't dwarf his own standing. The makings of a bitter quarrel were slotting into place. Battle-scarred by his notorious 1878 libel suit against Ruskin and bruised by recent confrontations with the shipping magnate F. R. Leyland (who only paid half his fee for the Peacock Room commission), Whistler's jeal-ousy ripened into *The Gentle Art of Making Enemies*, an attack on his younger frenemy.[48]

As if in a fairy tale in which an artist's pencil could actually be a wizard's wand, Du Maurier's 1880 *Punch* drawings transformed Wilde's reputation almost overnight. At a stroke, Du Maurier moved him from the fringes of aesthetic culture—where he had by then made his name as an occasional art critic and a friend to the famous—to the centre. Once a lord-in-waiting biding his time, Du Maurier's drawings cata-pulted Wilde to the position of Aestheticism's heir apparent.

Yet there had been no magic: all that had happened was that Wilde caught Du Maurier's eye. So far, his exciting new life was only an artist's impression. Little in his real life had changed. Indeed, it was said in some circles that the Aesthetic Movement didn't exist at all 'save in the brain of Mr. Du Maurier.'[49] Wilde felt tired of living like this, he complained to a friend.[50] Becoming nothing while trying one's hand at everything was an exhausting proposition. Years later, his experience of unemployment provided the outline for the hero of 'The Model Millionaire,' the story of a young man who surrounds himself with beautiful people, has but £200 a year, and can't find work. He was 'a delightful, ineffectual young man with a perfect profile and no profession,' Wilde wrote.[51] 'Ultimately he became nothing.'

By 1881, Wilde still hadn't found a profession, a fact Du Maurier satirized by picturing Maudle as a paradoxical guidance counsellor advising that 'to exist beautifully' was a career in itself.[52] '*What?*' his prim interlocutor replies, not for 'a *nice, manly* boy.' Already, Aestheticism hinted at some vague defect in masculinity. The choice of a profession was not Maudle's only muddle, *Punch* implied.

Newly arrived in London, the Polish actress Helena Modjeska dared to utter the unspoken question about this hanger-on that was then undoubtedly on many people's minds. 'What has he done, this young man, that one meets him everywhere?' she asked. 'Oh yes, he talks well, but what has he *done*? He has written nothing, he does not sing or paint or act—he does nothing but talk. I do not understand.'[53] Even Wilde's friend, the poet James Rennell Rodd, was quick to point out that 'he had accomplished little to entitle him to other recognition than that which his ready wit and deliberate eccentricity commanded.'[54]

Meanwhile, Maudle and Postlethwaite were continuing to do their work to raise Aestheticism's profile. For more than a year, new cartoons regularly stoked readers' interest.[55] Although Du Maurier kept a steady stream of aesthetic antics coming, Anglo-Americans could not get enough of Maudle and Postlethwaite. The aesthetic craze coincided with a boom in artistic style that would continue for over a decade. In the shops, there were loose tea gowns for the ladies, and bohemian-looking fabrics for men's clothes. A popular manual, *The Art of Dress*, encouraged people to think of their fashion choices as outward signals of their artistic sensibilities.[56] Home decoration followed suit. Shops like William Morris's sold delicate wallpapers ornamented with aesthetic emblems such as lilies and sunflowers. Aspiring aesthetes bought blue and white china, sunflowers and lilies, peacock's feathers, and Japanese fans.

This was not to everyone's taste. Wilde's mother criticized aesthetes for preferring wallpapers that looked to her like 'sliced pickles powdered with decayed carnations chopped fine.'[57] When she looked at their rooms, she thought the décor ought to be called the 'High Art Model trimmed with mud moulding.' As for the murky colours aesthetes favoured for their clothes, Speranza advised that 'tints of decomposed asparagus and cucumber do not suit the long, pale English face.'[58]

While the aesthetes' ways were being plucked from the pages of *Punch* and pulled into shops and homes, they were also being pushed onto the London stage. First *The Grasshopper* and then *Where's the Cat?* poked fun at the movement, to audiences' rapturous applause. In February 1881, the editor of *Punch*, F. C. Burnand, joined in by writing *The Colonel*.[59] None of these were great plays. At best, they were hasty remakes of old plots with aesthetes thrown in to give them a novelty twist. The storyline in *The Colonel*—a bourgeois family threatened by fraud but saved in the nick of time by the intervention of a military man—had served many times before. This time, however, it had ridiculous art-lovers and an American Colonel for a hero.[60] That was enough to make it a runaway hit even though the critics snubbed it. 'A Grand Play for the Philistines,' the *Illustrated London News* called it.[61]

English audiences were eager to see contemporary society portrayed on stage, so by the day's humdrum standards for drama, *The Colonel* seemed fresh.[62] The first production racked up 550 performances and a second company was hastily put together to take it to the provinces. This was good going for a threadbare remake of a mid-century French comedy with a patchy Professor of Aesthetics thrown in. The play's astonishing success signalled how much audiences wanted the stage to mirror current events and social trends. When one of the actresses in *The Colonel* went out in London dressed in an aesthetic costume similar to the one she wore on stage, nobody batted an eye.[63] Inside the theatre, however, spectators had giggled and snickered openly at her outfit.

It is hard to underestimate the force of the aesthetic craze that seized Victorians. Spurred by a caricaturist's pen, it became an unstoppable cultural phenomenon. Its next beneficiaries were two of the biggest names in English theatre, Gilbert and Sullivan, who brought out *Patience, or Bunthorne's Bride* in spring 1881.[64]

This timing was extremely fortuitous for Wilde: it put aesthetes in the limelight just as he was trying to publish his first volume of poetry. 'Possibly my name requires no introduction,' he told a publisher he hoped to entice.[65] The 26-year-old Wilde was not yet a household name, but he had a new-found currency on which he was now trying to trade. It worked. A year earlier, *Vera* had been nearly impossible to sell. But now the London publisher David Bogue was willing to be persuaded to print *Poems*, Wilde's first book.

When it was published, in June 1881, it was beautifully bound in white and gold, for Wilde had borne all the expenses of publication. *Poems* was intended to herald the arrival of a poet of distinction. Reviewers, however, condemned it. 'Mr. Oscar Wilde has published a shameful little book,' one said, but 'to arraign this young man solemnly at the bar of public opinion, to try him in wig and gown, would be a little cruel and a little ridiculous. His case is a sad one.'[66] Others said *Poems* was so imitative that Wilde sounded like 'a lyric parrot.'[67] Oxford critics were no less severe, sniffing at the collection as a vanity project. The Oxford Union refused an inscribed copy because an undergraduate described Wilde's verses as actually 'by a number of better-known and more deservedly reputed authors' including Shakespeare, Sidney, Donne, Byron, Morris, and Swinburne.[68] This was Wilde's second rejection from his alma mater, and a reminder that though he had distinguished himself academically, the university had resolutely closed its doors to him.

Punch joined the jeering chorus of reviews and added an unexpected twist. It mocked *Poems* by picturing Wilde as a thick-lipped, sunflower-faced Christy minstrel (see Plates 13 and 14).[69] Christy minstrels were blackface entertainers who pontificated absurdly and postured outlandishly. They crooned melodramatic songs about their broken hearts and pipe dreams. The performers were usually white 'Americans, stained black, who play & sing Negro songs, with grimaces,' Queen Victoria noted, when she described a minstrel show in her diary.[70] The funny 'Ethiopéans' she admired had been popular on both sides of the Atlantic since the century's early decades. In England and the United States, minstrel songs were whistled by workers, hummed by students, shrieked by children, carolled by civic associations, sung around the family piano, and intoned by royalty.

If we look forward one year to 1882, minstrelsy and sunflowers would become a big part of Wilde's story. For the moment, however, *Punch* stopped short of blackening Wilde's face. But the sketch was a black mark on Wilde's reputation as a poet, and made him look as if he could only warble the most hackneyed tune in the Victorian repertoire. 'Oh,' he sang in the cartoon, 'I feel just as happy as a bright sunflower.'[71]

Evidently, he was not. 'My life is full of pain,' he cried at the seaside in 'Vita Nuova,' one of the verses in his maligned poetry collection.[72] Describing how the waves drenched him with spray, he seemed baptized into a new life and 'a sudden glory' arose 'from the black waters of my tortured past.' Sure enough, August 1881 brought sunny news from across the Atlantic. The *New York Times* praised Wilde to the heavens, favourably comparing his *Poems* to those of Lord Tennyson, Queen Victoria's Poet Laureate.[73] 'Ave Imperatrix,' his ode to England, was singled out for 'grasping the idea of Great Britain and her colonies as one living empire and pouring out a majestic lament for her dead.' This gave cause to reconsider 'this much ridiculed "Maudle"' and see him as legitimate, according to the *Times*. 'In Wilde,' the review concluded, 'England has a new poet.' There could be no higher accolade.

The career of a poet was still a precarious one, and this was especially true for one who preferred the finer things in life. 'The highest form of literature, Poetry, brings no wealth to the singer,' he observed.[74] His mother knew this dilemma well. 'Writing for money is a very dull thing compared to writing for a Revolution,' Speranza complained.[75] Given the family's weak finances, she was writing for the *Pall Mall Gazette*, *The Queen*, the *Burlington Magazine*, and *Lady's Pictorial* while sharing rented London lodgings with Willie. Many men of Wilde's age had settled into a career and marriage. He had no profession and therefore no wages, no wife, and therefore no dowry. Would he prefer to ride the cultural wave that was about to come crashing down on him?

In summer and autumn 1881, the aesthetic craze gathered more momentum. One sign of how significant Aestheticism had become was that Queen Victoria ordered a Royal Command performance of *The Colonel* at Abergeldie Castle in Scotland and invited over two hundred of her associates, servants, and tenants to the show.[76] It was a 'very clever play, written to quiz & ridicule, the foolish aesthetic people,' the Queen thought.[77] What the Queen called foolish was fashionable to a younger set, like the Prince and Princess of Wales, who had loaned the actors a few of their own aesthetic baubles to fill out *The Colonel*'s scenery.[78] The rest of the play's furnishings were simply bought from a conventional Edinburgh store that stocked them, because aesthetic commodities were by then widely available.

Of all the aesthetic satires, Gilbert and Sullivan's *Patience* was far and away the finest.[79] It felt fresh, relevant, contemporary and, as a result, it soon outran its rivals. Its plot lines were pulled direct from cartoons and newspapers.[80] The show was a double feature about England's aesthetic craze and imperial current events. *Patience*'s Dragoons stood in for recent British victories in the 1879 Anglo-Zulu War and the 1880 Anglo-Afghan War. As Britain prepared for the Anglo-Egyptian war of 1882, the opera maintained its newsworthiness. But *Patience*'s soldiers also enabled Gilbert and Sullivan to editorialize about the war of the sexes. The opera pitted red-blooded military men against artistic pretenders of dubious masculinity in a battle for ladies' affections. In a light-hearted way, the show played out the real-life conflicts introduced by Victorian women's growing cultural clout. More and more, cultivated women had the authority to say what was attractive and what was not. Having taste was a way of wielding 'soft power' and exerting control over men—even over soldiers, as *Patience* demonstrated to comic effect when the Dragoons, frightened by the possibility that women might no longer find their uniforms irresistible, scramble to make themselves look more stylish. It's one of the opera's funniest scenes: the soldiers reappear on stage dressed as sunflower-wearing aesthetes. The manly makeover poked fun at military ideals and dramatized gender troubles in a way that resonated with Anglo-American audiences. *Patience*'s face-off between traditional imperial values and an artistic, youthful counterculture was an allegory for the oppositions that beset the age.

The opera's up-to-dateness and hummable melodies catapulted it to the top. Its best-loved song was a catchy send-up of impostors. Wilde's laughable alter ego, Bunthorne, reveals that the secret to appearing sophisticated is to become fluent in nonsense:

If you're anxious for to shine in the high aesthetic line as a man
of culture rare,
You must get up all the germs of the transcendental terms, and
plant them everywhere.
You must lie upon the daisies and discourse in novel phrases of
your complicated state of mind,
The meaning doesn't matter if it's only idle chatter of a transcen-
dental kind.
 And every one will say,
 As you walk your mystic way,
'If this young man expresses himself in terms too deep for *me*,
Why, what a very singularly deep young man this deep young
man must be!'[81]

The melody, the lyrics, the confession of what everyone already
suspected: it was an instant sensation. Once listeners heard the song's
rolling, thumping rhythms, they couldn't get it out of their heads or off
the tips of their tongues. Bunthorne was the nineteenth-century's
great pretender, a tongue-in-cheek tribute to Wilde who gave him
more visibility. But it was a mixed blessing to gain the fame he craved
at the expense of his artistic credibility.

Patience's success relied on its polarized depiction of Victorian England.
By pitting soldiers against aesthetes, and the Establishment against
bohemian freethinkers, *Patience* made itself interesting to all these
groups. No member of the audience could watch without wanting to
take a side—even Wilde himself. 'A party of my friends and myself
went to see *Patience* on the first night,' he said.[82] 'We laughed, or jeered,
at it as it deserved.' He had already seen all the other aesthetic satires
including *Where's the Cat?* and *The Colonel* (a 'dull farce,' he thought).[83]
It was as though he was an understudy preparing for a role.

Soon enough, the English theatre impresario Richard D'Oyly
Carte had three companies performing *Patience* in Europe, another in
Australia, and two in America. Wilde's growing fame as the face of
English Aestheticism made him the obvious choice to advertise *Patience*
across the Atlantic. D'Oyly Carte's newest venture was shipping British
lecturers and celebrities across to entertain the American public. The
war correspondent Archibald Forbes and the beautiful Lillie Langtry
were already on his books. Few of Carte's speakers suspected, however,

that they would be displayed as if in a circus. According to a contemporary, Carte's method was to present them on a 'Barnum platform' where like 'curiosities they are exhibited.'[84]

By late June 1881, American newspapers were saying that Wilde was coming to lecture, yet he hadn't been offered a contract.[85] Three months later, an agent from the Richard D'Oyly Carte Opera Company cabled from New York.[86] Would he accept a fifty-lecture engagement tour in the United States? Wilde slept on it, and cabled back the next day, 'yes, if offer good.'[87] Carte's Company undertook all the risk.[88] They would pay for any losses, though Wilde would have to meet his own expenses. At the end of the tour, Wilde would receive a third of the net receipts.[89] In a few months' time, Matthew Arnold would be offered the same terms. From Wilde's point of view, Carte's offer was magnificent. But accepting it meant putting aside his immediate hopes of a literary career. As those who knew him pointed out, 'his literary and dramatic gifts were developed later.'[90] Wilde's motives for accepting Carte's offer were personal and mercenary. The alternatives were lacklustre and his finances were stretched. The invitation to lecture in America could not have come at a better time. It was not quite the only option, but was by far the best.

Because of the extraordinary wave of interest in Aestheticism, Wilde found himself brought to market on the crest of enormous demand. '*Patience* has given Mr. Wilde the chance of an American career and success,' Americans were saying.[91] The arc of Wilde's life had been redrawn by a caricaturist and was presently redirected by a stroke of luck. It would make for a singular opportunity—if he could take advantage of it, rather than letting it take advantage of him. Wilde grabbed his chance with both hands. Very soon he would be telling a New York reporter, '*I* am the original of Maudle, the poet.'[92]

PART TWO
1882–1883

To mature its powers, to concentrate its action, to learn the secret of its own strength and of England's weakness, the Celtic intellect has had to cross the Atlantic.... What captivity was to the Jews, exile has been to the Irish. America and American influences educated them.

– Oscar Wilde on the Irish in America, Pall Mall Gazette, 13 April 1889

Chapter 5

Colonel Morse's Campaign

On Christmas Eve 1881, a 27-year-old Oscar Wilde wrapped himself in a fur cloak and boarded the SS *Arizona* at Liverpool. The sealskin coat would be his constant companion. Other than that, he ventured out alone. He was tired of his life in England. 'Anything is better than virtuous obscurity,' he thought.[1] A peek inside his luggage reveals a set of peculiar clothes: knee-breeches, silk stockings, and patent leather pumps. Also, an outfit inflected by the colours of his native Ireland: a dark-green Prince Albert coat, a clover-coloured kerchief, and a matching cravat. About a week later, the liner would deliver him to New York, where he would begin a new chapter. 'I shall endure,' he wrote in a poem, 'and sell ambition at the common mart, and let dull failure be my vestiture, and sorrow dig its grave within my heart.'[2]

It was days since the *Arizona* had set sail. Wilde didn't confine himself to the ship's stylish state-rooms and saloon. He ventured below decks and entertained himself by speaking to the other passengers and emigrants he found there. When a Romanian girl caught his eye, he approached and tried to woo her with his 'superlatively aesthetic' attitude to life. His sweetheart failed to be impressed when he told her he was a 'consummately soulful' young man.[3] The flirtation was lost in translation. To pass the time, he paraded along the ship's decks in front of the other passengers, as though he were walking down Piccadilly. He told anyone who would listen that the sea was disappointing. The mighty Atlantic had not met his expectations because he longed for it to roar, or for a storm to rise and sweep away the ship's bridge. Meanwhile, the ship's Captain, George Siddons Murray, contemplated giving his annoying passenger a better view of the ocean. 'I wish I had that man lashed to the bowsprit on the windward side,' Capt. Murray reflected.

On New Year's Eve, Wilde was still at sea. Meanwhile, in England, Queen Victoria was trying to be optimistic about what 1882 held in store for her and for her empire. Such hopes didn't come easily to the 62-year-old. On the last day of the year, she summed it up as 'a terrible one, full of horrors & sorrows.'[4] Her beloved Prince Albert had been dead for over two decades, and fresher losses troubled her. She wrote in her diary that 1881 had 'taken away 2 of my valued friends,' Prime Minister Disraeli and the Dean of Westminster, 'and many other acquaintances and old faithful friends.' She continued her gloomy catalogue of the year's troubles, adding to it 'the Emperor of Russia's horrible assassination, and that of [American] President Garfield, the dreadful state of Ireland, with "Irish Atrocities."' There was also 'the shocking Dunecht outrage,' in which the Earl of Crawford's corpse was stolen from its Scottish grave, and the burning of Vienna's Ring Theatre 'with nearly 400 people perishing.' Victoria concluded her dismal tally in disbelief at the unluckiness of 1881. 'All, occurred in this year!'

Some amusement was necessary to lighten the sombre mood. What better way to lift the spirits on New Year's Eve than with a singalong? Inside Osborne House, the royal family gathered around Princess Beatrice at the piano. They merrily sang airs from *Patience*, the Gilbert and Sullivan romp with which Wilde was becoming conspicuously associated. 'The words,' Victoria thought, 'are so very funny.'[5] Prince Leopold and the Assistant Keeper of the Privy Purse took the male solos. Queen Victoria and Princess Louise sang the chorus. Victoria couldn't resist the opera's cheer, and developed something of a lifelong passion for *Patience*. She learned the solos and duets by heart and would go on singing them until her death.[6] The Queen's subjects were equally enthusiastic about the rollicking opera. In England, even serious intellectuals liked to round off an evening with a group singalong of *Patience*, as an unsuspecting American student of Professor Max Müller discovered one night when the distinguished Oxford don invited him over for dinner and merry-making.[7]

It was because of *Patience* that Wilde was now sailing to the United States. As he stood on the prow of the SS *Arizona*, he had no idea what awaited him in the New World. Floating somewhere in the mid-Atlantic, Wilde was probably trying to muster some cheer for the New

Year. He knew only that he had decided to leave failure behind him. As for what lay ahead, he was optimistic about the opportunities for self-invention that America might afford him. For now, during the last days of December 1881, it was all still a marvellous adventure. The *Arizona* ploughed on, carrying Wilde and his cargo of hopes across oyster-grey waters. He thought of himself, he later said, as 'a man who stood in symbolic relations to the art and culture of my age.'[8] He had decided this 'at the very dawn of my manhood, and had forced my age to realise it afterwards.' In the New Year, he would declare his genius to the New World. Past disappointments would be buried. The future, when it came, would begin a new life.

3 January 1882, New York. Legend has it that on his arrival in the United States, Wilde breezed through customs and said to officials, 'I have nothing to declare but my genius.' We have no proof that he said this because the anecdote was first 'recorded' thirty years later.[9] We can be certain, however, that the New York newspapers—the *Sun*, the *Herald*, the *Times*, and the *Tribune*—were keen to get a soundbite from Wilde as he emerged from the SS *Arizona* wearing a felt hat and a huge cape that billowed in the wind.[10] Interviewers jostled towards him, questions at the ready.

'How old are you?' one enquired.

Twenty-six, he said, shaving a year off his real age.[11]

'What are aesthetics?' another journalist asked.

Wilde name-dropped his favourite artists and poets including Edward Burne-Jones, Dante Gabriel Rossetti, William Morris, Algernon Swinburne—the men who had established the Aesthetic Movement's credentials. Before long, the reporters turned to personal matters.

'When do you get up in the morning?'

'Do you like eggs fried on both sides or only on one side?'

'Do you trim your finger-nails in the style of the Empress of Japan?'

He had arrived in the land of accelerated intimacies and instantaneous familiarity. The press had never examined him so closely before. In England, newspapers were only 'dreary records of politics, police-courts, and personalities,' Wilde wrote in a letter.[12]

After the barrage of interviewers, there were throngs of men and women pressing forward, eager to have a look. Of course, he looked back, and was curious to find out who the American people were. New York City was then the biggest city in the United States with a population of more than 1.2 million.[13] The United States counted over fifty million people—twice the population of England and Wales, or ten times the population of Ireland.[14] America was a crucible of humanity. A stirring song about the melting pot revealed its ingredients to the tune of *Patience*:

> If you want a receipt for the mystery national,
> Known to the world as the Ameri*can*—
> Take all the elements cranky, and rational,
> Found in each nation and climate and clan:
> The pluck of the Britisher, dashing and metally, . . .
> Rollick of Irishman, German solidity. . . .
> Chinese rapidity, Tatar vitality,
> African jollity, Japanese oddity, . . .
> Zuluish strategy, Grecian address, . . .
> Language Shakespearean, spoken quite nasily, . . .
> Arabic luxury, western *elan*,
> And the mixture of all is the Ameri*can*.[15]

To Wilde, it seemed that even walking down the street would be a different experience here. Policemen held the crowds back so that he could clear a path through them.[16] 'It is delightful to be a *petit roi*,' he wrote to his confidante Mrs Betty Lewis, the wife of his solicitor. On pale-blue paper (the colour favoured by royalty), he explained that he felt he had become a prince and the gawkers his adoring subjects. Referring to the Prince of Wales, he told Mrs Lewis, 'I now understand why the Royal Boy is in good humour always.' Wilde felt like he had conquered the United States and added it to his dominions. Before long, he fancied the entire world would be his.[17]

Standing over six feet tall, Colonel William Francis Morse had a splendid moustache sprouting from underneath his Roman nose. Hired to be Wilde's manager and accomplice, the 40-year-old war veteran and theatrical manager had the unmistakable bearing of a military man. Before Wilde's arrival, Colonel Morse had been *Patience*'s New York business manager, and he looked like a natural to play one of the opera's Dragoon Guards.[18] He was accustomed to conquests and campaigns of all kinds. When the American Civil War broke out, in 1861, he had already been in the army for four years. As a 20-year-old lieutenant-colonel, he led his regiment in Minnesota's Indian campaign. During one battle, Native Americans surrounded his camp. Six hundred of Chief Little Crow's fighters appeared out of the tall grass. As the horde descended, Morse saw the gleam of a double-barrelled gun aimed directly at him.[19] More than 700 men died in the clash, but Morse survived. 'It was as though a flash of lightning had illuminated a curtain on which incidents' of his life were projected, he recalled.

Now Colonel Morse worked in New York City for Richard D'Oyly Carte, and he would be responsible for arranging Wilde's lectures.[20] He undertook his obligations with the aplomb of a seasoned military man—planning Wilde's itinerary and schedule, booking theatres, writing advertisements, and fixing ticket prices. He wasted little time marshalling Wilde, whose first lecture was only a week away. On the day of his arrival in America, Morse marched Wilde to the Hotel Brunswick for a hearty breakfast and then put his new lecturer in training.[21] 'The lecture is far from being ready yet, and he will have to spend the next four or five days working on this,' Morse told a *Tribune* reporter that afternoon. Nothing would be allowed to 'distract him from labour,' Morse said.

Colonel Morse managed his army of one with military precision. The first order of business was to make Wilde look like an apostle of beauty. A tailor called Wirtz took measurements for Wilde's new outfits. 30 inches from the groin to the knee. 38½ inch waist.[22] Fitted knee-breeches were made up and low-cut silver-buckled pumps were ordered. He would have to wear black silk stockings on his lower legs because of his abbreviated trousers. Colonel Morse described this costume as 'the court suit of the English private gentleman,' but many thought it actually made Wilde resemble a court jester.[23]

Morse's second order of business was publicity. To carry out this manoeuvre, he had chosen a photographer with a military name— Napoleon—who was almost as small as the Emperor himself. Despite his stature, Napoleon Sarony had an enormous reputation as the celebrity photographer of the day, and he claimed to have photographed upwards of 30,000 performers. The most famous were paid handsomely for agreeing to pose. The actress Fanny Kemble demanded $300, the singer Adelina Patti $1000, and the legendarily slender Sarah Bernhardt a fat $1,500.[24] The non-famous had to pay, and so Morse agreed a fee. Sarony had another condition, however. Nobody else would be allowed to take pictures of Wilde.[25] For the duration of his tour, Sarony would have the exclusive rights to Wilde's image.

When Wilde arrived at Sarony's studio in Union Square, the frisky little man in the big red fez set about arranging him into various picturesque attitudes. Wilde had brought his new outfits, including a white cane. Yet it was his sealskin cap that captivated Sarony. His first picture re-created the way Wilde looked when they first met on that cold January day, bundled in the fur-lined overcoat (see Plate 15). 'Ah, here is a picturesque subject, indeed!' Sarony exclaimed, pirouetting around Wilde.[26]

As he looked into the eye of Sarony's camera, Wilde smiled, laughed, and relaxed. At the photographer's suggestion, he reclined languidly on a fur pelt and prominently displayed his legs on a Turkish carpet. Wilde was docile as Sarony obsessed over the right attitudes and postures in which to arrange him. Like Dorian Gray, 'there was nothing that one could not do with him. He could be made a Titan or a toy.'[27] In each photograph, Sarony created a new Wilde. In a close-up headshot, here was the soulful-eyed young man of Gilbert and Sullivan's *Patience*. In white tie and tails, here was the Oxford gentleman, the guest at sparkling dinners, the friend of English high society. In his long fur coat and velvet jacket, here was the London dandy and man about town. A finger in his book of *Poems*, and another hand gently resting against his temple, here was the author, the serious man of letters. Each pose captured an aspect of his personality (see Plates 16 and 17). Wilde was thrilled with the photographs.[28] Sarony made him 'beautiful,' he told Lillie Langtry.[29]

The demand for Wilde's pictures rapidly outstripped supply.[30] Sarony's portraits were transformed into trade cards for products ranging from cigars to ice cream, a development that would later be impossible in the age of copyright. They flew into shopfront window displays, were glued into scrapbooks, and carried in Americans' pockets. In addition to the authorized photographs, tens of thousands of unauthorized copies were snapped up.[31]

We know this because two years later, Sarony filed for copyright infringement and accused the Burrow-Giles Lithographic Company of printing 85,000 unauthorized reproductions of Wilde's portraits. The landmark Supreme Court case enshrined American copyright protection of photographs.[32] According to the Circuit Court of New York, Wilde's image was Sarony's creation because the photographer had made the picture 'entirely from his own original mental conception, to which he gave visible form by posing' Wilde like a mannequin in front of his camera.[33] Years later, when he came to write 'The Portrait of Mr. W.H.,' Wilde winked at Sarony's creative genius in his story of a forged portrait creating a new identity for the sitter. Yet it was in *The Picture of Dorian Gray* that he captured the mysterious effect picture portraits had on society. Because they seemed so intimate, portraits gave viewers the false impression they knew the sitter personally. This is exactly what happens in Wilde's novel when Lord Henry's wife meets Dorian for the first time. Rather than greeting him as a stranger, she welcomes him like an old acquaintance. 'I know you quite well by your photographs,' she tells Dorian, 'I think my husband has got twenty-seven of them.'[34]

In the first weeks of January 1882, Colonel Morse made Wilde work all day and then sent him out into the night where he hobnobbed, dined with journalists, and sometimes managed to visit as many as three receptions in one evening.[35] Thanks to the press coverage and the lecture advertisements Colonel Morse had placed, Wilde was the talk of the town.

'Pah!' the New York literary critic and financier Edmund Clarence Stedman confided to his diary.[36] 'This Philistine town is making a fool of itself over Oscar Wilde.' Scowling in private was less satisfying than doing it in a letter, so a few days later he repeated his withering critique to Edward Henry Clement, the editor of the *Boston Evening Transcript*. 'Our rich people here,' Stedman wrote, 'see *no difference* between writers, between Longfellow and Emerson—and Bryant—and Wilde!' According to Stedman, 'our *soi-disant* intelligent and fashionable classes' could not discriminate between real artists and a minor foreign personality. 'I do not blame a clever humbug, like Wilde, for taking advantage of their snobbery and idiocy, and making all the money *he* can.' This was too good a scoop to pass up. The *Evening Transcript* editor promptly published Stedman's letter.

Most Americans made no distinction between Wilde's actions and those of his managers. To the outside world, it was difficult to tell them apart. However, Wilde's friends noticed that Colonel Morse and D'Oyly Carte were handling him like a puppet.[37] Behind the scenes, they saw his managers as 'humbugs' pulling strings, and exploiting their contractual rights to manoeuvre him as they wished. A few nights before his debut, they compelled him to attend *Patience* at New York's Standard Theatre. The show was in full swing when Wilde and his entourage noisily entered the theatre, an incursion calculated to produce the maximum disturbance.[38] At first, the aesthete sat out of sight, but then he created a second commotion by moving to a seat where the audience could observe him. When Bunthorne walked on stage, Wilde announced loudly, 'this is one of the compliments that mediocrity pays to those who are not mediocre.' The entire audience turned to look at him. For the rest of the performance, he ignored what was happening on stage and chatted with the ladies seated around him. After the show, a crowd gathered in the theatre lobby in anticipation of meeting the aesthete. Fifteen minutes ticked by and still Wilde did not appear. Finally, Colonel Morse, the whiskered ex-combatant, walked into the lobby to tell the spectators they were not going to see the smooth-cheeked aesthete again that evening. He had slipped away by another exit.

Colonel Morse had planned the stunt from start to finish, accompanying Wilde into the theatre and watching him carry out his role. He seemed to be a puppetmaster intent on making Americans see Wilde as his Pinocchio for *Patience*. 'He isn't vain at all, or he wouldn't go to see what is supposed to be a caricature of himself,' Morse told a reporter about his compliant aesthete's visit to the Standard Theatre.[39]

Morse's tactics were creating a sensation. Before long, tickets for Wilde's debut were sold out. 'Mr. Wilde has been so well worked up by his management here that there is an absolute craze to see and hear the apostle of aestheticism,' New York newspapers said.[40] There was just one more thing that needed to be done before the premiere of 'The English Renaissance,' and Morse could not do it for him: Wilde's lecture still had to be written. 'It had been assumed that he had a message to deliver, and one had to be found,' his friend Rennell Rodd recalled.[41] 'What he was to tell the lecture-loving public in the States he hardly knew himself.' With only two days to go, Wilde was in a frenzy about the lecture. 'If I am not a success on Monday I shall be very wretched,' he confided to Mrs Lewis.[42]

By the end of the nineteenth century, Americans had gained a reputation for being superior public speakers. Whether as lecturers, orators, or elocutionists, they were known as compelling presences at the podium. It had not always been so. Early in the century, Americans generally remained under the sway of eighteenth-century British rhetorical traditions.[43] By mid-century, however, the demand for a more democratic style reflective of American society led to a surge of oratorical ingenuity and enthusiasm. Emerson, Henry Ward Beecher, and abolitionists like Frederick Douglass, Wendell Phillips, and Colonel Thomas Wentworth Higginson enthralled audiences with their rhetoric.[44] Emerson advised beginners to speak to the audience as though in conversation with them. Scholars, he cautioned, must avoid 'cataloguing obscure and nebulous stars of the human mind' and should use everyday English.[45] Colonel Higginson, who had watched Wilde recite his prize-winning poem in Oxford, agreed that popular audiences had no patience with subtlety or profundity. 'Your cheapest efforts may tell better than your choicest,' he counselled in *Macmillan's Magazine* in 1868.[46] Lecturing Americans required 'your broadest common-sense, your heartiest sympathy, your manliest courage.'

Elocution—the art of felicitous expression—trickled down to every man. It became an indispensable part of training for those who hoped to rise in American society.[47] For a dime, inexpensive guides to public speaking promised a complete compendium of declamation for the School, the Exhibition, the Parlor, and the Fireside.[48] Training was integrated into educational curricula. By 1883, college freshmen, sophomores, and juniors could expect to perform weekly declamation and reading exercises, while seniors wrote essays and speeches that they delivered before their peers.[49] Students were taught to present their ideas in a neat and engaging way because it was thought that effective speaking and writing went hand in hand. In the century's final decades, American students were routinely instructed in oratory and elocution, with debating proving increasingly popular. The cultural work of this training was impressive: by the dawn of the twentieth century, oratory was thought of as an American art. Its history had been thoroughly rewritten. Now lecturing was considered a native tradition or, as some put it, 'an indigenous plant in America.'[50]

Wilde's debut lecture, 'The English Renaissance,' was to be more like a sermon than anything else he would ever write. 'The English Renaissance' was a synonym for Aestheticism and the Aesthetic Movement. In a letter to the poet James Russell Lowell, he solemnly declared his mission to America as a commission 'to give a course of lectures . . . on the modern artistic movement in England.'[51] But what, exactly, would he say? His old sidekick, Whistler, advised against earnestness. 'That you should take yourself seriously is unpardonable,' the painter cautioned.[52] At the start of his tour, Wilde was still terribly sincere about what he wished to achieve, and scholarly in how he went about it. He was, after all, fresh from university, and still hankering to become a serious author. Four copies of 'The English Renaissance' lecture survive—one of them written entirely in Wilde's hand.[53] These drafts hint at how much he struggled to gather his thoughts. They show that he approached his daunting task by drafting what can best be described as a long report—dry, detailed, and excruciatingly thorough. 'The English Renaissance' offered a comprehensive history of Aestheticism, a movement made familiar to his audience mostly as an object of ridicule. 'You have listened to *Patience* for a hundred nights and you have heard me only for one,' he would say. 'It will make, no doubt, that satire more piquant by knowing something about the subject of it, but you must not judge of aestheticism by the satire of Mr. Gilbert.'[54]

So he described the movement as an intellectual and artistic family that had roots in Oxford thinking, and personalized his version with anecdotes plucked from the men he claimed as his spiritual kin. Art is as true as life, he said: 'I remember Mr. Swinburne insisting on [that] at dinner.'[55] Later, he added, 'I remember once, in talking to Mr. Burne-Jones about modern science, his saying to me, "the more materialistic science becomes, the more angels shall I paint." '[56] He name-dropped with abandon. 'I remember William Morris saying to me once,' he swaggered, though he had only met Morris the once, and hadn't made a good impression.[57] ('I must admit,' Morris told his wife after meeting Wilde, 'that as the devil is painted blacker than he is, so it fares with O.W. Not but what he is an ass: but he certainly is clever too.')[58]

The future of Aestheticism was central to Wilde's lecture. 'Our English Renaissance,' he said, 'is indeed a sort of new birth in the spirit of man' that aims to improve life.[59] It was a way of living with passionate attention to beauty, and seeking out new experiences, whether in art, the mind, or imagination. He compared Aestheticism to the Italian Renaissance in the fifteenth century and to ancient Greece.[60] 'There is something Hellenic in your air and world,' he would tell his American audience, as though the nineteenth century might be a further phase in Greek history.[61]

The lecture evolved organically, and was soon sprawling in all directions, leaping off at angles and tangents from its main idea. As he drafted it, his thoughts turned to memorized passages from Ruskin's *The Stones of Venice*, Morris's *Hopes and Fears for Art*, and Pater's *Studies in the History of the Renaissance*. Pater's words rang in his ears: the professor's emphasis on the importance of 'new experiences, new subjects of poetry, new forms of art' was appropriated by his diligent student as 'new subjects for poetry, new forms of art, new intellectual and imaginative enjoyments.'[62] Wilde hastily reread Ruskin's early works and was spotted with *Fors Clavigera* (Ruskin's didactic letters to British workers about the perils of capitalism) and *The Poetry of Architecture* (the observations he had made as an 18-year-old about the relationship between buildings and nature).[63] Something of this, too, would later wend its way into Wilde's growing lecture.

9 January 1882, New York. The Chickering Hall box office put up a placard announcing the lecture was 'standing room only.' At 8 o'clock, ticketless hopefuls were turned away. Located in the entertainment district around Union Square, Chickering Hall was going to be filled to the rafters. In the hour before the curtain rose on Wilde's first lecture, private coaches drove through the frosty streets towards the theatre's entrance on 5th Avenue and deposited Manhattan's smart set, those who could easily afford the pricey $1 ticket. Inside the elegant red brick and marble Hall, they joined a throng of more than 1,200 ticketholders, including the 'representatives of families conspicuous in the fashionable world,' as the *New York Times* put it.[64] Looking around the horseshoe-shaped auditorium at the people on show in the seats, one could see that New York's ladies and gentlemen were wearing their finest. 'Opera glasses were levelled toward all points,' the *Times* observed. 'People more and more showed an interest in one another.' It was rare for such a first-rate audience to gather in one place.[65] To maximize the audience's visibility beyond the theatre itself, the *New York World* published a list of prominent ticketholders' names so that even those who hadn't been at Wilde's lecture could see the fashionable folk in attendance.

This was the fashionable world upon which Edith Wharton would open *The Age of Innocence*, her Pulitzer Prize-winning novel about complicated love in high society. In the first scene, Wharton satirized fashionable 1870s New Yorkers for whom most of the fun of a night at the theatre derived from inspecting the other members of the audience. She cast a knowing, sidelong glance at 'what the daily press had already learned to describe as "an exceptionally brilliant audience" '—a gem of a phrase that leaves no doubt that the performances happening in the theatre's seats easily rivalled the ones on the stage.[66] Wharton was born in a stylish home five minutes away from Chickering Hall; her supremely wealthy family was the origin of the phrase 'keeping up with the Joneses.' For the fashionable denizens of Fifth Avenue, there could hardly be anything better to do than turn away from the stage, peer through one's opera glass at the others in the audience, and tut-tut about Countess Ellen Olenska's awfully low-cut dress.

Standing in the wings of Chickering Hall, Colonel Morse watched Wilde take the stage. From this vantage point, he could see both his protégé and the audience. When Wilde appeared, they looked at him sceptically at first, Morse observed. The spectators murmured, then softly teased him, and finally, mocked him openly. Throughout the heckling, 'Mr. Wilde was perfectly cool and collected—not nervous, as many of the most prominent speakers often are,' Morse said in his account of the night.[67] The mood of the room suddenly shifted, and in a matter of moments, Wilde had Chickering Hall hypnotized. According to Morse's memoir, Wilde's demeanour quickly swayed the audience. 'As he went on, the calm, persuasive, convincing manner of the man had its effect,' he recalled. 'At the end of the first five minutes,' Morse claimed, 'a kind of gasp of astonishment and incredulity swept over the house.' A swell of applause filled the Hall. After calmly soldiering through five minutes of torment, 'his audience was captured' and America was at his feet.[68]

In the showman's version of Wilde's biography, it was a five-minute miracle: there was a brief trial in which a valiant hero immediately subdued and converted hostile spectators into adoring fans. If only it had been that easy. Perhaps Morse felt it inopportune to tell the truth, which was that Wilde's American tour had actually lurched from drama to drama. Instead, he created a myth and granted Wilde a fairy-tale experience that he did not have.

Here is what really happened on Wilde's first night in New York: he had worked hard at his lecture and by the time he reached the podium he had eighty-eight pages of notes to show for it.[69] 'I will not try to give you any abstract definition of beauty,' he promised before launching into his abstract definitions of beauty.[70] Glittering cultural references spangled the talk. He mentioned Balzac, Baudelaire, Beethoven, Blake, Byron, Chaucer, Coleridge, Dürer, as well as Gautier and Goethe, Homer and Hugo, Mazzini and Michelangelo, Napoleon, Rousseau, Scott, Theocritus, and Wordsworth. He scampered through centuries of history and culture—English, French, Greek, Italian, and Japanese. Even the most sympathetic members of the audience struggled to follow him. His thoughts were as dazzling as a sparkler but they veered off in as many directions as a pinwheel firecracker. After two hours of this, the lecture ended with a fizzle, not a bang.

Though his range was encyclopaedic, his delivery was bungled. 'Wilde sounded like a schoolboy scanning Horatio's first ode,' thought the *Washington Post*.[71] His voice, the *Chicago Tribune* reported, was 'an odious intoning and a half smothering of the Queen's English peculiar to Oxford men.'[72] To Americans, it sounded like he was speaking a foreign language. The lecture was 'painful,' the *New York Times* concluded.[73]

Colonel Morse was not the only storyteller to reframe the New York debut into something much greater than it really was. 'Great success here,' Wilde wrote to London friends days after the first lecture, 'nothing like it since Dickens.'[74] That was wishful bombast, and hinted at the half-truths with which he would frame his autobiography. His letters home show a young man in thrall to his managers' hype and dazzled by the speed of his own transformation. During those heady first days, he had every reason to believe Colonel Morse had his best interests at heart, and he still had everything to win by being docile and obeying his puppetmaster.

Wilde boasted in his correspondence that he 'had an audience larger and more wonderful than even Dickens had.'[75] The comparison was far-fetched at best, for the best-selling novelist had been responsible for a revolution in public lecturing. He had set a precedent by developing the lecture-reading form into a whole new way for the author to address his public.[76] 'He impersonates the characters of the story he reads,' *Harper's* reported with delight in its 1867 review of Dickens's second American tour.[77] 'He does not only read his story,' another contemporary said, 'he acts it.'[78] Wilde said he assumed that America had 'changed greatly since Dickens's visit' but he had no idea how much it had.[79] Ever since Dickens's second American visit, in

1867, Americans had come to expect lecturers to *perform* their script with the liveliness of an actor. Dickens was not the first to do this, but he was responsible for developing what was described in his own day as 'a novelty in literature and in the annals of "entertainment." '[80]

Before Dickens, very few authors performed in such a manner, and audiences were only rarely given the occasion to visit the creators of beloved literary characters. By the 1870s, it was common for authors to imitate Dickens by reading from their own works.[81] New styles of authorial performance evolved, absorbing aspects of the popular entertainer's humorous lecture (a style in its own right, which would lead to vaudeville, stand-up comedy, and performance art).[82] The best lecturers, like Dickens, were actors at heart. In his younger days, Dickens wanted to be a performer and he had channelled that dramatic sensibility into his writing practice.[83] His daughter Mamie secretly witnessed her father's frenetic, athletic writing process. As she looked on, she saw him do some quick scribbling at his desk, jump up, rush to the mirror, and examine his face in 'some extraordinary facial contortions which he was making,' and speak 'rapidly in a low voice.' On the public readings circuit, when faced with an audience, Dickens deployed his histrionic powers to the full.

Dickens's legendary delivery was no accident. Prior to his second departure for America, he practised by conducting trial reading tours in England, Scotland, and Ireland. To enhance his performance and acoustics, he developed a transportable stage-rig so he could stand behind his desk on stage, with carpeting underfoot, and gas lights shining on him.[84] An entourage of six—manager, valet-dresser, gasman, and other staff—attended to him. Nothing was left to chance. Henry Wadsworth Longfellow referred to these performances as 'Actings' rather than 'Readings.'[85] Over the course of seventy-six readings, Dickens entertained over 100,000 listeners, and made £19,000 in profit.[86]

One of these listeners was Mark Twain.[87] After Dickens's death, in 1870, Twain protested against the fashion for public readings that the English novelist had popularized. 'The nation is to be lectured to death,' Twain worried.[88] Though many British authors tried to repeat Dickens's feat, few succeeded. The sensation writer Wilkie Collins followed in the footsteps of his best friend and collaborator, but eventually discovered that Dickens's shoes were too large to fill. Collins had acting experience, prepared in advance, and sat to Sarony for promotional pictures in New York in 1873.[89] None of this made up for the fact that Collins was not half the actor Dickens was and so, in the end, he only made about a tenth of Dickens's earnings.[90]

Wilde's approach was nothing like Dickens's or Collins's. Everything they had done, he hadn't—including writing best-selling novels that made their names familiar to Americans long before they came to the United States. With no prior acting experience to speak of, a rambling script, and barely any practice, it was unlikely that Wilde was going to be able to continue drawing crowds beyond his first lectures. Besides, his script had been sent in advance to all the members of the press, and had been widely reprinted.[91] That would satisfy those who wanted to know what 'The English Renaissance' was about, but it was unlikely to make them buy a ticket to hear his lacklustre delivery. A celebrated American Professor of Rhetoric reminded his students that they had to do more than write something to read out. They had to give listeners a performance worth coming out to hear. Otherwise they 'might as well have stayed at home till it was printed.'[92] Across the Atlantic, Wilde's mother sensed he was in trouble when she read the transcript of his lecture in the newspaper. 'Your lecture is too *abstract*. Nothing to catch the attention. Give some *personal descriptions*,' she advised from London.[93]

For the time being, Wilde would stick to his script. In the days following his New York lecture, he had numerous conversations with American journalists. The interviewers took down his every word, and were more considerate and attentive than most of his audiences would be. When he spoke to journalists he had an easy wit that dried up when he stood at the podium. During these one-on-one chats he may have sensed that he had found his medium. But how could he turn these interviews to his advantage? If he could figure that out, it might prove a silver lining to the ominous clouds gathering over his tour.

Meanwhile, *The Nation* had already sniffed out the D'Oyly Carte Company's ruse. The aesthete's dismal lecture would be excellent for business, the magazine predicted, because it encouraged parody and satire. That, in turn, would be a boon for the Company's main bread-winner, *Patience*. 'You hear the true gospel at Chickering Hall, and join the mocking laughter of the heathen at the absurdity of it at the Standard Theatre.'[94] The Company's calculation was obvious. 'The same manager "runs" the lecture tour of the aesthete and the operatic company which heaps ridicule upon him,' the magazine explained. To D'Oyly Carte, Wilde was expendable. This set up a conflict between

Wilde's intentions (to use the tour to convey a serious message about art) and his managers' (to rake in profits). If his lectures boosted *Patience*'s box office but killed his reputation, they would merely consider it collateral damage.

Soon enough, the magnitude of the situation he had blundered into became apparent to him. 'My delivery has often been criticized *very* severely, but I confess it is abominable,' he told one interviewer, 'I cannot help it. I have never studied elocution.'[95]

'Americans are natural orators,' he pouted to another.[96] 'I never heard a spontaneous burst of oratory until I came to America and listened to an American.' At the end of the interview, the truth tiptoed out of his mouth. 'I had never spoken in public until I lectured in New York. I then found out what a difficult task I had undertaken.' He was no Dickens, and his life was not going to be one of Morse's five-minute fairy tales.

Chapter 6

Oscar Dear

'Interviewers are a product of American civilization, whose acquaintance I am making with tolerable speed,' Wilde remarked soon after his arrival in the country.[1] He did not suspect it, but he was poised on the edge of a cultural and journalistic revolution: the interview. As this new form of reporting swept him up, he would become one of the era's most interviewed people. Interviewing would turn journalism into a gossipy, tell-all medium. The keynote of New Journalism was its more intimate tone.[2] For Wilde, it would do two things: make his name familiar to millions, and make them feel like he was speaking directly to them. This added to what photography and technologies of mass reproduction were already doing to make him visible to millions. Now the printed interview was going to make him accessible and familiar. It would enable readers to 'hear' his voice on the page as they read their newspapers over breakfast. And that, in turn, would make him a phenomenon, a celebrity author whose book of poems was sought after and widely discussed.

For newspaper readers, the interview provided the enjoyable thrill of eavesdropping on private conversations without the worry of being discovered. It seemed almost possible to overhear intimate chats when you were not in the room, or were even an ocean away. Wilde's nosy mother, for instance, could listen in from across the Atlantic to her son's conversations because of the newspaper clippings he dutifully sent her. 'The *interviewing* is awful & how will you get through it?' she wrote, despairing at the vulgarity of the form.[3] But she changed her tune when she saw how interviews enabled her son to script his success. After reading his latest Q&A, she told him, 'Your responses were all so clever.'[4]

Wilde was finding a way to turn intrusive conversations with journalists to his advantage. Ever the doting mother, Speranza was pleased to have extra information about her son, but soon became addicted to the steady drip-feed of personal information and complained when he was slow to send the American newspapers on. 'I trust you are well for report got into the papers that you were ill and I am very anxious.'[5] In London, she would scour the latest article for details of Oscar's progress and offer unsolicited advice. Soon she was suggesting he could enhance his interviews by curling his hair every morning before journalists arrived. Give them something to write about, she thought.[6]

Wilde had ideas of his own about how to make his conversations with journalists noteworthy. His interviews were more theatrical than his lectures, and showed him in a more flattering light. In his hotel suite, one-to-one with a reporter, he had all the charisma that vanished when he faced large audiences. Up close, he was spellbinding. That temporary magic gained staying power when the interview was published in newspapers. His witticisms retained their crackle and fizz on the printed page. Slowly but surely aphorisms would come to define him and would eventually revolutionize his writing.

Over the course of twelve months in 1882–3, Wilde was interviewed at least ninety-eight times. How many times had he been interviewed before? Zero. How many interviews would he have during the rest of his life? Five. So 95 per cent of his lifetime interviewing experience occurred in one American *annus mirabilis*. Its effect on him was profound, but it was his writing that benefited most. Constant interviewing drastically improved his ability to write good dialogue. This was not then part of his skill set, as his first play, *Vera*, had amply demonstrated. Stilted and staid, it didn't yet have the humour and flexibility of Wilde's own repartee. While on tour, Wilde regularly read newspaper accounts of his lectures and interviews. This enabled him to 'hear' the sound of his voice in print, and to compare what he had said against how his conversation sounded on the page. The effect of this repeated, regular exercise trained his ear for witty dialogue. The unstinting attention he lavished on his interviews paid off. With each successive interview, his diction grew more precise, his soundbites sharper. Later, the characters in his society comedies would talk like him.

When Miss Mary Watson of the *San Francisco Examiner* turned up at Wilde's hotel room, she was looking for a story. The journalist was hoping to write one that would enable her readers 'to picture Oscar Wilde's at-home manner,' she said.[7] By the time she reached his door at the Palace Hotel, she was thinking of herself as a big-game hunter seeking her prey. 'I saw the lion in his lair,' Watson later said, 'saw him stirred up, poetically speaking, and an interesting process it was.' Intrepid in the discharge of her professional duty, she had prepared questions to fire at him. Now all she had to do was wait for him to appear.

As soon as he entered the room, he and his valet began to perform a disarming routine. When Wilde dramatically threw off his cloak, his valet pounced behind him and caught it just before it hit the floor. This choreography complete, the aesthete's next big move was to throw himself down on the sofa. Then, as if only for Miss Watson's benefit, he arranged himself in the languid half-reclining posture made famous by Napoleon Sarony's photographs. She had come looking for a lion but found a purring pussycat instead.

Miss Watson took a moment to compose herself. She was as baffled as Alice in Wonderland when she met the grinning Cheshire Cat on the bough of a tree. Wilde's performance could easily fluster an interviewer, let alone a lady like Watson, who was concerned, as she demurely put it, to carry out her duties 'without transgressing any social rules.'[8] With steely determination, 'soon I regained my ordinary frame of mind.'[9] There was no accepted way to 'do' the interview, no pre-agreed format, no standard to follow. Interviewing was still new, and women interviewers particularly so. Not until the 1890s would interviewing become widely acceptable as an activity for women. The proper thing to do, Miss Watson must have thought, was to remind the aesthete that he was in the presence of a lady, and make him aware of the rules of engagement.

'You have never met a lady reporter,' she said.

'No,' he replied coyly, 'I have not. We do not have them in our country.'

Wilde lolled on the sofa in front of her. 'Not, of course, lying down,' Watson reassured her readers, 'but in a careless posture, with his arm thrown carelessly over the pillow.'[10] And, just like that, the social rules appeared to have fluttered out the window.

There was nothing to do but grit her teeth and continue. Miss Watson asked about his *Poems*. 'An animated conversation, and especially about himself' ensued.

'Are you pleased at the newspaper reports of yourself and the reporters' interviews?' she asked.[11]

He laughed at her question before replying.

'I read them all, and not only here but all over America I have been quite amused at the struggle each of the gentlemen have had to write what I did not say; but I have the most sympathy with the writers of the articles which strive to be what is called here in the United States "funny." Their hard work has been so apparent.'

To him, *sprezzatura* was all: it was important that everything look easy. Effort must never show. Yet Wilde was working hard to impress Miss Watson. Now and again, he rose to show her a picture of his mother, or a volume by his friend, a young poet named James Rennell Rodd. He opened up his cabinet of curiosities, and showed her the intimate objects he carried on the road to remind him of faraway friends and family.

Soon Miss Watson was under his spell. They were treading new ground together, skirting some difficult social boundaries, and making it up as they went along. Just as his flirtation was having an effect, his valet burst in on their heart-to-heart with an album that urgently needed the aesthete's autograph. At this Wilde made a great show of breaking off his conversation with Miss Watson to attend to the relentless demands of celebrity autograph-hunters. She watched him arrange himself into 'a posture which excellently expressed "thought",' then suddenly glance up at her with a flustered look. He was so agitated, he confessed, that he had forgotten the lines of his own poetry that he wished to quote. He waved away the obligation, and said he would deal with the album later. 'I am too much engaged just now,' Wilde told his valet, with a pointed glance at the lady interviewer.

The frisson between the pair electrifies Miss Watson's account. Today, Wilde's semi-seduction seems surprising because we think of him as a homosexual, and not—as Victorians did—as a lover of women. Yet there is ample evidence to show that his contemporaries were right. During the summer of 1875, he persuaded a young woman to sit on his lap. Her mother entered the drawing room and caught the pair together. Later, the mother caught Wilde kissing her daughter in the hallway. 'Oscar,' she scolded, 'the thing was neither right, nor manly, nor gentlemanlike in you.'[12] And then there was Eva, who wrote saying she would accept a marriage proposal, if he was serious. He wasn't. By the next summer, he was enamoured of Florence Balcombe. At Oxford, he had been captivated by William Ward's sister, Gertrude. After arriving in London in 1879, he conquered an auburn-haired girl called Violet Hunt. 'Mr. Oscar Wilde allowed me to monopolize him for a couple of hours,' she swooned.[13] 'We will rule the world—you and I—you with your looks and I with my wits,' he promised.[14] He also proposed to Charlotte Montefiore, the sister of an Oxford friend. 'With your money and my brain we could have gone so far,' he told her when she refused him.[15] If he could not have her, there would be another.

By the time he boarded for America, Wilde left a pretty, grey-eyed girl called Constance Lloyd waiting for him in London. Undeterred, Violet Hunt lived up to her surname and continued to pursue Oscar by hounding his mother. During one of Miss Hunt's visits, Speranza slid a picture of 'Costume Oscar'—as she called the Sarony photographs—under the infatuated girl's eyes.[16] It was more than she could handle, Miss Hunt admitted in her diary. Oscar looked so very appealing in his knee-breeches! Speranza was obviously fanning the flames. Wilde's older brother, Willie, was 30 years old and still a bachelor. After all, she wanted to see at least one of her sons married.

Regardless of their state of wedlock, American women were having a public love affair with Speranza's younger son. Where he went, they followed. Ladies—groupies, really—clustered outside his hotels. Sometimes, they could be seen rushing towards his room, 'anxious to catch a glimpse of its inmate' in the words of an eyewitness.[17] When an attendant admitted reporters to Wilde's suite, he held the door open long enough to give the fans an opportunity to glimpse their idol. Wilde's powers of attraction quickly passed into legend. A thumbnail biographical sketch sold on trains told of how fathers watched in amazement as, before their eyes, their daughters became 'love-sick maidens' who declared Wilde a 'perfect raving angel.'[18] In these accounts, Wilde was the prey, not the hunter.

And so his name quickly became associated with a shocking rumour—women were acting on their desires. Newspapers made up stories about the effect of Wilde's lectures on young ladies.[19] Legend had it that under Wilde's influence they were breaking the age's taboos about what ladies should not do. Satirists mocked their indiscretions.

How did the girl caught kissing a carpenter explain herself to her old-fashioned father?[20]

She said it was 'the Oscar Wilde style.'

And the wife whose husband caught her giving sweets to a house painter?

Why, she said it was 'the Oscar Wilde style.'

Men swore they'd make him pay for being 'the perverter of our wives by means of your idiotic art twaddle.' Naturally, Wilde had little patience for such unsporting complaints. 'America is the only country in the world where Don Juan is not appreciated,' he countered.[21]

Wilde took to pronouncing on women's looks as if conducting his own personal Miss America contest. Journalists exploited the appetite for his opinions. Asking for his views on women's attractiveness became routine. Sweet-talk replies were always forthcoming. He would tell a Southern reporter it was true that Boston ladies were 'hard to beat for beauty,' and would hastily add that the women who lived south of the Mason-Dixon line were some of the most beautiful he had seen in the United States.[22] In Wilde's local beauty contests, almost every woman could be a winner. He raised the stakes by ranking American girls against their English sisters. 'I am charmed with American beauty,' Wilde declared.[23] Then, as though attempting to put his finger on what, exactly, made them transcendent, he would put his hand to his own face and say, 'there is a charm about this curve here.' Placing his finger on his cheek, he languorously traced its contours down to his chin. American women, he concluded, 'possess a certain delicacy of outline surpassing English women.' What American woman wouldn't be delighted to learn she had won the crown in this international beauty contest? Yet the real winner was Wilde, who gloried in the attention he attracted. 'I am obliging beautiful young ladies,' he said, as he signed autographs for his female admirers in front of the man from the *Albany Argus*. 'I make it a point to grant my autograph to no others,' he assured the reporter.[24]

Many women preferred aesthetic men. Advertisers capitalized on this by using aesthetes to market intimate women's products. Fanciful business cards then referred to as 'trade cards' sometimes used the aesthete's sex appeal to promote their merchandise. Coraline Corsets encouraged customers to let the aesthete get close to their skin. 'It CANNOT be broken,' the advertisements boasted, 'A REWARD of $10 will be paid for every strip of Coraline which breaks with four months ordinary wear.' But their trade cards depicted no ordinary event. They portrayed a manly, barrel-chested aesthete judging a female beauty contest with adorable cupids as his romantic sidekicks. Turning over the card, you discovered one little winged love messenger snuggling into the corset's bodice. Meanwhile, another cupid raised a tiny glass of champagne as though toasting the union of a happy couple. Distributed by stores, slipped into parcels by merchants, and collected into scrapbooks by customers, trade cards such as this one were portable reminders of the aesthete's sexual currency (see Plates 18 and 19).

Innovations such as the interview and the trade card amplified women's flirtatious admiration for Wilde and his poetry. Only a year earlier, English critics had turned their noses up at Wilde's *Poems*. Now American women were head over heels in love with them—and with him. When Wilde's lectures meandered, his audience's eyes wandered. They gazed at his hair and stared at his legs; they gawped at the tightness of his trousers and noted the smoothness of his cheek. And so, in overheated lecture theatres, as the evenings grew long and the lecturer long-winded, Americans ogled him. At six feet four inches and about two hundred pounds, he was imposing yet elegant. Audiences gossiped about his 'mashing'—late nineteenth-century American slang for behaving as a womanizer by arranging himself in seductive postures. Wagging tongues made much of his flirtation with the audience.[25]

His *Poems* encouraged readers to speculate how a man who wore his hair long and his breeches short spent his days and nights. 'I have made my choice, have lived my poems,' he wrote. Lines written in the first person were all the encouragement some readers needed to imagine the trysts behind his lyrics.[26] The content of Wilde's poems and his own self-presentation stimulated romantic, personal interpretations. The work was simply 'the *author* "confiding" in us,' readers assumed.[27] Some Victorians had championed this biographical way of reading. The best kind of reading, Ruskin thought, was a sort of eavesdropping that connected the reader to the thoughts of great men. 'You can be hidden behind the cover,' Ruskin promised, 'and listen all day long.'[28]

Poems turned nature into an erotic playground. Under Wilde's influence, a yellow iris offers its throat to a dragonfly's kisses, trees stoop to peck a swooning nymph, and lilies air-kiss the wind.[29] But it was what Wilde appeared to be confessing about his own love life that fascinated Americans. 'I am too young to live without desire,' one poem declared. Besides, said another, his sweetheart's lips were 'made to kiss.'

The beating heart of *Poems* is 'Charmides,' a 650-line love story in rhymed iambic pentameter. This was Wilde's favourite, the one he thought most perfect.[30] It opens with the hero sailing back to Athens:

> He was a Grecian lad, who coming home
>   With pulpy figs and wine from Sicily
> Stood at his galley's prow, and let the foam
>   Blow through his crisp brown curls unconsciously[31]

The 'pulpy figs and wine' hint at the poem's bacchanalian flavour. Wilde's Charmides has little in common with the eponymous young man of Plato's dialogue, who is an embodiment of moderation. As soon as Wilde's Charmides lands in Athens, he declares his genius by crowning himself with olive branches, buying a new outfit, and seducing a statue of the goddess Athena. A few lines later, he is undressing the warrior queen. The conquest is told from Charmides' point of view, not hers. Through his eyes, she is a 'Gorgon' but he is attracted to her nevertheless. Athena's chastity is 'pitiless,' her maidenhood 'terrible.'[32] Yet he acts as if he believes this icy, armour-clad virgin goddess should turn her 'blood-less lips' over to him. Never mind that Athena gives Charmides every signal that this is not her wish. Never mind that she is 'armed for battle.' Never mind that she defends her body with a 'long lance of wreck and ruin flared like a red rod of flame.' Never mind that her pet owl, the symbol of her legendary wisdom, is blinking and hooting with alarm. The poem doesn't endow her with the power of speech but her defensive body language clearly signals her distress. Yet brash Charmides thinks Athena's *no* means *yes*. The poem asks rhetorically, 'for whom would not such love make desperate'? Then, it licenses Charmides' roving hands.

> Ready for death he stood, but lo! the air
> Grew silent, and the horses ceased to neigh,
> And off his brow he tossed the clustering hair,
> And from his limbs he threw the cloak away,
> For whom would not such love make desperate,
> And nigher came, and touched her throat, and with hands violate

Undid the cuirass, and the crocus gown,
And bared the breasts of polished ivory,
Till from the waist the peplos [robe] falling down
Left visible the secret mystery
Which to no lover will Athena show,
The grand cool flanks, the crescent thighs,
the bossy hills of snow.

It is not difficult to imagine the objections a prudish nineteenth-century reader might raise to Wilde's poem, or what it might have suggested about his own sexual practices. At the moment of Charmides' climax, Wilde turns away from the scene and, as if facing his reader, delivers this sexy aside:

Those who have never known a lover's sin
Let them not read my ditty, it will be
To their dull ears so musicless and thin
That they will have no joy of it, but ye
To whose wan cheeks now creeps the lingering smile,
Ye who have learned who Eros is,—O listen yet a-while.

To read between the lines would be to find out about Wilde's life between the sheets. To emphasize the point, Wilde penned another aside about erotic delights:

They who have never seen the daylight peer
Into a darkened room, and drawn the curtain,
And with dull eyes and wearied from some dear
And worshipped body risen, they for certain
Will never know of what I try to sing,
How long the last kiss was, how fond and late his lingering.[33]

Wilde's English publisher, David Bogue, thought these lines too risqué. In 1882, he censored both asides.[34]

But the authorized American editions retained them. In fact Wilde's American publisher, Roberts Brothers of Boston, touted *Poems* by advertising Wilde's 'notoriety'.[35] It was an apt word for what he had by then achieved: white-hot fame tinged with shadiness. Advertisements promised *Poems* would lay bare 'the most talked-about man in London literary circles,' as *Publishers' Weekly* breathlessly described him. The book's first American edition sold out in a matter of days. A second edition swiftly appeared. Soon, the demand for Wilde's *Poems* far exceeded what Roberts Brothers could supply, and other publishers stepped in. At the time, American copyright law only protected works by US citizens. Emboldened by the absence of international copyright, rogue publishers turned to piracy. Across the country, their editions of *Poems* were quickly bought up.[36] At an impromptu press conference in a train depot, a reporter asked Wilde for his thoughts on the international copyright question. 'A country gets small good from a literature it steals,' he shot back. 'In all your [train] cars I find newsmen selling my poems—stolen!'[37] The first international copyright act would pass in 1891.[38] Until then, unauthorized editions proliferated.

American women wanted to win Wilde's heart, so composers did their utmost to spin their countrywomen's romantic dreams into songs. Monroe Rosenfeld, a 21-year-old ex-journalist, freely adapted rumours into a rowdy song with a jaunty tempo and 'Oscar Dear!' became a hit (see Plate 20).[39] It was one of the most popular novelty compositions because it played on Wilde's ladykilling reputation.

'Oscar Dear!' was an invented story full of innuendo about a character called Oscar, his wandering hands, and the girl who loved him despite them. 'Oscar dear, Oscar dear!' she sings in a lively voice that simultaneously conveys alarm and delight at his familiarity.[40] 'Take your hand away, sir,' she tells him as he tries to grab her by the waist though, in the next breath, she admits that she doesn't mind. Her real concern is that they'll be discovered. Of course, that's a foregone conclusion. At this point, she might gesture to the audience watching Oscar paw her on stage. 'Don't you see them looking, love?' she would insist, pointing to the spectators. The song is a portrait of amorous confusion that reels and rollicks around her mixed message as she goes back and forth between rejecting and inviting his advances. Trepidation vies with excitement, decorum with indecency, prudishness with sensuality. Two gawkers stroll into the scene. 'Catch on, old gal,' one cackles, encouraging her to let Oscar have his way. 'Ain't it g-g-great?' his pal stutters, gleefully tripping over his words as he observes the naughty scene. The sheet music cover for 'Oscar Dear!' sums up the story's winks, nudges, and contradictions. In the illustration, the girl stares straight out at the viewer, her eyes agog, her hands protectively placed over her body. Meanwhile, Oscar towers over her tiny frame and furtively touches her. The moral is that behind this great big man there is a little lady who puts up with quite a lot of cheek.[41]

The song was an instant success. It cheerfully encouraged men to find their inner Oscar and to become, as the song put it, 'just a little "wild".' In no time, Wilde heard men in the streets serenading him with Rosenfeld's tune. 'Oscar! Oscar, dear,' they clamoured.[42] 'Put out your head and let us see you,' men hollered as his carriage rolled past. At times, when Wilde didn't comply, a fellow was apt to leap up and squash his face against the carriage window.[43] On one such occasion, Wilde turned to the journalist seated next to him inside the carriage. 'It is so everywhere,' he said wearily. Americans usually behaved this way when they saw him, he explained. 'In Europe the people are less curious about public characters, and they are not rude.'

'Oscar Dear!' captured the feelings of the time. Now, when Wilde entered a reception, the orchestra struck up his song. The melody encapsulated the cloud of erotic possibility that swirled around him. Soon every street urchin could whistle the libertine tune.

One day, an interviewer stood outside Wilde's hotel and whistled the hit song to himself as he watched the aesthete arrive.

> Oscar dear, Oscar dear,
> How flutterly-utterly-flutter you are.
> Oscar dear, Oscar dear,
> I think you are awfully 'wild.'[44]

Moments later, when the reporter was ushered in to Wilde's hotel room, he noticed a powerful odour of rum in the air. Dressed in his tight clothes, the aesthete was lolling on a sofa in the languid pose he had adopted in Sarony's famous photos.[45] The posture had become his standard way of receiving interviewers, whether male or female.

Chapter 7

Mr Wild of Borneo, or The Paddy

For a long time, British and American publics had been fascinated with 'primitive' cultures. A year before Oscar Wilde came to America, the Norwegian ethnologist Carl Bock claimed to have discovered the 'true aborigines' of Borneo, the country now known as Indonesia.[1] In his 1881 travelogue, *The Head Hunters of Borneo*, Bock portrayed dramatic encounters with cannibals, 'savages', and headhunters. 'Their existence has long been known, but no European before myself ever saw one of the women of the race,' he boasted, illustrating his find with a hand-drawn colour portrait of one of these bare-breasted women. The line between 'freak hunter' and 'true ethnographer' was then blurry, but the book was confirmed as sound anthropological science when one of the leading theorists of evolution, Alfred Russel Wallace, gave it a positive review in *Nature*.[2]

By 1882, the arrival of an Irishman in a fur coat who purred nonstop about 'The English Renaissance' further gratified the public's curiosity about exotic creatures. 'Mr Wild of Borneo' was born. In the days after Wilde's first lecture, American press opinion grew polarized. On one side, there were those who took Wilde and his message seriously. And then there were the others—such as the *Washington Post*, *National Republican*, and *Harper's Weekly*—that printed vicious caricatures in pictures and prose. These satires were extreme, but because they appeared in respectable publications, their mockery was granted legitimacy and attention. And while they also raised Wilde's profile, they drastically demeaned his image, too. Soon 'Mr Wild of Borneo' would replicate, spawning ever more outlandish, warped characterizations. Before long, they would become part of a viral campaign threatening to destroy 'The English Renaissance' lecture tour.

It all began innocently enough. To kick off the New Year, *Harper's Weekly* put a sunflower-worshipping monkey dressed as Wilde on the front of the January 1882 issue (see Plate 21). The magazine didn't let its reputation for quality impede its expression of what are now considered odious ethnic and racial ideologies. The drawing stimulated other American maligners and, in England, had a full-page reprint in the *Lady's Pictorial*.[3] A South Carolina photographer named J. A. Palmer was inspired by *Harper's* to produce a series of stereoscopic cards each depicting a real African American man or woman in the Wilde role.[4] Palmer posed his models worshipping a sunflower and added a monkey-shaped jug to emphasize the association between Wilde's Aestheticism and monkey business. He titled the cards 'An Aesthetic Darkey.' When the *National Republican* discussed Wilde, it was to explain 'a few items as to the animal's pedigree.'[5] And on 22 January 1882 the *Washington Post* illustrated the Wild Man of Borneo alongside Oscar Wilde of England and asked 'How far is it from this to this?'[6] (See Plate 22.)

The *Washington Post* answered its own question with another: 'If Mr. Darwin is right in his theory, has not the climax of evolution been reached and are we not tending down the hill toward the aboriginal starting point again? Certainly, a more inane object than Mr. Wilde, of England, has never challenged our attention.' It concluded that 'Mr. Wild of Borneo, doesn't lecture, however, and that much should be remembered to his credit.' All of these publications compared Wilde to animals and primitives, with the *Post's* comparison recalling the way in which human exhibits were often presented in popular sideshows and exhibitions.

No doubt it was the *Post's* spectacularly effective headline, 'How far is it from this to this?,' that caused the most damage to Wilde because it exploited an obvious similarity with the well-known banners 'What is It?' and 'What Can They Be?' under which nineteenth-century curiosities and evolutionary spectacles were exhibited. P. T. Barnum routinely used such headlines to flag his ethnographic shows. Styling himself the greatest showman on earth, Barnum's 'Little Men of Borneo' were well known decades before Bock published *The Head Hunters of Borneo*. Many other promoters offered similar spectacles in their museums of wonders, but Barnum vouched for the authenticity of his exotics by claiming that they had been captured off the 'rocky coast of the Island of Borneo.'[7] Although they were actually brothers from Ohio, showmen like Barnum did not trouble themselves with facts. Their business was a sensational version of show-and-tell in which they did the showing and paying audiences did the telling. All Barnum and Co. had to do was encourage viewers to do the guess-work by framing their shows with a leading question like 'The Wild Man of the Prairies, or What is It?,' another of Barnum's popular human exhibitions. 'What is It? Or "Man Monkey"' would work just as well (see Plate 23).[8]

'What is It?' was performed in late 1840s London by Hervey Leech, an acrobat whose right leg was six inches longer than his left. His spe-ciality was leaping and climbing like a monkey. By the 1860s, Leech was replaced by William Henry Johnson, a microcephalic African American from New Jersey. He performed at Barnum's American Museum in New York under the name 'Zip' (a nod to Zip Coon, dandy of minstrel show fame). Eager to reproduce this success, Barnum increased the number of creatures at which to marvel. Another human exhibit titled 'What Can They Be?' offered a reward of one thousand dollars to anyone who could classify the 'strange and mysterious ani-mals' which Barnum said he had found 'in the hitherto unexplored Wilds of Africa.'[9] These 'missing link' performances exploited the fascin-ation with the evolutionary relationship between animals and men.

Barnum made the most of definitional uncertainty by further diver-sifying his offerings: in the 1840s, he added minstrel shows to his roster, as well as an African American woman he claimed was George Washington's 161-year-old nurse. He also adapted for blackface minstrels a version of Harriet Beecher Stowe's bestselling anti-slavery novel *Uncle Tom's Cabin*. His shows capitalized on contemporary American debates about the humanity of enslaved peoples, in which the arguments of the doubters served as a justification for the continuation of chattel slavery.

So by the time the *Post* enquired 'How far is it from this to this?' it was actually asking Americans to consider a weightier issue than whether Wilde reminded them of a monkey. He had been framed as one of a long line of Irish primitives and Paddies, and behind the *Post*'s cartoon there lurked ominous questions about the place of the Irish in Anglo-American society's evolutionary trajectory. Overnight, Wilde became an emblem of racial ambiguities that had arisen from new scientific research, as well as from old-fashioned ethnological displays and performances. How far was it from a simian animal, to a primitive creature, to an Irish Paddy, to a blackface minstrel? In 1882, not far at all.

'The Age of Darwin,' the ethnologist Bernth Lindfors observes, 'was a century of aggressive imperialism compounded by great biological confusion. One notion underlying the confusion was the belief that Africans were at least as close to the animal world as they were to the human.'[10] In the nineteenth century, the term 'African' often extended to include almost anyone with dark skin. Measuring how far it was between man and monkey intrigued scientists and enthralled audiences: the 'missing link' became a favourite subject of popular spectacles on both sides of the Atlantic.[11] But the fascination with racial hybridity goes back much further than the nineteenth century. The ancient Greeks proposed a Great Chain of Being that classified humans in relation to the animal kingdom, and over the following centuries evolutionary models and racial definitions varied wildly. Throughout the ages, one thing hasn't changed. 'Civilization' remains *the* enduring criterion. And it determines the 'cultural pecking order.'[12]

'I have already civilised America,' Wilde announced in 1882.[13] So why was his civilizing mission linked with evolutionary debates? In an age when being civilized put one at the top of the racial hierarchy, why was Wilde placed at the bottom with the uncivilized, the primitives, and the animals? And what did his position in this classification owe to the proliferation of ethnological hoaxes and popular performances?

In the United States and Britain, popular performances anticipated what evolutionary science could still only speculate about. It took an enterprising showman to make a spectacle out of such speculation, and P.T. Barnum was one of the most imaginative when it came to missing-link performances. 'No one was ever a better judge of what the public wanted than that eminent practical psychologist, P. T. Barnum,' the historian Arthur Lovejoy notes.[14] And what the ladies and gentlemen of the public wanted was to wonder at their relationship to other creatures in the animal kingdom.

Almost two decades before Darwin published *On the Origin of Species* in 1859, a version of the theory of evolution was already being played out before spectators. Hypotheses about the workings of inheritance were flourishing, setting the stage for daring new spectacles. Barnum loved the complexity of evolutionary science, and loved even more the public's willingness to pay to be perplexed by it. So he turned himself into a specialist in ambiguity and intermediacy. In his Museum, he exhibited mermaid bodies alongside specimens he claimed were the missing links between the seal and the duck, or the bird and the fish.

The publication of On the Origin of Species boosted interest in missing-link performances. Riding Barnum's coat-tails to tremendous popular success, other dime museums offered their own versions of 'What is It?' and the Wild Men of Borneo. When the American novelist William Dean Howells reviewed the panoply on show, he was impressed. Under one roof, one could listen to lectures by the inventor of perpetual motion and the fire escape, consult a fortune teller, watch a contortionist, or see 'a colored brother' in blackface performing an Irish emigrant's story.[15] One could also stare at five caged macaws, two apes, and a whole Australian family, who looked 'a good deal gloomier than the apes,' Howells noticed. The mixture of feelings such sites aroused in viewers was as ambiguous as the exhibits themselves. Within the dime museum, amusement, curiosity, and scientific interest shaded into Schadenfreude.

Barnum's 'What is It?' and the Washington Post's derivative 'How far is it from this to this?' were visual conundrums, puzzles designed to provoke. The Post put Wilde under its masthead to attract curiosity and popular speculation, and to ridicule him as an evolutionary throwback. In a letter to the Editor, Wilde's manager condemned the caricature as slanderous. The comparison between Wilde and the Wild Man of Borneo, wrote Colonel Morse, was 'a senseless exhibition of gratuitous malice.'[16] The Post printed his letter in full and then escalated its assault. Wilde was one of the 'great social evils,' it claimed, which was why he deserved to have his picture published 'in conjunction with that of his relative of Borneo.' There was still another reason for the comparison: 'we didn't invite the Wilde man of England to Washington, nor for that matter to America. He came of his own accord to exhibit at so much per head, his colossal cheek and diminutive wit.' Wilde was a primitive wild man aping an Englishman the newspaper argued. 'He is nothing, and in England he merely passes at his value.'

According to the Post, Wilde represented an interloper in Americans' midst: initially as an Irishman passing for an Englishman, but also as the year's most conspicuous symbol of a class of immigrants towards whom American nativists had grown increasingly hostile. The paper warned of the brutal consequences Wilde would face for impersonating an English gentleman. 'All true Englishmen will be glad if we can terrify him back to Britain, so that they may kill him,' the *Post* wrote, making a threat that would become more real as his tour progressed.[17] By accusing Wilde of ethnic trespass and by menacing retributive violence, the paper invoked a racial logic that would not have had currency in Britain. Yet this was not gratuitous violence against Wilde, the *Post* assured readers, but a matter of national and ethnic pride. The British would feel just as Americans now did, if an impostor 'should break into the mother country as a representative of American manners, life or thought,' the *Post* explained. 'We but resent for the Saxon spirit of England an unjustifiable insult.'

The attack moved Wilde to the centre of a long-standing international conflict that was still raging as he toured the United States. The immediate context for the *Post*'s invocation of a Saxon heritage shared by Britain and America was the Irish Land War of 1879–82, an Irish revolt against English control sparked by resentment of the landlord system, and the growing influx of Irish to the United States. The *Post*'s accusation of racial and sexual trespass on 'the mother country' was an unusual gesture of allegiance to Britain from within one of her former colonies. Stranger still, it was in America, not Britain, that Wilde's hybridity was persistently considered a threat.

Barnum's 'What is It?' deliberately didn't 'tell his audience what to think, opting instead to maintain a highly visible, self-effacing silence in the middle of heated popular controversy.'[18] But the *Post* used the opposite tactic and told readers exactly what to think. It told them to think of Wilde as a degenerate, a sign of human regression towards the primitive. 'Nature never makes any gross mistakes,' it asserted. 'She never puts the brains of a man of mental brawn and vigor into a cavity faced by such a physiognomy as that of Oscar Wilde's.'[19] Here the *Post* deployed science as a weapon, invoking Darwinism alongside phrenology to corroborate the notion that Wilde represented an evolutionary regression.

According to the tenets of the scientific fad known as phrenology, people's skulls and faces revealed the hidden secrets of their character. By studying an individual's facial features and bodily lineaments, phrenologists claimed they could discover his true nature. The *Post*'s diagnosis extended to its logical conclusion what other American publications were only saying tentatively. Already, it had become routine for publications of all kinds to describe Wilde phrenologically, which is to say to catalogue and classify each part of his face. One representative account itemized 'a large and well-developed nose, a broad mouth, with full lips opening over large, prominent teeth, the upper lip a shade too short, and eyes very full, large and handsome and an apology between gray and blue, are arched by delicately lined eyebrows.' It concluded with the diagnosis that his features were 'almost effeminate in apparent lack of vigor and force.'[20] Attentive accounts like this one served two purposes: on one hand, they enabled fans to get up close and personal with the aesthetic celebrity, but on the other, they reinforced the era's pseudo-scientific principles. The journalists' minute observations blurred the line between detail-obsessed fandom and anthropological scrutiny.

Each feature was logged as though it might be a piece of meaning-ful data: Wilde's long face (Celtic?), the fullness of the lips and broadness of his smiling mouth (Negroid?), and the arch of his brow (effeminate?). The questionable value of this accounting became glaringly obvious as soon as anyone attempted to draw conclusions from it. For instance, where the *Post* read degeneracy in Wilde's face, the *Philadelphia Inquirer* found signs of 'the highest Celtic type' with an air of refinement and good breeding.[21] The same evidence yielded riotously contradictory interpretations. Scientific 'truth' was in the eye of the beholder, not the face of the beheld.

Reading Wilde's Irish face was part of a crude attempt to link him to his race and to its social history. It was a kind of Victorian biomet-rics, a blunt instrument in the hands of those seeking greater control over America's increasing ethnic diversity. Half a century later, American scientists were perfecting these methods of social classifica-tion, and a controversial Harvard Irish study was experimenting on 'the Celtic type.' Using a larger sample size, researchers classified the typical Celt as long-faced, light-skinned, with blue or grey-blue eyes, and brown hair.[22] In short, the Celtic type looked precisely like Wilde. That's not the most arresting feature of the study, however. What is even more surprising is that, in the 1930s, the Harvard Irish Study was still basically using the same racial idiom that had been used against Wilde half a century earlier. As a result, the Harvard findings were vir-tually identical to those of run-of-the-mill nineteenth-century report-ers and five-cent phrenologists.

The Harvard scientists reached two conclusions: first, that race was visible chiefly in the face, and second, that it could be correlated to

sociological profiles. It was this second element that made their findings provocative. Their work suggested a direct link between a person's
facial profile, his ethnic profile, and his social profile. 'The Keltic type
is by far the most poorly educated type in Ireland. It has the highest
proportion of illiterates,' the researchers said.[23] Ninety per cent of this
type were Catholic. 'Occupationally, also, it is the most lowly type.'[24]
Men with Celtic faces were predominantly hired labourers, tinkers,
navvies, farmers, herdsmen, and factory workers. They were unlikely to
be found among the merchant or professional classes, the research concluded. It was nothing short of scientifically sanctioned ethnic predes-
tination. According to the study, an Irishman's face spelled out his
social past, present, and future.

When Wilde was a student at Oxford, he read widely in contemporary
science. He would have known what the *Post* was driving at and understood its anti-Irish prejudice. In his student notebooks, he had combined
German idealism with Herbert Spencer's evolutionary theory, explaining that 'Hegelian dialectics is the natural selection problem and struggle
for existence in the world of thought.'[25] His entry for the 1879
Chancellor's English Essay Prize was a bold attempt to unite science and
art that aimed at nothing less than to merge the social and material
world. Better known as 'The Rise of Historical Criticism,' his thoughtful,
well-informed essay amply demonstrates that he knew his way around
Victorian scientific ideas. It brings Spencer's philosophy of history to
bear on Ancient Greece ('that wonderful offshoot of the primitive
Aryans'), and nimbly leaps from Polybius to Tocqueville to Spencer's
general law of Instability of the Homogeneous.[26] The essay's main idea
developed from Spencer's 1867 assertion that 'the condition of homo-
geneity is a condition of unstable equilibrium,' which is to say that existence always tends towards a heterogeneous state.[27] The keynote of 'The
Rise of Historical Criticism' is that social growth depends on diversity.

Wilde was a lifelong student of Victorian race science who advanced
his thoughts on the subject in the years following his American tour. In
1890, he turned to the topic in 'The Critic as Artist,' an essay claiming that

the scientific principle of Heredity has become, as it were, the
warrant for the contemplative life. It has shown us that we are

never less free than when we try to act. It has hemmed us round with the nets of the hunter, and written upon the wall the prophecy of our doom. We may not watch it, for it is within us. We may not see it, save in a mirror that mirrors the soul.[28]

A year later, in 'The Soul of Man Under Socialism,' he emphasized the point. 'Evolution is the law of life,' he wrote, 'and there is no evolution except towards Individualism. Where this tendency is not expressed, it is a case of artificially-arrested growth or of disease, or of death.'[29] This talk of doomed souls, latent inheritance, and individualism is informed by ethnological science and a moral pessimism that almost certainly drew on his American experience.

Likewise, his later fiction internalized what the *Post* said was written on his body in 1882. 'Dorian, this is horrible! Something has changed you completely,' the painter Basil Hallward says when he witnesses his friend's transformation.[30] When Dorian examines the ugly, disfigured portrait of himself, he looks at it with 'scientific interest,' an approach that is entirely in keeping with his belief in Darwinism.[31] Dorian is astonished to discover that the laws of science apply to him for he had imagined he was immune to them. 'That such a change should have taken place was incredible to him,' Dorian thinks.[32] 'And yet it was a fact. Was there some subtle affinity between the chemical atoms that shaped themselves into form and colour on the canvas, and the soul that was within him?' Wilde's question exposes what Dorian can't quite bring himself to believe, namely that the science he once studied now pertains directly to his own life.

In an 1882 interview with an American reporter, Wilde said he was deeply interested in sociology and that he had 'read and greatly admired' the writings of Herbert Spencer.[33] Later that year, however, when Spencer visited the United States, he had nothing to say about Wilde. To his astonishment, the press promptly fabricated views for him. In an effort to set the record straight, Spencer told the *Chicago Herald*, 'I have expressed no opinion whatever concerning Mr. Oscar Wilde.'[34] As for the dubious practices of American newspapers, he said, they 'mix much fiction with what fact they report.'[35]

At the beginning of their relationship, in New York City, Colonel Morse had used Wilde for a compare-and-contrast publicity stunt when he arranged for him to attend *Patience*, as the real-life foil to the aesthetes on stage. Wilde's manager was courting gawkers, the people fresh from Gilbert and Sullivan's aesthetic musical, who laughed along at the sexual topsy-turvy, and wanted above all to be entertained. They would flock to see Wilde if they thought of him as an amusing riddle to be solved. Audiences might find 'The English Renaissance' lecture perplexing, but if framed in the right way, Wilde's indeterminate ethnicity and sexuality could be a draw.

A few weeks later, Colonel Morse's boss, the theatre producer D'Oyly Carte, decided to repeat the comparison. This time he wanted to set Wilde up as the antithesis to another of his lecturers, Archibald Forbes. The middle-aged Scotsman was a hard-boiled reporter of the Franco-Prussian War, the Serbo-Turkish War, the Russo-Turkish War, the Anglo-Afghan War, and the Anglo-Zulu War. He was 'the hugest, of the war correspondents,' according to Rudyard Kipling.[36] Wilde said he had read Forbes's books, and would do as D'Oyly Carte bid him. 'I was not particularly interested,' Wilde told him, 'but I would go.'[37] On the way there, Forbes met Wilde on a train, provoked a spat and, in the end, Wilde did not attend his lecture. But that hardly mattered to the promoters. The public quarrel was great publicity and cost D'Oyly Carte nothing.[38]

By the end of the first few weeks of his tour, Wilde must have begun to question the wisdom of his managers. Once again, they had set him at a disadvantage. A pattern was emerging. He didn't have to rack his brains to see that they were trying to drum up crowds by any means possible, regardless of the personal consequences to him. Their practices suggested they were running a comedy act, not a respectable lecture tour. Meanwhile his reputation was sinking lower and faster, declining to the very bathos of ridiculousness.

His managers were running a bankrupt system and he was locked into it. 'Aren't you sorry for Oscar?,' Lillie Langtry gasped to James McNeill Whistler.[39] 'They don't seem to treat him very seriously do they?' While Wilde endured the betrayal, he began to take counsel from friends, and would soon be contacting his solicitor. The Dublin-born playwright Dion Boucicault laid out the managers' sly manoeuvres in detail for Mrs Betty Lewis, the wife of Wilde's solicitor and a mutual friend. 'This is not fair,' Boucicault fumed. 'Mr Carte has not behaved well.'[40]

Suddenly a rumour started to make the rounds that Colonel Morse was responsible for the Wild Man of Borneo cartoon. It had been seen on his desk at D'Oyly Carte's New York headquarters before it appeared in the *Post*. When he heard this, Boucicault immediately saw through the operation and accused Wilde's managers of leaving him 'at the mercy of the Press, making a market of their caricatures.' As a fellow Irishman, Boucicault knew exactly what was being suggested with the caption 'How far is it from this to this?' As a playwright, he could see that the caricature drew on the ape-like stage Irishman, an English stereotype designed to denigrate the Irish.[41] When it was imported to the United States, it served the same purpose.

'Oscar is helpless,' Boucicault despaired.[42] Wilde's experience resonated with his own history with showmen. Back in 1859, Boucicault's *The Octoroon, or Life in Louisiana*, a play about racial passing, had been performed alongside 'What is It?' at Barnum's American Museum.[43] The melodrama centred on a free mulatta sold into slavery to save her family from economic ruin. To make the production more controversial, Barnum revised Boucicault's play and juxtaposed it with pro-slavery exhibits. As a result, the slaver's drama was co-opted into Barnum's museum of ethnic and racial variations. Art, science, and politics performed together in a compromised alliance. That brush with Barnumism must have been running through Boucicault's mind as he described Wilde's managers to Mrs Lewis. Boucicault seemed to be reliving his own nightmare as he watched Wilde's take shape. 'I cannot help feeling that so long as Carte...thought Oscar was only a puppet—a butt,' the manager was 'charming,' Boucicault said.[44] Yet Wilde had more strength of mind than his puppetmasters suspected. It was now becoming apparent to Colonel Morse and D'Oyly Carte that the toy boy who had initially appeared so docile was, in fact, a self-possessed man who preferred to make up his own mind rather than take orders. They were 'taken aback' to find out that the aesthete was no fool, Boucicault observed.

Publicly, Wilde showed a brave face. Although he allowed himself to make a few pointed remarks to journalists about the American press's low standards, he didn't give away the game. 'English papers are founded on facts, while American papers are founded on imagination,' he observed.[45] 'Your newspapers are comic without being amusing.'

In his correspondence, he was not nearly as measured. He was incensed. He would consent to have his image manipulated—up to a point. The *Post's* vitriol distinguished it from comparatively light-hearted caricatures elsewhere. It was racial, violent, and threatened murder. Wilde sent Colonel Morse two letters reproaching him for his mismanagement of the Borneo incident. The hostile newspapers, he informed Morse in the first of these, were 'accusing *me* of encouraging the attack on me and of having "corrected the proofs of the Washington attack and approved of the caricature before it was published." '[46] Morse's double-dealing proved him a traitor to Wilde's cause. Morse's lie could not have been more blatant: he called the *Post* caricature insulting and denied any involvement. Yet he had essentially planted the evidence on Wilde and left the press to draw its own conclusions. This was stooping too low.

Morse, however, had more tricks up his sleeve. To Wilde's great annoyance, the Colonel referred to the satire again in a ghostwritten article which claimed Carte's management company was on the side of the angels. Wilde seethed at Morse's hypocrisy and shot off a second letter. 'You, *without consulting me*,' he complained, 'said it was an insult to Mr. Carte to caricature anyone under his management. I regret you took any notice. The matter was mine and should have been left for me to decide on.'[47] Going forward, Morse should author no more misleading news. For now, Wilde preferred silence over publicity, and advised Morse to let the matter blow over. 'No mention should have been made of the cartoon at Washington. I regard all caricature and satire as absolutely beneath notice,' he said. 'Nothing could be worse in every way. It is quite stupid and gross and will do me much harm.' The Colonel's strategy was folly. By hijacking Wilde's image, Morse was turning the lecture tour into a kamikaze mission. It would be impossible for Wilde to recover if his manager stayed the course.

So far was he from enjoying the publicity, so unnerved was he by the *Post's* threats, that at the height of the debacle Wilde steadied his nerves by downing nearly $30 of wine over the course of three days (over $700 in today's money).[48] He grew bullish, and cabled his solicitor in London. Then he went above Morse's head and wrote directly to his boss, D'Oyly Carte, to tell him what he thought of his operation. First, Wilde spilled the beans about his two-faced manager. 'The whole tide of feeling is turned by Morse's stupidity,' he grumbled.[49] Then, he informed Carte that he was in breach of contract. 'I must have, according to our agreement, Morse or some responsible experienced man always with me,' he wrote. Days before, Morse had cut corners by leaving Wilde with an inexperienced office boy. When the lad saw the nine reporters, seven telegrams, and eighteen letters he had to answer, he was overwhelmed and promptly ran away, leaving Wilde stranded. Wilde's letter to D'Oyly Carte ended with a simple plea. 'Please do not expose me to the really brutal attacks of the papers,' he begged. 'We must be very careful for the future.' The plural pronoun suggested he thought they could work together to fix this. At this point, Wilde and his managers were at loggerheads over whether or not to exploit the bad publicity in the *Post*. Of course, keeping the controversy alive was in his managers' business's interests. Yet the bigger issue they were all grappling with was who would control Wilde's image, even as it grew increasingly distorted by the racial veneer applied to it.

Even if D'Oyly Carte had wanted to, it would have been impossible to stop others from developing what Mr Wild of Borneo had started. The monster unleashed by Colonel Morse could hardly be stopped. Within journalists' hearing, a fashionable lady sidled up to Wilde and exclaimed, 'Well, I'm glad I've seen a gorilla at last!'[50] Increasingly, when Americans talked about Wilde's business in the United States, they doubted that he was meant to introduce them to a serious art movement and suspected he was destined for a dime museum freak show like Barnum's.

One day, as an African American porter walked an interviewer to Wilde's hotel room, he innocently enquired whether Wilde was an actor.[51] 'Oh, he's a lecturer, not an actor,' the interviewer informed the porter. This only increased the man's confusion. In dime museums, 'lecturers' were performers dressed in scholars' caps and gowns who talked about novelties and inventions. Was this what Wilde was? The journalist offered further clarification. 'He's an aesthete,' he said. The porter wasn't convinced. 'Is he, dough?' he asked. He had seen plenty of other men dressed up in glad rags, and they didn't call themselves aesthetes. 'I thought he looked like one oh dem fellahs wat tumbles in a circus,' said the porter. The journalist paused to reflect on the man's wise observation. Circus actor, dime museum lecturer, or aesthete, Wilde could have been any one of these. 'Mr. Wilde is like unto the chameleon,' the journalist concluded, adding his voice to the growing numbers who thought Wilde was an odd specimen performing for profit.

An English newspaper editor who visited the United States at the time of Wilde's tour gave a buoyant account of what he had seen there. Any

Englishman would feel 'as much at home' in America as in England, William Edwin Adams wrote in *Our American Cousins*.[52] He was, however, shocked to find out how undiscriminating Americans were in their hospitality. 'The peculiar position of the British Islands, and the consequent difficulties which surround the relations of the English and the Irish people, are not, I think, generally understood in the United States,' he observed.[53] As a result of their misunderstanding, they were vulnerable to Irish posers who passed for English. 'Even Oscar Wilde was entertained as if he had been a representative Englishman,' Adams complained.[54]

The origins of the Irish Question that preoccupied the British throughout the nineteenth century stretched back to the eighteenth century, when penal laws imposed by the British had prompted a wave of three thousand emigrants to America.[55] By 1790, nearly one in every six of the three million citizens of the new United States were of Irish birth or descent. The emigration caused by the Great Famine of 1845 intensified over the ensuing decades, holding strong until the mid-1880s. Families already established in America often sent back prepaid tickets to allow their relatives to join them. In the last quarter of the century, the United States became the principal destination for 84 per cent of Irish emigrants.[56] In Boston, New York, and Philadelphia, the enormous influx created the largest Irish cities outside of Ireland. By the 1890s, three million Irish were living abroad. Evelyn Waugh later quipped that for Irishmen there were only two final destinations: hell and the United States.

The Irish exodus generated an intense expatriate nationalism and, in turn, the anti-Irish reaction to which Wilde was now being subjected. The Irish in America frequently imagined themselves as defeated, displaced people. They identified with the archetypal biblical wanderers ejected from their promised land. 'What captivity was to the Jews, exile has been to the Irish. America and American influences educated them,' Wilde later wrote, forcefully articulating this group psychology.[57] One of the paradoxes of emigration was that it fortified Irish nationalism. Celtic national spirit at home was feeble, Wilde continued, but, in the United States, the Irish 'realized what indomitable forces nationality possesses.'

Wilde's youthfulness and singledom was another crucial factor that determined Americans' negative response to him. Like him, the majority of nineteenth-century Irish immigrants were unattached young adults, men and women in their twenties travelling without their families. They looked to America as a place where they might find employment and romantic fulfilment. Word-of-mouth, propaganda, advertising, and popular prints fostered a vision of the United States as a land of liberty and new possibilities. Ireland's youthful emigrants found employment in private homes, factories, and on the railways. Their industry was admired in some quarters, but they were vilified in others for their disorderly and boisterous ways. As many as a third of the immigrants spoke Irish, a fact that irritated American nativists and anti-Catholics alike.[58] While Americans generously contributed towards Famine relief in Ireland, they were reluctant to support the Irish in their midst.[59]

The Famine-era journalist Thomas D'Arcy McGee counselled Irish emigrants to buy Benjamin Franklin's autobiography before setting sail. 'Therein you will read how, by industry, system, and self-denial, a Boston printer's boy rose to be one of the most prosperous, honorable, and important citizens of the Republic,' D'Arcy McGee wrote.[60] 'It will teach you that in America no beginning, however humble, can prevent a man from reaching any rank, however exalted... These are lessons you should have by heart.' By the closing years of the century, the Irish had become a privileged immigrant group and had achieved a good measure of economic success. The Irish-American middle class would continue to grow in the new century. Yet deeply entrenched anti-Irish stereotypes and nativist rhetoric would perpetuate Irish exclusion from the higher echelons of American social and political life for decades to come.

'An entirely new factor has appeared in the social development of the country, and this factor is the Irish-American, and his influence,' Wilde wrote in 1889.[61] The Irish-American he had in mind was Charles Stewart Parnell. By then, Parnell had been politically active for more than a decade and was the focal figure of Irish politics at home and abroad, a reputation he achieved by courting Irish-Americans. Fittingly, Parnell could claim Irish and American parentage: he was born in Ireland and his mother was American. Ireland's 'first practical leader is an Irish American,' Wilde declared in an essay considering the role played by Americans in furthering Irish interests. 'To mature its powers, to concentrate its action, to learn the secret of his own strength and of England's weakness, the Celtic intellect has had to cross the Atlantic,' he wrote, as though detailing his own personal experience.

But first the Celtic intellect had to cross the Irish Sea. Parnell studied at Magdalene College, Cambridge in the late 1860s, where he acquired a pronounced English accent. He had the bearing of an upper-class gentleman, and he left without taking a degree. The family were descended from English merchants who had established themselves in Ireland in the seventeenth century. While at Cambridge, Parnell heard about the 1867 Fenian rising then going on. The Home Rule League, advocating Irish self-government, had dominated Irish politics from the mid-1870s, but its aims remained unrealized. Parnell won a seat as a Home Rule MP in the 1874 general election, and cultivated Fenian sentiment so successfully that by the decade's end he was the *de facto* leader of the Irish.

In 1879–80, he forged new Irish–American connections when he travelled around America on a fundraising tour—an idea derived from the vogue for British lecturers in the United States.[62] A year earlier, the republican Michael Davitt had garnered support for the foundation of his Irish National League with a lecturing visit to America.[63] Following in Davitt's footsteps, Parnell's expedition enabled him to enlist Irish-American political and financial backing for the Irish National Land League he was now leading. Parnell delivered his message in sixty-two US cities. His impassioned rhetoric captured the Irish nationalist imagination abroad as it had at home. In the United States, he fearlessly declared that he and his supporters would never 'be satisfied until we have destroyed the last link which keeps Ireland bound to England.'[64] Rousing to some and alarming to others, Parnell became the face of Irish politics.[65] The English press, meanwhile, condemned his tactics, disparaging the influence of Irish-Americans and their money over nationalist efforts at home.[66]

In the years before Wilde's arrival, Parnell's charismatic leadership gave him a strong following in the United States. A pan-European agricultural slump towards the end of the 1870s and the Irish crop failures of 1878–9 led to the outbreak of the Irish Land War in 1879. Tenant farmers' insurgency against landlords' contemptible practices (extortionate rents, expulsions, and obstinacy) generated the will to eliminate landlordism, and did so by harnessing nationalism to agrarian self-interest.[67] Campaigners demanded lower rents. Boycotting became the dominant tactic. At first, the British government responded with arrests. In the debates that followed, Parnell gathered support in Ireland and succeeded in making Gladstone's government recognize tenants' rights in the setting of fair rents. Despite these gains, Parnell continued to support activism partly because of the revolutionary tendencies of his Fenian allies. However, his refusal to end mass agitation led to his arrest and imprisonment from October 1881 until May 1882. So, for almost half of 1882, Parnell was in Kilmainham Gaol for provocative speeches against British legislative land reform proposals. With one controversial Irishman out of circulation, attention turned to another who was touring America.

Firm though Wilde was in his support of Irish Home rule, he often saw himself as British first, and Irish second. Moreover, he felt himself part of an international linguistic community for whom English was a *lingua franca* bridging ethnic and national divides. In America, however, where ethnic divisions were more numerous, such cosmopolitan ideas had little traction. There, Wilde was perceived as part of an ethnic community (the Irish) rather than a linguistic one (Anglophones).

In the United States, Wilde's politics met with little sympathy and much misunderstanding. His nuanced position as Irish by birth and British by choice was taken as equivocation. It suited neither Irish-Americans nor those descended of Anglo-Saxon stock. In an article whose title promised to reveal 'Who Oscar Wilde Is,' Washington's *National Republican* alerted its readers to his alleged fraud. 'Mr. Wilde comes among us as an Englishman,' the newspaper protested, even though it was 'a fact that his first opportunities for studying the aesthetic were from the windows of his nursery in Merrion Square, Dublin.'[68] Meanwhile, Irish-American newspapers, which would have liked to claim Speranza's son, took issue with him for what they deemed a betrayal. The *Irish Nation* castigated him for lecturing on the *English* Renaissance while 'hideous tyranny overshadows his native land.'[69]

In Ireland, activism and attacks persisted during the winter and spring of 1882, while Parnell was in prison and Wilde toured America. On 2 May 1882, Parnell was released from Kilmainham Gaol. Less than a week later, Lord Frederick Cavendish, Gladstone's Chief Secretary for Ireland, was stabbed to death in Dublin's Phoenix Park. His under-secretary was also murdered. A nationalist group claimed responsibility for the assassinations and, in their wake, public support for radicalism declined dramatically.

The prevailing fear was that Parnell no longer controlled the terrorist Paddy, which some portrayed as a Frankenstein-like subhuman (see Plate 24).[70] Parnell persuaded the Irish National League to adopt a more moderate position and to align itself with the Home Rule Party in favour of constitutional nationalism. But radicalism had been renounced too late to save the Irish reputation. By then, the damage was done. The 1882 Phoenix Park murders reinforced the strong identification of the Irish Home Ruler as a violent Paddy. A bloodthirsty creature of simian appearance, he could be, by turns, peasant-like, Celtic, or Catholic, but was always a nightmarish distortion of the Irishman (see Plate 25).[71] In England and America, the Paddy was already in wide circulation.

The Paddy first appeared in the American press after the Civil War and remained a fixture into the twentieth century.[72] Such negative portrayals of the Irish shaped transatlantic public opinion. As Lewis Perry Curtis observes in his study of Irish caricatures, Victorians troubled by the implications of Darwinian science and 'disturbed by the prospect of being cut into apes and monkeys derived some temporary relief by treating the Irish and other lesser breeds around the world as a buffer or evolutionary cordon sanitaire between themselves and anthropoid apes. If there was any substance at all to the theory that gorillas were man's nearest relatives in the animal world, then it was quite possible to argue that some races of man were closer to them than others.'[73]

Open a nineteenth-century newspaper or magazine to its illustrated pages, and the consequences would be plain to see. The image of the Paddy dominated the public imagination of the Irish while confrontations between tenants and landlords soared, reaching their acme in the spring of 1882.[74] Around the same time, a recent technology made it possible to paint the Paddy in more eye-catching ways than ever before. The advent of inexpensive colour printing revolutionized the reproduction of caricatures and printed images such as trade cards. Chromolithography dramatically increased the circulation of comic and satirical magazines. The culture wars being fought in their pages mirrored the era's bitter political conflicts.

Bombarding Britons and Americans with caricatures like the Paddy, the stage Irishman, and fictional anti-Irish characters was tremendously

effective in forming public opinion. The satires made people assume
the worst, and they encouraged Anglo-Americans to view the Irish as
evolutionary throwbacks to the subhuman. One thing the satires
didn't do was reflect well on those who had created them, as one pro-
Irish newspaper pointed out. Rabid anti-Irish satire merely proved
'how accurately and appreciatively Irishmen are studied by those who
cater for the entertainment and instruction of the British public.'[75]

Colonel Morse's machinations were relentless. He seemed to believe
that there was no such thing as bad publicity. He saw matters from
a business perspective, not from Wilde's point of view. 'Wilde was
somewhat surprised at the way the newspapers received him here,'
Morse told the press in early January 1882.[76] 'I explained to him, however,
that journalism was not journalism here unless it had something personally descriptive about it, and he rather laughed after that.' But Wilde
was no longer amused.

A few weeks later, when a battle between Irish-American boxers
captivated the country, the press juxtaposed Wilde with America's first
professional bare-knuckle fighter, the Irish-American John L. Sullivan.
It was early February 1882 and Sullivan had challenged the Tipperary-
born heavyweight champion, Paddy Ryan. Sullivan v. Ryan was the
talk of every bar and barbershop.[77] Colonel Morse must have seen this
as an opportunity for his Irish aesthete to fight his corner by proxy, as
if the brawl would settle the matter of who wore the breeches, the aesthete or the athlete. Wilde begged to differ. This was not what he had
in mind when he said, 'it is a great fight in this commercial age to plead
the cause of Art.'[78]

On the day of the fight, Sullivan and Ryan each weighed in at two
hundred pounds, but Ryan was at a distinct disadvantage. Sullivan had
spent the past year fighting and was on top form. He made quick work
of Ryan, throwing him across his hip and then to the ground. Meantime,
false rumours circulated that Wilde's two hundred pounds of
Aestheticism had met Sullivan in Chicago, setting the scene for a con-
frontation between the two wearers of skin-tight knee-breeches.[79] The
Chicago *Tribune* used the opportunity to compare Wilde's effeminacy
with Sullivan's brawn, concluding that Sullivan's school 'cultivates the
muscle and develops a high type of physical manhood,' whereas Wilde's

elevates 'whatever is hideous.'[80] All of this amplified the ruckus that had started in the Washington *Post*.[81] The Carte Company scored another victory, and Wilde another embarrassing defeat.

Though Wilde had a well-known fondness for self-promotion, there were limits to what he would endure. 'How far is it from this to this?' had gone too far, and the Irish boxing gag further still. When Wilde next wrote to Morse, it was to lecture the showman on the errors of his ways. 'Do you think I would notice an article comparing me to a prize-fighter?' Wilde snapped.[82] His mission to civilize America could hardly be accomplished if his management insisted on associating him with the country's crudest entertainers. It must have felt like sabotage. 'To say I regarded my visit here as a mere speculation is grossly untrue and should not be said,' Wilde chastised Morse. He had enough of being mismanaged by a showman who turned against him every time there was a dollar to be made.

How low could Morse go? To be sold by an enterprising showman as a freak was hardly new—Barnum had been doing it since the 1840s—but it was not the kind of reputation Wilde wanted, and he was shrewder and more attentive to the politics of Irishness than his cynical merchandisers cared to be.

Meanwhile, P. T. Barnum had decided to develop a bigger, better, and more ambitious version of 'What is It?' He was drawing up plans for a 'Congress of Nations,' he told prospective agents.[83] 'I desire to carry out as far as possible an idea I have long entertained of forming a collection, in pairs or otherwise, of all the uncivilized races in existence.' He planned to show them alongside animals, reptiles, and other 'freaks of nature.'

By the autumn, he cheerfully told the Smithsonian Institution that he had secured twenty-five Nubian men, women, and children. Soon, he hoped to take delivery of '150 specimens of semi-civilized, or rather *uncivilized*, living specimens' from his agents in the Dutch colonies. 'My aim,' he said, 'is to exhibit to the American public not only human beings of different races, but also, when practicable, those who possess extraordinary peculiarities.' To this end, the Greatest Showman on Earth took a front-row seat at Wilde's lecture. The presence of this titan of the entertainment world testified to what Colonel Morse's mismanagement had accomplished. By now, Wilde was being appraised by Barnum as a spectacular showpiece. He had gone from a lecturing zero to a freakish hero (see Plate 26).

Chapter 8

Life Imitates Art

By the time Wilde was to deliver his sixth performance of 'The English Renaissance,' the lecture's infelicities were common knowledge. Word on the street was that students of Harvard College were planning to prank him when he came to lecture on 31 January at Boston Music Hall. Days before, newspapers said that sixty of the College's gentlemen scholars would attend dressed in imitation of him. Boston's sterner voices, such as the *Evening Transcript*, were apprehensive about how the gag would be received. 'Harvard students will not undertake to treat a Music Hall audience with any less respect' than it would be proper to show elsewhere, it was hoped. If they did, the *Transcript* warned, the students would learn just how efficient the Boston police could be.[1] It seemed the lark could only go one of two ways. Would Harvard 'display to a cultivated audience just exactly how scholarly gentlemen should carry themselves'? Or would they embarrass the audience and, by extension, the city?

Boston liked to think of itself as the Athens of America. It wanted to protect its reputation as an elite, refined, cultural centre. Days before the lecture, the mood wavered between sovereign disdain and outright paranoia. The editor of the *Atlantic Monthly*, the magazine that spoke for genteel New England, believed the best approach would be for Boston to ignore the visiting aesthete altogether. 'Nothing cuts a showman or a literary clown like no notice at all,' Thomas Bailey Aldrich thought.[2] Aldrich soon received a letter from New York in which the literary critic Edmund Clarence Stedman advised him that he should be much more anxious than he was. There was more on the line than the honour of his city, Stedman claimed. The whole country's reputation was at risk, he said, ratcheting up the stakes. 'I do hope that *Boston* will not aid New York in making America again the rightful laughing-stock of England. I suppose Wilde and Carte will cart away $100,000, and London will think us all d—d fools.'

The country was soon gripped by the notion that sixty students in knee-breeches and stockings could jeopardize the nation's international standing. It demonstrated how local views about Wilde could be catapulted into national news that would then govern conversations from coast to coast. It had already happened with the *Washington Post*'s Mr Wild of Borneo, and it was about to happen again. This time, however, Wilde was prepared to deal with the challenge.

On the evening of 31 January, a snowstorm descended over Boston. That might have deterred the audience for 'The English Renaissance' had it not been for the frenzy over the Harvard lark. Lo and behold, the hall was full. Nearly fifteen minutes after the scheduled start time, the crowd was still looking expectantly at the empty stage. Had Wilde decided to avoid the clash? Was he quailing in his room at the Vendome Hotel? At a quarter past eight, there was a commotion at the back of the Music Hall and people swivelled in their seats to catch sight of the action. Was it him? Necks craned to get a glimpse of the procession of Harvard gentlemen who solemnly entered. The leader was Winthrop Astor Chanler, a wealthy, Eton-educated Harvard student. Chanler was a member of America's unofficial aristocracy. The men following him wore floppy-haired wigs, dress coats, knee-breeches and green neck scarves (a nod to Wilde's Irishness). Everyone could see that they had gone to great lengths to deck themselves in Wilde's motley. No expense had been spared. They sauntered in gracefully, pausing occasionally to fix on the heavens gravely as if lost in thought. The audience erupted into laughter. According to one delighted spectator, it looked as though the students had just walked off the stage of *Patience*.[3] The night before, just a few paces from the Music Hall, the Globe Theatre had started its new run of the Gilbert and Sullivan opera.[4] The Harvard sixty had lilies in their buttonholes and sunflowers in their hands, just like Bunthorne. They were a spectacular warm-up act to Wilde's lecture.

Applause rippled across the room as the students took their seats. Then, as if on cue, Wilde took the stage. When the audience pivoted towards the front of the room and looked at the podium, they immediately noticed he wasn't wearing his usual *Patience*-inspired costume. Instead, he was dressed in black tie and tails, like any self-respecting gentleman on a night out. He had heard the rumours about the Harvard ploy, and chosen to wear conventional clothes. In doing so, he distanced himself from the students as well as from Gilbert and Sullivan's satire. It was a stroke of genius—his dandyish tactic cleverly marked out the difference between himself and his imitators. The audience's clapping grew louder. He basked in the warm reception a little longer before he spoke his first words. It seemed his luck had turned.

From the podium, Wilde coolly looked down on the assembly of pseudo-aesthetes. 'I see about me the signs of an aesthetic movement. I see young men who are no doubt sincere, but I can assure them that they are no more than caricatures,' he said.[5] He appeared practised, in control. It was a complete turnaround from his faltering New York lecture, less than a month ago. Wilde's appreciative but superior attitude made it look like he was exercising a visiting monarch's *noblesse oblige* by tolerating the fawning of his loyal American subjects. Wealthy and cultivated, Harvard's gentlemen scholars represented the country's elite. With these over-the-top imitations of himself sitting at his feet, he began his lecture.[6]

The next morning, Wilde awoke to discover he had conquered Boston. He had also made $1,000 in one night. The receipts were ten times what they had been at his previous lecture, in Albany.[7] It was a relief, especially after the terrible New York reviews. Boston, usually reserved in its praise, was in raptures. 'Mr. Wilde achieved a real triumph,' the *Evening Transcript* announced, 'and it was by right of conquest, by force of being a gentleman, in the truest sense of the word.'[8] When he chatted to interviewers, he said, 'what the young men did there was a mere piece of undergraduate high spirits. I received it in the same spirit, and my lecture at Boston passed off most brilliantly.'[9]

Yet Wilde's victory against the Harvard clowns had been assured from the start. The event was humbug, and the sixty students were, in fact, stooges. The commotion had been orchestrated from start to finish by Wilde and his management, who were in cahoots with sympathetic members of the student press. Together, they managed to hoodwink Bostonians and boost ticket sales by a healthy margin. Winthrop Astor Chanler, the undergraduate who had led the procession, was the business manager for the campus newspaper, the Harvard *Crimson*.[10] Orphaned at 14, he had already inherited a fortune, and was almost certainly the ringleader who had bought the sixty advance tickets and elaborate costumes.

Chanler was also the grandson of Samuel Ward—'Uncle Sam' to his friends—a wealthy New York lobbyist who felt sympathetic to Wilde's plight and probably wanted to save him from Colonel Morse's darker machinations. Years earlier, Uncle Sam had met 'my dear Charmides,' as he referred to Wilde, on a visit to Lord Ronald Sutherland Gower's cottage in England.[11] Wilde was accompanied by his Oxford friend, the poet James Rennell Rodd, and the pair charmed Uncle Sam. Now that Wilde was in the United States, Uncle Sam said he felt inclined to help him. 'I think him a sincere fellow with sweetness and dignity of manner and character.'[12] He summed up Wilde's predicament, saying, 'Here he is in a false position, having been imported as a speculation by D'Oyly Carte to revive the flagging public interest in *Patience*.' Although Uncle Sam liked Wilde, he hated the limelight. He did all he could to stay out of the papers and avoid the notoriety that would come from being publicly associated with D'Oyly Carte's aesthete. Instead, the lobbyist worked behind the scenes to engineer the coup.[13]

The ruse attracted one of the largest crowds Boston Music Hall had ever held. The stunt was textbook Barnum. But unlike 'What is It?' or Colonel Morse's 'How far is it from this to this?,' it didn't compromise Wilde's integrity or his message. The stunt bolstered it. Wilde was being initiated into the American art of spectacle-making. A few weeks earlier, his managers had turned him into an evolutionary joke, and they had simultaneously introduced him to showmanship on a continental scale. In doing so, they kicked the stakes up a notch. This was bigger than anything he had experienced before. Overnight, the name of the game became adapt or die. So in Boston, with Uncle Sam's assistance, Wilde used their tactics to his advantage. It was a sign of the compromises he was starting to make.

Showmen like Colonel Morse and D'Oyly Carte saw value in promoting Wilde as the living imitation of Gilbert and Sullivan's art, which was why they had brought him to see *Patience*'s pseudo-aesthetes in New York City. The Harvard stunt simply took the idea of life imitating art a little bit further. More than ever before, 'The English Renaissance' was descending into showmanship, with Wilde as an active participant.

Wilde's Boston victory made a reality of Americans' anxious fantasy about reputational damage. In this respect, the concerns of late nineteenth-century American cultural elites barely differed from those of their British counterparts. 'Gentlemanliness' ranked high among these concerns. According to the cultural historian Stefan Collini, 'the most sensitive dividing line in Victorian society was between those who were and those who were not recognized as "gentlemen."'[14] By the nineteenth century, 'gentlemanliness' was widely used as a euphemism to register Anglo-American anxieties about class and social standing.[15] The Boston incident represented in microcosm a fierce international rivalry between the United States and Great Britain over good manners. The legitimacy of each nation's claim to 'civilization' (a nebulous category that often used 'gentlemanliness' as a criterion) had long been contentious.[16]

Wilde's Boston lecture was construed as a test of the country's manners. The students' gag troubled the line between those who should be thought of as cultured gentlemen and those who should not. In Philadelphia, a city that rivalled Boston for culture, the prim, old-timey columnist for *Godey's Lady's Book* exaggerated the scandal, claiming that the Harvard undergraduates had made 'sech a dretful rumpus as I never heard anywhere afore. . . . No, not even at a minstrel show!'[17] On the other side of the social dividing line, working-class circles were gratified by the news that the country's foremost men were going a little 'Wilde.' In a New Jersey manufacturing town, the newspaper gloated over Boston's 'curiosity seekers, who went to see what sort of creature the lecturer was.'[18] As for the city's reputation as a bastion of higher culture, it predicted, 'Mr. Wilde will depart from the modern Athens with a very unfavourable impression of Boston "culchaw."'

News of the spectacle rippled across the country, growing increasingly distorted the farther it travelled.[19] 'Remember, young gentlemen,' a Texan paper moralized, 'it is the one who does a rude thing not the one to whom it is done who is degraded by it.'[20] 'If Boston culture is so thin a veneer,' a Californian worried, 'how can Mr. Wilde hope to escape pelting in the raw crudity of Chicago and San Francisco?'[21]

By today's standards, the Harvard students' behaviour would hardly raise an eyebrow. By nineteenth-century standards, just by paying attention to Wilde, they had embarrassed themselves and, by extension, brought shame on the entire class of gentlemen they represented. Wilde's triumph was spun into a neurotic fantasy, and interpreted as a sign of the imminent decline and fall of the American gentleman. It was reported that, in 1882, Harvard students were more devoted to fashion than to their studies, and that some were decorating their dorm rooms with aesthetic designs.[22] The country's most civilized young men now appeared to be under the sway of a young Irishman many believed to be an interloper and a sham.

Wilde's next stop was Yale, where the College's long-standing rivalry with Harvard stoked student interest. Senior administrators wrung their hands and worried about reputational damage, advising that Yale could prove its superiority to Harvard by ignoring Wilde altogether and threatening to punish any student who showed him disrespect. Yet the undergraduates prepared to outdo their rivals in a whole new way.[23] The controlled showman's experiment that had begun at Harvard was taking on a life of its own.

On 1 February, Yalies defied the administration and did not stay away. The audience for 'The English Renaissance' was enormous. That night, there were already over 1,000 people in attendance when a long line of aesthetically dressed Yale students sauntered into New Haven's Grand Opera House.[24] There were 200 gentlemen in the procession— Yale had more than tripled Harvard's numbers. But they went further still. Instead of being led by an aristocratic American like Winthrop Astor Chanler, the Yalies elected as their leader a black servant of the Trowbridge family, a prominent New Haven clan that had sent a long line of sons to Yale.[25] Out in front, the elderly black aesthete spear-headed the procession of young white aesthetes in knee-breeches and stockings. The audience was astonished.

'A College joke is something brilliant or at least new,' one Yalie explained.[26] To the students, the fun was in working out a more attention-grabbing response than Harvard's. Yet the Yalies' joke moved Wilde to the centre of a spirited game of one-upmanship that played on class and race. Old college rivalries traditionally played out on the athletics field were transferred to aesthetics.

Meanwhile, a gag biography was also juxtaposing Wilde with men and women of colour. In the ten-cent version of Wilde's life, as told from the perspective of an anonymous white gentleman narrator, the Irish aesthete's powers of attraction were so strong that 'our colored help stand speechless as he enters our hall.'[27] On the next page of the book, the point is illustrated in black and white. Wilde's fur-trimmed overcoat whirls open like a lily's petals to reveal his slim, black-clad body, and suddenly three adoring African American servant girls drop their work to make eyes at him (see Plate 27). At first sight, this seems to be a version of 'Oscar Dear,' a flirtation playing on Wilde's inter-racial appeal.

But look again. In the background, the drawing reveals another possible entanglement happening at the same time. Perched high above the women, a black butler watches the romantic scene unfold. Scowling, he carries on with his work. And this is when Oscar's expression comes into focus: this is when you notice that he actually looks quite indifferent to the swooning females in the foreground. Instead, he is gazing up at the man in the background. His face is screwed into an ambiguous expression that might mean he is lost in thought, or that he has set his sights on the butler.[28] The sketch bristles with illicit suggestion. By drawing into a tangle of romantic possibilities the race, class, and gender lines swirling around Wilde, it diagrams the many vectors that were then converging on him.

A few years earlier, a Yale professor named William Graham Sumner had begun to wonder about the proliferation of comic magazines directed at young men. He had noticed that there were more jokey periodicals than ever before, and he took a scientific interest in the influence they had on American boys. These were the kinds of questions that sociology was then beginning to tackle. It was still a new field, and Yale was its American headquarters. Professor Sumner was the discipline's leading exponent, and he firmly believed that sociology would eventually bring under the microscope social phenomena that humanity was still at pains to explain. He had trained for the clergy at Oxford, where he had fallen under the influence of Darwin, Huxley, and Herbert Spencer and converted to scientific naturalism.[29] 'My studies led me to the conviction,' he said in 1881, that sociology could 'do for the social sciences what scientific method has done for natural and physical sciences, viz.: rescue them from arbitrary dogmatism and confusion.'

In 'What our Boys are Reading,' Sumner analysed the influence of reading habits on young men's conduct. Disruptive behaviours—like those of the Harvard and Yale students at Wilde's lectures—were his main subject of interest. He noticed that teen magazines and boys' journals often featured vulgar stories of daredevils making mischief and being hailed as heroes for it.[30] This literature, he observed, was 'intensely stupid, or spiced to the highest degree with sensation.' Here, Sumner noticed, 'the most vapid kind of negro minstrel buffoonery' prevailed.[31] And school textbooks were no different. He observed that public-speaking primers intended to train the nation's young orators often praised tomfoolery and 'negro humor.'[32] Sumner was particularly concerned to assess the impact this sort of reading had on boys from privileged backgrounds—in short, the kinds of boys likely to go on to colleges like Harvard and Yale.

The Professor reached two alarming conclusions. First, he confirmed that life imitated art: he observed that young men tended to act out in real life the kinds of manners that they saw depicted in magazines and popular books. Certain types of culture nurtured negative behaviours even in good-natured boys, he noticed. What he had seen sufficed to show that such reading would 'poison boys' minds with views of life which are so base and false as to destroy all manliness and all chances of true success.'[33] This led Sumner to his second conclusion: that these humorous periodicals were putting the country's elite in peril.

Boys from good homes and from 'families which enjoy good social advantages' were at risk. Through their reading, the best boys were exposed to the worst men—tramps, rioters, criminals, gamblers, social delinquents, and 'low people who live by their wits.'[34] Letting 'our boys' associate with such people—even if only in print—was dangerous, Sumner implied, because it put America's social hierarchy in jeopardy. 'The law of the survival of the fittest, was not made by man,' he later declared.[35] 'We can only, by interfering with it, produce the survival of the unfittest.' From the lectern of his Yale professorship, Sumner preached social Darwinism. He took the view that 'the poor and the weak' were just emotional descriptors for people who should more accurately be called 'the negligent, shiftless, inefficient, silly and imprudent.'[36] By then, these terms had essentially become euphemisms for the working class—a group that contained a large proportion of Irish-Americans and African Americans.

Sumner's study offers a précis of what troubled some Americans about Wilde. In the popular stories that the sociologist condemned, the characters held up for youngsters' admiration were often 'swaggering, vulgar swells'—the proud and the pompous who pretended to be something they weren't.[37] At the same time, here was a foppish Irishman proposing to teach young Americans about 'The English Renaissance' and tricking good Harvard boys into misbehaving.

Class, ethnicity, and race go hand in hand: they cannot exist without each other.[38] Part of what Sumner noticed was that American popular

culture brought white, Anglo-Saxon men into contact with other eth-
nicities. Years later, in *Folkways*, Sumner examined blackface minstrelsy,
another popular social phenomenon. He was curious about the connection between what Americans thought about ethnic groups and
how they behaved.[39] Minstrelsy, Sumner explained, 'originated in fun
making by the imitation of a foreign group, whose peculiar ways
appeared to be ridiculous antics' but it was also 'used to burlesque and
satirize the weaknesses, follies, and affectations *of whites*.'[40] At the time,
this was a major step forward in understanding prejudice. Sumner's
ground-breaking insight was to notice that blackface minstrelsy wasn't
just about skin colour. It wasn't just about race. It was about much
more than that. It was a tool for ridiculing all kinds of 'foreign' and
'peculiar' people—which is to say people just like Wilde.

Wilde's affiliation with blackness would become stronger as his tour
progressed. For now, it was embodied in the practical, day-to-day part-
nerships he had with his valet and groom. For the duration of the tour,
his managers had hired these African Americans to work and travel
with him. Almost everywhere Wilde went in 1882, there were one or
two black men at his side. These men knew him intimately: they
dressed him, carried his luggage, and received the journalists who
interviewed him.[41]

Wilde first described his companions in a letter written shortly
after his arrival in the United States. Buzzing with pleasure, he talked
about drinking champagne in New York, writing autographs, and
sending out locks of hair to ladies. He was 27 years old and this was the
most exciting thing that had ever happened to him. He appeared to
have it all. 'I have,' Wilde bragged, 'a black servant, who is my slave—in
a free country one cannot live without a slave—rather like a Christy
minstrel, except that he knows no riddles. Also a carriage and a black
tiger [i.e. a groom in livery] who is like a little monkey.'[42] The thrill
wasn't about having servants—that was normal for a man of his standing—but about the novelty of having African American men tending
to him.

A few months later, Wilde was down to one servant. 'I have an
enormous trunk and a valet,' he told 'Uncle Sam' Ward's sister, Julia
Ward Howe, using a turn of phrase that made both the luggage and the

black man carrying it seem like portable property.[43] 'They need not trouble you,' Wilde reassured Mrs Howe about his chattels, 'I can send them to the hotel.' After this, Wilde's African American associates disappeared from his correspondence altogether.

We glimpse the man—or men—elsewhere, however. At several points during the tour, American journalists linger over them. At Jersey City, a reporter watches Wilde get off a train and leave the 'valet struggling hopelessly' with his luggage.[44] At Chicago, his 'stalwart African' gets an angry talking-to within earshot of a *Tribune* journalist.[45] In Charleston, South Carolina, Wilde's valet is 'a small but good-looking American citizen, a little off color.'[46] At Richmond, Indiana, he signs autographs for the aesthete's fans.[47] In Kansas, he is described as 'a mulatto of peculiarly soft brownish yellow complexion' who carries 'the [animal] skins and other aesthetic ornaments with which Oscar is wont to adorn his room' into a Leavenworth hotel.[48] In many cities, reporters like Miss Mary Watson witnessed an eye-catching choreography: as though on cue, Wilde's 'colored servant' would lay down a silk shawl and a bearskin on a sofa, then the aesthete would fling himself down on it, arrange himself into a dreamy posture, and indicate that he was ready for his interview.[49] In these vignettes, Wilde's men can be seen, but they are never heard. Specific names and identifying details never appear. Nineteenth-century journalistic practices reduced African Americans to absent presences or to jokes.[50] In its own way, advertising culture did, too. On one of the advertisements created to mock the sunflower aesthete, Wilde's African American dogsbody was portrayed as a little brown dog (see Plate 28).

Who were the men who worked for Wilde? The clues are thin, which makes them nearly impossible to trace. Although the story of the African Americans in Wilde's life still can't be told with certainty, it remains significant. They worked closely with Wilde, accompanied him on his travels, and helped him make his name. Even as a gap in the archive, they speak to the period's prejudice. (See the Appendix, 'The Mystery of Wilde's Black Valet.')

As for Wilde, he wasn't immune to Victorian racial bias. His letter and contemporary eyewitness accounts suggest that he thought poorly of his companions and treated them as joke-fodder, labouring underlings and aristocratic accessories. His Anglo-Irish racism shared a common vocabulary with American racism. In this transatlantic idiom, African Americans were synonymous with riddles and menial chores. His playful allusions to Christy minstrelsy and slavery freely mingled with notions of black inferiority and primitivism. They suggest that he did not imagine himself as having much humanity in common with these men. No, Wilde looked at his African American companions as though they had stepped off the stage of a Christy Minstrel show. In other words, Wilde saw them as life imitating art. William Graham Sumner's research was right after all.

Wilde's personal experiences in the United States amply supported Sumner's conclusions. By the end of the 1880s, the idea that life imitates art became a central Wildean principle. In *The Decay of Lying*, he named the interlocutors Cyril and Vivian, after his two young sons. Then he had his young gentlemen interview each other about life's relationship to art. Doublings such as these are usually a clue in Wilde that he is working through some element of autobiography. By then, all the world seemed to be a stage, and life itself a kind of perform-ance. 'Life imitates art,' he argued, illustrating his lesson by pointing to children's tendency to imitate what they read in books and stories.[51] To prove his point, he did not mention Harvard, Yale, or Rochester students but turned to an impersonal example, namely the phenom-enon of 'the silly boys who, after reading the adventures of Jack Sheppard or Dick Turpin'—eighteenth-century criminals—wreak havoc on unsuspecting citizens 'by leaping out on them in suburban lanes, with black masks and unloaded revolvers.'[52] Adults were no dif-ferent, he noted, except that their performances were more frequent and less ostentatious than children's.

To be a member of polite society, we all have to wear a mask, he claimed. 'In point of fact what is interesting about people in good soci-ety,' he wrote, 'is the mask that each one of them wears, not the reality that lies behind the mask. It is a humiliating confession, but we are all of us made out of the same stuff.'[53] He didn't think of himself as an exception to this rule. He told the poet Violet Fane that his essay was 'meant to bewilder the masses' but was 'of course serious.'[54]

In an era when sociology was only just establishing its credentials as a discipline, and psychology and theories of performativity were still a long way off, Wilde had touched on a profound truth about human behaviour in social situations. The laws of etiquette governing polite society were, in fact, a mask. Tact was merely an elaborate art of impres-sion management.[55]

7 February 1882. Rochester, upstate New York. When Wilde stepped on stage at the Grand Opera House, he looked out on an audience composed largely of students from the local university. By the beginning of the 1880s, the University of Rochester was a small, respectable college with three buildings, eight faculty members, and 143 students.[56] It was then still a young institution that aimed to include students who had 'hitherto been excluded from most of our older Colleges,' as the University's President, Martin Brewer Anderson, had put it in his recent commencement address.[57] An imposing man with a striking resemblance to Garibaldi, the General responsible for Italian unification, President Anderson thought his job was to be 'gentle and kindly as a woman in his relations to the students, and still be able to quiet a "row" with the pluck and confidence of a New York Chief-of-Police.'[58] Under his stewardship, the Rochester curriculum marked out a course of social meliorism. Those who were not gentlemen by birth or wealth could become gentlemen by training.

Discipline and good manners mattered a great deal to President Anderson, and so it must have been with a heavy heart that he read the local news on the morning after Wilde's lecture.[59] 'ROCHESTER'S DEEP DISGRACE,' the headline ran. 'Ill-Mannered, Boorish Young Men, Said to be Students, at Wilde's Lecture.'[60] Under that title, Anderson could discover the ungentlemanly chaos that a hundred of his students had caused the night before. They were called fools, rowdies, and mutton-heads.[61] The disaster immediately garnered attention across the United States as well as across the Atlantic.

On the evening of his Rochester lecture, almost as soon as Wilde began to recite 'The English Renaissance,' there was rowdy hissing, groaning, and hooting from the spectators. Wilde ignored the students and carried on. The ruckus grew louder. Finally, when they had drowned him out, he folded his arms across his chest and stopped speaking. It was what happened next that caused national embarrassment. Just when it seemed things could not get any worse, the students presented Wilde with a black reflection of himself.

On cue, the white Rochester students sent a lone African American aesthete strutting down the Grand Opera House's centre aisle. With all eyes on him, he pranced and postured, languidly dancing and occasionally pausing to turn his eyes heavenward. There was a great burst of applause, chuckles, and catcalling. Eager to outdo their Ivy league competitors, the students had commissioned a local known as 'Nigger

Pete' to act the aesthete. Born in North Carolina, Peter Craig had probably been enslaved as a child, had no education, and could neither read nor write.[62] After serving in the Civil War, he sometimes worked as a painter. By the 1880s he had fallen on hard times. Recently, the students had given the downtrodden 59-year-old a mortarboard and posted him at a busy Rochester intersection 'to furnish comedy for passersby.'[63]

Soon the excitement in Rochester's Grand Opera House had reached fever pitch. 'The negro enjoyed the lark, and carried out the part with so much zest that an unspeakable uproar followed,' reports said later. When the police arrived to calm the disturbance, a rowdy brawl ensued. Police reinforcements were called in, and then the gas was turned off. In the end, Wilde finished his lecture 'before a few people who had remained more to see the fun than to hear the lecturer.'[64] To add insult to injury, the night's take was $111.47—a tenth of what it had been in Boston.

When Donaldson Brothers' lithography firm in New York caught wind of Peter Craig's Rochester performance, they were reminded of Rochester's more famous former citizen, the 64-year-old ex-slave Frederick Douglass (see Plate 29). Freed by British supporters who had bought him out of slavery, Douglass was a legendary international orator who, by 1881, had published his third autobiography, *Life and Times of Frederick Douglass, Written by Himself*.[65] The comparison between the black aesthete and Douglass was outlandish, but that also made it eye-catching. It would be irresistible to the firm's advertisers. So the funsters at Donaldson Brothers re-created their own version of Wilde's Rochester lecture and turned it into a multicoloured trade card that would be used to advertise products including coach varnish (see Plate 30).

In this imaginative rendering, the black Oscar is someone who *looks* like a young Frederick Douglass, but *sounds* as illiterate as old Peter Craig. The young ladies and gentlemen on the front row appear ready to believe in him, though the white-haired man behind him on the far left looks astonished. Aestheticism is something beautiful, the black aesthete tells his 'belobed bredren' in broken English. Aestheticism is 'light and airy' like the flatulence-inducing bean, he says. To be clear: Donaldson Brothers' took the century's leading African American abolitionist, added Oscar Wilde, and came up with a punchline about passing wind. To them, black Oscar was nothing more than a windbag.

Increasingly, Aestheticism was being vulgarized, pushed towards the limbo between good taste and bad. More worrying still was the fact that the movement's associations were noticeably shifting toward to a visual politics rooted in the freak-show tradition.[66] What was happening to Wilde had happened to Douglass decades before. Indeed, in the 1840s, Douglass's career as a lecturer was negatively influenced by Barnumism and freak-show culture. As a fugitive slave, he was acutely aware that, for many in his lecture audiences, he was 'a curiosity' of the kind made famous by 'What is It?' and similar shows. He knew that they looked at him as an oddity, not a man and brother. 'Many came, no doubt, from curiosity to hear what a Negro could say in his own cause,' Douglass remembered. 'I was generally introduced as a "*chattel*"—a "*thing*"—a piece of southern "*property*"—the chairman assuring the audience that *it* could speak.'[67] Douglass's image, like Wilde's, was crudely framed by racial stereotypes. 'Negroes can never have impartial portraits, at the hands of white artists,' Douglass despaired. 'It seems to us next to impossible for white people to take likenesses of black men, without grossly exaggerating their distinctive features.'[68]

As antagonistic forces gathered around Wilde, his frustration grew. The victory at Harvard had been reversed at Yale and Rochester, and now it seemed that all was lost. Exposed and inexperienced, Wilde did his best to ignore what he could not change, and to improve as he could. He drew attention to the success at Boston, and minimized the pandemonium that came in its wake. He chuckled good-naturedly with reporters and made light of the Harvard boys, saying, 'You don't suppose for a moment that a movement of any importance can be affected by sixty young men?'[69] The Harvard sixty were not cause for concern, but the dangerous game of one-upmanship they had kicked off certainly was.

Although he put a brave face on, he was struggling. Failure, his greatest fear, seemed to be baying at the door, ready to devour him. More and more, he turned to drink to steady his nerves. That night, his tab would run to $28.75. A month later, in the suburbs of Chicago, his nightly earnings dropped lower than that. By March, his health would begin to fail.

Interviewers descended to hear Wilde's opinion of the Rochester catastrophe. Days before St Valentine's, one journalist found him already dressed up for the holiday in a red-collared silk smoking jacket with a red tie, handkerchief, and socks. Reclining on a couch covered in wild animals' skins, Wilde smoked as he endured the man's questions.

'In speaking of Rochester,' he said, 'I must say that I am trying to keep as good an opinion of your country as I can.' English audiences were so much more civilized, he informed the reporter between cigarette puffs. Americans' off-colour jokes were making it difficult to keep an open mind about the United States. 'Let a young man go to England and lecture on any subject he chooses, he will at least be treated with respect,' Wilde said, tossing away his cigarette with a disdainful gesture.

Chapter 9

Is it Manhood?

The nineteenth century was fixated on manhood. Much has been written about the constraints on Victorian women but gender expectations for men were no less real, although less pronounced. The debates swarming around Wilde were personal, but they also touched on fundamental questions about what made a man a man. Poetry was a battleground for masculinity, and Wilde had entered the fray.

'What is a man anyhow?' a then little-known poet called Walt Whitman asked at mid-century.[1] His reply came in the form of *Leaves of Grass*, an 1855 poetry collection that sought to establish the nobility of the American working man. Whitman's inclusive spirit and comprehensive range made his poetry nothing short of revolutionary. When he pictured seamen and horsedrivers, gunners and fishermen, he praised their blend of 'manly form' with 'the poetic in outdoor people.' Likewise, he assured readers that the ripple of 'masculine muscle' definitely had its place in poetry.[2] In Whitman's book, a working poet could be as manly as marching firemen, and wrestling wrestlers could be just as poetic. Every working man could represent what he triumphantly called 'manhood balanced and florid and full!'[3] He redefined who counted as a real man.

It wasn't long before the essayist Ralph Waldo Emerson was writing to congratulate Whitman. Emerson had given much thought to these matters. Decades earlier, in his celebrated 1837 'American Scholar' speech, he had observed that society rarely regarded a man as a whole person, but reduced him to less than the sum of his parts.[4] Now Whitman's poetry had restored men to their whole potential. *Leaves of Grass* 'meets the demand I am always making,' Emerson told

Whitman in 1855, praising his exceptionally brave handling of his materials.[5] Here, finally, was an American poet who embraced the totality of man, and celebrated him as a fully embodied individual. 'I greet you at the beginning of a great career,' Emerson wrote him.

For a long time, sexuality had been excluded from literature. No more. 'I say that the body of a man or woman, the main matter, is so far quite unexpressed in poems; but that the body is to be expressed, and sex is,' Whitman replied to Emerson.[6] The place to do it, he said, was in American literature. And the way to do it was by writing the truth about men's appetites, and rejecting the fiction known as 'chivalry.' At one time, chivalry designated medieval men-at-arms, but in Wilde's lifetime, it meant idealized gallantry, especially towards women, and a willingness to defend one's country. To Whitman, the notion felt clankingly old-fashioned. 'Diluted deferential love, as in songs, fictions, and so forth, is enough to make a man vomit,' he thought. Replace it with a truer picture of love and human nature, Whitman said, and 'this empty dish, gallantry, will then be filled with something.'

Whitman's ideas intrigued Wilde, who looked to the older poet as a role model and possible ally. If friendship and solidarity were too much to ask, there might at least be some positive publicity to be gained from courting Whitman's attention. By now Wilde realized that he had to advertise himself—it was a necessity if his lectures were not to be an outright failure. It was then that an enterprising young publisher named Joseph Marshall Stoddart suggested that Whitman and Wilde share an open carriage ride through wintry Philadelphia—a proposition designed to attract maximum publicity.[7] Stoddart had bought the American rights to Gilbert and Sullivan's operas; he therefore had a personal stake in the success of *Patience* and, by extension, in Wilde. When he pictured the pair rolling through the City of Brotherly Love, visible to all, Stoddart must have fantasized about the stunt's potential to make the dollars roll in. Whitman quickly put an end to that pipe dream. 'I am an invalid—just suffering an extra bad spell & forbidden to go out nights [in] this weather,' the 62-year-old replied, vetoing the invitation.[8] If Whitman read the *Philadelphia Press* a few days later, he would have noticed the aesthete fawning over him on page 2. 'What poet do you most admire in American literature?' the reporter asked.[9] 'I think that Walt Whitman and Emerson have given the world more than anyone else. I do so hope to meet Mr. Whitman,' Wilde said, so delivering his billet doux in public. 'I admire him intensely,' he continued. Then, gilding the lily, he added, 'Dante Rossetti, Swinburne, William Morris, and I often discuss him.' He was not above embellishing the truth, or insinuating that he might be Whitman's heir-apparent from overseas.[10]

Flattery has been known to open doors, and Wilde's lifelong habit of smooth talking those he wished to persuade may eventually have unlocked Whitman's. The key, this time, was one Wilde had not tried before: he used the press as a go-between, and it worked. The next morning, Whitman loaded a pen with black ink and shot off a quick note inviting Wilde to visit him that afternoon.[11]

When Wilde knocked on the door of 431 Stevens Street, a boyhood dream was about to be fulfilled. When he was 11 years old, he and his mother read *Leaves of Grass* together.[12] The book was not then in wide circulation, but Speranza managed to get her hands on one of the earliest copies and made a habit of reading passages aloud to her young son.

This boyhood Whitman was probably quite different from the edition which introduced the American poet to most British readers. William Michael Rossetti's selection of 1868 cut the book by half, excluding 'every poem which could with any tolerable fairness be deemed offensive to the feelings of morals or propriety in this peculiarly nervous age.'[13] Within a year, the sanitized Whitman had many admirers in England. Little did they know how much had been cut from the American *Leaves of Grass* to make the British version. 'I am a free companion,' Whitman proclaimed (and Rossetti excised).[14] 'I turn the bridegroom out of bed and stay with the bride myself, I tighten her all night to my thighs and lips,' Whitman wrote (and Rossetti deleted). Whitman called Rossetti's edition a 'horrible dismemberment of my book.'[15]

In the American *Leaves of Grass*, Whitman spoke for so many that his voice boomed like a chorus.

Walt Whitman am I, of mighty Manhattan the son,
Turbulent, fleshy and sensual, eating, drinking and breeding;...
Through me many long dumb voices;
Voices of the interminable generations of slaves;
Voices of prostitutes, and of deform'd persons;
Voices of the diseas'd and despairing, and of thieves and dwarfs;...
Through me forbidden voices;

Voices of sexes and lusts—voices veil'd, and I remove the veil;
Voices indecent, by me clarified and transfigur'd....
I keep as delicate around the bowels as around the head and heart;
Copulation is no more rank to me than death is.[16]

The modern ear may hear in these breathless enumerations a more-is-more exuberance. To Rossetti, such an earthy catalogue of potential conquests counted among the poems' 'deforming crudities.'[17] The repetitions at the beginning of successive clauses ('through,' 'voices') pump Whitman's red-blooded ideas through the poem with the insistence of a heartbeat. Such pulsating lines could not, the editor Rossetti explained, 'be placed with a sense of security in the hands of girls and youths, or read aloud to women.'[18]

Perhaps Speranza felt she could read them aloud to her son, however. Whitman was a daring choice of reading material for mother and son. In 'Song of Myself,' a poem Rossetti excluded, Whitman wrote:

I am enamoured of growing outdoors,
Of men that live among cattle, or taste of the ocean or woods,
Of the builders and steerers of ships, and the wielders
            of axes and mauls, and the drivers of horses,
I can eat and sleep with them week in and week out.

What is commonest, cheapest, nearest, easiest, is Me,
Me going in for my chances, spending for vast returns,
Adorning myself to bestow myself on the first that will take me.[19]

Speranza fostered 'adult' tastes in her son, and his growing independence enabled him to explore them to the full. So long as his adventures remained intellectual and sartorial, he was happy to share them with his mother. As an undergraduate at Trinity College Dublin, he would invite a friend to her salon in Merrion Square. 'Come home with me,' he said, 'I want to introduce you to my mother. We have founded a society for the suppression of virtue.'[20]

Upon entering Whitman's whitewashed chamber on 18 January 1882, Wilde noticed, first, just how small and bare the room was, and then, almost immediately, how large and majestic Whitman looked sitting in it.[21] As a result of a paralytic stroke, he seemed much older than his years. His snow white beard spread down his neck and onto his chest. But on the frontispiece of the most recent edition of *Leaves of Grass*, he appeared to have stopped the clock. There, forever fixed, he still appeared as a cocky 37-year-old workman-dandy—only a few years older than Wilde was now. There was good reason to see them as poetic alter egos, since their writings were, by now, both notorious for indulging in sensuality.

On that winter's day in 1882, Wilde was certain Whitman was 'the grandest man I have ever seen. The simplest, most natural, and strongest character I have ever met in my life.'[22] The younger man, eager to establish his kinship, told Whitman, 'I have come to you as to one with whom I have been acquainted almost from the cradle.'[23] But Whitman didn't immediately warm to him. He was usually stand-offish before he admitted an admirer into his life. Years before, on an index-card-sized scrap of paper entitled 'To a new personal admirer,' Whitman had started a list of questions he might address to a fan. 'Do you suppose you will find in me your ideal of manliness and of love?' he began.[24] Then, he paused, scratched out the word 'love,' and continued his enquiry. 'Do you suppose yourself advancing on real ground toward a real heroic man?' he wondered.[25] 'Do you think it so easy to have me become your lover?'

It was no coincidence that Whitman's list gave the impression of an interviewer preparing to give a subject a hard time. As a young journalist in the first half of the nineteenth century, asking questions had been the backbone of his approach. After leaving school at 11, he learned the printing trade, and by 18 he was working as a newspaper editor and journalist. Whitman's career, from the 1830s to the late 1850s, put him at the centre of the rapidly changing literary world. He belonged to the world of New York's popular press and was practised in interview-style reportage (as early as 1845 he wrote 'A Dialogue' between a convict and 'the people').[26] When he gave up journalism, he transferred his straightforward, vivid reporting style over to the craft of poetry. Often, his poems took the shape of a one-sided conversation, a sort of dialogue between himself and an imaginary interlocutor. Likewise, Wilde's experience of interviewing would later mould the dialogue in his plays and criticism.

No reporters were invited to witness the meeting between Whitman and Wilde. This was a strange choice for two dandyish men who loved self-promotion, but it was a canny one: they would each give separate interviews afterwards, and double the attention they received. In the two hours they'd spent together, both said they'd had a very pleasant time. 'One of the first things I said was that I should call him "Oscar," ' Whitman told a reporter afterwards.[27] ' "I like that so much," he answered, laying his hand on my knee. He seemed to me like a great big, splendid boy.' They had enjoyed a bottle of wine together and talked about poetry—about Swinburne, Dante Gabriel Rossetti, Morris, Tennyson, and Browning. The old poet had let the young aesthete hold forth on the intentions of his school of art. When Wilde asked about Whitman's poetic theories, the old man smiled and answered amiably, like the best of mentors. He had his private doubts about Aestheticism, but he was personally encouraging to Wilde. Whitman opened up about problems he was trying to solve in his own poetry—issues that included sensuality, which he thought essential and his critics thought obscene. Years later, Wilde amplified his appreciation for Whitman's fresh, uninhibited idea of sexuality, calling it 'the relation of the sexes, conceived in a natural, simple and healthy form.'[28] That made it sound wholesome and pink-cheeked. In his own works Wilde tried to tell the unvarnished truth, as Whitman did, when he described his poetry as 'the song of Sex, and Amativeness, and even Animality.'

Turning the conversation back to Wilde, Whitman was anxious to know whether this young aesthete was going to have the courage to do something new with his poetry and his art movement. Would he dare to question the age's pieties? What revolutions did he have in store? The white-beard urged the smooth-faced aesthete to have the courage of his opinions. 'Are not you young fellows going to shove the established idols aside?' he asked, as a goad to Wilde's revolutionary spirit. In the newspaper articles that inevitably followed this encounter, the poets endorsed each other. Whitman bragged that 'Wilde had the *good sense* to take a great fancy to *me*.'[29] The feeling was mutual. Wilde felt he had won Whitman's seal of approval. Years later, he told a friend, 'the kiss of Walt Whitman is still on my lips.'[30]

In 1881, shortly before Wilde set sail for the United States, Whitman published a new American edition of *Leaves of Grass*.[31] In his review, the critic Colonel Thomas Wentworth Higginson compared it to the previous ones and declared its 'somewhat nauseating quality remains in full force.'[32] Seizing the opportunity to tar Wilde with the same brush, Colonel Higginson described the aesthete as though he was the youngest English disciple of a Whitmanian society for the promotion of vice.

The reports about Wilde and Whitman's meeting in January 1882 gave the impression that the two poets had formed an alliance. It was reported that Whitman had given Wilde his blessing. 'I wish well to you, Oscar, and as to the aesthetes,' Whitman said, 'if you want my advice, I say "go ahead."'[33] Weeks later, in the wake of the widely publicized meeting, Colonel Higginson penned another article about the unwholesome pair of poets. Published under the title 'Unmanly Manhood,' it was a vicious attack. 'Their poetry is called "manly" poetry!' Higginson fumed.[34] 'Is it manly to fling before the eyes of women page upon page which no man would read aloud in the presence of women?' he demanded.

It was not just their poetry that Colonel Higginson objected to. He found both men personally abhorrent. Though they had not met, Higginson had been in the audience at Wilde's 1878 Oxford graduation, and had first heard him recite his prize-winning verse against the decorous backdrop of the Sheldonian Theatre. As Higginson read *Poems*, however, his doubts about Wilde's respectability grew. The 'offenses against common decency' committed by Wilde 'can indeed be paralleled in Whitman,' he decided. Worse still, from the Colonel's point of view, neither man had served in the military, nor defended their nations in wartime. 'Each of these so-called "manly poets" has had his opportunity of action and waived it,' he raged. During the Civil War, when Higginson was mustering ex-slaves into battle against the South, Whitman 'with all his fine physique and his freedom from home-ties, never personally followed the drum, but only heard it from the comparatively remote distance of the hospital' where he nursed wounded soldiers.

And Wilde's 'fine physique'? It, too, failed the 'test of manhood.' Speranza's poems about Ireland were powerful enough, Higginson thought, 'to enlist an army' and to spur young men to head for recruiting offices. But instead of following his mother's lead, Wilde had dodged his duty and followed the Irish exodus to America. Higginson reminded Americans that Wilde, like a fickle, careless lover, had fled Ireland at a time when she needed him most. Ireland now stood 'on the verge of civil war; her councils divided, her self-styled leaders in jail; she needs every wise head and brave heart she has ever produced, to contribute, according to their best light, to some solution of her hard problem,' Higginson wrote. He accused Wilde of being a traitor as well as a coward. 'This young Irish poet,' the pernickety veteran observed, spoke 'of "us Englishmen"' and of 'the so-called "English Renaissance."'

Is it manhood, Higginson thundered, to refuse to defend Erin when she most needs her men? The question rumbled throughout his essay like the crack and clap of a violent storm. *Is it manhood?* Like lightning igniting what it strikes, the question enflamed ongoing debates about virility.[35] Much had already been said about the ambiguousness of Wilde's body, but Higginson's essay reoriented the conversation by indexing it to a soldierly ideal that had its origins in ancient Greece.

Wilde loved the Greeks, but for different reasons. What had most deeply impressed him about Whitman's personality was how much it resembled the Hellenic ideal of harmony between body and mind, of athletic and intellectual development. 'I regard him as one of those wonderful, large, entire men,' Wilde said, 'strong, true, and perfectly sane: the closest approach to the Greek we have yet had in modern times.'[36] Whitman was the American incarnation of that ancient type of masculine excellence, and Wilde styled himself as the British version. At Harvard, he said that casts of Greek statues should be installed 'in all gymnasiums as models to correct that foolish impression that mental culture and athletics are always divorced.'[37] For the first time, Wilde was talking openly about what manhood meant to him. One way to express desire was by intercutting his present with ancient history. His affiliation with Whitman, a modern-day Greek, also gestured towards this strategy.

The age was demanding fresher, broader definitions of manhood than those put forward by Colonel Higginson. At the turn of the century, the rise of the New Man would release the Victorian gentleman from such narrow bounds and explode the pieties of gallantry and chivalry.[38] Wilde's desires were ahead of his time. For now, he wanted to be true to himself, but he needed to be careful. Until the mid-twentieth century, sodomy was a serious crime in England and the United States.

The word 'Greek' also hinted at Greek love—homosexuality. In the private notebooks he kept at Oxford, Wilde wrote that 'the refinement of Greek culture' had been arrived at 'through the romantic medium of impassioned friendships' between older and younger men.[39] For Wilde (and for men who shared his sympathies), the Greeks were a lifeline. Emotion could be contained by history, and intimacy rationalized. By taking the long view and making a friend of the past, it became possible to tolerate the loneliness, the secret struggles.

Meeting Whitman had stirred him deeply. When he left Whitman's side and climbed into the carriage waiting outside the door at 431 Stevens Street, the publisher J. M. Stoddart observed that he seemed a changed man. Profoundly moved by Whitman's example, Wilde sank into a meditative silence, breaking it only occasionally to speak of the old poet's grandeur, 'his struggles and triumphs.'[40] Ten days later, the spell remained unbroken. His face glowed enthusiastically as he talked to an interviewer about the author of 'Song of Myself.' Yet his gushing ended with an ominous offhand remark. 'Probably he is dreadfully misunderstood,' Wilde said. 'He only wants one thing, to be understood.'[41]

Certainly Wilde's own existence was troubled by similar misunderstandings. His sense of who he could love was fluid—there were all those pretty girls, those marriage proposals—but he had his preferences. The lobbyist Sam Ward remembered seeing Wilde together with an attractive Oxford poet named James Rennell Rodd, a few years earlier, at the cottage of Lord Ronald Sutherland Gower, a well-known reprobate and lover of men.[42] Meanwhile, Sam's sister, the poet Julia Ward Howe, worried about Wilde's predilection for Greek love, or 'the poison found in the ancient classics' as she gingerly put it.[43]

Wilde kept no diary in which he confessed his desires (though his mother told him to), and his letters to friends and family were littered with half-truths downplaying disasters and trumpeting successes.[44] Paradoxically, it was in conversation with interviewers that he could be most himself. Some of his most astonishing self-revelations came about when he gushed about Whitman. By talking about another poet, he talked about himself by proxy. By thinking through Whitman, Wilde exposed his own loneliness and desire for intimacy. He admired Whitman because he had dared to publish 'the drama of a human soul,' because he had gone 'on record' about his true feelings.[45] That qualified Whitman as a personal hero.[46] Up until now, Wilde hadn't been quite so bold, especially when it came to his feelings for men. But he was thinking about how those feelings might be put into print, perhaps with Stoddart as the publisher. When that book eventually saw the light of day, it was called *The Picture of Dorian Gray*.

At times, the 1882 chats Wilde had with interviewers resembled a rudimentary 'talking cure,' the therapy that Sigmund Freud, then a newly qualified Viennese physician, would evolve into psychoanalysis. Although Wilde preferred to live his life on the surface, the published interview transcripts suggest some of the depths below. Like tectonic plates moving at the bottom of the sea, things were shifting deep inside him. Six weeks after meeting Whitman, Wilde sent him a letter declaring 'there is no one in this wide great world of America whom I love and honour so much.'[47]

More than a decade later, in 1895, the stories of Wilde's loves were outed in London's Old Bailey. Wilde stood accused of violating Section 11 of the 1885 Criminal Law Amendment Act, which forbad 'acts of gross indecency between men.' At his trial, the prosecutor, Charles Gill, asked him whether 'the love that dare not speak its name' related to natural or unnatural love.[48] Wilde's response had the power to send him back to prison, where he had already spent a month. He had lied in reply to some of Gill's other questions. But now he told the truth, and went on record about the dramas of homosexual souls across the ages, including his own.

> 'The Love that dare not speak its name' in this century is such a great affection of an elder for a younger man as there was between David and Jonathan, such as Plato made the very basis of his philosophy, and such as you find in the sonnets of Michelangelo and Shakespeare. It is that deep, spiritual affection that is as pure as it is perfect. It dictates and pervades great works of art like those of Shakespeare and Michelangelo, and those two letters of mine, such as they are. It is in this century misunderstood, so much misunderstood that it may be described as the 'Love that dare not speak its name,' and on account of it I am placed where I am now.
> It is beautiful, it is fine, it is the noblest form of affection. There is nothing unnatural about it. It is intellectual, and it repeatedly exists between an elder and a younger man, when the elder man has intellect, and the younger man has all the joy, hope and glamour of life before him. That it should be so, the world does not understand. The world mocks at it and sometimes puts one in the pillory for it.

With this speech, Wilde placed himself as one of the latest in a line of misunderstood men stretching back millennia. The courtroom broke out into applause, but hisses were audible, too.

By the time Wilde was convicted, on 25 May 1895, the ambiguity that had hovered around Aestheticism in 1882 had hardened into a hideous diagnosis. To some, it felt like the Aesthetic Movement itself had been tried, found guilty, and condemned. 'The aesthetic sunflower dude, over whom the giddy girls of this country raved a few years ago, has just been sent to prison for two years at hard labor in London, on conviction of a beastly crime,' Indiana's *Farmland Enterprise* newspaper stated, gleefully mocking Wilde's fate.[49] Elsewhere, it was reported that 'the aesthetic dude has been sentenced to two years in prison at hard labor for a crime that la-da-dahism leads to.'[50]

For the time being, in 1882, Wilde's homosexuality was still a secret. But Higginson's accusation of 'Unmanly Manhood' threatened to let the cat out of the bag. Already, the persistent incursions of military men in Wilde's life were giving him a taste for battle. The betrayal of Colonel Morse, the rank scurrility of the war reporter Archibald Forbes, and now Colonel Higginson's latest attack were having their effect. Only recently, he had rebuffed Forbes in a letter saying 'you have to speak of the life of action, I of the life of art. Our subjects are quite distinct and should be kept so.'[51] But now he changed his mind. There could be no peace without war, he realized, and he was ready for combat. He was determined 'to be a part of the living world and of the great currents of interest and action.' Aestheticism was on the march.

His honour needed protection, and several American friends flew to his defence with a press campaign designed to shame Colonel Higginson into silence. First, on 10 February 1882, there was a letter in the *New York World* from a flamboyant poet and frontiersman named Joaquin Miller. 'My dear Oscar,' he began, 'I read with shame about the behaviour of those ruffians at Rochester at your lecture there.'[52] The so-called civilized parts of the United States were rougher than the wilderness, Miller said. 'Don't you lose heart,' he wrote. 'My heart is with you; and so are the hearts of the best of America's millions.'

Then William Henry Hurlbert stepped in. As the editor-in-chief of the *New York World*, Hurlbert had been pestering Wilde to name his persecutors (preferably in his newspaper, of course).[53] So far Wilde had been too proud to accept Hurlbert's offer. He had preferred to endure the humiliation, and honourably refused to be lured into public quarrels. But now he was coming around to the view that the public could only be sympathetic to him if they knew about these distressing attacks. Strain and fatigue had a mollifying effect. He looked burdened, tired, thin and anxious. He was reaching breaking point.

The *New York World*'s editor-in-chief had been watching from the sidelines long enough to know that playing the silent stoic was no way to win against Colonel Higginson—and Hurlbert knew the Colonel very well. Intimately, even. Nearly half a century earlier, when they were Harvard theology students together, in the 1840s, the Colonel had been 'Dear Wentworth' to him.[54] The affectionate feeling was mutual. That was when Dear Wentworth was an opium-smoking dreamer who thought Hurlbert was 'a young man so handsome in his dark beauty that he seemed like a picturesque Oriental; slender, keen-eyed, raven-haired, he arrested the eye and the heart like some fascinating girl.'[55] The pair soon developed a passionate friendship. By the time Wilde met Hurlbert, he was a portly gentleman with a walrus mustache, a comb-over, and heavy-lidded eyes. Although he hadn't married, he was known as a 'randy bachelor' who could conquer women with his conversation.[56] By 1882, the Colonel had all the trappings of success. Along with a distinguished military record and a seat in the Massachusetts legislature, he had become, for the first time, a father at the age of 59 (his wife was 38).

To help Wilde, Hurlbert attacked the Colonel in the *New York World*. The editor suggested his old friend go take a look at himself in the nearest mirror to see what 'unmanly manhood' really looked like. 'It is not so very long, if the traditions of Harvard may be trusted, since Mr. Higginson wore his own hair long,' Hurlbert explained, pointing to the similarity between Wilde's long hair and his soldier-critic's youthful locks.[57] The resemblance was still more thoroughgoing, Hurlbert revealed, for years ago Higginson had also cared deeply about beauty. It was a case of the pot calling the kettle black.

Hurlbert implied that the Colonel's own masculinity had once been less than assured, and he knew of what he spoke. As students, they had been close until, one day, Hurlbert gently but firmly sought to end their loving relationship.[58] But Higginson would have none of it. He never accepted that their friendship was over. Years later, he wrote Hurlbert longingly about the evenings they had shared. He wanted Hurlbert to know how much he missed him. 'Out of the depths of my heart I still love you,' the Colonel told him in a letter. When he mentioned that he wished 'to spend a night at your room again,' his neat script slanted forward as if leaning towards his old friend.[59] 'I have never loved but one male friend with a passion,' he explained.[60]

As the World's editor-in-chief, Hurlbert knew that fuelling a debate between the Colonel and Wilde was bound to sell newspapers. That it also settled a personal score was a fringe benefit. His plan worked like a charm and his editorial created a sensation. 'It is impossible for anything to be livelier than Hurlbert's article in today's World,' Sam Ward gushed to his sister, Julia Ward Howe.[61] Ward then sent the article on to Longfellow, who would surely find it amusing. 'As a "free lance" journalist,' Ward wrote, Hurlbert 'hits all around. But, the objective point, Higginson, he hits in the bull's eye.'

Two weeks later, Wilde followed up by allowing a private letter to be published in the World. He had never done this before, but the Colonel deserved special measures. 'Who, after all, is this scribbling anonymuncule in grand old Massachusetts who scrawls and screams so glibly about what he cannot understand?' Wilde railed.[62] 'Scribbling' had a particularly nasty ring to late nineteenth-century New England ears because it echoed Nathaniel Hawthorne's legendary scorn for the 'damned mob of scribbling women,' his more successful female competitors.[63] Women and children scribbled. Men wrote. And Wilde was only warming up. Who is 'this apostle of inhospitality, who delights to defile, to desecrate, and to defame the gracious courtesies he is unworthy to enjoy?' he wrote, delivering alliterations rat-a-tat like hostile gunfire.[64] Although Wilde didn't name Higginson outright, he didn't need to. Everyone knew who his target was. The Colonel knew he was beaten and immediately ceased hostilities.

All this sensation hadn't improved ticket sales one jot, and by early spring Wilde's box office receipts were continuing their spiral towards oblivion. 'Such a fiasco as the last ten days have given should be avoided,' Wilde told Morse in early March.[65] He felt wasted by 'wearying my voice and body to death' in front of negligible audiences and hoped that Morse would soon send him some showy new clothes. That might be a draw at the box office. To recover, the tour would need much more than a novelty costume, however.

In interviews, Wilde projected unshakable self-belief despite the private worries he shared with Morse. 'I know that I am right, that I have a mission to perform. I am indestructible!' he told the American press.[66] No matter how much he was struggling, he was determined not to let the public see it.

   Privately, he was falling to pieces. A look at Morse's accounts and Wilde's itinerary provides further clues to Wilde's fraying state of mind. In a little over two weeks in mid-February, he lectured in twelve different cities—a relentless schedule by any standard. Despite all that hustling, the take at the box office was miserable. His health was declining. One night, he collapsed on stage from sheer exhaustion.[67] 'It's so depressing and useless lecturing for a few shillings,' he told Colonel Morse in another desperate letter.[68] Sometimes he must have felt that the world was against him—the audiences and the newspapers certainly were. By 6 March, Wilde had reached his all-time low. In a small town south of Chicago, his lecture brought in just $18.75. That night, he bought himself some medicine and went to drown his sorrows at the bar.[69] He had hit rock bottom.

Chapter 10

The War of Art

'What a tempest and tornado you live in!'[1] Even from a distance of four thousand miles, Speranza sensed her youngest son was in dire straits. As usual, she had words of advice at the ready. '*Don't* rush about so rapidly. Take more rest,' she instructed. But with opponents closing in on him and jeopardizing his tour, this was no time to take to his bed. Wilde wasn't giving up, but he was drinking hard and thinking tactically about his next move. Since his early twenties, his aim in life was 'Success: fame or even notoriety.'[2] Perhaps his greatest fear was that he would become a failure—an anxiety embodied for him by his older brother, Willie, a layabout alcoholic who, at the age of 30, still sponged off their mother. She, in turn, depended on the money Oscar regularly sent her. It was typical of Speranza to compare her two sons and to remind Oscar, in one of her letters, to 'take warning by Willie.'[3] Willie was a dark shadow to Oscar. He worked as a journalist and writer, sometimes relying on his little brother to feed him the plots for short stories he signed 'Frère Sauvage,' a pseudonym that hinted he was not so much his own man as he was 'Wilde's brother.'[4] That year, Willie was acting as an extension of Oscar by distributing his brother's photographs to London actresses and socialites, and lecturing at their old school in Enniskillen on 'The Aesthetic Movement of Oscar Wilde.'[5] Part alter ego, part PR agent, Willie's tragedy was that he looked so much like his brother, yet had so little of Oscar's work ethic or wit.[6]

Success, fame, notoriety. For Oscar, they would be the gold, silver, and bronze medals in the game of life. By now he had achieved fame and notoriety, and seen up close that everything that glittered wasn't golden. He knew notoriety's devouring power and felt at first hand fame's horribly distorting effects. But 24-carat-gold success still eluded him. Of course, Speranza had ideas about that, too. Her dream was to see Oscar come home to a brilliant but settled life or, as she put it, 'literature & lectures & Parliament—Receptions 5 o'clock for the world—& small dinners of genius & culture at 8 o'clock.' None of that would be possible if he came home from the United States with his tail between his legs.

In the early weeks and months of 1882, Wilde was without a plan or a formula. He had run himself ragged for the benefit of his untrustworthy managers and unappreciative audiences. There had been little time to pause and reflect on what was being done to him or how he might get what he craved. Change was in the air, however. Gone were the days of meekly submitting to the will of D'Oyly Carte or agreeing to play a part in Colonel Morse's latest hare-brained scheme. Those compromises had got him into a rut. Pushed and pulled by these external forces, he had been made into a parody of himself, a vile curiosity.

He didn't have to be the person—or the creature—they were creating. But who was he, really? And what would he fight for? By playing by other people's rules, he had only succeeded in losing himself. To win, he must take an even bigger risk: he had to be true to himself. That more difficult route lay ahead, but he resolved to take it. He had gathered allies in the newsprint and book publishing worlds, and they could help him carry out the paper warfare he was now planning. Now that he had the *New York World*'s editor, William Henry Hurlbert, and American publisher J. M. Stoddart in his pocket, he took steps to prove once and for all that he was worth taking seriously as the leader of the Aesthetic Movement.

According to his nemesis, Colonel Thomas Wentworth Higginson, one of the big 'tests of manhood' was seizing the opportunity for 'action.' To the Civil War veteran, that meant warfare, but the aesthete knew that not every battle was about ballistics, gunpowder, and beating drums. Wilde's war was about Art. Prompted by relentless accusations of charlatanism and unmanliness, he was bringing his Art crusade to the fore, and preparing a print war that aimed to silence his opponents once and for all. He was going to publish his first art manifesto.

Before leaving for the United States, Wilde had promised his Oxford friend James Rennell Rodd that he would find an American publisher for his 1881 poetry collection, *Songs in the South*. He quickly fulfilled his promise by enlisting J. M. Stoddart to the cause. But on the way to getting something for his friend, he also secured something for himself. Together, he and Stoddart took control of the American publication of Rodd's poems, making high-handed editorial decisions that would eventually make the book look more like Wilde's than anyone else's. The changes were small but meaningful. First, Rodd's title was changed to the more aesthetic-sounding *Rose Leaf and Apple Leaf*.[7] Next, Rodd's modest dedication, 'For my father,' was scrapped and replaced by an extravagant tribute to Wilde.

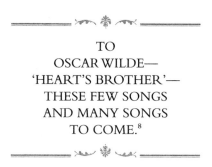

TO
OSCAR WILDE—
'HEART'S BROTHER'—
THESE FEW SONGS
AND MANY SONGS
TO COME.[8]

'*Look at dedication*,' Wilde winked at Stoddart when he sent him the manuscript.[9] The next step in the makeover was to make Rodd's book of poetry look like Costume Oscar himself. Printed in brown ink on white parchment interleaved with green tissue paper, the book's eccentric design would prompt many to compare its appearance to Wilde's get-up.[10] The book's front page was stamped with Wilde's bright red seal—a Grecian profile of a curly-haired young man with a bow at his neck.[11] There was also an over the top *edition de luxe*: it was autographed by Wilde, and printed on US Government paper remaindered from printing American money.[12] *Rose Leaf and Apple Leaf* instantly became an advertisement for his own aesthetic mission.

Important though these changes were, they would probably have gone unnoticed were it not for the strange preface called *L'Envoi* that Wilde added to *Rose Leaf and Apple Leaf*.[13] At thirty pages, it made up a significant proportion of the book and explicitly confirmed what the volume's bizarre aesthetic get-up implied: this was Rennell Rodd's poetry in drag as Oscar Wilde. The preface insinuated that Wilde was the original inspiration for Rodd's poetic tribute, and therefore his 'heart's brother.'

As a manifesto, *L'Envoi* sounded like a declaration by the leader of a band of aesthetic brothers in arms, the marching banner for a legion of art warriors. It was a *cri de guerre*. Wilde called his retinue of male followers 'young warriors under the romantic flag' who were fighting on behalf of culture and art. Suddenly he sounded like a general reviewing a phalanx of artistic troops, and pausing to single out Rodd as the dearest of 'the many young men in England who are seeking along with me to continue and to perfect the English Renaissance.'[14] He invoked the rhetoric of heroic, martial masculinity with purpose: the American publication of Rodd's poems became the occasion to declare war against Philistinism. It seemed Wilde had taken to heart Colonel Higginson's belief that action was the real test of manhood after all.[15]

James Rennell Rodd and Wilde had so much in common, they seemed destined to become friends. Four years Wilde's junior, Rodd followed behind him at Oxford and was a fellow Mason. At the university, Rodd attended Ruskin's over-full lectures and met with Pater ('a weird exotic individuality,' he thought).[16] In 1880, the fine-looking young poet won the Newdigate Prize, just as Wilde had before him.[17] By nature 'an instinctive pagan,' it was in Greece that Rodd felt most at peace, he said.[18] He had lived abroad and was less conventional than many of his peers. His natural 'spirit of revolt,' as he called it, was encouraged by his reading of Swinburne's erotic *Poems and Ballads* and Whitman's *Leaves of Grass*.[19] 'There were hardly any time-honoured institutions which I was not ready to denounce in debate, and no scheme of reform which seemed too revolutionary,' he recalled.[20]

'Looking back from far away at those great days of youth and discovery' at Oxford, Rodd later reflected that he 'must have seemed abnormal to the average sturdy barbarian.'[21] In his memoirs, he confessed to having a fundamentally divided nature in which the vigorous, manly elements in him constantly warred against his sentimental impulses. Likewise, he felt torn between his desire for personal liberty and his feeling of obligation to family tradition.

When Rodd was introduced to Wilde by a mutual friend, he was immediately fascinated by 'the unconventional freedom of his brilliant conversation and his sureness of himself.'[22] Rodd described Wilde's early influence on him like Lord Henry's on Dorian Gray, writing that 'the attraction of his dominant personality took a strong hold upon me.'[23] By this time, Wilde had experienced romantic friendships with men, including the actor Norman Forbes-Robertson and Frank Miles, the portrait painter with whom he had shared a London house. His first homosexual encounter, with the Anglo-Canadian student Robert Ross, was still more than a decade off, however.[24]

During their 1879 holiday together, Rodd and Wilde travelled on foot through the vineyards of the Loire. They rambled the hills, sketched barges along the river, lay together in the long grass, and may have shared a travellers' romance.[25] Wilde sent his solicitor's son, the 12-year-old George Lewis Junior, a jolly letter describing the adventure in child-friendly terms. They had an enjoyable time in Paris—'a large town, the capital of France,' he tutored his young correspondent, omitting the fleshpots of Paris and its dusky Babylon. Likewise, he didn't mention Rodd's name but only said that he was travelling incognito with 'a delightful Oxford friend.'[26] They had made up names for each other, he told young George. 'As we did not wish to be known, he travelled under the name Sir Smith, and I was Lord Robinson.' Since Wilde tended to lord it over Rodd anyway, he naturally gave himself the higher honorific ranking.

'Sir Smith' and 'Lord Robinson' shared a common goal. They were both 'ambitious of recognition' Rodd said.[27] Reading Henri Murger's *Bohemians of the Latin Quarter* together as they travelled, they took inspiration from the book's stirring descriptions of artists as unstoppable adventurers who lived every day as if it were a life and death battle for their creed.[28] 'Ambition keeps their wits always on the alert, sounds the charge, and urges them on to the assault of the future; invention never slackens, it is always grappling with necessity, always carrying a lighted fuse to blow up any obstacle so soon as it is felt to be in the way.'[29] Tucked inside Murger's romance of artistic life, there was an omen of things to come for Wilde and Rodd. 'The battle of Art is very much like war in some respects. All the fame goes to the leaders,' Murger warned.

For now, they were still on the same side. Together, under the French sun, the pair decided they were going to wage war for art. They envisioned great artistic futures for themselves. Wilde called these their 'plans *pour la gloire, et pour ennuyer les philistins*'—plans for glory and to annoy the Philistines.[30] Rodd wanted to become a painter or a poet, but his family already had claims to glory and plans for his career. He was the grandson of a Vice-Admiral and a Cornish Major's son; becoming an artist would mean breaking with the family's military tradition. When the end of the summer came, he decided to do the sensible thing and defer his plans to annoy his parents. He returned to Oxford for the final year of his degree and graduated with a second-class in Greats, a result that came as a tremendous personal disappointment to him. If Wilde felt sorry for his bosom friend, he had a strange way of showing it in the letters they exchanged. 'A Second is perhaps for a man of culture a sweeter atmosphere than the chilly Caucasus of an atheistical First,' he told Rodd, offering a condescending reminder of his own superior achievement at Oxford. It was a way of saying it was very lonely at the top—and that Rodd wouldn't be joining him there.[31] Wilde's inconsiderate reply hinted at the haughty attitude that would ultimately doom their friendship. For Wilde, it seemed, Rodd's Oxford second was merely the occasion for Wilde to reflect on himself and his own lofty double First. Good-natured, humble, self-effacing Rodd excused his friend's vanity because he had, by then, become accustomed to it. As he recalled in his memoirs, he knew only too well that Wilde had a 'really genial and kindly nature which seemed at times a strident contrast with his egotism, self-assertion and incorrigible love of notoriety.'[32] After graduation, Rodd put all his energy into pursuing the bohemian career he had postponed. He made friends of Morris and Burne-Jones, moved in London's artistic circles, and painted along-side Wilde's friend, Whistler. Through Wilde's publisher, David Bogue, he published *Songs in the South*, his first book of poetry. Rodd was following his dreams, but he was also following closely in his older friend's footsteps—perhaps too closely for Wilde's tastes.[33]

The poetry they wrote separately around this time already showed signs of just how differently they understood the artistic mission they had concocted together in France. Wilde imagined himself alone as the leading poet of his generation, a fantasy he played out in 'Bittersweet Love,' by picturing the early nineteenth-century Romantic poet John Keats anointing him as his heir:

Keats had lifted up his hymeneal curls from out the poppy-seeded wine,
With ambrosial mouth had kissed my forehead, clasped the hand of noble love in mine.
And at springtide, when the apple-blossoms brush the burnished bosom of the dove;

Two young lovers lying in an orchard would have read the story of our love.[34]

With the seal of this kiss, Wilde turned Keats into a Greek lover.[35] Indiscreet reviewers read between the poem's lines. *The Nation* speculated that 'the procedure thus described has by no means been confined to Keats.'[36]

Though Wilde was out for himself alone, Rodd still envisioned himself joining forces with a brother in arms conjured from recent personal experience. In correspondence with others, he described love as a metaphysical bond uniting two friends in service of an honourable shared principle.[37] He believed love was not merely about passionate desire but about sharing ideals and working together to make them a reality. His vision already imbued his art. 'By the South Sea,' his 1879 poem, ventriloquized the words of an unnamed travelling comrade with whom he had entertained the fantasy of a joint artistic career:

> But you say, Let us go unto all wide lands,
> Let us speak to the people's heart!
> Let us make good use of our lips and hands,
> There is hope for the world in art!
> ...
> Shall we get hence? O fair heart's brother!
> You are weary at heart with me,
> We two alone in the world, no other:
> Shall we go to our wide kind sea?[38]

Rodd unintentionally revealed the identity of his poem's 'fair heart's brother' when he later handwrote these words as a private inscription into Wilde's copy of *Songs in the South*.

Since the sixteenth century, sodomy had been a crime in England. Over the centuries, men who loved men had found ways around this. By the Victorian era, shared labour and passionate idealism, muscular Christianity and Greek friendship had become encoded into a romantic pattern of discreet signals for love between men. Whether kissing a dead poet or joining hands with a nameless brother, the telltale actions in both Wilde and Rodd's poems point to some of the typical routes followed by Victorian men in their efforts to describe forbidden feelings for other men.[39]

So when Wilde drafted *L'Envoi* in 1882, he evidently thought carefully about how to introduce Rennell Rodd to readers. He explained
that they had holidayed together, but signalled their competitiveness
by mentioning their game of 'matching our reeds in sportive rivalry' as
they roamed the Loire's riverbanks, a phrase lifted from his own poem,
'The Burden of Itys,' where he played the same erotic riverside sport
with a woman.[40] Wilde's double trouble was embodied in that poem's
invocation of a creature 'who is not boy or girl and yet is both.'[41]

Wilde hesitated over how to describe Rodd, phrasing and rephrasing
the passage in the manuscript of the manifesto. 'The best likeness to
Rennell Rodd's poetry I ever saw was in the landscape of the Loire,' he
first scribbled. Perhaps using his surname sounded a touch too impersonal, so Wilde tried again. This time, he rewrote the sentence and called
Rodd a 'young brother poet.' But that sounded rather familiar. It also
implied some equality between them, and, as he was still in the first flush
of his American celebrity, perhaps it no longer rang true to Wilde. So he
took a hard look at the word 'brother,' and decided to cross it out.[42] So
much for the brotherhood, and their communal plans for glory. At the
third attempt, he finally managed to articulate what Rodd meant to him
now. He was, in the final version, merely a 'young poet.'

When Wilde sent J. M. Stoddart the manifesto in manuscript, he
enclosed a note to alert the publisher to the magnitude of what he was
about to read. 'The preface you will see is most important, signifying
my new departure from Mr. Ruskin and the Pre-Raphaelites, and marks
an era in the aesthetic movement.'[43] Only a little while ago, Wilde had
been happy to tell journalists that 'many of my theories are, if I may say
so, Ruskin's theories developed,' but that was all over.[44] Wilde's manifesto made Rodd incidental to his personal mission to prise the English
Renaissance from the influence of Ruskin. 'The rule of art is not the
rule of morals,' Wilde declared, discarding a central Ruskinian tenet.[45]
Ruskin's philosophy of ethical art was the vessel that had carried Wilde
across the Atlantic but, now that he had landed on American soil, he
seemed eager to burn that particular ship. (Of course, his claim about
divesting himself of Ruskin was to be more of a rhetorical pose than
anything else. Even Wilde's conception of the warrior-artist stemmed
from Ruskin and the Pre-Raphaelites' crusade to reform the British
Philistine and improve English public taste.)

L'Envoi announced that the time had come to promote 'the sensuous element in art.'[46] Freely adapting the ideas of Walter Pater, another

of his Oxford influences, Wilde modelled parts of his mission statement on *The Renaissance*. The new warrior-artist would 'be always
curiously testing new forms of belief, tinging his nature with the sentiment that still lingers about some beautiful creeds, and searching for
experience itself, and not the fruits of experience,' Wilde said, pilfering
from Pater's golden book.[47]

Nowadays the manifesto is rarely read, even by Wilde's most ardent
fans. It doesn't appear in most popular editions of Wilde's works and
even scholars have more or less forgotten this formative episode in
Wilde's war for art. Yet *L'Envoi* presents a rare opportunity to watch
Wilde's early shape-shifting up close, and to see him gradually trans-
forming himself into a legitimate cultural leader. In some quarters, it
earned him the title of 'a profound thinker.'[48] *L'Envoi* was a milestone
on the way to becoming a critic. About a decade later, when he penned
his famous second manifesto, the 1891 Preface to *The Picture of Dorian
Gray*, his reputation would be more established. It was at the suggestion of J. M. Stoddart that Wilde wrote the novel. By then, even his
antagonist, Colonel Higginson, had conceded that Wilde was one of
the age's 'serious and important authors.'[49]

Over dinner, in 1882, Wilde proudly showed off *Rose Leaf and Apple
Leaf* to the *New York World*'s editor-in-chief, William Henry Hurlbert,
who had once been Colonel Higginson's heart's brother. 'He was
charmed,' Wilde told Stoddart; 'you should send him a copy to review.
He will write something delightful about it.'[50] Most of the reviews
were negative, however, and critics were horrified by the preface.
'Oscar Wilde's Protégé,' *The Critic*'s headline read. The story followed:

> Mr. Rennell Rodd dedicates his verses to Mr. Oscar Wilde—
> 'heart's brother;' and in his lines there certainly breathe a sweet-
> ness and an innocence that may account for the situation. For
> Mr. Wilde has made himself so prominent with his 'Introduction'...
> he is so patronizing to poor Mr. Rodd; he so postures and poses
> as the would-be leader of the English 'jeunes guerriers du dra-
> peau romantique,' that all that is left to the poet whose work he
> is commending is to wish for some cave in which to hide his
> belittled head.[51]

The accusations of unmanliness that had been levelled at Whitman's *Leaves of Grass* and Wilde's *Poems* were now levelled at Rodd's *Rose Leaf and Apple Leaf*. 'Is he a man,' some asked, 'or some romantic girl in the costume of the page and troubadour?' Rumours swirled around Wilde and Rodd's alliance.

Rodd suffered most from the scandal that ensued. Abused by the press and neglected by Wilde, the book's appearance caused him terrible embarrassment. Rodd was annoyed at being 'identified with much that I have no sympathy with,' he told Stoddart.[52] He complained to the publisher that Wilde's dedication was 'too effusive.' Early in their friendship, Wilde had advised Rodd to stay away from another artist because he was 'not a man in whose company we could afford to be seen.'[53] The humiliation over *Rose Leaf and Apple Leaf* made Rodd put this advice into action. He took to the *New York Tribune* to announce that he 'now disdains any connection with the aesthetic school, and lets it be known that he had nothing to do with the amazing dress in which his verses appeared.'[54] Then he severed ties with Wilde once and for all. Shortly after the *Rose Leaf and Apple Leaf* debacle, he gave up on art altogether. He joined the British diplomatic service and built a successful career that took him out of England to posts in Abyssinia, Athens, Berlin, Cairo, Paris, Rome, Stockholm, and Zanzibar.

Meanwhile, in 1882, Wilde's star was on the rise. Despite the stories being whispered and printed, *L'Envoi* bolstered Wilde's claim to being the leader of the Aesthetic Movement. He saw no harm in what he had done, only in Rodd's bad reaction to it. He no longer referred to Rodd as his 'heart's brother,' nor even as a 'young poet.' Now he called him a 'false friend.'[55]

Gross indecency (a euphemism blanketing a host of sexual acts between men) became a crime in the United Kingdom three years after the fiasco over Wilde's manifesto. Officially called Section 11 of the Criminal Law Amendment Act 1885, it was commonly referred to as 'the blackmailer's charter' because it made homosexual men vulnerable to extortion, intimidation, and prosecution by the unscrupulous. So it was that Wilde would come to sit in the witness-box in London's Central Criminal Court, in April 1895. A few weeks later, as the judge delivered a guilty verdict, he said to Wilde, 'it is no use for me to address you. People who can do these things must be dead to all sense of shame, and one cannot hope to produce any effect upon them.

It is the worst case I have ever tried.'[56] With that, he sentenced Wilde to two years in prison for gross indecency.

On Valentine's Day 1905, Rodd broke his silence on his feelings towards the 'heart's brother' of his youth. By then, he was nearly 50 years old. In reply to a bibliographer's enquiry, he briefly summarized his version of events on paper headed *British Legation, Stockholm*. Despite the decades that had passed, his friendship with Wilde remained a painful subject. His neat black cursive explained away the manifesto as part of a reckless phase, but admitted that his anger had turned to bitterness. By pushing him aside, Wilde had crossed the boundary between ambition and egoism. As a result, Rodd said, he had taken steps to prevent the book from circulating in England.

In his letter, Rodd claimed that he hadn't followed Wilde's 1895 trial for gross indecency. Nevertheless, he offered his opinion on it, saying that the tragedy had been both predictable and unavoidable. After that, he shut the door on the whole matter, and wished nobody would rattle the lock again.[57] Rodd's letter didn't mention that he had married, nor that his first son was born in 1895, the year Wilde went to jail.

Rodd and his wife eventually had six children. During the First World War, he played a pivotal ambassadorial role in persuading the Italians to join the allies. He was awarded British orders of chivalry and foreign honours for his extraordinary service. Later in life, he was elevated to the title of Baron Rennell of Rodd. He died in 1941.

Homosexuality was decriminalized in England in 1967.

Chapter 11

Ain't Nothing Like the Real Thing

With the publication of his first art manifesto, Wilde lost his 'heart's brother' Rennell Rodd, but in 1882 there were many other men claiming kinship with him. Professional imitators were drawing huge crowds and delighting spectators with their imaginative take on his sexual and ethnic ambiguities. *What is he?*, Americans wondered. Thanks in part to Colonel Morse and the *Washington Post*, the guessing game captivated the country. Journalists performed interpretative guess-work, submitting hypotheses in editorials and articles, and letting the public decide for themselves. *Is he a man or a woman?* Interviewers became investigative reporters who studied Wilde's body for clues. His 'soft effeminate flesh' and 'graceful form' baffled them.[1] 'The almost boyish fullness and effeminacy of his face' was a puzzle.[2] Why did this 'tall and manly figure' have 'a certain womanly air'? they wondered.[3] *Could he be a 'she'?* 'It was easy to detect a something which gave an effeminate shade to his masculinity,' they said, but impossible to inter-pret with certainty what it signified.[4] Some said Wilde's voice was feminine and his body masculine.[5] Others said just the opposite, claiming that he 'conveyed at first the appearance of a woman in male attire, [but that] his strong masculine voice quickly dispelled that illusion.'[6] 'Have you seen *her*? Well, why not say "*she*"?' some asked, as though a simple change of pronoun would resolve the entire matter.[7]

While Americans scratched their heads over Wilde's 'half of man and half of woman' physique, a showman called Colonel Jack Haverly was concocting a new minstrel show for his company.[8] Haverly's entertainment empire was so vast that he was hailed as 'Colonial Jack.'

His latest innovation would make a spectacle out of the aesthetic puzzle no newspaper had yet solved.

'I've got only one method,' Haverly explained, 'to find out what the people want and then give them that thing.'[9] *Patience Wilde; or Ten Sisters of Oscar* was born. Haverly's Consolidated Mastodon Minstrels, one of the era's pre-eminent troupes, dramatized Wilde's mystique and turned it into a colossal joke featuring The Only Leon, the biggest star in female impersonation (see Plate 31). It was a burlesque of Gilbert and Sullivan's *Patience* muddled together with a novelty act that mugged and winked at Wilde's ambiguities. Both visionary and delightfully trivial, *Patience Wilde* was a crowd-pleasing confection that held audiences in open-mouthed wonder. Haverly had a winner of a show.

'Mighty! Wondrous! Artistic! The greatest Minstrel organization in existence!'[10] With The Only Leon dancing the lead in *Patience Wilde; or Ten Sisters of Oscar*, the spectators and the dollars were rolling in. As Wilde's buxom 'sister,' The Only Leon converted sexual bewilderment into amusement. Born around 1840 in New York City to Irish Catholic immigrants, Francis Patrick Glassey had been a Jesuit choirboy and studied ballet as a teenager. As 'The Only Leon,' he earned his living as a wench who sang and danced her way across the world's stages. Leon's soprano voice, delicate physique, and the hundreds of dresses in his wardrobe made him his generation's most bewitching, genteel, refined female impersonator.[11]

Man by day, woman by night: Leon's protean performances made the counterfeit pass for real. One moment he could be the white women's rights reformer Elizabeth Cady Stanton and the next he would become *Lucretia B. Orgia* for a burlesque of a Donizetti opera. When he danced, he left audiences awestruck. White now, black later, and everything in between, Leon's women could range across the racial spectrum while dancing on *pointe* like the best of ballerinas.[12] 'Heaps of boys in my locality don't believe . . . it's a man,' one spectator marvelled.[13] In the Australian outback, Leon performed in the country's first blackface production of Gilbert and Sullivan's *HMS Pinafore*. Advertisements promised the mostly male audiences, 'Mr. Leon will wear some of the handsomest dresses ever seen.'[14]

As soon as he returned to the United States, in 1882, Leon leapt onto the stage for *Patience Wilde; or Ten Sisters of Oscar*.[15] Touted as 'an aesthetic hit' that made 'the ladies scream with laughter,' the extravaganza included seventy performers, and sometimes more because, to Haverly, bigger was always better. Visual overload was one of his company's hallmarks.[16] Promising enormous casts on stage was a huge draw at the box office.[17]

One of *Patience Wilde*'s peculiarities was that its fictional storyline gestured at the true history of Aestheticism in the United States. Since Shakespeare's day, gender fluidity had been a dramatic commonplace, rich in farcical potential and occasions for sexual exploration. As audiences watched The Only Leon in *Patience Wilde* they might become conscious that Aestheticism signalled strange new gender worlds—or they might not. Either way, their laughter would be unencumbered, not uncomfortable. Leon wasn't attempting to answer the questions hovering around Wilde's Aestheticism, he was just playing at asking them. Musical theatre seemed a good way to do it. His staged sexuality was not a litany of agonizing worries performed in song. After all, Leon was an actor, not an activist.

Although Wilde and his managers never acknowledged Haverly's aesthetic spectacular, it would have been impossible for them to ignore it because *Patience Wilde* played many of the same places where Wilde lectured.[18] Their audiences were probably similar except for the fact that Leon's were gigantic, and Wilde's were not. Listeners were walking out of Wilde's orations, but Leon could keep them captivated 'until the last air in the final burlesque,' when they demanded encores and jumped to their feet to give him standing ovations.[19] Leon earned $100 a week for his over-the-top imitations in 1882—the highest salary of any minstrel performer.[20] The impersonator had eclipsed the original.

From about 1850 until the early 1880s, minstrelsy was *the* premier entertainment on both sides of the Atlantic. The mix of theatre, dance, and music became the go-to entertainment for everyone from working-class men to well-to-do ladies and children (see Plate 32). It was said to have originated early in the century, when the father of minstrelsy, T. D. Rice, appeared on stage as Jim Crow, a character made up from his impressions of Southern black men. Dressed in tattered clothes, he sang, talked in primitive dialect, and embodied a raggedy 'aw, shucks, massa' slave stereotype.[21] Rice's idea wasn't entirely original. He jumped into a culture where blackface clowning was already popular, and in European theatre there was a long-standing tradition of 'black-ing up' dating as far back as Richard II's fourteenth-century court performers. Make-up routinely served to highlight tricksters for view-ers.[22] But Christy minstrelsy distinguished itself from previous prac-tices in one unmissable way: it consistently referenced slavery and alluded to racial hierarchies, two of the nineteenth century's foremost preoccupations.

The mid-nineteenth-century pinnacle of minstrelsy's popularity intersected with the rise of new racial science and ideologies that emphasized black inferiority.[23] Even after the end of the Civil War, blackface shows usually depicted slaves as content, and their masters as generous. African Americans with aspirations were routinely mocked. While standard blackface characters like Uncle Tom and Sambo crooned about their supposedly happy lives in bondage, the well-dressed Dandy Jim, Long Tail Blue, and Zip Coon were satirized because of their highfalutin' talk about book larnin', fashion, and city life. Minstrelsy reduced black characters to two polarized types—the plantation fool and the city fool. Like tailor's mannequins, they could be dressed up to suit the fashion of the day, attracting audiences who would pay to see their latest antics and watch the show exploit contrasts between the haves and have-nots. As a result of their currency in Anglo-American popular culture, they seemed to leap off the stage and into people's minds. The twentieth-century novelist and leader of the National Association for the Advancement of Colored People, James Weldon Johnson, observed that minstrelsy 'fixed the tradition of the Negro as only an irresponsible, happy-go-lucky, wide grinning, loud-laughing, shuffling, banjo-playing, singing, dancing sort of being.'[24]

For decades, minstrelsy was considered wholesome family fun. Even blackface female impersonators, like The Only Leon, were thought to provide respectable entertainment. The American minstrel stage became one of the century's most prominent venues for gender-bending per-formances.[25] The reasons for this are complex, but they certainly include the age's love affair with the artificial and its anxieties about the real thing. At the time, a white simulation of blackness was thought to be funnier than real African Americans could be.[26] By the same token, men simulating womanhood were deemed more attractive (and less dangerous) than the real thing. Without a doubt, the nineteenth century's 'romance of the real' was accompanied by a hot and heavy reliance on simulation.[27]

Playing a woman was a tough job, a muscular female impersonator in a pink satin dress complained. 'I think I earn more than my salary wearing these duds.'[28] In the 1880s, innovations in 'dressmaking for men' made it possible for even larger-bodied impersonators to become sex-changing stars. Still, becoming beautiful could be an ordeal, some men complained. It wasn't easy to come out singing the *Magnetic Waltz* in a ladylike fashion while wearing a low-cut gown when, backstage, the hairdresser had just been swearing at you like a pirate.[29]

Shows like *Patience Wilde; or Ten Sisters of Oscar* performed mesmerizing gender alchemy. Talented cross-dressers like The Only Leon were like 'magicians, able to conjure themselves across gender boundaries that all observers believed to be fixed and immutable.'[30] Guessing the gender of the buxom divas and graceful ballerinas on stage was part of the pleasure. It was not uncommon to feel a frisson at a minstrel show, as Henry James noted in his memoirs. The distinguished novelist recalled that, as a small boy in the 1850s, he had been transfixed by the blackface performer's 'swelling bust encased in a neat cotton gown,' a singular sight otherwise rarely available to a young man from a buttoned-up family.[31] Sixty years later, he cherished the happy memory and could almost still smell the scent of peppermint and orange-peel that pervaded the room in which he had watched the blackface show. Barnum's American Museum, he said, was 'the true centre of the seat of joy.'

The ubiquity of minstrelsy made it tremendously effective in distorting whites' perceptions of blacks. Its degrading outlook insidiously crept into everyday idiom. By the 1880s, it wasn't unusual for someone like Wilde to think of his African American valet as a source of humour more than as a human or, as Wilde put it, 'like a Christy minstrel, except that he knows no riddles.'[32]

Derogatory, reassuring, and comic, blackface grew to mean much more than just a popular form of entertainment. It embodied a white attitude to blackness. In the visual and commercial arts, it would have a huge number of spin-offs ranging from the blackface characters used to advertise soap and stove polish all the way to 'proper' theatre and literature, where minstrelsy inflected representations of black characters in Mark Twain's *Huckleberry Finn* and Harriet Beecher Stowe's *Uncle Tom's Cabin*. Minstrelsy's afterlife on TV and in twentieth-century cinema is well documented, and its troubling legacy still haunts the

British High Street today, where Minstrels brand chocolate candy is widely sold.

Colonel Jack Haverly wore diamonds in his shirt-front so that people knew by looking at him that he was one of the wealthiest men in show business.[33] For a long time, he was the king of the American minstrel show. He had ten travelling companies named after him, and he owned theatres in New York, Chicago, Philadelphia, and San Francisco. While running the country's biggest troupes, he added opera companies, mining companies, and a London agency to his portfolio. In 1880, his troupe played for England's royalty. In 1881, one of his blackface troupes took part in US President-elect James Garfield's inaugural parade and, later the same year, they also performed in his funeral procession.[34]

Increasingly, Haverly was diversifying his entertainment empire, moving out of blackface minstrelsy and into legitimate theatre. A year before Wilde's arrival in the United States, the D'Oyly Carte Company joined forces with Haverly's Theatre in Chicago to stage an authorized production of Gilbert and Sullivan's *Patience*. On the back of that local success, the authorized production toured throughout the country for several months.[35] The business manager of that tour was none other than Wilde's manager, Colonel Morse.

Being a sharp-minded businessman, Haverly contrived to get even more out of the bargain. Old habits die hard. Haverly didn't give up blackface shows just because he had the official *Patience* in his theatre. Instead, he created another new show to run alongside the legitimate one: it was a blackface version of *Patience*. He called it *Black Patience*. Leon played the blacked-up milkmaid and soon the burlesque was crowned 'the greatest hit of the season.'[36]

The name of the game was diversification. Naturally, there were other American showmen who had the same bright ideas as Haverly. In fact, there were already more than nineteen unauthorized versions of *Patience* touring the United States. The illegitimate *Patience* market was very crowded, and even a big player like Haverly had to jostle for position. So within weeks of Wilde's arrival in the United States, Haverly had already set up a third burlesque. This spectacular new show incorporated actual events from Wilde's American tour. Ripped from real life and taken to the stage, Haverly's New Mastodon Minstrels evolved a semi-biographical show called *Oscar's Arrival*. It included an aesthetic reception and a flamboyant parody of his Harvard imitators titled 'Rude Disturbers of the Peace.'[37] Art imitated life imitating art.

All of this may seem to have been happening a long way off from Wilde and his American tour, but it wasn't. The public was flocking to see his imitators, not him. They were real competition, and he could not easily dismiss them. The *Norfolk Virginian* said that Wilde looked like a cross-dressed impersonator, while the *Salt Lake Weekly Herald* said he wasn't quite as entertaining as female minstrels.[38] Pressure from competitors meant Wilde had to show Americans that he was the original aesthete—more authentic and true than any imitator could ever be.

In early March 1882, Wilde collapsed from exhaustion on a stage in suburban Chicago. Around the same time, it became obvious that what he needed to resurrect his tour was a new lecture. His mother had been telling him so for weeks. 'You must give some *new lectures* on living & modern celebrities in England,' she insisted, suggesting they should cover

> Poets & artists, teachers & thinkers & philosophers—
> All the painters.
> All the poets—
> Ruskin—Mill—Carlyle.[39]

Her command hadn't met with immediate compliance, so she reminded him, a few days later, to 'give a lecture on the leading intellects of England.'[40]

Late nineteenth-century show business demanded constant innovation to keep audiences coming back. Haverly and his blacked-up Wilde imitators were formidable opponents. In pursuit of his ambitions, Wilde needed to outwit them. It was a moment of crisis, when he might have given up. He dug deeper, pushed on, and wrote two new lectures. 'I will begin with the door-knob and end with the attic,' he cryptically answered a journalist who asked for a preview. 'Beyond that there only remains heaven, which subject I leave to the church.'[41]

In February and March 1882, he premiered the two new lectures, 'The House Beautiful' and 'The Decorative Arts.' They were clearer than the previous talk, and showed that he could communicate complicated ideas in simple English. His training at the podium was paying off. Having won his battle with his script, he carried his campaign back into lecture theatres. He was still fighting his war for art, and in his latest lectures he argued that the life of action and the life of art were one. 'Wars and the clash of arms and the meeting of men in battle must be always,' Wilde told Americans.[42] But art, he said, would also protect nations from one another by promoting cosmopolitan sympathies. 'By creating a common intellectual atmosphere between all countries [art] might, if it could not overshadow the world with the silvery wings of peace, at least make men such brothers that they would not go out and slay one another for the whim or folly of some king or minister.'

The new talks were hands-on and how-to. They were crammed with practical decoration advice for the fashionable homeowner. But they also seethed with contempt for the culture of imitation that was taking hold of American life. Wilde took aim at the creeping shams that insinuated their way into American homes, turning what could have been a beautiful house into an ugly counterfeit. Rather than attacking his imitators directly, Wilde made an impassioned argument against the fakes that cheapened home life. The essence of his aesthetic message hadn't fundamentally changed, but he had adjusted it to his American audience. His first lecture, 'The English Renaissance,' had been theoretical and abstract—as though offering a blueprint for Aestheticism. 'The House Beautiful' and 'The Decorative Arts' were more like show homes into which Wilde invited his audiences. As the aesthetic lord of the manor, he opened the door onto a more gracious domestic scene and invited them to come in and see how much their lives would improve if they surrounded themselves with real beauty. If they followed him inside his imaginary House Beautiful, they would immediately notice that he had removed all the fakes that usually filled their homes. Here, he told them, there would be none of the usual objects he had seen in American homes: no taxidermied animals, no artificial flowers, no embroidery-covered piano, no cast-iron stove, no carpeted floors, no clashing colours, no Gothic furniture, 'no great flaring gas-chandelier,' nor 'horrible pictures of historical scenes.'[43] In sum, he proposed to get rid of their obnoxious clutter. He would fill their windows with stained-glass. Their floors would be tiled in red brick and strewn with Far Eastern rugs. Their rooms would be decorated with inlaid marble tables, carved ornaments, delicately blown glass, Queen Anne furniture, handsomely bound books, and casts of ancient Greek works, like the Venus de Milo. His well-intentioned advice was not enthusiastically received, however (see Plate 33). The *Chicago Tribune* summed up his lecture as 'Nothing in America but Muddy Streets and Ugly Buildings.'[44]

What Wilde wanted his audience to appreciate was that 'an honest age' didn't have 'dishonesty and hypocrisy' in its workmanship.[45] He meant that their shabby imitations and second-rate copies mocked the uniqueness that real artists brought to their craft. Why should they consent to live with 'articles of furniture which tell a lie every moment of their existence' and 'so-called works of art that are unpunished crimes?' he asked them.[46] 'Every home should wear an individual air in all its furnishings and decorations.'[47]

There was a better way to live, he suggested. Good, honest works would increase in value over the years. The most important thing was that they banish fakes from their homes. 'Let there be no sham imitation of one material in another, such as paper representing marble, or wood painted to resemble stone,' Wilde said. Like a biblical commandment of the 'let there be light' variety, his suggestion rang with authority. Because individuality was the symbol and guarantee of true artistry, imitation was therefore far less noble.

Half a century later, the philosopher Walter Benjamin articulated similar concerns in his celebrated 1936 essay, 'The Work of Art in the Age of Mechanical Reproduction.'[48] Benjamin recognized photography as a democratic art that made it easier for images to reach mass publics. But he warned that the 'aura' of the original work of art would be threatened by the proliferation of fakes. This was precisely what Wilde was experiencing: he was feeling what it was like to *be* a reproducible work of art in the age of minstrel show reproductions. Long before Benjamin, Wilde recognized that because he lived in the age of imitation, he had become easily reproducible.

Wilde's transformation into a blackface imitation coincided with his inception as a celebrity. But it also made him reducible to a set of symbols like sunflowers, lilies, knee-breeches, and silk stockings. All of these became Oscar's emblems. This was catnip for copycats. It also meant that the proliferation of counterfeits couldn't be stopped. All he could do was find ways of dealing with them.

In his new lectures, Wilde wasn't just talking about interior decoration, he was talking about himself by proxy. While fulfilling his duties as a D'Oyly Carte Company employee, he was also signalling the catch-22 in which he was mired. The lectures became allegories of the distortions his existence had taken on. By arguing against shams, he indirectly protested against the culture of imitation in which he was entrapped. His pointed advice was a way of taking out his frustration on Americans' tacky tastes, and projecting his despair onto their walls. 'The House Beautiful' was part funhouse, part house of horrors.

Next, Wilde took his campaign against imitation into his conversations with journalists. In interviews, he sermonized and scolded, turning newspaper columns into pulpits from which he preached a more beautiful, honest way of life. If he had his way with American interiors, he told one interviewer, he would abolish ersatz and 'place things of beauty, things of delicacy, in the houses of all our mechanics as well as of the wealthy.'[49] He would banish the cast-iron stove, that most 'horrid dreadful thing.' As for the press's hostility towards him, he said, 'at first I was greatly annoyed, and with difficulty restrained my feelings, but latterly I have schooled myself not to notice them.'[50]

His whole posture had changed. Gone was the sycophancy of his early days. 'Everything looked "second-class"' in the United States, he now declared.[51] The best way to please the American public, he had discovered, was not to try to please them at all. 'Having shown America what gentleness is,' he declared, 'I am now determined to discard forbearance, and defend myself.'[52] What was the manliest art of self-defence he knew? Dandyism. His weapon of choice? Irony.

By spring 1882, Wilde had become a type of man with the most exquisite manners who also happened not to give a damn about anyone else's. That, to him, was the true definition of the dandy.[53] Attitude mattered far more than the cut of a velvet coat or gorgeous patent pumps. Wilde's dandyism was a state of mind. By speaking ironically, he was inventing a way of coping with an intolerable situation. This is because irony says one thing, but it signals another: when we speak ironically, we speak in two voices simultaneously. In 1882, Wilde was exploring the tension between them. Rather than internalizing his attackers' distortions, he played against them. His irony yo-yoed interviewers back and forth. It was a push–pull exercise, he soon discovered: even as his words pushed people away, it pulled them back for more. He kept reporters on edge and kept their readers guessing at what he meant.

Increasingly, he existed at an angle to American society, as if to better critique it. At any moment he was liable to unsheathe his secret weapon: a rapier wit, a sharp tongue, a mind mightier than any sword. In his society comedies, his best characters would do the same. 'The future belongs to the dandy,' he would later have Lord Illingworth declare in *A Woman of No Importance*.[54] ('If you can bear the truth,' he told the actor manager Herbert Beerbohm Tree, Lord Illingworth 'is *myself.*')

He was becoming a version of himself more reliably surprising and spectacular than any of his imitators—even those in blackface and drag. Wilde had created something original. Cool, detached, uncompromising, and tough-minded—the ironic dandy would become synonymous with his name forever.

'To the world I seem, by intention on my part, a dilettante and dandy merely,' Wilde explained in a letter he wrote in the 1890s.[55] 'It is not wise to show one's heart to the world…folly in its exquisite modes of triviality and indifference and lack of care is the robe of the wise man. In so vulgar an age as this we all need masks.'

Fifteen years after the end of American slavery, 'Colonial Jack' Haverly judged that the time was right to build a living history showcase to the cause. His extravagant project was to give post-Reconstruction Northern audiences a taste of antebellum Southern life. On the toy plantation he erected in Boston, life continued as though the Civil War had never happened. Haverly had over a hundred African American citizens re-enacting slave scenes from the recent past when they were considered chattels. During the 1879–80 season, audiences could watch 'overseers, bloodhounds, and darkies at work.'[56] This was only one of Haverly's many outlandish undertakings. Around that time, he bought another minstrel troupe called Callender's, invested in too many theatres, and generally spread his finances thin. When he lost a pile in Colorado mining, his debts were rumoured to be more than $100,000.[57]

By spring 1882, Colonial Jack's empire was bust. In desperation, he turned to his apprentice, a 26-year-old called Charles Frohman, to bail him out. Instead of wearing a diamond stud in his shirt-front like his boss, Frohman wore a faded hand-me-down suit that sat awkwardly on his pudgy frame. He had a shy, unassuming demeanour and seemed about as different from his brash, dashing boss as could be.[58] Born to an itinerant pedlar in Sandusky, Ohio, Frohman was a rosy-cheeked Jewish boy who loved the theatre. Under Haverly's tutelage, he had learned the rudiments of running a successful show business. At the beginning of their association, Haverly told him, 'you and I will work the public, all right.'[59] He was true to his word. Soon Frohman was sitting in on the Mastodons' rehearsals and had dramatically changed his style. On show days, he dressed up in a silk hat, frock coat, and lavender trousers like the performers that made up Haverly's Consolidated Mastodon Minstrels. Then little Charles Frohman, the company's usually quiet treasurer, would go out and drum up business by parading through the city streets alongside them.[60]

Frohman quickly learned that showmanship relied on getting the public to imagine extravagant things that weren't exactly true, but *might* be. So, for example, he purchased a three-foot safe and had it gilded with large letters spelling out, 'Treasurer, Haverly's Mastodon Minstrels.' During tours, four heavies lifted the safe conspicuously to the top of the troupe's mountain of luggage so that, when the pile was wheeled into hotels, the golden coffer never failed to attract gawkers. When the crowd had grown sufficiently large, Frohman would appear out of nowhere with a fist full of dollar bills and allow them to watch as he ceremoniously deposited them in the strongbox. 'Gee whiz!' someone invariably said, 'that Haverly show has got so much money!'[61] The gimmick peddled a shinier, better version of the truth. Of course, the safe was never used except for this performance. Frohman made himself indispensable to Haverly, who rewarded him with more and more responsibility. Frohman was at the helm of Haverly's Mastodons when they marched into England for the first time in 1880 to make Her Majesty's Theatre ring out 'with the old-time plantation melodies of the American negro.'[62] And it was a silk-hatted Frohman who received the Prince of Wales and a party of royal children when they came to see the spectacle.[63] Soon, Frohman had achieved prominence as a minstrel promoter and was ready to strike out on his own.

By 1882, 'Haverly in Trouble' was headline news.[64] Colonel Haverly came begging for help, but Frohman refused to go back as an employee, offering to buy one of Haverly's minstrel troupes instead. A deal was struck and Frohman became the owner of Callender's Minstrels.[65] With the help of his brother, Gustave, Frohman planned to pull together a showier, flashier display and to take Callender's Consolidated Spectacular Colored Minstrels on the road across the United States.

Frohman had made a close study of Haverly's crowd-pleasing give-'em-what-they-want business model, and what he did next proved that he had an ingenuity all his own. For a long time minstrelsy was populated with fakes: 'blacked-up' whites offering spectators a surrogate version of black reality. Frohman's big idea was to give audiences authenticity. The men in his company had no need to 'black up' because they were the real thing. He could boast that his performers were 'genuine Negro' minstrels. In the 1880s, this counted as a novelty, and one that Frohman gladly exploited. If Haverly's replicas of blackness enraptured viewers, then Frohman's men would push them to the point of delirium (see Plate 34).

The aesthetic craze was another fad on which he capitalized. During the 1882 season, Frohman's performers pranced on stage with an act called *The Utterly Too Too's, or Parodies on Oscar Wilde*.[66] They promised 'the fun of the circus, the sobriety of the platform, the intellect of the Greek play' for three hours every night.[67] The spectators and the money poured in.

'All black, all beautiful, all accomplished, all gentlemen of color!'[68] Frohman's tagline was no embellishment. Many of his men were among the country's most educated African Americans, students of the Hampton Institute, an educational establishment founded after the Civil War to educate freedmen. They were black America's elite, or as the ads put it, 'THE PICK OF THE EARTH'S COLORED TALENT.'[69]

Wilde had many more rivals in minstrelsy besides Haverly and Frohman. Their troupes were only two of the most prominent outfits running knock-off Oscars. In fact, there were at least four others (and probably several more), and each had its own peculiar way of imitating the aesthete.[70] There were small-timers like Hyde and Behman's Minstrels, who produced a travelling 'takeoff on the Oscar Wilde rage,' and accessorized it with exaggerated Irish brogues, slapstick, and green accessories conventional for the role of an Irishman on stage.[71] There was also John T. Kelly, an Irish-American who made a speciality of Irish impersonations. He was performing 'in make-up à la Oscar Wilde.' In addition to these smaller operators, there were well-established companies like the San Francisco Minstrels, a troupe that had dominated the New York scene for almost a decade. The San Francisco Minstrels were versatile and talented instrumentalists, dancers, and

singers who ad-libbed nightly to full houses. By 1881, they were playing *Patients, or Bunion Salve's Bride*, a freewheeling Gilbert and Sullivan
spectacle full of blackface men playing aesthetic maidens. 'Scream
power turned on at 8 p.m.,' ads shouted, and when the curtain went up
the San Francisco Minstrels delivered a raucous three-hour feature on
'Aestheticism run mad.'[72] Their slapdash scenery trivialized Wilde and
his cause by reducing it to a set of knick-knacks that included his
trademark sunflower, alongside tin pans, gridirons, and stuffed dum-
mies.[73] Looking at this stage, viewers saw Aestheticism at its tackiest.
It was the opposite of what Wilde advocated in 'The House Beautiful.' It
was The House Ugly. 'The burlesque terminates with a solemn warning to Aesthetic Poets, and it will haunt you in your dreams,' the San
Francisco Minstrels ads announced.[74] They were such a hit that they
were immediately booked for a long run.[75]

Another of Wilde's big rivals was offering a blackface simulation
they christened *Oscar Wilde's Lecture*. Thatcher's Minstrels billed themselves as the 'best playing band of minstrels under the sun, courting the
criticism of the intelligent and the patronage of the refined.'[76] A
Thatcher's Minstrels variety show delivered 'a kaleidoscope of brilliant
wit, humor, melody, and mirth.'[77] Its array was as dazzling as it was
eager to please. The troupe had impressed President Grover Cleveland,
as well as celebrities such as Sarah Bernhardt.[78]

An evening of Thatcher's copycat Aestheticism began with the
orchestra striking up *Patience*'s theme to warm up the audience. Then
minstrels would dance to old-timey plantation favourites and the audience would join in the cracker barrel fun. Next there would be a
comic medley—including, for instance, dancing gladiators, opera, a
fat men's ball, synchronized acrobats on pedestals, a sketch about the
telephone (long distance service began in 1878), and a gigantic 'garden
party in an aristocratic cull'rd neighbourhood.'[79] Once the audience
was primed, Thatcher's brought out their Wilde imitator, Hughey
Dougherty (see Plate 35).

Unlike the other novelty outfits, who tried to best Oscar by being
more bizarre, Dougherty didn't bother to invent anything new. He
simply delivered Wilde's own lectures, 'The House Beautiful' and 'The
Decorative Arts.' If those words were good enough for the genuine
aesthete, they were good enough for his impersonator.[80] Dougherty
started doing the act he called *Oscar Wilde's Lecture* and *Oration a la*

Oscar Wilde when Wilde was only in the third month of his American tour, in March 1882. The crowds immediately loved it, and Dougherty played Wilde nonstop for a whole year. The satire's authenticity made it a runaway success. 'The Orator of the Day,' in his new speech, 'A LA OSC-COR WILD' was bringing down the house night after night.[81] Soon Dougherty's imitation aesthete was doing two shows a day. Dougherty delivered *Oscar Wilde's Lecture* in folksy pseudo-dialect. He occasionally riffed on items gleaned from Wilde's interviews and ad-libbed with rhetorical nonsense of his own. Sometimes his act became a stream of consciousness monologue into which news items floated like driftwood. In Maryland, for example, Dougherty's 'Wilde' talked about local waterway administration. He 'gave some pat references to the proposed ship-canal' that were probably Pat references—allusions to Wilde's Irishness and to the Paddy's native talent for blarney.[82] One night his subject could be politics and Transcendentalism, and on another it could be electricity and lost umbrellas.[83] Dougherty contorted his deeply creased face to bring Wilde's lecture to life. As the pompous blackface orator, his elastic mouth stretched and spewed long sentences short on sense. He complemented his platitudes with aesthetic postures and attitudes.

Dougherty made his name as a stump speaker, a blacked-up comedian specializing in mocking orators and politicians. The stump speaker's clownish costume—enormous shoes, strange hat, shabby coat, and large umbrella—made him instantly recognizable.[84] Long before he began delivering his *Oration a la Oscar Wilde*, Hughey Dougherty was already one of minstrelsy's top stars. Originally, 'Oration' was an Irish word for an uproarious commotion. In the stump speeches that made him famous, Dougherty brought that definition to life. 'In my lecture this evening on the great and interesting subject of Oratory,' he announced one night, 'I will first consider the derivation of the word.'[85] Then he unpacked an outrageous made-up etymology, like a clown pulling enormities out of a tiny suitcase.

Dougherty was of Irish extraction, like so many of the minstrels who performed as Irish cheats, thugs, and tipsy talkers. The Irish dominated American minstrelsy, where they could play out racist ideas and be paid for it.[86] They also performed in blackface shows that took the Irish as their subjects and denigrated them as a race of drinkers and fighters who spoke in sentences peppered with the expletive 'Begorra!'[87] The pressures that drove Irish performers to perpetuate such stigmas are closely tied to the century's immigration and labour history. On their arrival in the United States, Irish immigrants discovered that, contrary to their expectations, they would continue to be perceived as a subject race, even beyond Britain. Irish-Americans were at the bottom of the social scale, but they were not alone: from 1865, a newly emancipated class of African Americans also hoped for upward mobility. The poor living and working conditions Irish immigrants encountered in America boosted their racial identification with whiteness. The enmity between blacks and Irish originated in competition for jobs as labourers on canals and railroads, but soon contaminated other aspects of life, especially in popular culture such as minstrelsy. The Irish were often lumped in with blacks, as an 1876 *Harper's Weekly* demonstrated, by literally hanging both in the balance (see Plate 36). To many Americans, the two groups were equal. As the sociologist Richard Williams explains, 'because blackness was the badge of the slave in America, people from Ireland who went there entered the free labor system, which made them part of the dominant race. As unskilled workers, [however] they occupied the lowest place within it. Ethnicity marked the spot.'[88] The fact that the Irish had white skin did not guarantee that they would be treated as whites in America; it merely gave them the opportunity to earn that privilege.[89] The paradox of the American Irish for much of the nineteenth century was that they were optically white, but socially blacklisted.

Yet whiteness still conferred privileges. However denigrated the Irish were on stage and in actual fact, their whiteness nevertheless gave them options that people of colour did not have. In Wilde's case, he could choose for himself how to contest his imitators. Blackface operators like Thatcher's Minstrels and Haverly's Mastodons were a competitive threat because they played cities throughout the Northeast and Midwest where he also lectured.[90] Soon, he would be rethinking his politics and, especially, his Irishness.

Chapter 12

Son of Speranza

'I am of noble birth, treat me as becomes my station—with respect,' Wilde was heard shouting at a stagehand after one of his lectures.[1] A few nights later, he told the Minnesotan audience at his lecture on 'The Decorative Arts' that most of the things he saw in the United States were 'confoundedly, gorgeously vulgar, from cast-iron gate-posts all the way up to soup tureens.'[2] The following evening, on 17 March 1882, he took the stage in St Paul, Minnesota to deliver a St Patrick's Day speech, and addressed the crowd of farmers, labourers, Irish patriots, and clergy as 'my countrymen, a race once the most aristocratic in Europe.'[3]

Minnesotans measured progress in people, acres, and energy. Recently, St Paul had seen electric light for the first time.[4] 'ELECTRICITY IS LIFE!' was the message put out by merchants of electro-voltaic gadgets, who flogged electricity's merits in preventing disease and death.[5] Although St Paul had been the state capital since 1849, it was still a sparsely populated town more than three decades later, when Wilde visited. Roughly 40,000 people then called it home. That was equivalent to 2 per cent of New York City's population at that time (today, about the same number of people live in Times Square alone).[6] Largely rural and agricultural, Minnesota was then considered a frontier state. Its direct neighbours, North and South Dakota, would only join the United States towards the end of the decade. According to John S. Pillsbury, Minnesota's Governor, the state's priority was the 'peopling of its uninhabited unoccupied territory and the culture of the idle soil.'[7] To this end, land prices were enticingly low—$2 an acre in 1880.[8]

In New York City, a couple would pay the same price to attend Wilde's lecture.

'The contrast between city life in New York and country life in Minnesota is, indeed, remarkable,' Philip H. Bagenal, a visiting Anglo-Irish journalist, observed in his 1882 book on *The American Irish and their Influence on Irish Politics*.[9] 'It was hard to keep from the mind's eye the squalid poverty of the crowded haunts of the Irish in eastern cities,' Bagenal said of his western journey, where conditions for the Irish were far better. In the 1850s, a positive press campaign in Ireland's newspapers succeeded in attracting large numbers of settlers to St Paul, and by the late nineteenth century Irish-Americans dominated the city.[10] Bagenal noticed that Irish-American settlers had intensely romantic feelings for their native land. Even the second generation, who looked and spoke like Americans and had never seen Ireland's shores, spoke 'with as ardent an affection for Ireland as the most National native-born inhabitant of Cork, the very capital of Irish nationality.'[11]

Wilde had been rehearsing for this moment from the cradle. 'The Irish will love you,' his mother had told him encouragingly when he left for the United States.[12] Thankfully, Wilde's Minnesotan country-men did not know that Speranza had called Irish emigrants 'outcast weeds to be flung on the shores of America, a helpless crowd of crushed, dispirited, unlettered peasants.'[13] In St Paul, he had been introduced as 'a son of one of Ireland's noblest daughters,' a '48er whose patriotic writings they still gratefully remembered.[14]

By 1882, according to Bagenal, the revolutionary writings of the '48ers had become 'the political creed of the Irish in America.' The literature of 1848 was, he claimed, singlehandedly responsible for keeping 'alive the flame of Irish nationality with such intense fervor at the distance of three thousand miles.'[15] Closer to home, newspaper reprints of Speranza's late 1840s writings reminded Americans of the patriotic flavour of the Wilde family's politics. As a young poetess, she had used her pen to declare Ireland at war with the brutal English oppressor. 'We appeal to the whole Irish nation,' she wrote, 'is there any man among us who wishes to take one further step on the base path of sufferance and slavery?'[16]

Certainly not her own son, Oscar. As he stepped onto the podium on St Patrick's Day in St Paul, his exquisite clothes announced him as a master, not a slave. Even before he was introduced to the crowd, his bearing and aristocratic costume made it plain for all to see. Encased in a fitted purple velvet coat with white lace cascading down his neck, he looked sovereign. His attire had been chosen as carefully as the patriotic words he was about to speak. Its regal elegance and colour was the exact opposite of the stage Irishman's raggedy peasant's costume. No green caubeen, no swallow-tailed coat, no corduroy breeches, nor blue worsted stockings for him.[17] In short, nothing that countless works of theatre and fiction had conditioned audiences to think of as 'Irish.' Whereas the stereotypical Irishman made familiar by the minstrel stage would be in filthy brogues, Wilde's impeccable shoes were tied with bows.

This was no accident. Wilde adored sartorial symbolism. On this occasion, he had commissioned Colonel Morse to secretly get his outfit from a dealer in theatrical costumes and ordered a tight-fitting suit designed to 'excite a great sensation.'[18] He got it. Dressed like an early sixteenth-century Frenchman under King Francis I, Wilde's carefully chosen raiment subtly gestured to the monarch's legacy, for he had been responsible for initiating the French Renaissance. Even more significant for Wilde's immediate purposes on St Patrick's Day was the fact that Francis I had overseen a period of Irish politicking with continental allies against the English.[19] This was a visual clue to the theme of Wilde's talk—a eulogy of Irish culture and cosmopolitanism against the brutish English—and a signal that he favoured Home Rule.

Although journalists breathlessly detailed his regal costume, many of the historical subtleties of his carefully tailored message were lost on his audience. They noticed, however, that his hair had grown down to his shoulders, the style worn by rugged adventurers.[20] He reminded Midwesterners more of swashbuckling frontiersmen like General Custer and Buffalo Bill than anyone else. Custer's long hair was still remembered, as was his personal flamboyance and the elaborately adorned uniform he wore. Likewise, Buffalo Bill wore his hair long and preferred black velvet suits finished with lace.[21] These homespun examples of manly dandyism influenced how St Paul saw Wilde.

The night before, Wilde had worn almost exactly the same thing to deliver his St Paul lecture on 'The Decorative Arts.' Tonight, he made one tiny but symbolic change. (Remember he would later build a whole philosophy of fashion around the importance of a carefully thought out buttonhole.) On St Patrick's Day, those who leaned in and

THE ÆSTHETIC CRAZE.

What's de matter wid de Nigga ?   Why Oscar you's gone wild !

Plate 1. Currier and Ives, the nineteenth-century's most prolific American lithography firm, vividly illustrates 'The Aesthetic Craze' that took hold during Oscar's 1882–3 tour of the United States.

Plate 2. Advertisers, collectors, and scrapbookers favoured handy little colour lithographs, such as these cartoons. Drawn by E. B. Duval to coincide with Wilde's visit, the six 'National Aesthetics' cards depict him as Irish ('Begorra and I belave I am Oscar himself'), Chinese ('No likee to callee me johnnee, callee me Oscar'), French ('Mon dieu! I feel utterly too-too'), German ('I vas aesthetic aint it'), black ('Ise gwine for to wuship dat lily kase it sembles me'), and, finally, as a white American.

Plate 3. By the age of 26, Oscar's father, William Robert Wills Wilde, was already a medical doctor, explorer, and travel writer. J. H. Maguire sketched the handsome, dreamy-eyed gentleman of science in 1841.

Plate 4. Oscar's mother, the poet and essayist Jane Francesca Agnes Wilde, loved to dress dramatically and favoured headdresses, like the one in this 1864 portrait by Bernard Mulrenin.

Plate 5. Born in 1854, Oscar was about 2 years old when he posed for this picture. During her pregnancy, his mother was certain that her baby would be a girl, so she dressed him in girls' clothes until he was about 10 years old.

AESTHETICS V. ATHLETICS.

AESTHETE. THIS IS INDEED A FORM OF DEATH, AND ENTIRELY INCOMPATIBLE WITH ANY BELIEF IN THE IMMORTALITY OF THE SOUL.

Plate 6. At Oxford, Oscar didn't care for the activities that fascinated other students: sport, public debating, politics, and music left him cold. A college cartoon mocked him as an awkward aesthete who believed athletics were 'a form of death.'

Plate 7. In March 1876, during his second year at Oxford, Oscar posed for this photograph with his close friend William Ward.

Plate 8. During spring 1877, Oscar toured Italy and Greece, where he posed in Greek national costume. 'Seeing Greece is really a great education for anyone and will I think benefit me greatly,' he said.

Plate 9. There were greater student celebrities than Oscar at Oxford. Born in Sierra Leone, Christian Cole was one of the university's first black African graduates and was known as one of the 'Great Guns of Oxford.'

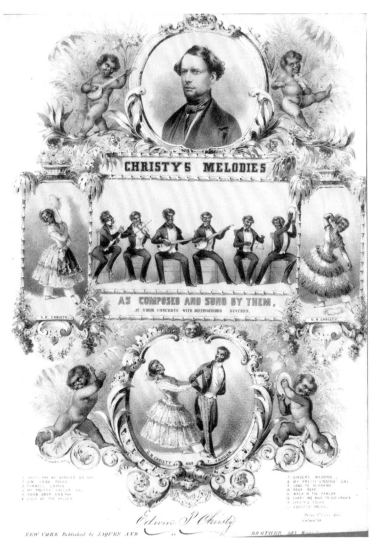

Plate 10. From the 1840s, E. P. Christy (top) became synonymous with black-face minstrelsy, a showcase for racialized songs, dances, and gender-bending performances (bottom). One of the show's standard features was the line-up of joking gentlemen trading witticisms (centre). Minstrelsy was the century's most popular entertainment in the United States and Britain.

Plate 11. Dressed as dandies, the Delmanning Brothers demonstrate typical blackface make-up. White performers—many of whom were of Irish descent—dominated black-face minstrelsy.

Plate 12. In 1880, George Du Maurier introduced caricatures of Oscar the poet (far right) and the painter James McNeill Whistler (second from right) into his *Punch* cartoons. Although women appreciated the duo, conventional men tended to be suspicious of their claims to fame.

"O. W."

" O, I feel just as happy as a bright Sunflower ! '
Lays of Christy Minstrelsy.

Æsthete of Æsthetes !
What's in a name ?
The poet is WILDE,
But his poetry's tame.

Plate 13. When Oscar's first book of poetry was published in 1881, it met with harsh criticism. *Punch* joined the jeering chorus and pictured him as a thick-lipped, sunflower-faced Christy minstrel singing one of the show's signature songs, 'The Big Sunflower.'

Plate 14. Decades before the sunflower became the Aesthetic Movement's symbol, the Original Christy Minstrels made 'The Big Sunflower' famous. Singers usually wore a ring of wide yellow cardboard petals around their blackened faces.

Plate 15. For the duration of Oscar's tour, only the celebrity photographer Napoleon Sarony was allowed to take pictures of him.

Plate 16. Sarony posed Oscar like a mannequin, capturing him in the eccentric costume he wore to lecture North Americans on 'The English Renaissance of Art.'

Plate 17. To highlight Oscar's attractive legs, Sarony had him recline on a sumptuous fur rug. Later, Oscar adopted the same sensuous pose for interviews. It was a case of life imitating art.

Plates 18 and 19. Advertisers capitalized on women's interest in Aestheticism. To market their corsets, Warner Brothers sent a manly aesthete to judge a beauty contest and gave him cupids as his romantic sidekicks.

Plate 20. 'Oscar Dear!' was a hit song full of innuendo about an eccentric called Oscar, his wandering hands, and the girl who loved him.

VOL. XXVI.—No. 1310.
Copyright, 1882, by HARPER & BROTHERS.

NEW YORK, SATURDAY, JANUARY 28, 1882.

TEN CENTS A COPY.
$4.00 PER YEAR, IN ADVANCE.

THE ÆSTHETIC MONKEY.—ENGRAVED, BY PERMISSION, FROM THE PICTURE BY W. H. BEARD, IN THE POSSESSION OF MR. HUGH AUCHINCLOSS.

Plate 21. *Harper's Weekly* put a sunflower-worshipping monkey dressed as Wilde on the cover of its January 1882 issue.

HOW FAR IS IT FROM

THIS

TO

THIS?

We present in close juxtaposition the pictures of Mr. Wilde of England and a citizen of Borneo, who, so far as we have any record of him, is also Wild, and judging from the resemblance in feature, pose and occupation, undoubtedly akin. If Mr. Darwin is right in his theory, has not the climax of evolution been reached and are we not tending down the hill toward the aboriginal starting point again? Certainly, a more inane object than Mr. Wilde, of England, has never challenged our attention, whose picture. as given herewith is a scrupulously correct copy of a photograph put out with his sanction and which may be seen in all public windows. Mr. Wild of Borneo, doesn't lecture, however, and that much should be remembered to his credit.

Plate 22. On 22 January 1882, the *Washington Post* boosted the trend for comparing Wilde to animals and primitives. It placed Oscar alongside the Wild Man of Borneo and asked, 'How far is it from this to this?'

"WHAT IS IT?"—OR "MAN MONKEY".

ON EXHIBITION AT BARNUM'S MUSEUM, NEW YORK.

*This is a most singular animal, with many of the features and clear characteristics of both the HUMAN and BRUTE Species. It was found in Africa, in a perfectly nude state, and with two others captured.— The others died on their passage to this country. At first it ran on all fours, and was with difficulty learned to stand as usually erect as here represented. It is the opinion of most scientific men that he is a connecting link between the **WILD NATIVE AFRICAN, AND THE ORANG OUTANG.***

Plate 23. Popular guessing games like Barnum's 'What is It?' made audiences pay to try to figure out a human exhibit's ethnicity.

THE IRISH FRANKENSTEIN.

"The baneful and blood-stained Monster ∗ ∗ ∗ yet was it not my Master to the very extent that it was my Creature? ∗ ∗ ∗ Had I not breathed into it my own spirit?" ∗ ∗ ∗ (*Extract from the Works of C. S. P-RN-LL, M.P.*)

Plate 24. Violent attacks persisted throughout winter and spring 1882, when the leader of the Irish National Land League, Charles Parnell, sat in Kilmainham Gaol. *Punch* fuelled fears that Parnell no longer controlled his terrorist Paddy by depicting him as a Frankenstein-like subhuman.

Plate 25. The Irish were imagined as America's most violent new immigrants. Satires of the Paddy were tremendously effective in forming public opinion.

Plate 26. In 1882, P. T. Barnum transported Jumbo the African Elephant to the United States, where the animal superstar dwarfed Oscar.

A Symphony in colovr

Plate 27. A popular biography illustrated by Charles Kendrick portrayed Oscar as especially attractive to African Americans.

Plate 28. Wilde's public affiliation with blackness became stronger as his tour progressed. He worked closely with an African American valet, whom he described as 'a black servant, who is my slave.' In this trade card, E. B. Duval portrayed Wilde's dogsbody as a little brown dog.

Plate 29. Bought out of slavery by British supporters, Frederick Douglass was a legendary abolitionist, editor, international orator, and resident of Rochester, New York.

Plate 30. Advertising made Oscar look like a young Frederick Douglass. Here he tells his 'belobed bredren' in broken English that Aestheticism is 'something beautiful.'

Plate 31. Man by day, woman by night, Francis Patrick Glassey earned his living as 'The Only Leon,' a wench who sang and danced her way across the world's stages. The Irish-American danced the lead in *Patience Wilde; or Ten Sisters of Oscar*.

"Minstrelsy is an art, and Haverly's Mastodons are the artists."—*London Telegraph.*

Even Her Majesty's Royal Family

Went to see HAVERLY'S GREAT ORIGINAL World-Famed UNITED MASTODON MINSTRELS when this Company were in London, England, just the same as

The President of the United States and his Family

Go and see them in America, and everybody else and their family.

The Royal Family as they appeared while visiting on several occasions HAVERLY'S GREAT ORIGINAL WORLD-FAMED UNITED-MASTODON MINSTRELS, at Her Majesty's Theatre, London, England. The only Minstrel Company ever visited by Royal persons, and the only Minstrel Company visited by so many distinguished Americans and the Public in general.

Remember !   Remember !   Remember !

Haverly's Great Original World-Famed United-Mastodon Minstrels, in all their Full Force and Power of Attraction, remain here but a short time.

Their Brief Stay Plainly Printed in Clear Color on First Page.

Plate 32. For much of the nineteenth century, minstrelsy was thought to be fun for everyone from working class men and well-to-do ladies right up to royalty and American Presidents.

THE BRIC·A·BRAC MANIA.

Dat's fine piece 'broke yer back' Missis Jonsing. Whar you got him ?

Plate 33. Wilde criticized Americans for cluttering their homes with bric-a-brac. In this satirical Currier and Ives poster, a blackface imitator admires a fine piece of 'broke yer back.'

Plate 34. Minstrel troupes exploited the fascination with Oscar by producing aesthetically-themed extravaganzas. Callender's Colored Minstrels produced a show called *The Utterly Too Too's, or Parodies on Oscar Wilde*. The performers were African American.

Plate 35. One of blackface's top stars, Hughey Dougherty, impersonated Oscar for Thatcher's Minstrels.

Plate 36. To many Americans, Irish-Americans and African Americans were equal as this 1876 *Harper's Weekly* cover shows.

Plate 37. Wilde idealized the picturesque Rocky Mountain miners for their dress sense and good looks. 'The most graceful thing I ever beheld was a miner in a Colorado silver mine driving a new shaft with a hammer; at any moment he might have been transformed into marble or bronze and become noble in art forever,' Wilde said.

THE ÆSTHETIC DARKEY.

*YES SIR! LAST YEAR USED ASHLEY PHOS-
PHATE ON DE PLANTATION, AND OB COURSE
HAD GOOD CROP: I SPECS TO DO DE SAME
DIS YEAR. WEAR GOOD CLOTHES, AND DE-
VOTE CONSIDERABLE TIME TO DE FINE
ARTS.*

Plate 38. In American ads, aesthetes wore their sunflower lapels like badges of social mobility. The aesthetic sunflower symbolized the good life. Ashley Phosphate promised its fertilizer would boost your crops as well as your prospects by making you rich enough to 'wear good clothes, and devote consider-able time to de fine arts.'

Plate 39. Decked out in aesthetic finery, Dandy Jim (right) was more attractive to women than his down-at-heel rival, Jim Crow (left). In popular culture, the dandy invited viewers to measure for themselves the social distance he could travel—from raggedy to well-heeled, from romantic zero to hero.

Plate 40. 'This is my view at present from the Windsor Hotel, Montreal,' Wilde wrote on 12 May 1882. Seeing his name in six-foot-high blue and magenta letters confirmed his fame.

Plate 41. Constance Wilde and Cyril, aged about 4, in 1889.

Plate 42. During summer 1891, Wilde was introduced to Lord Alfred Douglas. The angel-faced 21-year-old Oxford student went by the nickname 'Bosie' and looked like Dorian Gray come to life.

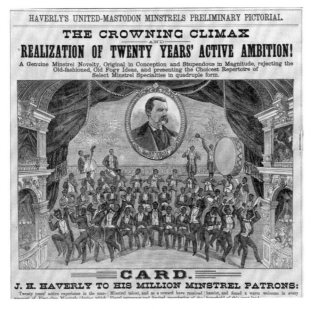

Plate 43. The seated line-up was one of minstrelsy's set pieces. Dressed in tuxedos, the Interlocutor and his endmen traded conundrums, jokes, and one-liners.

Plate 44. Wilde's society comedies looked and sounded like minstrelsy. The best reason to see *A Woman of No Importance*, *Punch* said, was 'to hear the Christy-Minstrel epigrammatic dialogue.' It illustrated the point by putting Oscar at the centre of a seated minstrel line-up as the Interlocutor, 'Massa Johnson O'Wilde.'

Plate 45. *The Illustrated Sporting and Dramatic News* portrayed Wilde as a blackface Interlocutor whose characters ask 'conundrums, as though "society" were a Christy Minstrel troupe.'

THE WORLD: SUNDAY, MAY 9, 1897.

nd brilliant Career in ♦♦ OSCAR WILDE SOON TO BE FREED FROM PRISON. ♦♦ His Visit to the Unite
Raised /

SURROUNDED BY ADORING MAIDENS WHEN HE WAS PROPOUNDING HIS ÆSTHETIC THEORIES; DESERTED BY THEM NOW WHEN HIS JAIL
LIFE HAS LEFT ITS MARKS UPON HIM.

Plate 46. Wilde's imprisonment destroyed his reputation. He told the Home Secretary in 1896 that his 'wife, children, fame, honour, position, wealth' were lost. Days before his 1897 release, the *New York World* predicted that his female fans would shun him since he had lost his looks.

Plate 47. Charles Frohman's 1902 production of *The Importance of Being Earnest* lined up the actors playing John Worthing and Algernon Moncrieff as though they were minstrel men.

Plate 48. Towering a little above the crowd in his top hat and red tie, Wilde (right) was the centre of attention in W. P. Frith's *The Private View, 1881*. The painting was exhibited at the Royal Academy in 1883, when Wilde returned from America, and a protective railing had to be installed to control the massive crowds.

looked closely noticed that Wilde was wearing a single white kid glove, like some precocious 1880s anticipation of Michael Jackson's famous single white glove in the 1980s. In Wilde's day, however, white gloves were characteristically worn by gentlemen—but also by blackface performers. And in the United States, those performers were usually Irishmen in glad rags and blackface playing servile, slave-like roles on stage. For all its restraint, the glove was a show of dissent, a meaningful detail that made all the difference. His finery announced the many Irish identities he wore in America, where he was simultaneously treated as a king and a court jester.

St Patrick's Day was the right time to say this, and St Paul's Opera House was the appropriate place. Months before, his antagonists, The Only Leon and Haverly's Original Mastodons, had already performed on the same stage.[22] The cross-dressed blackface *Patience* had taken St Paul's Opera House by storm. The whole town had turned out. Hundreds had been turned back at the box office. Now, Wilde was taking back that stage and taking a stand against his imitators too. By 17 March, at St Paul's Opera House, he had fashioned himself into a manly, well-groomed solemn defender of Ireland. He was going to make Speranza proud. Wilde's speech would extol Ireland's faded glories.

'There was a time,' he began, as if telling his Minnesotan kinsmen a fairy tale, 'when Ireland stood at the front of all the nations of Europe in the arts, the sciences and genuine intellectuality.'[23] Ireland had been the university of Europe, he told them. Then, she led all other nations in goldsmithery, architecture, and literature. All that was lost because of the English.

The English, Wilde explained, were responsible for exterminating Irish art. 'Those proud monuments to the genius and intellectuality of Ireland do not exist today,' because 'when the English came they were burned,' he said. 'With the coming of the English, art in Ireland came to an end, and it has had no existence for over 700 years,' because art cannot flourish under tyranny. All that remained of Ireland's glories were 'blackened mouldering walls.' The only source of hope, he told the Irish-Americans gathered in St Paul, was for the Irish to commemorate their history and to work for an independent Ireland. Home Rule was the best thing that could happen to Irish art. 'When Ireland gains her independence, its schools of art and other educational branches will be revived and Ireland will regain the proud position she once held among the nations of Europe.' He electrified the crowd, who filled the hall with thunderous appreciation. On the other side of the Atlantic, Speranza waited for news of his St Patrick's Day speech. When she received it, 'Oscar Wilde on Irish Art' was proudly pasted into the Wilde family scrapbook.[24]

Meanwhile, Colonel Morse was laid up with malaria and neuralgia, though that didn't put him out of action.[25] From his sickbed, he continued to orchestrate Wilde's tour. He seemed to picture Wilde as his plaything, and himself as a general pushing a toy soldier figurine across the map of the United States. So, on his first day out of bed, he booked Wilde for California. It was a typical Colonel Morse move, his general attitude being to shoot first and think later.

A few days later, on 21 March 1882, Wilde dutifully boarded a train at Omaha, Nebraska and settled in for the 1,918 mile journey to the Pacific Coast.[26] At 18 miles per hour, it would take nearly a week to reach San Francisco, where he would deliver his usual aesthetic lectures and a special address on 'Irish Poets and Poetry of the Nineteenth Century.' As the train made its westward crawl, it stopped at over 230 stations. Until recently, this land had only been populated by Native Americans. More than thirty years ago, the pioneers and goldrushers known as the '49ers had been propelled towards California by the promise of the fortunes to be found there. Much of the West had not yet formally become part of the Union. North Dakota, South Dakota, Washington, and Montana would join in 1889, followed by Wyoming and Idaho in 1890, and Utah in 1896. The south-western block made up of Oklahoma, New Mexico, and Arizona would come into the Union in the 1900s.

Wilde passed the time by befriending some of his fellow passengers, including John Jerome Howson, the actor playing Bunthorne in the official touring production of *Patience*.[27] Sometimes Wilde stepped out of the train to stretch his legs and amused onlookers by walking the platform in his wide-brimmed white sombrero. Sometimes Howson would put on his Bunthorne costume and cakewalk along instead, impersonating Wilde and delighting the crowds.[28] P.T. Barnum and other showmen were known to use similar tactics to boost ticket sales, marching their companies down Main Street in full regalia to garner attention.

Every station offered a new potential audience. Crowds waited hours for the thrill of watching Wilde's train pass or glimpsing him through the carriage window.[29] In *An Ideal Husband*, Wilde had Lady Markby say that her good reputation was just big enough 'to prevent the lower classes making painful observations through the windows of the carriage.'[30] Sometimes Native Americans appeared at his carriage window selling trinkets. In Iowa, one tried 'through the window to force me to buy a pair of bead slippers,' he told Mrs Beere, an English actress he had seen under the proscenium arch in *The Green Bushes; or, A Hundred Years Ago*, a much-loved play about a bigamous Irishman's tryst with an Indian huntress on the banks of the Mississippi.[31] Wilde joked that the pushy salesman in scarlet feathers looked as fearsome as *Patience*'s librettist or *Punch*'s editor, and was about as likely to malign him. When the Native American tried to close the deal, Wilde saw him signal to his companion 'to tomahawk me if I refuse[d].' On another occasion, Wilde bought an astonishing piece of taxidermy: an ornate birchbark fan decorated with a stuffed black bird and bright yellow feathers. It was a grisly beauty he described as 'a fanciful thing of feathers' made up to look like a sunflower.[32]

Looking out from his train window, he saw America's landscape and those that peopled it as though watching them from a good seat at a West End theatre. The squaws and papooses that appeared at the train car's window in Sioux City were, he said, but 'poor imitations' of scenes from *The Green Bushes; or, A Hundred Years Ago*.[33] To him, the genuine Native Americans out West were merely uninteresting versions of merely 'Indians' he had seen on stage in London's West End.

The expedition to California was 'excessively long and tedious,' he said.[34] As the train cut across the landscape, he watched buffaloes lumbering along and red antelopes scampering.[35] There were blue skies and pine trees for days on end. Vultures shrieked from high above. 'I don't know where I am,' he wrote en route, 'but I am among coyotes and cañons.'[36] Preferring art and civilization, all this natural scenery bored him.

By late March 1882, the chilly Eastern winter and the snowy Sierra Nevadas were finally behind him. In San Francisco, peach and apple trees were blooming, the sky was bright, and the ocean warm.[37] At Wilde's request, hundreds of his photographs had already been dispersed throughout the city. On 27 March, Wilde disembarked at

Oakland, California. The welcome he received was as warm as the weather. Hundreds descended to the train depot to greet him, some clutching sunflowers, lilies, and Japanese parasols. Soon California clothiers would be stocking knee-breeches, 'the Finest, the Latest, the Most Artistic Styles of Elegant Clothing' for gentlemen.[38]

He looked dishevelled and tired by the long journey. A drooping boutonnière pinned to his chest symbolized his mood.[39] Wilde's wilting sunflower buttonhole told of the ardours of the long journey. 'To wear this paltry age's gaudy livery,' he had written in 'Taedium Vitae,' 'I swear I love it not!'[40] The signs of weariness suggested by that poem were playing themselves out on the train platform. Wilde had written that it was 'Better to stand aloof from these slanderous fools who mock my life knowing me not,' and now looked anxious to keep moving. He was impatient of the attentions of the hundreds of curious men and women who had gathered at the train depot to inspect him. As he shuffled towards the ferry, the crowd of San Franciscans followed.

He wore a snug black velvet frock coat that 'showed off strong, square shoulders, manly waist and hips,' a journalist for the San Francisco Examiner noticed. Nearby, a throng gathered around to inspect Wilde's fur overcoat, the original 'made famous by Du Maurier's sketches in Punch.'[41]

'Mr Wilde!' the journalist called out. He had tracked Wilde from the moment he had emerged from the train, pursuing the aesthete through the depot, and onto the ferryboat. As they cruised across San Francisco Bay, it became a floating press conference. Rather than seeing Wilde as the real version of a caricature, however, the reporter thought he resembled Chaucer's soldierly paragon of manhood. Like the 'gentil knight' in The Canterbury Tales, Wilde was 'courteous, deferential, and self-possessed' with the 'quiet, dignified courtesy of a gentleman and a man of the world.'[42]

What poem voiced his political creed?, the journalist asked.[43]

'If you would like to know my political creed,' Wilde told the intrepid journalist, 'read the "Libertatis Sacra Fames."' The choice signalled his changing politics. The sonnet's Latin title translates as 'The Sacred Hunger for Liberty' and although it begins as an encomium to democracy, it rapidly evolves into a defence of monarchy. 'Better the rule of One, whom all obey,' Wilde wrote.[44] The sestet reveals the poem's main concern: preventing the barbarous destruction of 'Arts, Culture, Reverence, Honour.' In the end, Wilde's Sacred Hunger for Liberty turns out to be a holy terror of anarchy.[45]

San Francisco was a crucible of nations in which almost every ethnicity was represented, and where the Irish dominated. They had been among the earliest settlers because of the city's roots as a late eighteenth-century Roman Catholic mission. The Irish who came during the Gold Rush of the 1840s rapidly became part of the city's social fabric and shaped the Bay Area's development even more substantially than the Irish in Boston or New York.[46] By the time of the 1880 US Census, 80,000 San Franciscans (one-third of the city's population) claimed Irish heritage. San Francisco's Irish population was one of the biggest outside Ireland and, unlike most of their counterparts on the Eastern seaboard, they were exceptionally well-off. Wilde had found his sweet spot—a city full of his countrymen, and wealthy to boot. He was invigorated by California's warmth. 'I fancy that I shall be greatly pleased with California,' he told the *San Francisco Examiner*.[47] After his exhausting journey West, he felt relieved to exchange winter for 'summer here, groves of orange trees in fruit and flower, green fields, and purple hills, a very Italy without its art.'[48]

Wilde chose to make his most significant pronouncement on Irish culture and politics in San Francisco. During the long journey west, he had composed an oration on the heroism of the Irish. The trip across the continent had given him a sustained period of reflection, when he could meditate on such matters. Since his arrival in America, more than two months earlier, he had had precious little rest. He had been in a state of tension for so long that the transcontinental journey presented a meditative pause. During the train expedition to California, he seemed to have concluded that his imitators were more than a minor annoyance; they were an insult to him and to all self-respecting Irish. This marked a decisive change in his attitude. Far from Colonel Morse's reach, he glimpsed an opportunity to speak his mind more forcefully.

For months now, he had had it both ways: playing the English aesthete for pay, and keeping quiet about Ireland (except on St Patrick's Day). He had little choice in the matter if he wanted to stay on D'Oyly Carte's payroll. The brief biography Colonel Morse broadcast to America announced him, in its very first line, as 'Mr. Oscar Wilde, the young English poet.'[49] Introduced as an Englishman, it became natural for orchestras to strike up 'God Save the Queen' when he entered American receptions. Though he knew only too well the atrocities that the reign of the English had visited upon Ireland, he did not object to the triumphalist anthem, 'Happy and glorious, Long to reign over us: God save the Queen!' Precarious as the family's finances were, his once radical mother did not stand on ceremony either; Speranza was only too happy to hear that her progeny was being fêted.[50]

But current events, Irish history, and personal honour were forcing Wilde to a crisis. Irish nationalists could no longer countenance his divided politics. 'In a time like this,' they said, when Ireland has the

> hand of the landlord robber at her throat, when she is girt around about with English bayonets, when her most honored sons are found behind prison bars, and when a supreme effort is being made to bust the bonds of ages, and give free homes and lands to a free people...such a man as Oscar Wilde could better employ his time...than in turning his teeming thoughts to the discussion of the merits of a picture, a statue or a poem.[51]

So in early April 1882, when San Francisco's Irish-American community invited him to speak specifically about the Irish poets of 1848 and Young Ireland, he faced a difficult decision: he must resolve the matter of his divided English and Irish allegiances. But how? Here was a test of character that would demand courage and ingenuity. To get up on the stage and address this particular audience would require him to reconcile the English aesthete he had played since his Oxford days, and the native Irishman he actually was. A few years earlier, in her book on *The American Irish*, Speranza declared, 'no Irishman returns from America loyal to monarchy. On the contrary, he laughs to scorn in the old bonds of servile feudalism, with all its superstitions of class worship.'[52] Oscar described the 1878 book as 'a political prophecy.'[53] Now he was going to experience for himself just how right his mother was.

Activism and unrest in Ireland were rampant in the spring of 1882. The markets had recently been flooded with low-cost American grain, and Irish prices were tumbling. Irish tenant farmers found themselves unable to meet their rents, and thousands were facing eviction. Irish-Americans who learned of their kin's distress rallied, offering political support for the nationalist cause.[54]

Visits by Irish leaders to America were still a recent memory in 1882. The republican Michael Davitt had used his 1878 tour to organize

Clan na Gael, a secret, nationalist movement supportive of Charles Parnell's Irish Parliamentary Party. California was the high point of Davitt's visit. In San Francisco, thousands of ardent nationalists welcomed him.[55] In 1879–80 Davitt's charismatic countryman, Parnell, followed him to the United States for a well-publicized visit to fundraise for the Irish National Land League. Bankrolled in part by Irish-Americans, radical and moderate nationalists came together and found a middle way. Together, they aimed to give Ireland an independent parliament and Irish peasants ownership of their lands.

Two years later, while Wilde toured America, Parnell and Davitt were both in prison.[56] 'What are your feelings with regard to the Land League?' a reporter asked Wilde, who was quietly sipping a glass of mineral water and smoking a cigarette.[57] The question enthused him. 'As regards the general principle, that the only basis of legislation should be the general welfare of the people,' Wilde replied, 'I am entirely at one with the position held by the Land League.' The next day, the *St. Louis Globe-Democrat* headline read, 'A Home Ruler: Oscar Wilde Has Some Well-Settled Opinions on the Irish Question.' Meanwhile, in England, the press disparaged the Land League's work, and claimed that Ireland's problems could be attributed to 'fundamental flaws in the Irish character.'[58]

The influence of Parnell's Land League in America coincided with a renewed interest in Young Ireland, the Anglophobic, Irish nationalist movement that Speranza had enthusiastically supported in her twenties.[59] Speranza's Young Ireland and Parnell's Home Rule set the scene for Oscar. American newspapers implied that both had been a formative influence on the aesthete. Like the Parnells, the Wildes were landowners. Charles and Oscar both had an Irish Protestant upbringing, genteel manner, upper-class English accent, and Oxbridge pedigree. Following in Parnell's footsteps, it was in the United States that Wilde would become more vocal in his support for Home Rule.

Only a few years earlier, at Oxford, Wilde's politics had become more moderate than his mother's. Then, he had made a habit of eliding the difference between English and Irish.[60] But his politics shifted again in the United States. Increasingly, Wilde aligned his ideology with Speranza's, resurrecting her patriotic youth to alert Americans to the Wilde family's allegiances. The first edition of her poems was conveniently reissued. Newspapers reprinted her incendiary Young Irelander writings.[61] As a result of the Famine, the Land War, and Parnell's imprisonment, what she had written in 1848 sounded even more inflammatory in 1882.'Do your eyes flash—do your hearts throb at the prospect of having *a country*?' she asked her fellow Irish.[62] 'You have never felt the pride, the dignity, the majesty of independence. You could never lift up your head to Heaven and glory in the name of Irishman, for all Europe read the brand of *slave* upon your brow.'

Politics dominated Wilde's San Francisco visit.[63] After months of lecturing about English Aestheticism, Wilde rediscovered his Irishness and spoke with greater candour about his politics than he ever had—or ever would again.[64] He delivered four lectures in San Francisco—more than in any other American city. For his final appearance, on 5 April, he spoke about 'Irish Poets and Poetry of the Nineteenth Century,' a statement of national pride for which his St Patrick's Day speech in St Paul, Minnesota had been his dress rehearsal. 'The Irish Poets of '48' strongly emphasized two points: that Irish poetry had flourished despite terrible political upheavals, and that Wilde was a proud Irishman, the son of Speranza through and through. The very first words he spoke were a call for Home Rule. 'Since the English occupation we have had no national art in Ireland at all, and there is not the slightest chance of our ever having it until we get that right of legislative independence so unjustly robbed from us; until we are really an Irish nation.'[65] Styling himself the son of Young Ireland, Wilde recited poems composed by the poets active in the 1848 rising. 'I wish I had a good Irish accent to read it to you,' he apologized before declaiming one of their poems, 'but my Irish accent was one of the many things I forgot at Oxford.'[66] He now regretted he had erased the accent of his birthplace. A similar bout of cultural repression had marked his revolutionary mother's Irish youth, Wilde told his San Francisco audience. As a young girl, the future poetess of the Young Ireland movement 'had been brought up in an atmosphere of alien English thought, among people high in bench and senate, and far removed from any love or knowledge of those wrongs of the people to which she afterwards gave such passionate expression.'[67] Thomas Osborne Davis's patriotic poems first opened her eyes to her country's suffering.

The dandyism he and his mother shared was also a point he emphasized in his speech. Dandyism, he claimed, was a trait native to Irish poets. He was only the most recent example of a long-standing tradition that had started when Irish peasants could only dress in drab monochrome, whereas the poet was allowed colours 'and encouraged in fact to wear whatever kind of clothes he thought the nicest.'[68] He was tailoring his dandyism to his politics, and refashioning English Aestheticism to suit his own Irish form. Then, with a nod to his own fabulous outfit, he added that it was 'a state of things which I am sure I would wish to see revived for the benefit of modern poets.'

In his oration, he resorted to his preferred method of confronting the present: by talking about the past. Only recently, in interviews about Walt Whitman, he had talked about ancient Greek love rather than his own feelings for other men. Similarly, when Wilde talked about Young Ireland and the revolutions of 1848 in his San Francisco lecture, he intended his listeners to relate his homeland's distant history to the country's more recent travails. Here again Speranza's influence was at work. She had also adopted this strategy in her recent book, *The American Irish*. 'She remembers the days of old with a vengeance,' one reviewer noted, complaining that more than half the book was about Irish history and criticizing her for reiterating decades-old nationalist dreams, when what was really wanted from her was an account of present-day politics.[69]

Oscar's lecture on 'The Irish Poets of '48' adopted a similar approach, but achieved happier results. The talk was a safe way of addressing the explosive situation playing out in real time back home. Rather than mentioning leaders like Parnell and Davitt directly, he talked about eighteenth- and early nineteenth-century notables like Thomas D'Arcy McGee, John Mitchel, William Smith O'Brien, Daniel 'The Liberator' O'Connell, and Speranza, of course. Under the cover of history, he spoke the truth about his own day.

For the benefit of his Irish-American listeners, Wilde personalized his roll call of Irish history's greats. Many of them were real flesh and blood men with whom he and his family had a shared history.[70] The Wildes knew the poet John Savage (who was active in the 1848 rising and escaped to the United States where he worked as a New York journalist and organized the Fenian movement), Charles Gavan Duffy (under whose editorship *The Nation* was suppressed because of Speranza's subversive 'Jacta Alea Est'), and the poet Thomas Davis (a patriotic versifier for *The Nation*, he was the unofficial leader of Young Ireland). Like the lace handkerchief he sometimes secreted into his pocket only to brandish it dramatically later when he spoke, Wilde flourished his personal affiliations with the generation of '48.[71] 'As regards the men of '48,' he said, 'I was trained by my mother to love and reverence them as a Catholic child is the saints of the calendar, and I have seen so many of them also.'[72]

By drawing historical parallels, he reframed current events in Ireland as part of a vast, cosmopolitan panorama of world events unfurling across time and space. By these lights, he reckoned that the Celtic imagination was responsible for 'all the great beauties of modern literature' in Europe. Its 'chords of penetrating passion and melancholy,' had touched 'men so widely different as Goethe and Napoleon, influencing the work of every poet from Byron to Keats and Lamartine.' Even now, England's poet laureate, Alfred Tennyson, 'has nothing better to do than put into exquisite verse the old Celtic legends of Arthur,' Wilde said. Diverting the conversation from Celts to cosmopolitans, deflecting from the present to the past, from this to that, from X to Y—these manoeuvres were to become his lifelong strategy for discussing topics that were personal, emotional, or controversial.

In St Paul and San Francisco, Wilde performed as Speranza's son, which legitimized him as an Irish aesthete and gave him the opportunity to recite military verse, such as Speranza's poem, 'Courage.'[73] He was a red-blooded revolutionary after all. Making light of his transformation, he told the Fenian poet John Boyle O'Reilly that his mother's poetry would be very popular in the United States because 'it is so unlike the work of her degenerate artistic son.'[74] Then, turning serious, he said, 'I know you think I am thrilled by nothing but a dado. You are quite wrong, but I shan't argue.'

Ultimately, Wilde's real passion was for the politics of aestheticism, but there could be no doubt that America had encouraged his Irish republicanism. England has 'hands dabbed in blood,' he told journalists, and an Irishman would find it 'hard to shake hands with her.'[75] As for current events, 'she is reaping the fruit of seven centuries of injustice.' Ireland's struggle, as he saw it, was essentially one between its native culture and English colonial barbarism. 'There is no lack of culture in Ireland, but it is nearly all absorbed in politics,' Wilde told the *San Francisco Examiner*.[76] 'Had I remained there my career would have been a political one.'

The news of Wilde's Irish-American triumph was greeted with joy in London, where 'Bunthorne's Mama,' as the American press now called Speranza, approvingly noted her son's transformation. She had dreamed that Oscar would one day have a career in politics.[77] 'What a tour!!' she enthused.[78] There would be no more doubt as to his legitimacy, she thought. 'How changed you will be—I shall feel quite nervous having you to dinner.' She proudly watched his growing reputation eclipse her own. When he returned to London, she predicted that she would be known as 'the Mother of Oscar.'[79]

Chapter 13

Underground Men

Leadville, Colorado, was not for the faint of heart. Founded in 1877 and made rich by its mines, by the time Wilde made his way there it had a reputation as the richest, roughest, and most wicked town on earth. Leadville was run by cowboys and miners—a shaggy, broad-built bunch with large hands that gripped yours in a handshake that felt like a vice. They had feet the size of small cradles, and thighs so brawny that half a dozen children could easily sit on their laps.[1] Their pastimes were whittling wood, chewing tobacco, loafing in bar-room armchairs, and brawling, sometimes with the help of a gun. Toughness was a way of life.

When Wilde arrived in snowy Leadville late on Thursday, 13 April 1882, there were bluebirds in the snow-caped mountains, but there was nobody to greet him at the station. As he sank into the carriage trundling towards his hotel, he was gripped by a wave of nausea and a violent headache. Outside, snowflakes churned into a blizzard. By the time the carriage reached the Clarendon Hotel and Wilde was secreted into his room through the ladies' entrance, he was desperate for a doctor's attention. Lying on the bed, he panted as he awaited the diagnosis. It was a case of altitude sickness, the physician decided, a common ailment for visitors to the town.

Located more than 10,000 feet above sea level, Leadville is the highest city in the United States, and sits at about half the altitude of Mount Kilimanjaro, the highest mountain in Africa. The reduced amount of oxygen can induce symptoms including weakness, headache, and nausea. To remedy altitude sickness, it is recommended to avoid alcohol, tobacco, and overexertion. That evening, Wilde would follow none of this advice.

No doubt the uppermost thing on his mind that night was avoiding getting murdered. Before his arrival, he had heard that locals might try to shoot him. Rumours were flying that 'hard characters' and 'Western "bad men"' were planning to threaten him at his lecture.[2] Perhaps they had imagined a Wild West version of what the students had done at Rochester. Days before Wilde's visit, a murder had taken place in front of the Tabor Opera House, where he was scheduled to speak. A jilted husband had challenged a womanizer to a shoot-out for being too friendly towards his wife. It was a good omen for Wilde that the womanizer had won.

As the doctor was ushered out of Wilde's room at the Clarendon Hotel, a journalist was promptly shown in. From his sickbed, Wilde submitted to a full interview for the *Leadville Daily Herald*. The reporter filed it under the title 'Oscar Dear,' the hit song about the aesthete's legendary talent for womanizing.[3] The citizens of Leadville knew it well. On many nights, it had been on the lips of Miss Erba Robeson, a local singing sensation who performed decked in diamonds.[4]

By now, lecturing to unappreciative small-town audiences felt like a death sentence to Wilde, who had recently told an interviewer that he felt '*condemned* to go on the platform.'[5] He wanted his Colorado audience to know exactly how things stood between him and them. If 'mischievous young men will make it hot for me,' Wilde declared, 'then will I bid farewell to my vow of peace. I am resolved to no longer tamely submit to being made a target for rude youngsters.'[6] He had bought a gun, he threatened. From his train window, he was taking target practice on sparrows.'My aim is as lethal as lightning,' he warned.

That evening in Leadville, Wilde faced a double challenge: delivering his lecture with a whirling head, and not getting killed while doing it. The snow turned to slushy rain and then back again. At the Tabor Opera House, most of the 888 seats were filled despite the hostile climate. Leadville had a clutch of genteel folk who wanted to show that their town could lay claim to being just as refined and courteous as any other.[7] 'There is now a good chance to show some towns which pretend to endless "culchah"'—the word stood in for refined cities like New York, Boston, Chicago, and London—'that our people are not wholly lacking in good manners, [even] if they do live in the mountains,' an editorialist said. One-upmanship was the order of the evening. Local advertisements promised Wilde's 'Art Decoration!' lecture would be 'the event of the season!'[8]

That night, Wilde dressed in his usual knee-breeches and black stockings, stumbled onto the Opera House stage with 'a stride more becoming a giant backwoodsman than an aesthete,' and started his talk on interior decoration.[9] It was an auspicious beginning. His lumbering gait surprised Coloradans, who saw that he wasn't at all the effete aesthete they had been told to expect. Wilde's appearance was 'not so effeminate as some people would have the public believe,' they said.[10] In fact, they thought he looked like one of their men. Working Westerners saw his body differently from Northeastern and Midwestern urbanites.[11] They called him 'the athletic-looking aesthetic,' and said that he moved like a coal-heaver, which was a compliment in that part of the world.[12]

When Wilde spoke in the West, he encouraged listeners to aspire to a higher level of culture than circuses and popular entertainments offered them. They didn't need galleries like Barnum's museum of wonders, or exhibits like those in 'the dreadful modern museum where you find a stuffed and very dusty giraffe face to face with a case or two of fossils.'[13] It was far better, he said, to put their minds to building a museum of art, for it would enrich their lives.

On their days off, he thought American workers should spend their time in art museums. 'Where the workman can see clay, marble, wood, or glass specimens of the best decorative art,' he promised, 'he may come to know what is simple and true and beautiful.' Their British counterparts did this, he said, hinting at the cultural rivalry so keenly felt in the United States. 'In London, one of our strongholds of strength is the South Kensington Museum,' he explained, alluding to the art galleries now known as the Victoria and Albert Museum.[14] On any given Sunday, Wilde assured Americans, they would find British 'workmen going round and examining every ornament, every specimen of beauty that men of past ages have wrought.'

Once Americans had trained their eyes by looking at art, he promised, they would begin to see beauty in everyday life. Even today's 'men at the docks unloading some beautiful ship' would make fine models for a Graeco-Roman artist or 'ancient sculptor' of gods and goddesses. Some months before, he had told Harvard students that they should install casts of Greek statues in their gym to prompt them to remember, while they exercised, that bodies like their own had once inspired artists.[15] His examples suggested how fuzzy the line between art and life was to him by blurring the distinction between museum objects and dockside-workers, sculptures, and students.

America's art future was all around them today. 'I do not ask you to bring back the thirteenth century,' he said, but to use today's technology and to ennoble contemporary life by looking at it artistically.[16] Generations of European artists had merely transformed the beautiful bodies they saw around them into breathtaking sculptures. In ancient times, Greek and Roman artists made myths out of the quotidian. Americans should do the same. 'Wherever in your fields you find men driving cattle or women drawing water, there you will find models of beauty' fit to be transformed into art or into 'gods and goddesses,' he said. Wilde encouraged quasi-magical thinking about everyday realities, however modest. That's precisely the kind of thinking that, in *The Picture of Dorian Gray*, makes the third-rate actress Sybil Vane seem divine to Dorian. When they see Sybil's mesmerizing performances, 'common rough people, with their coarse faces and brutal gestures, become quite different,' Wilde wrote.[17] Art works in invisible ways, and transforms viewers by changing their minds.

On the evening he spoke in Leadville, as he was telling them this, there was a piercing cry from the audience. Wilde paused, as though deciding whether to brandish his pistol. Then, scanning the audience, he located the shrieker. It was a youngster, he noticed, so he spared the bullet and shot at him with humour instead. 'I wish the juvenile enthusiast would restrain its raptures until the end of the lecture,' he said, and carried on speaking over the wail of the crying baby.[18]

At the end of his Leadville lecture, Wilde stepped away from the podium unharmed. Later, from a distance of 4,000 miles, he made light of Colorado's 'hard characters' and their murder threats. 'I was told that if I went there, they would be sure to shoot me,' he said, regaling British audiences with his Leadville adventures in 'Personal Impressions of America,' a lecture he delivered throughout England, Scotland, Wales, and Ireland for the better part of the 1880s.[19] Murder was no idle threat in Leadville, he informed audiences, because men carried guns. But, he boasted, he hadn't been cowed. 'I wrote and told them that nothing that they could do to my travelling manager would intimidate *me*.'[20] He and the miners had hit it off, he claimed. They invited him along to a dancing-saloon, where he learned the fate that awaited performers who didn't live up to the miners' expectations.

Over the saloon's piano, he saw a notice printed with what he called their 'rational method of art criticism':

PLEASE DO NOT SHOOT
THE PIANIST.
HE IS DOING HIS BEST

'The mortality among pianists in that place is marvellous,' Wilde said.

While in the United States, he had planned to write another book of poems but quickly discovered that his hectic schedule made that impossible.[21] Still, his long train journeys gave him the opportunity to do more than shoot hapless sparrows. He read voraciously from the library of books that his valet lugged from place to place. He pored over the newspapers, hunting for copy about himself, analysing his interviews and snipping articles. He filleted the best of the press (and, sometimes, the worst) and sent the clippings to his friends and mother. This handmade newsfeed often included opinions and commentary. 'Even the papers, though venal and vile,' he editorialized for the benefit of his correspondents, 'often repent and write sensibly about me. I send you an extract from the last place I lectured at before this. It is full of common sense.'[22]

To a gifted social observer like Wilde, the tour was a unique opportunity to study American women and men from all walks of life.[23] During the course of his journey, he met thousands of them, getting a coast-to-coast overview. As Wilde rode the rails, he took mental notes. 'The greatest thing a human soul ever does in this world is to *see* something, and tell what it *saw* in a plain way,' his Oxford tutor, John Ruskin, believed.[24] 'To see clearly is poetry, prophecy, and religion,—all in one.' Wilde's train's carriage window became a changing picture frame through which he examined Americans in their natural habitat. Seated in a carriage chugging across the country, it must have been impossible to ignore the moving panoramas that unspooled before his eyes, or the human dramas that played out on train platforms as people arrived and departed. When he reached Colorado, he told a journalist that he was making notes on the many new things he had experienced. He said he was planning to write them up when his tour was over. 'Whatever I have seen to impress me in America, whether of the beauties of nature or of men and women, I will write and give America credit for it.'[25]

When Wilde looked at American society, he saw a gender revolution in progress. He took his sociological observations back to England, where he turned them into essays—on 'The American Invasion' and 'The American Man'—as well as a lecture, 'Personal Impressions of America.' According to these arresting portraits, the turn-of-the-century American man was a creature who, in his natural habitat, was perpetually overworked and culturally undernourished. Wilde saw the American father as a man who 'passes his life entirely in Wall Street and communicates with his family once a month by means of a telegram.'[26] He saw the American husband as a man who paid no attention to his wife and despaired at the thought of a tête-à-tête with her.[27] Consequently, these men showed alarming symptoms of intellectual, artistic, and personal impoverishment. They were pitiful figures, sordid materialists who knew the price of everything and the value of nothing, Wilde believed.[28]

The inequalities between American men and women startled him. In modern life, a clear division of labour was emerging: women were becoming the tastemakers, men the moneymakers. 'It is only the women in America who have any leisure at all,' Wilde disapproved.[29] Enterprising and creative women were pouncing into the foreground of American cultural life. Meanwhile, men were receding into a hinterland of bank balances and Broadway stores. He believed they cared too much about steam engines and telephones, and not enough about art, leisure, and culture. All work and no play made American Jack a very dull boy indeed. Perhaps that was one reason the number of divorces had more than doubled in the last decades.[30] 'The American man marries early,' Wilde wrote, 'and the American woman marries often.'[31]

His diagnosis of the American scene was damning. To him, the typical American man was a Philistine. 'Industry without art is simply barbarism,' Wilde warned Americans in his 1882 lectures.[32] An American man's life began with devotion to money-making and ended in philistinism. Like Matthew Arnold's dreaded philistine in *Culture and Anarchy*, the classic 1869 defence of culture, the American seemed to believe 'that our greatness and welfare are proved by our being very rich.'[33] Oblivious to all that he was missing, he seemed as ridiculous as someone condemned to go through life expressing himself by using only the most limited of alphabets—say, the letters between 'M' (for Mammon and Money) and 'P' (for Philistine and Plutocrat). Such an impossibly doomed creature would hardly notice that all he had left to enjoy was 'N-O'. Nothing much. No leisure. No culture. No point, Wilde thought.

As ever, he believed art could provide a solution to these woes.'The artist comes forward as a priest and prophet of nature to protest, and even to work against the prostitution or the perversion of what is lofty and noble in humanity,' Wilde said.[34] Although he had evidently borrowed a little inspiration for this riff from Ruskin's phrase about seeing being equal to 'poetry, prophecy, and religion,' Wilde had also added a few beats of his own. Alliterations are usually a clue to the vigour of his views. When he delivered this message, the thrusting energy of the plosives—priest, prophet, protest, prostitution, perversion—chugged the ideas along and out of his mouth, as if the sounds were a series of miniature explosions bursting from his lips and flying into listeners' ears to persuade them of his idea.

By the end of the twentieth century, Wilde predicted that women would run the United States. 'The whole culture of the New World will be in petticoats,' he believed.[35] The novelist Henry James agreed that, in the absence of men, American women were leading the nation's cultural development and, as a result, they were dominating the scene.[36] By then, it had become so unusual for American men to take an interest in culture that American women who visited Britain were astonished to see men taking the time to dine out and socialize. Maude Howe was one such tourist. 'At home,' the Bostonian recalled, men had 'little time for society' and so she was surprised to discover that British men thought of it as 'part of the relaxation all intellectual workers must find.' [37]

In the wee hours of the morning, on Friday, 14 April 1882, Wilde was in a Leadville saloon celebrating his survival by watching buxom dancers in tiny red skirts. It was one of the town's many pleasure palaces, a place where men could gamble and gawk. Wilde was drinking heavily, smoking cigars, and placing bets at the gaming tables. He had changed out of his lecturer's costume and into a corduroy coat, trousers, and a wide-brimmed hat. Bystanders thought he looked like 'a Texas ranger who had struck it rich.'[38] Outside, drunken men and dead-eyed musicians lined the walls. Painted ladies walked up and down the wooden walkways, as though in a scene from 'The Harlot's House,' his poem about loiterers outside a brothel spying prostitutes making merry.

Around 1 or 2 o'clock in the morning, Wilde was having a liquid supper—mostly wine—when someone suggested that they have dinner at the bottom of Governor Horace Tabor's Matchless Mine. Tabor was a peculiar specimen. Large and ungainly, he lurched along, often in a drunken stupor. An enormous longhorn moustache sat atop his upper lip, and his whiskers looked as if they had been shaped into a personal tribute to the Colorado mountains where he had made his multimillion-dollar fortune. Tabor's name now graced the opera house where Wilde had just delivered his lecture. Leadville silver mining had been his first success. Known as the 'Croesus of Colorado,' his empire comprised several mines, railroads, theatres, newspapers, a stagecoach line, and a bank.

A few evenings earlier, in Denver, Wilde was having supper—broiled fish, potatoes, omelette, mutton chops, bread, and Bordeaux wine—when Tabor barged in and introduced himself. The millionaire soon extended an invitation to visit his silver mine in Leadville's mountains. 'I shall be delighted,' Wilde replied.[39]

Now, Wilde and his entourage are more than a mile outside Leadville. Tabor's miners are lighting the way with torches as they climb up the mountainside above Leadville in the dark.[40] Below them, the town's yellow lights glow like stars against the snowy landscape. When they reach the Matchless Mine's entrance, the superintendent hands Wilde a full body outfit of India rubber. This is the obligatory costume for those going underground. Wilde has the honour of donning Tabor's own rubber suit, and stepping into the great man's clothes. As he pulls on the outfit, it becomes obvious that it was made for a man as wide as Oscar is tall. He continues dressing himself, even though the suit's gummy expanse drapes and folds over him unflatteringly. Even now—especially now—he uses his imagination to improve the situation. 'This cloak reminds me of the togas worn by the Roman senators,' Wilde drawls, making the best of his new costume. There is

room for aesthetic improvement, however. The lining could be purple satin, Wilde suggests. Some Japanese styling would be nice, too.
He proposes embroidering storks on the rubber flaps and ferns along
the edges.[41] Nearby, the man from the *Denver Tribune* is scribbling
notes and he will file a report saying that Wilde looks fetching in
India rubber.

Next, Wilde climbs into the bucket that will take him down into
the Matchless Mine's Number 3 shaft. The liquid courage he drank
in the saloon is helping ease his nerves. The mine's superintendent
climbs in with him and they are off. Wilde is laughing loudly and grab-
bing at the bucket's rope. 'Impossible to be graceful' in that rickety
contraption, he later says.[42] As they sink down deeper and deeper into
the shaft, plunging into total darkness, the superintendent shines his
lamp here and there, pointing out the subterranean sights, high and
low-grade ore. 'The finest sight in the world,' Wilde burbles as the
superintendent's lamp spotlights the walls.

At the bottom of the shaft, in the heart of the mountain, a surprise awaits. As the bucket is lowered to the ground, Wilde glimpses
faces and bodies. Twelve silver miners watch as he clambers out of
the bucket. Each man has a bottle in his hand. Circling around him,
they explain that the twelve bottles will make the rounds until they
are all empty. After a few turns, signs of intoxication soon become
noticeable. Most are struggling. Some are looking distinctly unsteady
on their feet. But not Wilde. He has his head about him and stands
tall, as if nothing could shake him. All at once, there is a great stamping of feet. A clapping, hooting blast of joy explodes from the men
buried deep inside the mountain. He has passed their test.

'A perfect gentleman!' they cheer.[43]

'A bully boy!'[44]

From rock bottom—*de profundis*—they have hailed Wilde as a hero,
a man's man. In this pit, the miners have taken Wilde into their hearts,
and embraced him as one of their own.

He will dine out on this story for years to come. 'I found these
miners very charming and not at all rough,' he will tell the *Manchester
Examiner and Times*, pointing out that he had never had a more attentive audience.[45] 'One reason I liked them was because of their magnificent physiques,' he will explain to a *New York World* reporter.[46]

A year later, in Britain, he will tell audiences at his 'Personal
Impressions of America' lectures an embellished version of this Wild

West adventure. He will describe their underground meal as 'supper, the first course being whisky, the second whisky and the third whisky.'[47] He will also say that he gave the Matchless men a talk about the Ethics of Art. 'They are miners,' he will tell audiences. They are not minors, not under-age boys, but 'men working in metals,' he will point out, pausing to clarify a distinction visible on the printed page but lost when the word is spoken. 'I read them passages from the autobiography of Benvenuto Cellini and they seemed much delighted.' Then he will add, 'I was reproved by my hearers for not having brought him with me. I explained that he had been dead for some little time which elicited the enquiry "Who shot him?"'

The episode will become a turning point in Wilde's personal version of his American story. Almost immediately, he talks about the manly miners in his interviews, his correspondence, even his lectures. During his talks, he suddenly parachutes the Leadville men in, and describes them as though they are gods of the underworld, saying:

> The most graceful thing I ever beheld was a miner in a Colorado silver mine driving a new shaft with a hammer; at any moment he might have been transformed into marble or bronze and become noble in art forever.[48]

He parades the workers as prime examples of American men who have 'attained the beautiful,' in spite of their lack of so-called 'civilisation.'[49] Eventually, they become *the* highlight of his 'Personal Impressions of America' lecture (see Plate 37).

This moment exemplifies how, slowly but surely, Wilde remade his personal history: by rewriting it himself. Keep Wilde's authorial hand in sight, watch its furtive re-scripting of this moment, and you may have noticed that he has repeated a trick you've already seen him perform. Indeed, it was the same imaginative sleight-of-hand that had turned Tabor's rubber worksuit into a Roman senator's toga. And it was performed by the same illusionist who had once looked at a dockman and seen a god. Wilde's quasi-magical thinking remade the miners into paragons of manhood. His visit to the mine became a kind of abracadabra moment when—ta-dah!—the light of Aestheticism was brought to one of the darkest places on the earth.

Yet America's underground men of culture were Wilde's invention. His compelling hocus-pocus entailed some nimble legerdemain, but it didn't manage to make the truth vanish entirely. Two letters about Leadville remain and they hint at how much he exaggerated the ennobling power of culture. In the first letter, he confessed that while he spoke about Florentine art in Leadville the men had dozed off.[50] In the second, more detailed letter, he announced in neat black cursive on cream paper, 'I have met miners.'[51] He described the workers as lovable lugs—'big-booted, red-shirted, yellow-bearded and delightful ruffians'—who treated him just as most American men did, which is to say that they couldn't care less. In this version, when he told them about Italian art, they didn't ask after Benvenuto Cellini. And when he mentioned 'early Florentine art they unanimously declared they could neither trump or follow it.' This time around, Aestheticism was jokey gibberish to them. So the miners were typical American men after all. Still his imaginative process transformed the leaden facts of his Leadville visit into a bright, twinkling triumph: the moment when refined masculinity won with a pen rather than a pistol.

By dint of Wilde's retelling, his enhanced version of the incident became the definitive one. In his 'Personal Impressions of America' lectures, he turned it into a myth marking his tour's triumph. The tale would be repeated again and again for years to come until, more than a century later, it would become the opening scene of *Wilde*, a 1997 film in which the actor Stephen Fry, as a fur-wearing Wilde, clambers into a bucket and goes down to visit Leadville's bare-chested underground men.

By then, the apocryphal story had become gospel. Sinking down into Tabor's mine became part of the story of Wilde's rise to aesthetic greatness. There is more at stake in this transformation than a little embellishment. By spangling the facts with fancy, the miners took on symbolic dimensions. And Leadville, in turn, became a parable about Art's civilizing power—about how sweetness and light can pierce through darkness and dirt.

Chapter 14

Going South

Before the summer started, he had delivered over eighty lectures in seventy-four different locations across the United States. Now his train was speeding South. It was early June 1882 when Wilde crossed the Mason-Dixon line, once the symbolic division between southern slaveholding states and northern non-slaveholding states. The South greeted Wilde with clear skies and sweltering temperatures. He would take the stage in New Orleans, Louisiana, Texas, Alabama, Georgia, South Carolina, and Virginia, making at least twenty-three individual stops before the end of July. His valet at his side, Wilde soldiered through the humid summer in a velvet jacket and silk stockings. When they reached the coast, he found relief by bathing in the Gulf of Mexico.[1]

Colonel Morse had delegated management of the Southern part of the tour to Peter Tracy, an Irish-American showman with a sideline in printing.[2] Tracy promptly draped Wilde's Pullman car with a huge white banner that read O-S-C-A-R-W-I-L-D-E in big black letters. That gimmick ensured no publicity opportunity would be wasted on any mile of the journey. As the train moved across the horizon, everyone would see the great aesthete was coming their way. O-S-C-A-R-W-I-L-D-E literally became a coming attraction.

Because of Wilde's interviews and lectures, Southerners now imagined the aesthete as an ambassador of two interest groups: the Irish and the working man. Readers of *The Atlanta Constitution* were informed 'that Mr. Wilde was thoroughly celtic in sentiment and regarded the Irish as his own people.'[3] As a result of such reports, the press began a new spate of degrading attacks, which included reprinting the *Washington Post*'s caricature of Mr Wild of Borneo. All of this amplified the perception of Wilde as a negrified Paddy.

Earlier in the century, particularly in cities, the Irish often worked alongside African Americans in low-paid jobs.[4] As a result, the two groups were thought of as interchangeable. African Americans were called 'smoked Irish.'[5] It was said that the Irish were 'white niggers' or 'negroes turned inside out' who would 'slave like a nigger.'[6] That same association presently haunted Wilde and his black valet as they travelled together. When a Georgia newspaper referred to his valet as 'an Irish negro,' his manager, Peter Tracy, played along by signing them in as 'Oscar Wilde and servant of Ireland' on the hotel register.[7] The associations that attached to Wilde were also attached to Aestheticism. Increasingly, its signature symbols became emblems of working-class aspiration that cut across the colour line.

For marketers and consumers alike, Aestheticism had become shorthand for brighter futures. In ads, the African American aesthete wore his sunflower lapel like a badge of his social mobility (see Plates 38 and 39). From stove polish promising to beautify your home, to boots promising to improve your romantic prospects, the aesthetic sunflower symbolized the good life. And if you weren't yet an aesthete, these seductive ads promised to turn you into one. By buying crop-boosting fertilizer from Charleston's Ashley Phosphate Company, for instance, 'The Aesthetic Darkey' promised that you, too, could become rich enough to 'wear good clothes, and devote considerable time to de fine arts.'[8]

Wilde's train plunged down the length of the country towards Tennessee, then followed the Mississippi River through the bayous of Louisiana. When he reached New Orleans, his lecture took a back seat to reports about his fascination with people of colour. 'OSCAR WILDE,' the *New Orleans Daily Picayune* headline read, 'The Negro, the Indian and the Sunflower His Theme.'[9] He was surprised that painters and poets had paid so little attention to 'the negro as an object of art,' he told the reporter. 'I saw them everywhere, happy and careless, basking in the sunshine or dancing in the shade, their half-naked bodies gleaming like bronze and their lithe and active movements reminding one of the lizards that were seen flashing along the banks and trunks of the trees,' he said, as though describing creatures set in an exotic pastoral scene.[10] On one hand, his admiration put African Americans on a pedestal. On the other, it objectified them like a buyer at an auction might. The news item concluded that 'nothing in the way of animal life, however, seemed to please the poet and art reformer so much as the young negroes.'

Soon a more tragic theme was emerging in the coverage of Wilde's Southern tour. Oscar Wilde 'was made a guest at a lynching entertainment,' newspapers across the country claimed.[11] 'A crowd of obliging white men...wanted the distinguished English aesthete to see one of the[ir] chief amusements.'[12] Others punned on his art credentials, saying that 'he no doubt gained some new ideas on the subject of aesthetic hangings.'[13] In Louisiana, where the incident was rumoured to have taken place, racial tensions were high. The lines between black and white were troubled. The problem of the colour line took many different forms. One of them was lynching—a line of rope knotted into a deadly noose. And now, among the picturesque bayous and magnolia trees, a peculiar thing happened: that noose began to hover closer and closer to Wilde, threatening him more than ever before.

'Southern trees bear strange fruit, blood on the leaves and blood at the root, black body swinging in the Southern breeze,' Billie Holliday sang in the 1930s.[14] About half a century before, systematic records on lynchings were non-existent. In 1882, the *Chicago Tribune* and the Tuskegee Institute began collecting data in response to anecdotal evidence about the rising number of such murders. They soon quantified a gruesome trend that began in the 1880s and would continue until the 1930s, when Holliday first recorded her haunting song.[15] This period has become known as the Age of Lynching. 'What made the age of lynching distinctive is that a particular type of society was born then,' historian Ashraf Rushdy explains, 'a society in which two regions of the country achieved postbellum reconciliation through a tacit agreement about the fate of African Americans, a society in which mass media, mass transportation systems, government officials, and business elites cooperated with and abetted mobs that were too frequent in appearance, too regular in strategy, and too pervasive to be thought of as spontaneous.'[16]

Lynching became a means of putting into action visceral, inchoate feelings about domestic, foreign, and social policies. It was both a symptom and a gauge of the country's troubles. From the 1880s to the early 1890s, on average, the United States lynched 180 of its black citizens every year. Sometimes the numbers were as high as 235.[17] In Louisiana, during the year of Wilde's visit, twelve lynchings were recorded.[18] One of them took place in Bayou Bonfouca, where Wilde was said to have witnessed it. The incident was never properly investigated and the victim is rarely identified in histories of lynching.[19] As for Wilde's role, nobody ever looked into it. Yet this story reveals how the hatred directed towards him caused him to be framed as an accessory to another man's murder.

Bonfouca, Louisiana is a tiny picturesque community on the north shore of Lake Pontchartrain. Bordered by coastal marsh and pine forested wetlands, it is a haven for migratory birds and endangered species. Today, you can count all of the town's streets on one hand. In less than an hour, you can drive south and reach New Orleans.

A year before Wilde set foot in the United States, Bonfouca was still a marshland. But this was the great age of the railroad and engineers were devising a plan to connect this isolated region to New Orleans, by then a growing metropolis. By December 1881, works had commenced. A railroad would be laid across a trestle bridge over Lake Pontchartrain.[20]

The New Orleans and Northeastern Railroad Company took charge of the project. Everything was built from scratch. Wielding axes and shovels, men cleared and graded the road. They hewed the timber by hand and then oxen dragged the wood into place. Since the pilings, cross-ties, and timbers for the trestle bridge had to be treated with preservative creosote, a plant was built. Workers' accommodations were erected on the banks of the bayou. Hotels and boarding houses rapidly sprang up. Close by, in the town of Slidell, a brisk trade in food, clothes, and whisky broke out.

Despite the bustle of new activity, the area remained a rough and impoverished swampland frontier. The Civil War had left it in a calamitous state. Afterwards, it became a haven for Confederate refugees from New Orleans who refused to take the oath of allegiance to the Federal government. A Federal Order intended to starve the area into submission proved effective and by 1865 there was almost nothing left in St Tammany Parish. Those who had survived seemed intent on destroying each other. For years to come, the region was wracked with violence and mayhem and, by the early 1880s, the parish's largest town had only a few hundred inhabitants. At the end of the decade, the area's salient features were 'a shattered economy, war ravaged infrastructure, and painful wounds associated with nearly twenty years of sustained violence.'[21]

It was here, in 1882, on the sloping banks of what was then still called Bayou Bonfouca, that a 15-year-old named Milan Howard came to work on the railroad that was being built through St Tammany Parish. Later on, in newspaper reports, he would be described as 'a Negro laborer on the Northeastern Railroad.'[22] This was the teenager whose fate would become intertwined with Wilde's.

Born around 1867 in South Carolina, Milan was the fourth child of farmers.[23] Neither of Milan's parents could read or write. Both were probably slaves before Emancipation. By Milan's first birthday, his mother had already given birth to another son and named him Mingo Jr., after his father. By Milan's third birthday, the Howards were farming in Darlington, a rural area settled in the eighteenth century by Welsh, Scottish, and British cotton farmers and developed thanks to the labour of enslaved African Americans.[24] During the Civil War, the county's population and its livelihood had been devastated and, more than a decade later, Darlington still counted fewer than 1,000 inhabitants.

Even in a tiny place like Darlington, the privileges conferred by whiteness were obvious. The Youngs, who lived next door to the Howards, provided a stark contrast to the poverty verging on destitution in which Mingo Sr. and Harriet Howard were raising their children in 1870. The Youngs were the only white family in the neighbourhood, and by far the wealthiest, with a personal estate valued at $50. That wasn't much, but it was more than anyone else around, and enough to send 12-year-old Mary Young to school, making her the only child in a community of nearly eighty to receive any education that year. These statistics capture the locality's stagnancy and suggest some of the challenges Milan undoubtedly faced. Nobody in Darlington seemed equipped to go very far from where they had started off in life. Milan's little brother, Mingo Jr., followed in his parents' footsteps and became a farmer. When he died, at the age of 83, he was buried close to the town where he was born.

As a teenager, Milan must have wanted a different life for himself. Less than a hundred miles westward from Darlington, there was Myrtle Beach's coastline. Travelling the same distance eastward could carry him to Columbia, the capital of South Carolina. If he made his way to either place, neither held him for long. Almost a century later, Bruce Springsteen's record-breaking 1984 album, *Born in the U.S.A.*, memorialized Darlington as a great place to escape from. 'Driving out of Darlington County, my eyes seen the glory of the coming of the Lord,'

Springsteen sang, telling the story of another of the town's escapees. As a teenager, Milan appears to have been driven out from Darlington by the Lord. Aged 13, he took to the road as an itinerant preacher. Perhaps it was this calling that led him south to Louisiana, where the locals garbled his name and sometimes called him 'Amilia' and 'Mealy.'

Itinerant preaching brought little reward and he soon became a desperado.[25] Two years later, his wandering feet stopped in Bayou Bonfouca. He was only 15 by then, but since he looked and acted much older than his age, he was able to get a job with what was then the most exciting new venture in town, the New Orleans and Northeastern Railroad. But that didn't change the fact that he was in a bad state by the time he made it to Bayou Bonfouca. A local said that the teenager looked so weathered he could easily pass for a man in his mid-twenties. The rest of Milan's life is a mystery which can only be pieced together from the few remaining records. What is nevertheless clear is that by the first week of June 1882, he had nothing to lose.

Milan Howard's final days, as we know them, began on the afternoon of Saturday, 10 June 1882, when a white man went to visit his mother in a town several miles away.[26] While the man was away, his wife—'a respectable lady'—allegedly stayed alone in their isolated house near the Bonfouca sawmills.[27] That night, Milan supposedly visited the house, breaking through the bedroom window with an axe. According to press reports, he saw 'the defenseless wife was sleeping, seized her by the throat to stifle her cries for help, choked her into unconsciousness, and brutally outraged her person.'[28] Since the nearest neighbour lived a mile away, nobody heard the woman's cries for help. If she had tried to run, it would have taken her about ten minutes on foot to reach the next house. This made it possible, reports inferred, for Milan 'to commit the crime without interruption' before escaping back to the New Orleans and Northeastern Railroad Company camp to gloat about what he had done.

During the Age of Lynching, the media became accustomed to framing lynching theatrically, as a drama with conventions of its own. These often involved a sensationalized rape, a manhunt, and grisly play-by-play accounts with editorial commentary.[29] All of this dramatic framing was about to be applied to Milan. In fact, the news reports and coroner's records cling so closely to the standard lynching script, they make his demise look inevitable. By these lights, his calamity almost writes itself. The only real anomaly is that Wilde is part of it.

Milan's story follows the standard lynching pattern so perfectly that it is both unique in its particulars and totally predictable in its general outline. And that should make us suspicious about the so-called 'facts' of his case. The story's sensationalism suggests that the truth was twisted, adulterated, and moulded into a tale that would fit the era's preference for the spectacular. This development was consistent with the values of a culture fascinated by participatory spectacles like minstrel shows (where, for a long time, the audience regularly clambered on stage to jump Jim Crow alongside the blackface performers) and ethnographic exhibits like P.T. Barnum's 'What is It?' that invited spectators to question the humanity of the 'creature' set before them.

Late nineteenth-century Americans imagined lynchings as spectacles—public performances of torture where mobs were invited to join in.[30] Even when individuals didn't participate in person, the press invited them to do so by proxy through gory human interest stories that actively engaged readers. By 'setting the scene, assigning motivations to actors, predicting action, and explaining or justifying it,' these new forms of journalism fed the public's appetite for participatory drama.[31] The rise of the interview and the human interest story gave readers the ability to 'witness' lynchings as part of their everyday lives.[32] These sensationalized news reports brought home gruesome events with a level of detail never seen before. This was why the novelist Charles Chestnutt called them 'noospapers.'[33] Over breakfast, Americans could open the morning 'noospapers,' read about a recent stomach-turning murder, feel a jolt of shock, then put the paper down, go to their jobs, earn their daily bread and never give the lynching another thought.[34] The case was closed as soon as readers put the newspaper down.

But Milan Howard's real story was not an open-and-shut case. Back at the New Orleans and Northeastern Railroad Company camp, on the night of Saturday, 10 June 1882, he supposedly told one of his fellow-laborers about the rape. Before long, Bonfouca was up in arms. A search party was quickly assembled, and several suspects were arrested. The rape victim was 'still suffering from the injuries received' and so traumatized that she had lost the power to speak.[35] When she saw the suspects lined up, she said she did not recognize her assailant among them. It was conjectured that this was 'owing to the fact that the assault had been committed in the dark.' Next, one of Milan's fellow labourers was arrested and, to protect himself, he gave Milan up. A justice of the peace hunted the teenager down and set a date for his trial later that week.[36]

On Sunday, 11 June, the day after Milan's alleged crime, Wilde was nearly a thousand miles away, lecturing in Cincinnati, Ohio. In the days and nights that followed, Milan sat in St Tammany Parish prison awaiting his trial, while Wilde and his valet sat in a train chugging southwards towards New Orleans. He was scheduled to speak at the city's Grand Opera House at the end of the week. By then, Milan would be dead.

Wilde kicked off his Southern tour on 13 June in Memphis, Tennessee with performances that were even more theatrical than before. After the curtain rose, he sauntered onto a stage set up to look like an American drawing room, with a table and chair, as well as sofas and pictures. At a reception afterwards, he flirted with the pretty daughter of a wealthy Irishman who had come to the United States as a labourer and made his fortune by inventing a compress that could press a bale of cotton into half its size.[37] In Vicksburg, Mississippi, Wilde witnessed a coroner's inquest into a shootout between two men who had squabbled over a raft of timber. 'This was the first instance of murder that had come under his observation in America,' he told the *Daily Picayune*.[38] At Vicksburg, he visited the Civil War entrenchments that had sheltered the leader of the Union Army, General Grant, until he had ensured the Confederates' surrender and the end of the Civil War.[39]

On 15 June, Wilde's train headed towards the Louisiana border, towards the region where a sheriff was then accompanying Milan from prison to his trial. In St Tammany Parish, whites were then directing a great deal of hostility towards blacks. Recently, white vandals had twice broken into the 'colored' schoolhouse, stolen the chalk, poured the ink bottles over the tables and benches, and scratched obscenities over the door.[40] On their way to court, Milan and the sheriff were intercepted by sixty mounted men intent on revenging the rape. The mob had already decided the 15-year-old was guilty; it wasn't going to wait for the parish judge to tell them any different. The vigilantes took Milan hostage, placed a noose around his neck, and fastened it to the Bonfouca bridge. Then, he allegedly made a full confession, apologized for his crime, and begged for mercy.[41]

At this very moment, a Pullman with an enormous O-S-C-A-R-W-I-L-D-E sash allegedly came chugging down the track. From far off in the background, it rushed into the scene where Milan was pleading for his life. What happened next depends on which newspaper you believe. Some reports claimed Wilde was sympathetic to Milan's case, saying 'Oscar saw the hanging from a car window. The negro was a preacher, and his wild, eloquent appeals for mercy moved the aesthetic traveller greatly, but did not affect the lynchers, who quickly suspended him from a railroad bridge.'[42] About a week later, an enhanced report implied that Wilde's defence had provoked the vigilantes to a quicker kill:

> At Bonfouca, Louisiana, the train in which Oscar Wilde was travelling was stopped to give the passengers a view of a lynching. A negro preacher had made a criminal assault on a white woman and the mob had a rope around his neck. He was eloquent in his pleas for his life and his supplications deeply moved Oscar, but the lynchers were not made of aesthetic stuff: they yanked the miscegenating moke to a telegraph pole and made dead meat of him instanter.[43]

Few of the newspapers outside Louisiana mentioned Milan by name, but most of them mentioned Wilde. To be clear: it wasn't Milan's lynching that was newsworthy to these publications, it was Wilde's involvement. Of course, this was entirely in keeping with the period's conventions for sensationalizing lynchings. And it strongly hinted at foul play.

The day after the lynching, the Acting Coroner of St Tammany Parish filed his report. 'A yellow man, aged about 24 or 25 years of age, came to his death by hanging by the neck and sundry gun[shots] done in his body by parties unknown.'[44] The mob of sixty lynchers who had killed the prematurely aged 15-year-old was never identified. Black parishioners held a meeting to protest Milan's pitiless killing, but nothing came of it.[45] Milan Howard's mutilated body was finally laid to rest on the outskirts of Bonfouca. His case was never reopened.

And Wilde? Did he intervene? Wilde's train could never have stopped in Bonfouca because there were no railroads that went there. The railroad that Milan was working on was the only one that would have taken Wilde anywhere near Bayou Bonfouca, and it was still under construction in 1882. The line was not completed until March 1883, and the first train didn't roll along the rails until seven months later.[46] Instead, Wilde travelled on the Illinois Central Railroad for the north–south portions of his journey. His train would have skirted the marshy frontierland of St Tammany Parish, but it would not have come close to the place where Milan Howard breathed his last. Wilde could not have seen the lynching. The story was a hoax, a pseudo-event concocted by the media.[47]

Fake news like this tells us a lot about what people wanted to believe. Looking back, it almost seemed inevitable that a culture enamoured of celebrity razzle dazzle and panicked by race would stir Wilde into this gruesome mixture. The fake news about the lynching revealed what people were willing to imagine was true about Wilde.

Yet the hoax's mixture of fact and fiction also signalled a social problem greater than any Wilde and his managers might be able to master. By the century's last decades, Negrophobia and Celtophobia were as joined as the proverbial horse and carriage. That was the reason Wilde had been linked to Milan Howard. As one report put it, 'Oscar Wilde has found out that negrophobia is not yet extinct in the South.'[48] Nor was Celtophobia.

Linking together fears about the Irish and blacks was by then a long-standing practice. Among intellectuals and so-called advanced thinkers it had actually become common practice to align the two. Many considered it the logical outcome of the 'evidence' offered by the era's cutting-edge racial science. As a result, public speakers like Edward A. Freeman, the Oxford don who took to the American lecture circuit in 1881–2, found audiences surprisingly receptive to white supremacist ideas.[49] To persuade white Americans to see themselves as part of the imperial federation that he and other intellectuals had taken to calling 'Greater Britain,' Freeman correlated 'the Irish difficulty' in Britain to 'the negro difficulty' in America.[50] His exercise in comparative ethnology proposed a simple solution: lynching. 'Very many approved when I suggested that the best remedy for whatever was amiss would be if every Irishman should kill a negro and be hanged for it,' Freeman reported.[51] He claimed that dissenters only disagreed 'on the grounds that, if there were no Irish and no negroes, they would not be able to get any domestic servants.'

Freeman's virulence had been anticipated at mid-century by many others including the physician Robert Knox ('the source of all evil lies in *the race*, the Celtic race of Ireland,' he wrote), by Sidney and Beatrice Webb's comments on their visit to Ireland ('we detest them, as we should the Hottentots'), by Carlyle's belief that the solution to the 'Irish Question' was to 'black-lead them and put them over with the niggers,' and by Kingsley's return from Ireland 'haunted by the human chimpanzees

I saw along the hundred miles of that horrible country.'[52] Kingsley concluded, 'to see white chimpanzees is dreadful; if they were black, one would not feel it so much.'[53] Freeman would not be the last Victorian to make the correlation. Only a few years later, John Beddoe's *The Races of Britain* proposed an 'index of nigrescence' that proved the Irish were more Negroid than the English.[54] As for Victorian Oxford's most famous Irish undergraduate, Freeman said he had never heard of Oscar Wilde until he saw his name spelled out 'in large letters on the walls, as his photographs, and various attitudes, were to be seen in the windows, at Washington and at several other places.'[55] (See Plate 40.) It was only by travelling thousands of miles away from the university that Freeman eventually discovered the young Irish aesthete whose college rooms had once been less than a mile away from his own. When he declared that Wilde looked like the 'last of the Mohawks,' the *Oxford Magazine* made light of the slur by claiming that Freeman was only hostile to 'the negroes, the Irish, the Chinese, and Mr. Oscar Wilde.'[56]

16 June 1882, New Orleans. On the morning the *Daily Picayune* came to interview Wilde, his hotel room was scented with cologne water and he was in a good mood. The aesthete enthusiastically told the interviewer about the 'picturesqueness' of Southern Negroes and joked about owning a Louisiana plantation with pretty magnolias.[57] 'I have nothing to do with commerce and what is called progress. I am a student of art,' he said. That only partly explained why the South looked like an antebellum fantasia to him. The other reason was that his mother had probably spoon-fed him Southern pre-Civil War nostalgia alongside other titbits of her family folklore. Despite the prejudice swirling around him, he told his New Orleans interviewer that Southerners were 'more agreeable and courteous than Northerners.'

On the same day, thirty miles away, Bonfouca's Acting Coroner was examining Milan Howard's wounded corpse.[58] He made a note of the gunshot gashes in the teenager's body and the damage to his neck. In newsrooms around the United States, journalists would soon invent stories about how Wilde had 'been a spectator at a recent Louisiana lynching.'[59] Some would wryly editorialize that 'everything has been done to make his stay in the United States agreeable.'[60]

On that day in New Orleans, the contrast between the negrified Paddy 'Wilde' and the sophisticated Irish aesthete presently being interviewed by the *Daily Picayune* could not have been more egregious. But there were greater surprises in store. During this interview, Wilde suddenly opened up to the press about his white supremacist uncle, John Kingsbury Elgee. Speranza's adventurous brother had long been resident in Rapides Parish, close to where Milan Howard's body awaited burial. Elgee's name had once been legend in this Louisiana locality but now he was largely forgotten. Until this moment, Wilde had rarely spoken about his slave-owning uncle.[61] Yet now he felt compelled to brandish his family's Confederate history and bring America in on the secret.

Chapter 15

The Confederate

John Kingsbury Elgee's extraordinary rags-to-riches story was a familiar one in the Wilde family home. Born in 1812, John was nearly 10 years old when his little sister, Speranza, came into the world. Family life among the Elgees was tumultuous. Their passions ran high, as did their debts.[1] As a result, they often moved house. After a stint at Trinity College Dublin, John quickly married a woman a decade older than him, and fathered a daughter. By the time he was 19, John and his new family had emigrated from Ireland. They sailed from Belfast into New Orleans aboard the *Planter*, and the ship's name became John's destiny.[2]

By the age of 38, he had become wealthy: he owned a Louisiana sugar plantation and thirteen slaves, whose ages ranged from 3 to 55.[3] Judge Elgee, as he was known by then, had become a respected lawyer, politician, and a distinguished member of Southern society. After his first wife died, he took for his second bride a well-to-do French Louisiana widow almost two decades his senior. That union produced a handsome, dark-eyed son, Charles Ledoux Elgee, who attended Harvard Law School and later went to Mexico as a representative of the President of the United States.[4]

The lavishly decorated home of the Louisiana Elgees had three enormous libraries dedicated to its fine book collection. Financial concerns were no impediment to Judge Elgee's love of fine art. Rumour had it he had spent $1,200 on a single painting.[5] By 1860, his personal estate was valued at $405,000. It later grew to include three plantations, 9,600 acres, and 515 slaves. It was said to be worth almost a million dollars. Years later, when Wilde arrived in the region, some assumed he had come to claim his family inheritance.

When the Civil War broke out, in 1860, Judge Elgee defended his lands by leading the local breakaway movement.[6] Delegated to the 1861 Louisiana Secession Convention by his parish, Judge Elgee put his big, whirling signature at the centre of the state's 1861 Declaration of Secession from the United States. 'The union now subsisting between Louisiana and other States, under the name of *The United States of America* is hereby dissolved,' the ordinance read.[7] The state's citizens were thereby absolved of their allegiance to the American government and Louisiana declared herself sovereign and independent. Showing the family flair for art, Judge Elgee helped design Louisiana's Confederate state flag.[8] Its thirteen horizontal stripes and large star symbolized 'the star of Louisiana [that] has arisen to take her place in the political firmament,' Judge Elgee told delegates at the state convention.[9] Praising the defenders of the Confederate States of America, he predicted that 'their struggles, their trials, and the crowning achievement of their labors, shall live while civilization lasts in the memory of the philosopher, the statesman, the philanthropist and the Christian.'[10]

Judge Elgee essentially became a New World aristocrat. Defending the planter class was part and parcel of the Confederate agenda.[11] Southern patricians believed in 'a government of gentlemen, of men of money, men of brains who hold slaves,' historian Nancy Eisenberg observes. In short, they believed in 'a government resembling that of the aristocratic Old World.' During the War, Judge Elgee served as companion and civil adviser to Confederate General Richard Taylor, the Commander of the District of Western Louisiana. Judge Elgee's son, Charles Ledoux Elgee, joined the Louisiana Militia and served as General Taylor's chief of staff.[12]

1864 proved a painful year for the Louisiana Elgees and their Dublin kin. It was that year that Charles, who had earned a reputation for being a clear-headed, efficient officer with excellent judgement, jeopardized himself for the sake of a fellow soldier. While riding through hail and rain to his compatriot's rescue, Charles was captured by the opposing camp. Afterwards, he was driven to New Orleans, and imprisoned during the fever season. He soon fell ill. While in captivity, Charles was informed that his father, Judge Elgee, had died.[13] Eulogized by the *New York Times* as 'one of the most accomplished gentlemen in the country,'

Judge Elgee was remembered as a hero.[14] His rise to planter and political mover transformed him into a celebrated national figure. A few months later, in the autumn, Charles died of fever. He was 28 years old.[15]

Nearly two decades later, Oscar arrived in Louisiana amid rumours that he had come to take his share of the Elgee fortune. But by the time he reached New Orleans, in mid-June 1882, the million-dollar plantation had long disappeared. Before the end of the Civil War, it had been burned to the ground by federalists. Afterwards, it was revealed that Judge Elgee had heavily mortgaged the estate, and virtually sunk it into worthlessness. It was left to his heirs to discover the enormous loans on which he had built his lavish home and indulged his luxurious tastes. In the end, his descendants were left to split $10,250 between themselves.[16] The secret of his success was to live on credit.

Judge Elgee was proudly remembered in the South and so the more Wilde talked about his illustrious uncle, the more Southerners warmed to Aestheticism. News that the aesthete was 'a nephew of our former distinguished fellow-citizen' made them 'give him credit for having talent, upon the faith of his uncle's recognized ability.'[17] When Speranza heard that Oscar had paid public tribute to her brother, she beamed with pride. 'I am glad they remember Judge Elgee & receive his nephew so brilliantly,' she peacocked.[18] 'You are certainly making a mark in American history.'

While her son was basking in the glow of the American Elgees, the Wilde family was in trouble in England. 'You appear to have a career of triumph—we a career of endless descent,' Speranza complained in one of her typical letters.[19] Gifted with a prodigious imagination and a tendency to catastrophize, she envisioned the worst. When Oscar returned to London, she anticipated, 'you will find us bankrupt.'[20] Yet Speranza had legitimate cause for concern. Extravagance was a trait of Elgee men that, left unchecked, could lead to ruin. Her father's debts had to be paid off by her mother, her American brother's glory had been built on a heap of debt, and her own sons were accumulating a tidy pile of their own.[21] While Oscar was in the United States, his unpaid bills were arriving at his mother's door. Panicked, she took to signing her letters 'la povera Madre,' to drive home the idea of the family's poverty.[22]

Another Elgee family trait was a fondness for white supremacy. Speranza thought the English and the Celts were equal, first-class racial types that towered above other races, like pinnacles of humanity. She rejected England's domination of Ireland because she thought the people of both nations inherently equal. 'No other race on earth can now hope to rival or conquer them.'[23] Both the Irish and the English were 'preeminently the world-leaders,' she argued, and were 'destined to rule the world.' White Americans (specifically those of Teutonic-Celtic descent) would share this brilliant future, she believed.

The example of her Confederate brother, Judge Elgee, aligned with Speranza's own conviction that certain whites were destined to become 'the great levers of humanity.' She envisioned this as a eugenic purge of 'other races [that] are stationary or retrogressive... to build a better and nobler humanity.' In time, she pictured the Irish and the English dominating 'all other tribes and nations that stand in the way of these two great destined races.' She noted that the races she deemed obstructive and inferior were already 'disappearing from the earth—the half-souled Negro, the Red Indian of the prairies, the miserable Gnomes that guard the portals of the gold lands of the Pacific, as well as the luxurious, sensuous Oriental.'

Although she expressed her ideas dramatically, her vision of white power triumphant was not that eccentric for the time. The nineteenth century's imperialist Zeitgeist coincided with the popularization of the idea of 'Greater Britain,' a convenient moniker that bracketed Britain's worldwide colonies.[24] Advocates of Greater Britain sought to link the mother country to her white colonies through an imperial federation, and so Greater Britain basically became a polite way for the British to talk about places in the world where there were 'people like us.'

Greater Britain was a state of mind as well as a political philosophy—a broad phenomenon that encompassed Celtophiles like Speranza and Celtophobes like Edward A. Freeman, the Oxford don who didn't know Wilde but still thought him objectionable simply because he was Irish. The common denominators of both these positions were Negrophobia and white supremacy. For a long time, British imperialists had used their so-called 'racial and cultural superiority' to justify their dominance of Asian and African colonies.[25] They claimed that it gave Britain the right to lord it over countries populated by 'inferior' indigenous peoples. Fans of Greater Britain like Speranza and Freeman went a step further. They believed in a colonial pecking order based on skin colour and ethnicity. This resulted in a colour-coding of colonies whereby those with white skins migrated to the top of the British Imperial pile and those with darker skins gathered at the bottom. It was essentially white supremacy by another name. At the top of the heap were Britain's self-styled 'settler colonies' (modern-day Australia, Canada, New Zealand, and parts of South Africa) substantially populated by people of British extraction and therefore thought of as 'extensions of the British state transplanted to distant parts of the globe but retaining an organic connection with the mother country.' Americans were generally considered part of 'Greater Britain beyond the Atlantic,' as an English travel writer put it in *Our American Cousins*, his 1882 travelogue about his visit to the United States.[26]

The racism baked into Greater Britain was almost never acknowledged explicitly because it didn't need to be. To the Victorians, it was obvious that it was modelled on traditional racial hierarchies. The striking similarities shared by this imperialist mindset and the racist attitudes that propelled the Confederate States of America hardly need comment. However, they provide a clue to how a young Irishman—like Judge Elgee or his nephew Oscar—could come to the American South and end up admiring white supremacy.

Indeed, in Oscar's case, the process of indoctrination had begun at his mother's Dublin dinner table, where he first heard about his uncle and Irish nationalists like John Mitchel, Young Ireland's most fiery speaker. By the time Mitchel took a seat at the Wildes' table, in 1872, he had already lived in Tennessee and Virginia, owned slaves, and warred for the Confederacy. During the Civil War, he had been in the ambulance corps and edited a pro-Confederate newspaper.[27] Two of his sons gave their lives to the Southern cause. A die-hard believer in the Cause, he remained faithful to the South even in defeat. After the end of the Civil War, he was briefly imprisoned in Virginia's Fortress Monroe alongside Jefferson Davis, the President of the Confederacy, and Clement C. Clay, a suspect in Lincoln's assassination.[28] Mitchel recoiled from the popular Anglo-American association between Irishmen and blacks. In a speech about the Famine that had crippled Ireland, he asked his audience, 'Can you picture in your mind a race of white men reduced to this condition? White men! Yes the highest and purest blood and breed of men.'[29] He dreamed of a free Ireland that would own slave plantations. To him, the whiteness of the Irish was their badge of nobility. Only a few months earlier, in San Francisco in spring 1882, Wilde had flaunted his family connection to Mitchel, who was a hero to the majority of Irish-Americans. In his lecture, Wilde said that he had been impressed by Mitchel's 'eagle eye and impassioned manner' at his parents' table.[30]

More and more, Wilde began to defend his own whiteness by using logic that resembled Speranza's and Mitchel's. 'I do not wish to see the empire dismembered,' Wilde told the *New Orleans Picayune* in 1882, 'but only to see the Irish people free, and Ireland still as a willing and integral part of the British Empire' so that it would not be relegated to one of the 'weak and insignificant places in the panorama of nations.'[31] By the summer, Wilde was talking about the Confederacy, and comparing the situation of white Southern planters to that of the Irish at home. 'The case of the South in the Civil War,' he said, 'was to my mind much like that of Ireland today. It was a struggle for autonomy, self-government for a people.' When Wilde spoke about the Confederacy, Southerners sat up and took notice. The aesthete's idea of whiteness, it turned out, was not far off from theirs.

'Jefferson Davis is the man I would like most to see in the United States,' Wilde announced, making public his admiration for the man who would have been President if the South had won the Civil War.[32] No sooner had he made this declaration than his train was plunging through emerald green landscapes to Beauvoir, Davis's white-porticoed residence in Biloxi, Mississippi.

By now, Wilde's latest moves looked like tactical manoeuvres. Since his image had been darkened and distorted, he seemed desperate to assert his whiteness, his badge of nobility. The Davises were acquainted with Wilde's extended family: they had known Judge Elgee and Richard Henry Wilde, a distant relation on Oscar's father's side.[33]

Wilde's pilgrimage meant a detour of several hundred miles. 'That's a long way to go to meet anyone,' he said, 'but not too far to go to see such a man as Jefferson Davis.'[34] He told a New Orleans journalist that he 'had an intense admiration for the chief of the Southern Confederacy.'[35] That wasn't idle talk. He explained that Davis's 'fall, after such an able and gallant pleading of his own cause, must necessarily arouse sympathy.' Although he was talking about Davis's war, he could easily have been describing his own troubled mission. The Confederate's idealistic, aristocratic disposition and nobility in the face of disappointment may have reminded Wilde of his own temperament. Even in defeat, Davis seemed heroic to Wilde and, besides, it was more interesting to examine someone else's failures than to dwell on his own.

As a young man, Davis had been a high-spirited student at West Point, then a slave owner, planter, and a Mississippi Senator. Although he could demonstrate moderation, he was hampered by a cold, litigious nature and didn't have Abraham Lincoln's gift for speechmaking. He failed to inspire ordinary citizens to join his cause and alienated those who might have been his natural allies: planters (whose concerns about black emancipation Davis ignored) and poor whites (who resented that the Civil War had become 'a rich man's war and a poor man's fight').[36] At the end of the Civil War, Davis had been savagely lampooned because he attempted to escape capture by dressing in an unmanly disguise—his wife's coat and shawl. Davis's defeat held a gruesome fascination for Wilde, who had tracked the leader's 'career with much attention.'[37]

On his way to Beauvoir, Wilde acquired *Southern Poems of the War*, an emotional medley of nostalgia for the Lost Cause in which the Confederate President loomed large. 'Each heart-string that throbs at the South' throbs for Davis, one poem vowed.[38] 'In the name of God!' another cried out, 'Stand for the Southern rights!' Wilde read the poems en route, alongside *The Rise and Fall of the Confederate Government*, a 1,666-page history co-authored by Davis and his wife. He declared it 'a masterpiece' and told a reporter that he had read the book 'with the keenest interest and delight.'[39] Others flatly declared it unreadable, but Wilde would only concede that 'the elaborate detail of military manoeuvre is at times a little burdensome.'

On 27 June, Wilde walked through the Davises' white portico and was welcomed by Mrs Davis and Winnie, her 18-year-old daughter. A talented artist and musician, Winnie came to be known as 'the Daughter of Confederacy.'[40] She was fascinated by Irish history and would publish *An Irish Knight of the Nineteenth Century*, a book on Robert Emmet, the eighteenth-century Dubliner who led the last rising of the United Irishmen and went to his grave a national hero.[41] Wilde's visit passed pleasantly despite the fact that Davis made himself scarce. The aesthete's enthusiasm could not make up for the fact that his hero was a withered 74-year-old who had no interest whatsoever in him. But Oscar would not quit Beauvoir without leaving his mark. On the morning before his departure, he autographed a Sarony portrait of himself and placed it conspicuously on his host's bureau. When Davis picked up the picture, he learned that his guest's respect for him was as high as ever. 'To Jefferson Davis,' the appreciative inscription read, 'in all loyal admiration from Oscar Wilde, June '82 Beauvoir.'[42]

After they had lost the Civil War, Confederate veterans perpetuated the idea of the honourable South. The myth of the Lost Cause helped heal the wounds of the conquered by giving them a tradition to cling to. As historian William C. Davis explains, mythmaking is part and parcel of defeat. 'Out of any conflict, the losers create more myths than the winners. It is hardly a surprise. After all, winners have little to explain to themselves. They won. For the loser, however, coping with defeat, dealing with it personally and explaining it to others, places enormous strains on the ego, self-respect, and sense of self-worth of the defeated.'[43]

Wilde recognized in the Lost Cause a mentality similar to the idea of the lost Irish nobility. The Lost Cause was a powerful myth that memorialized the honourable South—just like the Celts whose destruction by the English Wilde had described in his lectures at St Paul and San Francisco. This was why he identified with a class of ex-combatants like Jefferson Davis who imagined their defeat had denied them their destiny. The kinship between Ireland and the South spoke to Wilde intimately. In his retelling, the Lost Cause and the Irish cause almost became one: the defeated white Southern planter aristocracy were the counterparts to his Irish kinsmen. This had the added benefit of encouraging Southerners to see him as white.

Now that Wilde was more experienced in the ways of the American press, he seemed to want white Southerners to see was that he was no different from them. His identification had a noticeable effect on how he handled interviews. When reporters angled for a soundbite on Confederacy, he deftly moved the question over to Ireland and Home Rule. The bait-and-switch tactic got him noticed all over the South. He might begin by praising Jefferson Davis, 'a man of the keenest intellect' with 'an enthusiasm that is as fervent as it is faultless,' he told the *Atlanta Constitution*.[44] But then he would immediately zig-zag towards Home Rule, saying, 'We in Ireland are fighting for the principle of autonomy against empire, for independence against centralization, for the principles for which the South fought.' Rounding up, he would return to the Confederates' Lost Cause, and call it a great one. 'So it was a matter of immense interest and pleasure to me to meet the leader of such a great cause....The principles for which Mr. Davis in the South went to war cannot suffer defeat.' The Irish Cause was the meaty issue but it was stuffed in between two white-bread slices slathered with compliments about the Lost Cause. It was a classic 'sandwich' approach. It worked. Soon Southern newspapers like the *Macon Telegram and Messenger* were on his side. 'OSCAR WILDE, Esq. is a hard-looking piece of humanity, but he has the highest respect for the late glorious Confederacy. That covers a multitude of sins.'[45] The intricacies of his pro-Confederate positioning eluded many Americans, however. For the most part, they continued to equate his Irishness with blackness and to show their distaste in poisonous ways.

On the fourth of July in Atlanta, Georgia, Wilde attempted to board a sleeping car with his African American valet. The pair intended to ride together to Savannah. Wilde was promptly informed that it was against company policy to let African Americans into the sleeping car. Wilde protested, and declined to change his itinerary or arrangements. According to the *Atlanta Constitution* and *New York Times* reports, 'Mr. Wilde said that he had never been interfered with before, and persisted in having his darkey retain his sleeping car ticket.'[46] Wilde was in the right. The 1875 Civil Rights Act had granted all Americans—regardless of race—the right to access public facilities, including public transportation, trains, restaurants, and theatres. Yet the sleeping car porter pulled Wilde's valet aside, and whispered that the train was routed to go through Jonesboro, Georgia and that 'if the people saw a Negro in the sleeper they would mob him.' The lynching threat proved effective and Wilde's valet disappeared into another carriage. Wilde's tour was not derailed, but a grim spectre hung over it.

For months now, the aesthete had been attacked by proxy. No longer. There were indications that some Americans wished to do to the visiting Irish aesthete exactly what the lynchers had already done to Milan Howard in Bayou Bonfouca.[47] One fake news report tracked the period's mania for macabre spectacle more closely than any other. Colorado's *Leadville Daily Herald* claimed that Wilde was dragged from the stage, thrown in jail, and charged with obtaining money under false pretences since his lecture wasn't worth the price of admission. Published under the title 'Oscar Wilde Hung,' the gruesome hoax claimed that his American lecture tour ended with his lynching.

PART THREE
1883–1900

To arrive at what one really believes, one
must speak through lips different from
one's own.

– *The Critic as Artist*

Chapter 16

Success is a Science

Shortly before Wilde returned to London, in January 1883, the first history of the Aesthetic Movement was published. Walter Hamilton's *The Aesthetic Movement in England* gave considerable attention to Wilde's career as an art lecturer in the United States, where his role was to explain '*real Aestheticism* [to] our rich, clever, but not particularly *cultured* transatlantic cousins.'[1] The Harvard pranksters were a case in point ('shallow-pated imbeciles,' according to Hamilton). Wilde, by contrast, was a thoroughgoing gentleman and 'scarcely the man to condescend to become an advertising medium' for a Gilbert and Sullivan opera. Hamilton capped his eulogy by praising Wilde's dandyism, although he regretted that 'what suits *his* figure might not in all its details be adapted for the everyday wear of ordinary mortals of less heroic proportions and statuesque form.'

Wilde's heroic proportions dwarfed the other men in Hamilton's book as well. *The Aesthetic Movement in England*'s longest chapter ran to thirty pages, and it was dedicated entirely to 'Mr. Oscar Wilde.' The importance of the giants on whose shoulders Wilde stood was reduced, and so their place in aesthetic culture shrunk proportionately. The Pre-Raphaelites got seven pages. Ruskin's *Complete Works* ran to thirty-nine volumes, but he only got ten pages. Whistler's name only appeared a handful of times. Wilde's growing reputation had crowded out his eminent predecessors. By making so much room for Oscar, Hamilton created a skewed but compelling narrative that would come to dominate the story of Aestheticism. Naturally, Speranza was delighted. She immediately sent for twelve copies of the book and wrote a letter about *The Aesthetic Movement in England* in which she congratulated her son for rewriting their family history.[2] 'You see the *Wildes* are destined for celebrity & pinnacles—Nothing will put us or keep *us* under a bushel!'

She predicted Oscar would be celebrated by mobs of fans on his return to England.[3] On board the transatlantic steamer, he told the *Liverpool Post*'s interviewer that 'his lecturing tour was the most successful undertaking of the kind ever known.'[4] As soon as the journalist tried to probe his claim, Wilde rebuffed him. 'Everything one says should be in mystery,' the aesthete replied, confounding the unfortunate interrogator, who dutifully wrote down Wilde's self-congratulatory opinion, published it, and let readers gulp it down as if it were fact.

When Oscar came back from America, Speranza was astonished at how much his reputation had changed. Inevitably, their relationship would be altered, too. 'I feel quite nervous,' she admitted to the famous man who was returned to her instead of the boy she had sent off.[5] Even the English acknowledged him now. 'How shall we entertain the great Aesthete—all the world here yesterday [was] talking of you. The last *Whitehall Review* says you have been paid £5000. This has greatly influenced London. They now look on you with awe.' But his awe-inspiring reputation was the result of another factual error. The dollar sign had been mistaken for the sterling symbol, and so his $5,605 earnings were magnified to five times their actual value, which was nearer £1,000.[6]

Wilde's success was post-truth. By then, such distortion had become the norm. Feelings fed rumours. Mistakes fattened into lies. An eager public snapped up these morsels of 'information' and swallowed them so quickly that they were rarely questioned. And this, in turn, plumped up his reputation. 'We hear in many quarters of your success & London *at last* is forced *to believe it*,' Speranza told him.[7] Random cab drivers asked her whether she was Oscar Wilde's mother. Even the milkman had bought his picture. The aesthete had made his mark.

One of Oscar's admirers sent a proxy to plead her case to Speranza months before her son's return to England. To encourage a match, Constance Lloyd's great-uncle paid Speranza a long visit and praised the girl wholeheartedly. Constance was a thoroughgoing aesthete: a student of the St John's Wood School of Art, a talented potter, and a collector of blue-and-white china who frequented the Grosvenor Gallery.[8] To top it all off, she had Irish parentage. Speranza was so excited that a marriage might be in the offing that she told Oscar she had barely managed to suppress her impulse to blurt out, 'I would like her for a daughter-in-law!'[9]

From the Lloyd family's point of view, Oscar's transformation made his union with Constance more plausible than it had been two years earlier, when the pair had met for the first time at a Dublin party. On his visit with Speranza, Constance's great-uncle noted that Oscar was 'quite a celebrity now.' That strengthened his earning potential, and made him a more likely prospect than a suitor with debts of £1,500 would otherwise have been.[10] Constance only had an allowance of £250 a year, so it was a necessary precaution for the Lloyds to ascertain whether Wilde could afford to keep a wife. As the courtship progressed, Constance's family warmed to Wilde, who had finally cut his long hair. 'They all think him so improved in appearance,' she said.[11]

'Prepare yourself for an astounding piece of news!' Constance wrote her brother on 26 November 1883; 'I am engaged to Oscar Wilde and perfectly and insanely happy.' Persuaded of the couple's suitability for each other, Constance's grandfather angeled the alliance with a £5,000 trust fund.[12] 'I am going to be married to a beautiful young girl called Constance Lloyd,' Oscar told Lillie Langtry.[13] He was as elated as his bride-to-be. He designed her engagement ring himself, forming a heart from pearls and diamonds (his favourite gemstone). He also gave her a pet monkey to keep her company while they were apart.[14] Constance and Oscar were married on 29 May 1884 in St James's Church, Sussex Gardens.[15] The gold wedding band he chose symbolized their unusual union. To the outside world, it appeared utterly conventional. But though it looked like one solid band, it was actually made of two interlocking rings. Applying a bit of pressure made them swivel apart. The ring's secret doubleness, with its portent of separate lives, would also have its place in their ill-fated marriage.

Financial concerns were the first to bring pressure to bear on the relationship. Before his wedding, a gruelling lecture tour across Britain and Ireland took him away from his fiancée to talk about his 'Personal Impressions of America' and 'The House Beautiful.'[16] Long into their marriage, he continued to travel widely to deliver his opinions on dress, art, and interior decoration. Although Wilde's celebrity didn't immediately translate into security, it did yield new opportunities to write and review. Another lucky break was the editorship of *Woman's World*, which he accepted in summer 1887.

By autumn, he had relaunched the magazine. Under his stewardship, *Woman's World* extended beyond the domestic sphere and much farther than 'the field of mere millinery and trimmings' that was then usual for ladies' magazines.[17] It would be more 'womanly' and less 'feminine,' as he put it in an ambitious statement of his vision for the publication. His boldest editorial move was to reject from the outset the idea of separate spheres for men and women. Instead, he aimed to produce content that would entice readers of both sexes. 'The cultivation of separate sorts of virtues and separate ideals of duty in men and women has led to the whole social fabric being weaker and unhealthier than it need be,' he believed.[18] This was not his mother's feminism. Although Speranza was extremely accomplished and well-read, she liked the Victorian idea that each sex had its own sphere of activity. 'If I were a Dictator, no girl should be taught to read and write. It is woman's mission to adorn life,' she told an interviewer.[19] Her son disagreed and adopted a more modern view of the matter.

Oscar's feminism was prompted by several positive influences. First among them was Constance. Married life gave him a privileged insight into the inner life of the kind of intelligent woman to which *Woman's World* would cater. By then, he and Constance had two young sons, Vyvyan and Cyril (see Plate 41). She balanced their care along with her work for the Rational Dress Society, her public speaking engagements to promote corset-free dressing, journalism, and reviewing for the *Lady's Pictorial*.[20] Wilde could be a hands-on father when it suited him. When the boys broke their toys, he fixed them.[21] He told them fairy tales, sang to them in Gaelic, and took them fishing. They loved playing tag with him, loved the smell of his cigarettes and eau-de-cologne, loved his beautifully tailored suits. Nothing delighted them more than seeing him on all fours on the nursery floor roaring like a lion, baying like a wolf, or neighing like a horse. To them, he was 'a smiling giant' who joyfully came down to their level.[22]

Another vital influence on Wilde's feminism were the changes in gender relations he had witnessed in the United States, and the friendships he formed with women's rights advocates like Julia Ward Howe. Wilde had met a great number of influential American women in 1882. During the first week alone, he met Jane Cunningham Croly, a feminist and journalist who introduced him to Louisa May Alcott, the author of *Little Women*. He also visited Mrs Paran Stevens, the wealthy Massachusetts-born leader of New York society, and attended receptions hosted by women philanthropists and art collectors. His advocacy of aesthetic culture made him familiar with women's sophisticated tastes. Editing demanded an attention to detail that was not natural to him, but it focused his eye, sharpened his style, and put him amid distinguished company (Thackeray and Dickens had been editors).[23] Being in a position to recruit writers enabled him to widen the circumference of his social circle to encompass leading women writers and socialites.

The prominence of American women in London had an improving effect on culture as a whole. 'The American invasion has done English society a great deal of good. American women are bright, clever, and wonderfully cosmopolitan,' he thought.[24] The magazine was to reflect this modern outlook. Luckily, he noticed that there wasn't a single periodical in England like the ones he had admired in the United States, he told Mrs Howe.[25] He had spotted a gap in the English magazine market and now he set about filling it.

From the beginning of his *Woman's World* editorship, Wilde planned to include portraits of the women making over America in their image, such as those, like Mrs Howe, who dominated the country's cultural life.[26] 'Nothing in the United States struck me more than the fact that the remarkable intellectual progress of that country is very largely due to the efforts of American women, who edit many of the most powerful magazines and newspapers, take part in the discussion of every question of public interest, and exercise an important influence upon the growth and tendencies of literature and art,' he explained in one of his first editorials.[27] American women were the role models. For their British sisters, there was *Woman's World*. In its pages, the woman reader was not addressed as an angel in the house, but as a thinking, feeling citizen. Her interests included happenings in fashionable London and Paris as well as in Oxbridge, and her ambitions telescoped to far-flung Egypt and Russia as well as to professions such as medicine, nursing, and elementary school teaching.

Thanks to the makeover Wilde gave it, *Woman's World* was heralded as 'the finest magazine with an exclusive appeal to women that has ever been published.'[28] Its high-society feminism was engineered to appeal to middle- and upper-class readers, but one year into Wilde's editorship, the magazine wasn't yet as profitable as the publisher wished it to be. That was probably because it was priced beyond the reach of its target readership. Instead of fixing that, the publisher took aim at Wilde. His behaviour was closely scrutinized. He was blamed for turning up late and leaving early. This was unfair. Though he bridled at regular office hours (his assistant described him as 'Pegasus in harness'), his creative commitment was clear. Besides, he had always preferred to look like a slacker while secretly grinding at his work. His editorship was no different. Over the last two years, on top of his editorial duties, he had produced seventy-two pieces for other periodicals and brought out a book of carefully crafted fairy stories, *The Happy Prince and Other Tales*.[29] By August 1889, the magazine's circulation had dwindled further. So, two years in, he quit *Woman's World* for good.

By a stroke of luck, it was around this time that the American publisher J. M. Stoddart popped into his life again. Stoddart had helped mastermind some of the American tour's coups—accompanying Wilde to visit Whitman and using Rennell Rodd's *Rose Leaf and Apple Leaf* to publish his first aesthetic manifesto. This time, in London, Stoddart would go one better. At first, Stoddart's proposal to introduce Wilde to Arthur Conan Doyle, an author then marginal to English literary society, hardly sounded like a date with destiny. Still, Wilde agreed to the meeting. The trio's evening went down in publishing history as the dinner that prompted Wilde to pen *The Picture of Dorian Gray* and Conan Doyle to write *The Sign of Four*, a sequel to Sherlock Holmes's first adventure.[30]

Critics and readers alike were scandalized by *The Picture of Dorian Gray*, his 'unclean, though undeniably amusing' 1890 novel about an older man's corrupting influence over a younger man with a fascinating personality.[31] 'Man is half angel and half ape, and Mr. Wilde's book has no real use if it be not to inculcate the "moral" that when you feel yourself becoming too angelic you cannot do better than rush out and make a beast of yourself,' the reviewer for the *Daily Chronicle* concluded.[32]

The following year, a second version appeared with a preface. It was his second manifesto. 'It is the spectator, and not life, that art really mirrors,' he wrote, as though warning the reader to look in the mirror if he did not like what he saw in the novel.[33] With polished, declarative sentences such as this one, Wilde attempted to deflect from the autobiographical elements of his tale. Ever since his American tour, deflection had been his go-to method for redirecting uncomfortable conversations and coping with personal, sensitive subjects. But closer inspection revealed cracks just beneath the preface's armoured surface. Despite his dandyish poker face, he sounded too defensive. It was an obvious bluff. By insisting that readers *not* look to life to find the experiences reflected in his novel, he was encouraging them to do just the opposite. And that was a risky way to introduce a novel made up of gleaming shards of hard, secret truth.

A few months later, during summer 1891, the poet Lionel Johnson dropped in on the Wildes and brought along Lord Alfred Douglas, an angel-faced 21-year-old Oxford student who went by the nickname 'Bosie.' (See Plate 42.) He looked like Dorian Gray come to life—beautiful, fickle, and amoral. Oscar was instantly infatuated. He treated him to tea and then introduced him to Constance. An illicit love story between Oscar and Bosie began that day. Though it was not the first scratch on the smooth, glassy surface of Mr and Mrs Wilde's domestic fairy tale, his relationship with Bosie was the one that would eventually crack his marriage and shatter it to pieces. Like a broken mirror held up to Wilde's reality, it reflected many facets of himself that he did not want to see.

'Life is a stormy sea, and my wife is a harbour of refuge,' he wrote in *The Wife's Tragedy*, the play he drafted that summer.[34] It was an ominous sentence that hinted at the precariousness of his marriage. Like Constance's wedding band, their two lives were swivelling apart. *The Wife's Tragedy* was also the title of a section of Coventry Patmore's 1854 poem, *The Angel in the House*, in which the angelic wife's 'tragedy' was her failure to satisfy her husband's desires.

Wilde dithered about his play's title, and later proposed to switch it to *A Good Woman*. In the end, he settled on *Lady Windermere's Fan*. From February 1892, with the play in rehearsals at the St James's Theatre, he headquartered himself in London's West End at the Albemarle Hotel. Soon he was no longer coming home to Constance. His publisher's premises were located close to the Albemarle, which was convenient because Wilde had recently fallen for Edward Shelley, a clerk who worked there.[35] The Bodley Head, the St James's Theatre, and the Albemarle Hotel became three coordinates forming a neat triangle that contained his increasingly messy life. Gradually, Wilde eschewed discretion, making grand gestures such as offering the 18-year-old clerk a signed copy of *The Picture of Dorian Gray* and taking him home to meet Constance.[36] Wilde's interest in the Bodley Head's clerk did not escape Shelley's colleagues, who referred to him as 'Miss Oscar' and 'Mrs Wilde.'[37]

From his experience in the United States, Wilde developed some distinctive ideas about drama and how to make a play succeed. His encounter with American popular entertainment had expanded his horizons.

In his early plays, there had been doubt and misdirection, but now a bracing tone of conviction invigorated his writing, and he had enough experience and know-how to carry off his plans. Having starry actors alongside his name on the bill would entice the public, but he knew that much more needed to be done to ensure a new theatrical venture didn't flop. 'What we want to do is to have all the real conditions of success in our hands,' he informed an actress shortly after his American tour. A play lived or died on the strength of its opening night, he told her. 'Success is a science; if you have the conditions, you get the result.'[38]

By now Wilde had an entourage in England, many of them younger men. He pressed them into service, just as he had done with the Harvard students so long ago. At the premiere of *Lady Windermere's Fan*, the American formula worked like a charm. It turned the play into Wilde's first successful dramatic production. Alongside it, he would launch his new symbol and use it to mark out his acolytes, just as the aesthetic sunflower once had.

'You have your place for the *première*?' he asked the painter-playwright Walford Graham Robertson in advance of the first night.

'Yes.'

'Now I want you to do something,' Wilde confided. 'Order a green carnation buttonhole for tomorrow night.'

'A green carnation? But there's no such thing.'

'No, I know there's no such thing but they arrange them some-how ... dye them, I suppose. I want a good many men to wear them tomorrow—it will annoy the public.'

'But why?' his young friend asked.

'It likes to be annoyed,' Wilde replied.

Robertson gave him a dubious glance. That was enough to make the whole evening's scheme tumble out of Wilde. On his play's opening night, he planned to astonish his audience. He would make life and art mirror each other.

'A young man on stage will wear a green carnation; people will stare at it and wonder,' Wilde said, alluding to Act 3 of *Lady Windermere's Fan*, in which a young dandy named Cecil Graham drops a hint about the strange flower's association with immorality. 'What on earth should we men do going about with purity and innocence?' Cecil Graham would ask. 'A carefully thought-out buttonhole is much more effective.'[39]

'They will look round the house and see every here and there more and more little specks of mystic green. "This must be some secret symbol," they will say. "What on earth can it mean?"'[40] Wilde knew what would happen next, he told Robertson. In his mind, he had already scripted the audience's reaction.

On 20 February 1892, at the opening night of *Lady Windermere's Fan*, both the actors and the audience performed exactly as Wilde had predicted. Inside the St James's Theatre, dapper young things like Robertson and Robert Ross swanned around with green carnations in their lapels. Those wearing the unnatural-looking flower looked like they'd been marked with a colour asterisk indicating their specialness. During the play, when Cecil Graham philosophized about his carefully thought-out corsage, he encouraged speculation about its coded meaning.

What was it? A new guessing game had been launched. Quite what the green carnation symbolized, everyone wanted to know. Some said the green carnation was a dainty sign for 'a specimen of epicene masculinity.' Others noted that every randy dandy was wearing it to 'each Randy-vous that's handy.'[41] The American science of success was working perfectly.

'I invented that flower,' Wilde later said.[42] It was another of his works of art, he claimed. In fact, the green carnation had been imported from Paris, where it was already fashionable among French men. For the fashionable young man 'in a state of Wilde-ness,' nothing would do but to join the vogue.[43] London's cosmopolitan set adopted it and, before long, Covent Garden and the Royal Arcade were doing a bustling trade in the unusual blossoms.[44]

What the common sunflower had been to the aesthetic 1880s, the green carnation would be to 1890s decadence. But unlike its predecessor the green carnation was a costly ornament. It symbolized Wilde's changing attitude to art and the coterie world to which he wanted to cater. At two to three shillings apiece, it was out of reach to most, and quickly became a status symbol.[45] His prerogatives had become more exclusive, and less populist. This was not Aestheticism for all, but Decadence for the few. As ever, imitations and impostors sprung up. Five minutes from the St James's Theatre, just off Piccadilly, a large sign in J. Pritchard's shop window announced, 'EXTRACT OF LILAC, Oscar Wilde *says*:—"It is the most delicate and delightful of all perfumes."'[46] The trade in fake green flowers blossomed, too. Fastening on a blue gardenia became the done thing among penny-pinching dandies who insisted 'that a title was a matter of temperament.'[47]

At the opening night of *Lady Windermere's Fan*, Wilde demonstrated to his audience exactly what a dandyish temperament was. So doing, he took the conditions of success into his own hands: he had written the play, but now he was also going to script its reception. By the time the curtain came down, the actors' lines had fizzed like crackers and burst forth like pinwheels, and the audience had laughed and clapped for a long time as the actors took their bows. It was then that Wilde came to the edge of the stage, struck a languorous pose, took a deep drag on his cigarette, paused, and exhaled. The whiff of his tobacco drifted across the theatre. There was a buzz of whispers, and the room swarmed with anticipation. Wilde looked out on the sea of appreciative faces, and calmly waited. The moment was his. 'Ladies and gentlemen,' he began,

> I have enjoyed this evening *immensely*. The actors have given us a
> *charming* rendering of a *delightful* play, and your appreciation has
> been *most* intelligent. I congratulate you on the *great* success of
> your performance, which persuades me that you think *almost* as
> highly of the play as I do myself.[48]

It had been a long time coming, but now he could spontaneously address crowds with all the wit he'd usually only been able to muster in private conversations and interviews. That night, he made it look easy.

But like everything else at the premiere, this had been carefully rehearsed. His little speech had probably been inspired by Aristophanes' *Clouds*, in which the poet steps forward from the chorus and candidly addresses the audience's vanity. 'It was because I believed you *sophisticated* spectators,' the bard tells his listeners, 'and took this comedy to be the cleverest of all my plays that I deemed it right for you to be the first to savour a work that caused me so much effort.'[49] Nobody noticed the similarity, however. And so what appeared to be an impromptu monologue passed into legend.

Like his 1882 lecture debut at which New York's glitterati crammed into Chickering Hall, the elegant white and gold St James's Theatre had been packed with a brilliant audience. There were plenty of recognizable faces including Lillie Langtry, George Bernard Shaw, Henry James, Frank Harris, Richard Le Gallienne, Mrs Bram Stoker (who, as Florence Balcombe, had been one of Wilde's first loves). Edward Shelley was also there. Wilde had slipped his 18-year-old lover a ticket along with a copy of *A House of Pomegranates*, the book of fairy tales he had recently published and dedicated to Constance.[50] Despite this touching acknowledgement, it did little to compensate for the callous disregard Wilde showed his wife. Only recently, his mother had stepped in, cautioning Oscar not to neglect Constance in public and, especially, at the opening night of *Lady Windermere's Fan*.[51] But Oscar was already far beyond her reach.

That night, Constance came to the premiere of *Lady Windermere's Fan* but she went home without her husband. It was not the first time she had done so and, by now, certain patterns were setting in. After the play, Wilde took Edward Shelley to a celebratory supper party.[52] Then he took him to bed at the Albemarle Hotel. 'It was very good of you,' the appreciative young man wrote afterwards to thank Wilde for the theatre ticket.[53]

On 29 June 1892, the 73-year-old American poet and activist Julia Ward Howe stood on the doorstep at 16 Tite Street.[54] Tucked near London's Chelsea Embankment, Mr and Mrs Wilde's red-brick, three-storey house resembled Mrs Howe's own bay-windowed Boston home, which Wilde had visited so many years ago. When she invited the aesthete to lunch in 1882, her scandalized neighbour, Colonel Thomas Wentworth Higginson, criticized her indifference to ladylike propriety. He grumbled openly in *The Woman's Journal*, where her name appeared alongside his on the masthead.[55] The function of 'women of high social position,' Higginson then wrote, was to act as guardian angels regulating the social turnstile.[56] A dereliction of duty such as Mrs Howe's jeopardized womankind, he catastrophized. Of course, Colonel Higginson didn't pass comment when men of equal social standing, like Mrs Howe's bon vivant brother, Sam Ward, lavished big New York City dinners on Oscar and dedicated poetry to him in the *New York World*.[57] It was only women's private largesse that threatened 'the public purity,' the Colonel scolded.[58]

Mrs Howe had heard it all before. It was just like Higginson, one of her late 'husband's old companions-in-arms,' as her daughters called him, to rattle the shackles in which her marriage had once held her.[59] Throughout her long marriage to Samuel Gridley Howe, an eminent philanthropist and humanitarian celebrated for his pioneering work with the blind, he had complained that her public work led to the dereliction of her private, domestic duties. Meanwhile, her husband

frittered away the wealth she had inherited from her New York bank-
ing family, interfered with her literary efforts and suffragist endeavours,
left her to bear the domestic burdens of their six children on her own,
and generally did his best to clip her wings. So when he died in 1876
and didn't leave her a penny or a house to live in, she began 'gadding
about, flapping her wings' again, as her children put it.[60] To earn money,
she lectured. And for two years she travelled the world, taking in
Europe, North Africa, and the Middle East, arriving in London for
the 1877 opening of the Grosvenor Gallery, popping in on Egyptian
princesses in Cairo, and meandering through the streets of Cyprus,
Jerusalem, and Bethlehem. Finally, she sailed back to Boston, where
her generous brother, Sam, had bought her a home.[61] Finally, as a
widow, she had a home of her own, to do with as she pleased. And in
1882 that included entertaining Wilde—more than once. It was, without
a doubt, the 'most sensational incident' of 1882, her daughter said.[62]

'When you are present,' Wilde told Mrs Howe in a private letter, 'the
air is cosmopolitan and the room seems to be full of brilliant people.'[63]
It was enough to make any woman blush (let alone one as old as his
mother). But Wilde went further still. He didn't want a room full of
people, he wanted to see her alone, he told her. 'There is no such thing
as dining with *you en famille*,' he wrote. 'No, *en famille* is impossible, but
to dine with you is one of the great privileges.' His flattering letters
brimmed with flirtatious appreciation. What passed between them was
like a look exchanged across a crowded room, a glance of mutual recognition that seemed to make everyone else vanish. While newspapers
gossiped about his possible marriage to her daughter, Maud, it was really
Mrs Howe who had captured Wilde's attention. When she defended
Wilde against Colonel Higginson in the press, Wilde read her piece,
and vowed never to forget 'the chivalrous and pure-minded woman
who wrote it.'[64]

He kept his promise. A decade later, in 1892, he welcomed her into his
London home *en famille* with Constance and showed off his 5-year-old
son, Vyvyan. He and Mrs Howe reminisced 'of old times, of his visit to
America,' she noted in her diary.[65] He also invited Mrs Howe to his private box at the St James's Theatre. Together, they watched how he had
settled their old score against moralizing puritans with his new play, *Lady
Windermere's Fan*, a drama that turns on social gate-keeping and sexual
double standards by poking fun at the idea that women's behaviour must
conform to impossible ideals, while men are free to gad about.

The play opens in Lady Windermere's home. She is hosting Lord Darlington, a dandy who has been paying her 'elaborate compliments.'[66] It was here, in the first act, that Wilde roasted an old Higginsonian chestnut for laughs. 'I will have no one in my house about whom there is any scandal,' Lady Windermere primly announces, testifying to the puritanical cast of mind that the play will gently but mercilessly demolish.[67]

When she saw the play, Mrs Howe had a private sense of *déjà vu*. She enjoyed Wilde's resolution to the drama's battle of the sexes. 'The *motif* not new, but the *dénouement* original in treatment,' she noted appreciatively in her diary.[68] In later life, Wilde was frank about the parallels he felt existed between his secret life as a man who desired men, and the women that society condemned as bad mothers, terrible wives, fallen women, or women with a past. He saw himself in them, especially in their vulnerability. In a letter, he told a friend that such gender nonconformists were no more 'unnatural and insane' than he was, and that they shouldn't be held to 'an alien standard' by people who didn't understand their lives.[69]

Lady Windermere's Fan became the talk of the town. At last, Wilde had fulfilled his dream of becoming a successful playwright. The box office was doing a booming business.[70] Within the year, English satirists were claiming a slice of his success. *The Poet and the Puppets: A Travestie on Lady Windermere's Fan* burlesqued his play and its songs mocked his biography.

> A Poet lived in a handsome style,
> His books had sold, and he'd made his pile,
> His articles, stories and lectures, too,
> Had brought success, as everybody knew.
> But the Poet was tired of writing tales
> Of curious women, and singular males;
> So soon he'd finished his Dorian Grey,
> He set to work at a four-act play.[71]

The comedian Charles Brookfield and the composer Jimmy Glover had cooked up the parody, and thrown some Christy minstrelsy into their dramatic melting pot. 'Nigger mighty happy when he's layin' in de corn,' Lord Gonbustus leads off, 'Nigger mighty happy when he hear de dinner horn' the Poet joins in. Soon they are all crooning together as though they were away down south in Dixie, rather than in England.[72]

When he got wind of the satire, Wilde was boiling with rage. *The Poet and the Puppets* was just like the parodies that dogged him a decade earlier. But back then, in the United States, there had been no Examiner of Plays enforcing moral and artistic standards on behalf of the nation. In England, there was. To make matters worse, in summer 1892 the Examiner had banned Wilde's erotic Bible play, *Salome*, from being performed on the English stage even though the French actress Sarah Bernhardt had come to England to rehearse the lead role. Angered by the censorship, Wilde suspended his nationality. 'I am not at present an Englishman, I am an Irishman, which is by no means the same thing,' he informed a reporter.[73] 'I will not consent to call myself a citizen of a country that shows such narrowness in its artistic judgment.'

But now the Examiner of Plays had 'licensed a burlesque of *Lady Windermere's Fan* in which an actor dressed up like me and imitated my voice and manner!!!' Wilde wrote to the painter William Rothenstein.[74] He rarely resorted to such emphatic exclamations, and they signalled how deeply the *Travestie on Lady Windermere's Fan* offended him. It was merely a farce pandering 'to the vulgarity and hypocrisy of the English people.' If anything ought to be banned from the English stage, he thought, it was caricatures of artists' personalities.[75] William Archer, a leading theatre critic, agreed. He protested against the Examiner's hypocrisy. It was unfair to bar *Salome* 'at the very moment when the personality of its author is being held up to ridicule, night after night, on the public stage, with the full sanction and approval of statutory infallibility.'[76]

But not everyone shared Archer's sympathies. The *New York Times* said that *A Travestie on Lady Windermere's Fan* made Wilde's 'philosophy dance a jig' and that it electrified 'his passion till it grins from ear to ear.'[77] Brookfield and Glover's show transferred to the United States, where it was part of 'a big laughing success' featuring 'legitimate act- ors' that gave audiences plenty to see, including a leg show ('marvell- ous invention!') and a line-up of joking gentlemen who 'range themselves like negro minstrels to exchange riddles instead of cyni- cism.'[78] The satire was such an obvious personal attack that some said it should have been renamed *The Reckoning up of Oscar Wilde*.[79]

Around this time, in June 1892, the American theatre impresario Charles Frohman returned to New York City. Frohman commanded the importation of foreign plays to the United States almost single- handedly.[80] Fresh from his latest European buying spree, he held an impromptu press conference when he disembarked from the SS *City of Paris*. He had secured *Lady Windermere's Fan* for the United States, he told reporters, calling the play an unqualified triumph.[81] 'Oscar Wilde is coming to this country a week or two before its production here,' Frohman announced. 'He has expressed himself as being exceedingly anxious and glad of the opportunity of paying another visit to America,' he boasted. 'It is the most striking dramatic success of the season. . . . The theatre is crowded nightly by the most fashionable people at the English capital.' He made it sound like he had bought the rights to London's most exciting play and got the playwright into the bargain.

Frohman had been watching Wilde's career from the beginning. About a decade earlier, Frohman had started off in hand-me-down suits as Colonel Jack Haverly's pudgy little apprentice minstrel manager. Now he was known as 'the Napoleon of Drama.' He had a theatre empire of his own, an English valet, and, when visiting London, he headquartered himself at the Savoy Hotel, which was also one of Wilde's favourites.[82] His ventures were bigger and more important than anyone else's in the country.[83] He could afford to brag. Frohman would eventually produce the authorized road tour of *Lady Windermere's Fan*.[84] But he would never get Wilde to come back to the United States to be his puppet.

Chapter 17

You Have Made Your Name

W ithin a year of his first society comedy being produced in 1892, Wilde was London's leading theatrical phenomenon. *Lady Windermere's Fan* and *A Woman of No Importance* were the tipping points in the story of his success. 'All the characters spoke in exactly the same way' in both plays, critics noticed, but the dialogue was so witty, smart, and distinctive that all was forgiven. Likewise, they pardoned the plays' second-hand plots (obviously borrowed from French melodrama).[1] Wilde seemed to have done the impossible. Nineteenth-century theatre was so staid, so full of old-fashioned scenarios that in the rush to recognize him as the era's most exciting new playwright, almost nobody stopped to ask how, exactly, he had accomplished such a feat. Few queried the origins of his plays' stylish dialogue, or wondered why the voices that came out of his characters' mouths sounded so similar to each other. Those few who did were generally not the established 'names' in the theatre world, not those with 'serious' reputations, and not those writing for the 'better' publications. No, the people who understood the secret of Wilde's transformation best were, well, professional jokers and members of the comic press.

For the better part of the 1880s, Wilde was preoccupied with lecture tours, editing *Woman's World*, publishing essays and reviews, and writing *The Picture of Dorian Gray*. Until the 1890s, he had never written a comedy, nor created English or American characters for the stage. He had imagined only dramatic tragedies and peopled them with Russian revolutionaries (*Vera*), sixteenth-century aristocrats in the Republic of Venice (*The Duchess of Padua*), and biblical avengers (*Salome*).

But he had some funny stuff stashed away. On his return from America, in 1883, he had imported a set of new ideas about comedy for his personal use. When he unpacked them in his correspondence, a few months later, he sounded like a seasoned professional. 'The drama appeals to human nature, and must have as its ultimate basis the science of psychology and physiology,' he announced.[2] The secret of good drama was to manipulate the audience's emotions, and to make them experience a gamut of feelings ranging from hysteria to tears of joy. 'A laugh in an audience does not destroy terror, but, by relieving it, aids it.' He counselled an actress, 'Never be afraid that by raising a laugh you destroy tragedy. On the contrary, you intensify it.' In their conversations, actors shouldn't talk *at* each other, but talk *to* each other. Good dialogue on stage was reactive. It was full of interruptions, of stops and starts, of zinging energy. 'As regards dialogue, you can produce tragic effects by introducing comedy.' Now he knew how to charm audiences and exploit their feelings by creating tension between laughter and seriousness.

Nowhere did he mention that these were also hallmarks of Christy minstrelsy. But none of this mattered to Wilde's plays until the 1890s. It was then that the actor-manager George Alexander encouraged him to write his first comedy. So Wilde raided his comic stash, turned his experience to his own ends, and—*voilà!*—he created *Lady Windermere's Fan*. To the outside world, the comedy's success seemed like a bolt from the blue, a first-timer making a huge hit on his initial outing on the comic stage. Now he was going to repeat the feat. The American rights to *A Woman of No Importance* were bought up in September 1892, even before he had finished writing the draft.[3] He set his new comedies in nineteenth-century England and populated them with brittle Anglo-Americans that were thinly veiled caricatures.

A Woman of No Importance made a comedy out of the modern-day tragedy of the 'woman with a past'—the 'bad' woman who fascinated Victorians heralded an 1890s craze for plays about two-timing wives, unwed mothers, sexual schemers, and penitent reprobates.[4] Seesawing back-and-forth between light-hearted frivolities and emotional bombshells, Wilde's dialogue judders and bumps along melodramatically as one woman's misfortune becomes fodder for amusement. The plot of *A Woman of No Importance* turns on the tension between Mrs Arbuthnot, a single mother whom society values at naught (as Wilde announces by her name), and the cynical dandy, Lord Illingworth, who fathered her child. Lord Illingworth is one of Wilde's most charming, misogynistic, and morally corrupt dandies. The play pits female virtue against male villainy and offers a tart commentary on the differences between the two.

More often than not, in Wilde's society comedies, dandies manage to rise above their pasts. With the help of their wits and a decent tailor, dandies like Lord Illingworth, or like Mrs Erlynne in *Lady Windermere's Fan*, can propel themselves into the future. 'She is absolutely inadmissible into society,' one woman complains about Mrs Erlynne, but she 'dresses so well, too, which makes it much worse.'[5] Lord Illingworth is a poisonous charmer whose easy swagger casually disappears inopportune questions. Like a frog swallowing a fly, the Wildean dandy can make a meal of his interlocutors and vanish them with a flick of the tongue. Those who dominate the dinner-table are destined to dominate the world.[6] Simultaneously superior and subhuman, Wilde's dandies belong to a class the poet Charles Baudelaire described as 'a new type of aristocracy.'[7]

The dandy was an essential part of the Christy Minstrel show, a standard character that audiences always expected to make an appearance. When he pranced onto the stage in his glad rags and flashed his shoddy credentials, his pretensions cued hysterics from spectators inclined to find humour in the juxtaposition of blackness and nobility. In minstrelsy, the blackface dandy was a character who had clambered to the top but whose origins were humble. Whether he went by the name of 'Dandy Jim,' 'Long Tail Blue,' or 'Zip Coon,' he could be counted on to raise a laugh. Strutting his sophistication in a morning coat and top hat, the blackface dandy could be Dandy Jim, a self-absorbed egotist admiring himself in a mirror before going a-courtin', singing, 'I'se de best lookin' nig in de county oh; I look in de glass an' I find it so,' while admiring his tight 'pantaloons strapp'd down so fine.'[8] Long Tail Blue could deliver romantic advice while showing off his fine blue coat-tails and crooning, 'if you want to win the Ladies' hearts, I'll tell you what to do, Go to a tip-top Tailor's shop, And buy a long tail blue.'[9] The dandy could also be a 'larned skoler,' like Zip Coon, who used his wits to 'hab de pretty girls.'[10]

In the last decades of the century, advertising capitalized on the blackface dandy's mock-success story by contrasting the shabby Jim Crow with a sunflower-wearing Dandy Jim type who had won the affections of an aesthetic young woman. Decked out in his raggedy finery, the dandy invited audiences to measure for themselves the social distance he had travelled—from slavery to freedom, from Jim Crow to Dandy Jim (see Plate 39).

Wilde's aristocratic dandies could also have humble origins. Halfway through *A Woman of No Importance*, Wilde planted an astonishing revelation about his lead dandy, Lord Illingworth. It turned out that his claims to nobility were just as flimsy as any blackface dandy's. For most of his life, Lord Illingworth had been plain old George Harford, and penniless to boot. Although he lorded it over the world, that was merely a stylish imposture.

When the actor-manager Herbert Beerbohm Tree saw what a great success Wilde had made of *Lady Windermere's Fan*, he requested a new play from him for the Haymarket Theatre. At first, Wilde hesitated to write for Tree. As a younger man, in the early 1880s, Tree had spoofed Wildean aesthetes in *Where's the Cat?* and *The Colonel*—the satires that had helped raise Wilde's profile enough to get him invited to lecture in the United States. That pattern was to repeat itself with other performers and managers who had lampooned him a decade earlier.

When he finished writing the manuscript of *A Woman of No Importance*, Wilde went up to Glasgow to party with Tree and his half-brother, the essayist Max Beerbohm. They had three days of non-stop 'laughter, badinage, partridges, oysters, champagne; feasts of no particular reason, flow of no memorable soul.'[11] Max recalled both Beerbohms found something irksome about Wilde, and they were relieved when another 'smart invitation' called him away. The feeling was mutual. Wilde knew he had compromised himself by agreeing to work with Tree, whom he called 'slippery and deceptive.'[12] In his private correspondence, he set about managing the tense relationship as he had years before: by working behind the scenes with a little help from his friends. 'I want you down here,' he told the actor Sydney Barraclough, inviting him to a working holiday at the seaside.[13] 'I need you too, and we will devise schemes and undermine the foolish Tree.'

During this period, Wilde became more distant from his wife. He was preoccupied with preparations for *A Woman of No Importance* but told his lover Lord Alfred Douglas that he wanted to run away with him to 'somewhere where it is hot and coloured.'[14] Wilde became increasingly cynical about the world of women. Likewise, Lord Illingworth talked to every woman as if he loved her, and privately held all women in contempt. To him, they were sphinxes without secrets. 'No man has any real success in this world unless he has got women to back him, and women rule society,' the dandy mentors a younger man, teaching him to see women as means to an end.[15] 'If you have not got women on your side you are quite over.'

By 1893, it was impossible for Constance to ignore the fact that her husband was in thrall to Douglas, and spending money far more liberally than he could afford.[16] For £3,000, he rented a country house in Goring, in the Thames Valley, where the lovers spent part of the summer alone before Constance arrived. On a warm day, the village vicar found Wilde and Douglas enjoying themselves in the yard, dressed only in towels, and playing around at spraying each other with the garden hose. Wilde's affairs weren't limited to Douglas. During a village firework display, Constance discovered her husband hugging a local boat-boy. There were other men as well.

'Things are dreadfully involved for me just now,' Constance wrote to a friend in September 1893. Despite her remarkable powers of composure, she was terrified by the publication of *The Green Carnation*, a satire written by Robert Hichens in which the main character, Esmé Amarinth, was closely modelled on Wilde. Amarinth smokes gold-tipped cigarettes, writes about 'The Wickedness of Virtue,' and makes observations about 'how tiring women are.'[17] London's men in green carnations 'revolve around him like satellites around the sun.' These men tend to waggle when they walk, tilt their heads coyly when they talk, and address each other with great familiarity, Hichens wrote. *The Green Carnation* met with great popular success, not least because the hero was a contrarian and an aesthete whose witticisms sounded so much like Wilde's. Constance's anxiety increased when *Punch* printed a cartoon subtitled 'A Colour Study in Green Carnations' featuring Wilde and Douglas as 'Two Decadent Guys' ready to be burned at the stake.[18] 'I am very distraught and worried, and no one can help me,' Constance told a friend on the day the caricature was published.[19] 'I can only pray for help from God, and that I seem now to spend my time in doing; some time I trust that my prayers may be answered— but when or how I don't know. Destroy this letter please.'

Since minstrelsy's inception, in the early nineteenth century, the show's signature act was the witty back-and-forth between three key characters:

the Interlocutor (a white aristocratic type who played the straight man and wore impeccable black and white evening dress) and Tambo and Bones, his two plainspoken blackface endmen (so named because they were seated at either end of a line-up of performers). Smack dab in the middle of the traditional minstrel show, there was always a sit-down conversation between this trio. The Interlocutor might shoot out a question—'Why is a woman like an umbrella?'—and let the endmen's answers ricochet back and forth. 'Because she's made of ribs and attached to a stick,' Tambo proffered.[20] 'Because she always has to be shut up,' Bones would say. 'I knew you couldn't guess,' the Interlocutor concluded, 'It's because she's accustomed to reign.' Another round could begin with an endman confessing, 'I don't know who I am.' Then he would spin a yarn about marrying a widow and ending up becoming his own grandfather. As the trio conversed, they zigged from comedy to tragedy, and zagged from puns to riddles to one-upmanship. Their hysterical back-and-forth was really a battle of wits.

During these bouts of verbal repartee, it was standard practice for the performers to be seated and lined up (see Plate 43). It soon became a recognizable visual cue. For decades, that distinctive arrangement signalled the start of the minstrel show's funny one-liners and riddles. By dint of repetition, audiences were conditioned to react to it. When they saw the line-up, they expected witty banter to ensue. Like Pavlov's dogs, who salivated every time their master rang a bell because they thought it meant they were about to be fed, the line-up primed spectators to laugh.

Imagine how the audience reacted when the curtain rose on *A Woman of No Importance* in 1893, and they saw that familiar cue. In minstrel show fashion, Wilde had his three characters seated on chairs, and then, like clockwork, the verbal sparring match began. Of course, in Wilde's version, the straight man Interlocutor was replaced by a priggish American. She was sandwiched between two English aristocrats who stood in for the two traditional blackface endmen. Their comic jousting set the tone for the rest of the play. And although Wilde only wrote a few stage directions, he made sure to keep cueing the audience with line-ups. He also called for a lot of sitting throughout the play. The second act opened with '*ladies seated on sofas*,' the third with men lounging, and the fourth in a sitting-room where Wilde's minimal stage directions nevertheless indicated exactly when characters were to sit.[21]

In the dramatic world Wilde created, all that sitting became more than just a visual cue. It also served his private purpose. By freezing his characters in place, Wilde made sure that his audience would concentrate on the conversation—which was where his talents lay. Talking to American interviewers taught him it was his forte. Now he had found another way to serve it up and dish it out. Wilde stimulated the audience's laugh reflex and delivered a feast of amusement. The Pavlovian crowd loved it.

To Victorians familiar with minstrelsy's sit-down displays of farcicality, the specific arrangements and characters in *A Woman of No Importance* spelled out a version of old-time comedy borrowed from the century's most popular entertainment. By now, it was hard to ignore the fact that something was up. Like the Interlocutor who presided over the minstrel show, Wilde's ever-truthful American girl was the only straight talker in the group. Moreover, his English characters tended to speak in enigmatic frivolities, like blackface endmen. His *dramatis personae* were obviously stock characters—the puritanical American girl, the overbearing Englishwoman, and her henpecked husband. The subject of their conversation, America versus England, was just as antiquated. Yet for all its prefabricated components, the play's talk was fresh and new because it was like listening to age's wittiest conversationalist—Wilde himself.

'You had better sit beside me,' the quintessentially English Lady Caroline instructs her husband, Sir John, in the first act.[22] That provided a neat pretext for her to quiz Hester, the young Bostonian, about the United States. The air of pseudo-seriousness was a set-up for the cultural conflict that the play teased out for laughs. Another trio of sitters soon joined the first and, once again, Wilde's stage directions cued up the American theme. Sure enough, Lord Illingworth, the arch-dandy, '*sits down beside Mrs. Allonby*,' the female dandy. Everyone is in position for the wisecracks to begin.

LADY HUNSTANTON: What are American dry goods?
LORD ILLINGWORTH: American novels.
LADY HUNSTANTON: How very singular!... All Americans do dress well. They get their clothes in Paris.
MRS. ALLONBY: They say, Lady Hunstanton, that when good Americans die they go to Paris.
LADY HUNSTANTON: Indeed? And when bad Americans die, where do they go to?
LORD ILLINGWORTH: Oh, they go to America.

Wilde's visual and verbal cueing worked perfectly. Victorian comic weeklies noticed it, saw that the set-up was modelled on blackface acts, and believed it served Wilde's society comedy well. *Punch* thought the best reason to go to *A Woman of No Importance* was 'to hear the Christy-Minstrel epigrammatic dialogue in the first two Acts.'[23] So did the writer for *Judy: or The London Serio-Comic Journal*.[24] But the only mainstream newspaper that credited Wilde for using the minstrel form was *The Guardian*. 'Those who expect a cascade of wit will hardly be disappointed,' the newspaper said, 'but may be amused at the naïveté with which Wilde marshalled his paradoxes, ranging his speakers across the stage in groups convenient for addressing the stalls, like a troupe of Christy Minstrels; nor did he fail to complete the resemblance by supplying a sparkling Massa Johnson in Lord Illingworth, and in Lady Stutfield an obtuse Massa Bones.'[25]

When these late nineteenth- and early twentieth-century critics watched *A Woman of No Importance*, they felt they were listening to dialogue drawn from Wilde's own troupe of '*Christy Minstrels of No Importance*,' as *Punch* renamed the play. To British devotees of minstrelsy, the American source of Wilde's sound was obvious (see Plate 44). Besides, this wasn't a mystery that anybody questioned, much less investigated. Instead of enquiring about the origins of his plays' snappy dialogue and clever staging, it was generally thought that he had simply borrowed a few things from French plays. By then, Wilde's American tour had been more or less forgotten, like a box of out-grown clothes (knee-breeches and such) consigned to eventual oblivion.

More often than not, it was assumed that Wilde had created his society comedies from whole cloth, and that he alone had originated these witty caricatures of Anglo-American society. It became increasingly common to suppose Wilde had effortlessly transferred his natural wit to the stage. 'He was a born playwright,' the theatre critic William Archer believed.[26] 'From his very first attempt, he seemed to have the tricks of technique at his fingers' ends, and to know by instinct what would be effective on the stage.' If only. Wilde's talent for comedy was not written in his DNA, and he didn't have showman's tricks at his fingertips until he had spent a year in the USA.

Wilde hated the stereotypes that plagued portrayals of the Irish on stage. He praised Yeats for rejecting ethnic caricatures that 'merely magnified an irresponsible type, found oftenest among boatmen, carmen, and gentlemen's servants, into the type of a whole nation.'[27] He believed 'the Celtic element in literature is extremely valuable, but there is absolutely no excuse for shrieking "Shillelagh!" and "O'Gorrah!",' as was then the norm.[28]

Before 1882, Wilde hadn't yet harnessed comedy in his writing. But in the world of showmen to which he was introduced, tragedy and comedy sat cheek by jowl. When he started writing plays featuring the English, he retained that sensibility. So he replaced the scruffy stage Irishman he deplored with arch, empty, Anglo-Saxon caricatures who were just as laughable. It was a switcheroo that invited the audience to measure the distance between the characters' high social position and their low morals. Under the cover of comedy, he laid bare the champagne and cucumber sandwich set.[29]

Here was social warfare on parade. He milked the comic potential of national and ethnic stereotypes by having his characters speak in riddles and constantly interrupt each other. His slyly derogatory farces anatomized English and American obsessions with class, sex, ethnicity, and gate-keeping. Although his plays had a veneer of reality, the society he portrayed was a parody of itself. His heroes and heroines spent their lives 'asking and solving conundrums, as though "society" were a Christy Minstrel troupe,' *The Illustrated Sporting and Dramatic News* noticed.[30] To illustrate the point, the weekly sketched Wilde in blackface and rechristened him 'The Interlocutor,' as though he was a minstrel show leader (see Plate 45).

From *Lady Windermere's Fan* and *A Woman of No Importance*, to *An Ideal Husband* and *The Importance of Being Earnest*, the presiding spirit of Wilde's society comedies was not drastically different from the spirit of caricature that animated minstrelsy. His outlandish men and women sounded almost like the real thing, only much funnier. Critical, ironic, and paradoxical, Wildean dandies spoke in minstrel-style riddles they made all their own. Exposure to Irish and black caricatures taught Wilde what he needed to know to turn his eye on *fin de siècle* Anglo-American socialites, and turn them into characters who quipped like minstrels. Their witty style transformed his writing and his reputation took off.

In the last decades of the nineteenth century, when it became more common for African Americans to perform blackface minstrelsy, it also became possible for skilled tricksters to interrogate their own oppression and use 'blackness as a vehicle of protest and dissent.'[31] Some of these performers also used whiteface as a way of attacking prejudices. As the critic Marvin McAllister has shown, whiteface minstrels took elite representations of whiteness and co-opted them in order to critique attitudes to class and race.[32] Under certain circumstances, whiteface and blackface make-up worked like a mask that enabled performers to speak truth to power.

Of course, Wilde hadn't worn either blackface or whiteface, but he had worn knee-breeches for D'Oyly Carte. In other words, he had been contracted to perform a version of himself: the English Renaissance's Irish missionary to the United States. Because of that, he had been portrayed as a Paddy. He knew that Irishness, seen through American and British eyes, was tantamount to blackness. To survive, he learned something of the trickster's craft, and doing so enabled him to outpace his blackface avatars and imitators. Although Wilde didn't mention these satirists in his correspondence, it would be absurd to imagine that he didn't know about them. Such an assiduous newspaper reader could hardly have overlooked the countless advertisements and reviews of shows that were promoted under his name and—worst of all—attracted gigantic audiences and became far more popular than his own lectures. All those dubious characters in 'make-up à la Oscar Wilde' had an effect. They taught him how to muster comedy in service of social tragedy. Satire became a weapon in the war of art.

Wilde didn't write blackface minstrelsy. Instead, he gave his characters masks and created his own kind of whiteface theatre. His minstrel-inspired approach was unusual, but it was not unheard of. Still, it was rare enough to be outside the mainstream of what was on offer in London's serious theatres at the turn of the century. The English theatre was then only beginning to contend with moral challenges. Around this time, risky dramas of ideas like Ibsen's *A Doll's House*, with its tormented heroine and unrelenting attack on domestic pieties, created a sensation but it also angered conservative critics when it was produced in 1889. Even though Wilde sugar-coated his subversion with humour, his society comedies were more than mere entertainments: they were experimental in their attempts to expose hierarchies and daring in their approach to the period's social prejudices. He exaggerated Anglo-Saxon identities into extreme versions of themselves. Through the mask of comedy, the plays challenged Victorian hypocrisy.

This was entirely consistent with the philosophy of art he promoted in the late 1880s and 1890s. 'A mask tells us more than a face,' he pointed out in his 1889 essay, 'Pen, Pencil and Poison.'[33] He continued that line of thought a year later in 'The Critic as Artist,' in which he argued that 'to arrive at what one really believes, one must speak through lips different from one's own.'[34] The following year, in 1891, he completed his long-running meditation with 'The Truth of Masks,' an essay that proves that masks ultimately reveal more than they conceal. 'The truths of metaphysics are the truths of masks,' he concluded.[35]

Theatre reviewers picked up on what his society comedies were doing (even though they had no idea how Wilde had managed it). The critic William Archer believed Wilde 'despised the stories he was telling, and took a cynical pleasure in fooling his public.'[36] Praising the 'verisimilitude' of Wilde's cynical society portrayals, *The Theatre* critic validated his deprecating attitude towards his high-society English characters. 'The section of society you have chosen to observe and reproduce quite justified your scheme of treatment,' the critic noted.[37] *The Spectator*, which was usually hostile to him, had to admit that his close study marvellously captured the pseudo-smartness of the nation's 'special class' of aristocrats and wannabes.[38]

It took Irish eyes to see the polarized reputation Wilde had achieved by these methods. The *Irish Times* observed that he was being heralded as an imitator by some, and as an innovator by others. 'One critic holds it to be a "Christy Minstrel Show," another places it "on the highest level of the English-speaking drama."'[39] It was a paradox. Gradually, one side won out, and a consensus about Wilde's talent emerged. Audiences voted with their feet. Popular opinion veered away from critical opinion. The minstrel comparisons began to fade away. The significance of his work could no longer be denied. His plays were being taken seriously, his comic dialogues heralded as truly original, and his portrayal of British high society as refreshing. As admiring reviews of Wilde's plays became more common, the laurels he had long hoped for were finally his. Influential reviewers hailed *A Woman of No Importance* as confirmation that Wilde had 'no rivals among his fellow-workers for the stage.'[40]

Before long, his reputation as the leading dramatist of the day was sealed. His high-society portrayals secured his standing as the foremost playwright of his generation. 'You are now the great sensation of London—& I am very proud of you,' Speranza wrote him in 1893, after the premiere of *A Woman of No Importance*. 'You have made your name, & taken your place and now hold a distinguished position in the circle of Intellectuals. *That* all your critics acknowledge.'[41]

Chapter 18

By the Throat

Wilde's society comedies remade the Victorian stage. They were the breath of life necessary to reinvigorate English theatre, notable then only for the fact that it was moribund. As the critic A. N. Wilson points out, 'there were no plays of any interest or quality written in English between the death of Sheridan [1816] and the emergence of Oscar Wilde [in the 1890s].'[1] Wilson's dismissal of Victorian theatre is swift, but it is fair. There's a good reason the Victorian era is remembered as the age of the novel, not the age of the drama.

The invention of new words like 'Wildean' and 'Wildese' in the early 1890s defined Oscar's place in the world. Those two words legitimated him as an artist because they associated his name with verbal pyrotechnics all his own.[2] Not only did the neologisms designate the particular rhythms and phrasing in his plays, they testified to his uniqueness. They put him in distinguished company, too: 'Dickensian' and 'Shakespearean' were also household words. Naming Wilde's signature style influenced what people thought of him. The neologisms announced a unique voice. When *The Importance of Being Earnest* premiered, in 1895, reviewers were virtually unanimous about the play's 'Wildean' originality and verve. In *Truth's* review of the play, the drama critic noted that 'all the *dramatis personae*, from the heroes down to their butlers, talk pure and undiluted Wildese.'[3] By this point, Wilde's voice was thought to be so original that it not only justified such neologisms, it required them.

The idea of Wilde's originality was becoming ingrained in Victorian consciousness. Today, it's common knowledge that labelling influences social perception. What we feel about certain words shapes how we engage with the things that they define. In 1895, Victorians were waking up to the idea that feelings—not just objective facts—shape public opinion. That year, the French social psychologist Gustave Le Bon published *The Crowd: A Study of the Popular Mind*, a prescient examination of the powerful influence of sentiment over mass psychology. Le Bon showed that words and the images they generate make an impression on the collective imagination and therefore act directly to influence popular opinion.[4] 'The power of words is so great that it suffices to designate in well-chosen terms the most odious things to make them acceptable to crowds,' he observed. Conversely, a well-chosen word could completely turn the tide of public opinion. 'The memorable events of history are the *visible* effects of the *invisible* changes of human thought,' he argued, because words have the capacity to provoke those invisible changes in popular thinking.

In 1895, the word 'sodomite' was about to provoke an unforgettable event in history. It was the word the Marquess of Queensberry used on the calling card he left at Wilde's club and, like 'Wildean' and 'Wildese,' it was another label that would define Oscar's place in Victorian society. 'For Oscar Wilde, posing somdomite [*sic*]' were the five words with which the poor speller chose to threaten his son's lover on 18 February 1895. The Marquess was a keen boxer, and if he had given Wilde a full-fisted punch instead, the consequences would have been far less disastrous. Days before, Queensberry had threatened him by prowling the theatre where *The Importance of Being Earnest* was playing. The police denied the Marquess entry when he appeared 'chattering like a monstrous ape,' with a prize-fighter in tow, Wilde later told Bosie, the Marquess's son.[5] A single misspelled word with biblical connotations of wickedness soon proved more terrifying still. 'Bosie's father has left a card at my club with hideous words on it,' he wrote to his friend, Robert Ross, at the end of February, adding that he felt he had no choice now but to turn to the law for protection.[6] 'My whole life seems ruined by this man.' Egged on by Bosie, Wilde grew insensible to friends' advice, and decided to sue for criminal libel. 'I had made a gigantic psychological error,' he later realized.[7]

The trial began on 3 April 1895. The Marquess of Quensberry's defence counsel was Edward Carson, whom Wilde had known since boyhood. Like Wilde, Carson was born in Dublin in 1854 to Anglo-Irish parents. As children, they played together at the seashore. As students at

Trinity College Dublin, they strolled arm in arm. But that friendship, like the sandcastles of their youth, had disappeared by 1895. In the Old Bailey, Carson argued to the all-male jury that Wilde had misused his position as a man of literary power to mislead younger, more vulnerable men.

'Do you think pleasure is the only thing that one should live for?' Carson asked Wilde during the cross-examination.[8]

'I think self-realization—realization of one's self—is the primal aim in life,' Wilde said, adding that in matters of pleasure he was 'entirely on the side of the ancients—the Greeks.'

Carson coaxed the jury to see *The Picture of Dorian Gray* as the perverse moral blueprint by which Wilde had lived his life. He read Wilde's private letters aloud to the courtroom, and produced a string of questionable male associates. He lined up witnesses, including a masseur who claimed to have seen a boy lying in Wilde's bed, and hotel servants ready to testify to the 'disgusting filth in which they found the bedclothes.'[9] Carson appealed to the jury's paternalism, saying, 'tell me that the gorge of any father ought not to rise if he believes, as is proved now, that his son was so dominated by Mr. Oscar Wilde that he allowed him to make love to him—a filthy, abominable love.'[10]

Despite being hampered by a cold, Carson was in fighting form. He destroyed Wilde, who lost his libel suit against the Marquess. Then the tables turned, and suddenly Wilde was being accused of criminal acts and prosecuted for gross indecency. Sir Edward Clarke stepped in and agreed to defend Wilde *pro bono*.[11] A devout man, Clarke had risen from modest beginnings to become one of the leading English barristers of his day. On the morning of Wednesday 3 April, 1895, Clarke pursued a line of questioning designed, first, to remind the gentlemen of the jury of his client's phenomenal ascent and, second, to arouse sympathy from the judge, an Irishman by the name of Richard Henn Collins who, like Wilde, had studied classics on a scholarship at Trinity College Dublin.

CLARKE: I think you are thirty-eight years of age?
WILDE: I am thirty-nine years of age.
CLARKE: Was your father the late Sir William Wilde a surgeon in Dublin... Chairman of the Census Commission?
WILDE: Yes.
CLARKE: ... Were you a student at Trinity College Dublin?
WILDE: Yes.

CLARKE: And at that University or College did you obtain a
        classical scholarship and the Gold Medal for Greek?
WILDE: Yes.
CLARKE: Then, I believe you went to Magdalen College, Oxford
        [and] there had a classical scholarship [and] obtained the
        Newdigate Prize for English Verse?
WILDE: Yes.
CLARKE: ... I believe as early as 1882 you published a volume of
        poems?
WILDE: I did.
CLARKE: And did you afterwards make a lecture tour in America?
WILDE: Yes.
CLARKE: And have lectured also in England, I think?
WILDE: Yes.
CLARKE: Have you since that time written many essays of different
        kinds?
WILDE: I have.
CLARKE: ... During the last few years you have devoted yourself
        specially to dramatic literature?
Wilde: I have.
CLARKE: I think I am right in mentioning *Lady Windermere's Fan*,
        A Woman of No Importance, *The Importance of Being Earnest*
        and *An Ideal Husband* as the four plays of yours which
        have been interpreted on the stage in this country?
WILDE: Yes.
CLARKE: And all of them successful?
WILDE: They have all, I am glad to say, been successful.[12]

None of those accomplishments could shield him. Already, his name
had become synonymous with shame. Within weeks, scandal unmade
him and society sent him to jail. Many of Wilde's associates turned on
him, and some, like the Pre-Raphaelite painter William Holman Hunt,
said 'the law treated him with exceeding leniency.'[13] But others saw
Wilde's downfall for the squalid disaster it was. 'His fall is hideously
tragic,' the novelist Henry James felt.[14] Wilde's friend, the painter
Louise Jopling, was driving home to Kensington when she heard a
newsboy shouting the verdict in the streets. She stopped her vehicle at
once. 'What is it?' she asked from her hansom. The child made a pitiful
face. 'Two years!' he replied. The pair looked at each other sadly.[15]

Wilde's sons learned about their father's imprisonment through the press. His eldest son, Cyril, who was then 9 years old, got his first inkling of his father's fate when he saw a placard in Baker Street.[16] When he asked what it meant, he got an evasive answer. It was by reading the Irish newspapers, a short while later, that he discovered the truth. After that, Cyril became a damaged, 'very solemn-faced little boy,' his younger brother recalled. Vyvyan's abiding memory of the time was coming home from school, at the age of 8, to find his mother crying over press-cuttings boldly headlined 'OSCAR WILDE.'

By April 1895, Wilde was forced to declare bankruptcy. The contents of 16 Tite Street were publicly auctioned. Everything on the premises had to be sold, and it all went—from Wilde's personal library and the children's toys, right down to the family's blue-and-white china and the housemaid's pails. While some bid on the hastily bundled lots, inquisitive members of the public roamed from room to room in search of revelations. 'Oscar Wilde's bedroom was the chief point of attraction,' the *Morning Post* reported.[17] Six months later, on the advice of the solicitor Sir George Lewis, Constance changed her surname and the two boys'. They became the Hollands, and went to Italy to live in exile.[18] Although there had been talk about moving to Ireland, Wilde's disgrace made that impossible. 'It was thought better, after all, that we should go and hide ourselves abroad,' Vyvyan recollected later in life.[19] 'There at least we could live unmolested' by the curious. Vyvyan and Cyril never saw their father again.[20]

1895 was also the year that two Frenchmen, les frères Lumière, built a motion picture camera. The brothers soon realized that their contraption could project images onto a screen, and their novelty signalled the birth of film. Meanwhile, Wilde sat in solitary confinement.[21] During those first thirteen months, his mind became like a private cinema. Deprived of human contact, he could do nothing but brood on the perversities that had 'brought him from high place and noble distinction to the convict's cell.'[22] Traumatic memories unspooled before his mind's eye as though from a gruesome showreel. One of his most painful memories was being dressed like a convict, handcuffed, and put on the midday train to travel from Clapham Junction to Reading with members of the public, he later told the Home Secretary. What made the experience truly harrowing, he said in a letter he wrote from Reading Jail, was his 'exhibition to the public gaze.'[23] On that train platform, his tragedy became a state-sanctioned public spectacle. He detailed the scene in *De Profundis*:

From two o'clock till half-past two on that day I had to stand on the centre platform of Clapham Junction in convict dress and handcuffed, for the world to look at. I had been taken out of the Hospital Ward without a moment's notice being given to me. Of all possible objects I was the most grotesque. When people saw me they laughed. Each train as it came up swelled the audience. Nothing could exceed their amusement. That was of course before they knew who I was. As soon as they had been informed, they laughed still more. For half an hour I stood there in the grey November rain surrounded by a jeering mob. For a year after that was done to me I wept every day at the same hour and for the same space of time.[24]

The humiliation broke him. It was the reverse of his strutting on North American train platforms under the admiring gaze of onlookers. The nightmarish Clapham Junction scene mocked that public peacocking. Dressed in a prisoner's uniform, he could no longer scorn the public with dandyish *hauteur*.

'I went to Reading, and saw poor O,' Constance wrote her brother in February 1896.[25] The change was heart-breaking. His mental health had declined drastically. 'They say he's quite well, but he is an absolute wreck compared with what he was.' During her visit, Constance informed Oscar that his mother had died earlier that month. Speranza's funeral was held at Kensal Green, London and she was buried in an unmarked grave. The family could not afford a headstone.

In prison, Wilde was spared few humiliations. Vilified by society, witness to daily spectacles of violence, he was condemned to walk a treadmill for six hours a day and sleep on a plank. The fingertips which had penned some of the century's most delightful criticism and plays grew dull with pain by shredding hard ropes. In a matter of months, he was destroyed in body and mind. In autumn 1896, he begged the Home Secretary for early release. 'Poverty is all that he can look forward to: obscurity all that he can hope for,' Wilde wrote, outlining his bleak future in the third person, as though on behalf of someone else.[26] Tallying his losses, he continued, 'he has lost wife, children, fame, honour, position, wealth.' With each biographical subtraction, a tiny piece of himself seemed to vanish. Worse still, he would never again have the youth, energy, and personal resourcefulness to recover any of it. 'There is of course before him no public life: nor any life in literature anymore,' he wrote, continuing his morbid calculation until, at last, having considered the great list of debits, he concluded that there would be 'nor joy or happiness of life at all.' The Home Secretary was unmoved by his plea.

He was denied early release, but allowed books to read. To occupy his agitated mind, he requested dozens—in English, French, Italian, German. Among them was *Illumination* by Harold Frederic, an American acquaintance who had worked as the *New York Times*'s London correspondent.[27] Frederic has the hero of his novel, Theron Ware, learn to consider popular cartoons more critically after falling in love with an Irish aesthete. Suddenly aware of how anti-Irish and anti-black caricatures corrupted him, the novel's hero opens his eyes to their prejudice. He recognizes lynched bodies and 'ape-like faces' as bigotry's bleak phantasms.[28] From jail, Wilde wrote to Robert Ross that *Illumination* was 'very interesting in matter.'[29]

When he was sent to prison Wilde instantly moved from the hub of a social circle to solitary confinement. Life as he knew it ended, and the grim life of convict C.3.3 began. It was like a death sentence. It also felt like a surreal lynching, one in which he was simultaneously the victim and an observer of another man's gruesome hanging. 'There are moments,' Wilde later told a young Irish poet named Chris Healy, 'when life takes you, like a tiger, by the throat.'[30] There was a connection, he felt, between his 1895 mauling and *The Ballad of Reading Gaol*, the long poem that grew out of his incarceration. But Wilde's 109 stanzas owed as much to the execution by hanging he claimed to have witnessed in prison. The hanged man was Charles Thomas Wooldridge, a Dragoon Guard who had slashed his wife's throat. 'The man's face will haunt me till I die,' Wilde told Healy.[31] In the poem, he described Wooldridge as an alter ego.

> Like two doomed ships that pass in storm
> We had crossed each other's way:
> But we made no sign, we said no word,
> We had no word to say;
> . . .
> A prison wall was round us both,
> Two outcast men we were.[32]

The *Ballad of Reading Gaol* darts from realistic dreams to lucid night-mares, constantly tightening the bond between the hanging victim and the inmate who watched him die, until they become twin bodies with one shared soul:

> And as one sees most fearful things
>   In the crystal of a dream,
> We saw the greasy hempen rope
>   Hooked to the blackened beam,
> And heard the prayer the hangman's snare
>   Strangled into a scream.
> And all the woe that moved him so
>   That he gave that bitter cry,
> And the wild regrets, and the bloody sweats,
>   None knew so well as I:
> For he who lives more lives than one
>   More deaths than one must die.[33]

Prison broke him, but it had not silenced him. Against the odds, Wilde recovered his voice. His face flamed with anger when he described the squalid conditions, the hard labour, and the ignominy of it all to his friend, Healy.[34] His jailers were animals, Wilde said, comparing them to ferrets, apes, rats, and sheep. But at least they had not succeeded in making an animal of him. 'It was when I was in the depths of suffering that I wrote my poem,' Wilde told Healy. Making a ballad out of Reading had been a way out of jail.

When the time came to publish *The Ballad of Reading Gaol*, Wilde proposed that Wooldridge should be remembered for his military ser-vice. He thoughtfully considered how the poem might be presented so that people realized it was based on real events. Perhaps 'Hanged in Reading Gaol' might be added to the dedication.[35] Otherwise, he told the publisher, 'people might think it was all imaginary.' Then, he sug-gested that an epitaph with Wooldridge's initials and the inscription 'late of H. M. Dragoon Guards' could be added to the poem. Years before, Gilbert and Sullivan's Dragoon Guards had been the anti-aesthetes in *Patience*. It was probably those redcoat soldiers that made Wilde imagine Wooldridge's coat as scarlet, when in fact it was blue.[36]

Wilde hoped that the *New York World* would pay him richly for 'my American poem,' as he then referred to *The Ballad of Reading Gaol*.[37]

But William Henry Hurlbert, *The World* editor who had been his ally in the old days, had died while Wilde was still in prison. When Wilde's American agent, Elisabeth Marbury, read the poem, it sounded to her as if he had written it from beyond the grave. She said it had made her weep until great tears rolled down her cheeks.[38] Although she tried to sell it in the United States, no one would touch it, not even 'the most revolting New York paper,' Wilde told his friend Ada Leverson. Marbury suggested having the poem illustrated, but Wilde categorically refused that.[39] Finally, Leonard Smithers agreed to print it.[40] The London publisher had an eye for eccentricity. 'The popularity of the poem will be largely increased by the author's painful death by starvation,' Wilde joked bitterly in a letter to Smithers. 'The public love poets to die in that way. It seems to them dramatically right. Perhaps it is.'[41] The typography of the first edition of *The Ballad of Reading Gaol* suggested a tidy symmetry between the poem's soldier-dedicatee, C.T.W., and the poem's anonymous author, C.3.3, the number of Wilde's prison cell.

The sweeping vistas of hindsight can be terribly seductive, particularly when they pertain to autobiography. It's easy to see why. It replaces a life's disarray with composed lines lying neat and still on the page, tidy as a manicured garden. Emotional wildernesses have been contained. Messy feelings have been trimmed into sentences that fall into line as neatly as boxed hedgerows. Autobiography delivers the illusion of order, but it's not the kind that occurs in nature or in real life.

After he had lost everything, in 1897, Wilde reminisced, 'the gods had given me almost everything. I had genius, a distinguished name, high social position, brilliancy, intellectual daring.' Known as *De Profundis*, the autobiographical letter Wilde wrote Lord Alfred Douglas from prison is a poignant document of his disgrace. It is also a testament of his self-invention that illustrates the legend he created about himself. Yet some of its truths are as thin as the translucent blue paper stamped 'Reading Prison' on which he wrote them.

> I was a man who stood in symbolic relations to the art and culture of my age. I had realised this for myself at the very dawn of my manhood, and had forced my age to realise it afterwards. Few men hold such a position in their own lifetime, and have it so acknowledged. It is usually discerned, if discerned at all, by the historian, or the critic, long after both the man and his age have passed away. With me it was different. I felt it myself, and made others feel it.

When Wilde wrote *De Profundis*, he had to raise himself out of the slough of despond. In such a situation, order was precious: it helped delineate a new perspective. From this point of view, truth and fact appeared to converge, like the illusion of parallel lines appearing to meet at a distance. So in *De Profundis*, there were 'turning points' and 'symbolic relations' where real life had sowed doubt and disaster. Such signposting imposed order on the chaos, but it also signalled the thickets of experience that had been cut down to size or cleared altogether to create a well-ordered panorama.

In 1897, from behind the bars of Reading Jail, Wilde accused his callous ex-lover of being responsible for his imprisonment. Douglas's lack of empathy for the macabre display he had witnessed in the court-room was almost as unforgiveable. 'Even the spectacle of me behind the bars of a wooden cage,' Wilde wrote, as though his prison cell were the cage for a freak show, 'could not quicken that dead unimaginative nature.' He expanded the metaphor by comparing Douglas to an insensitive, dull audience. 'You had the sympathy and the sentimental-ity of the spectator of a rather pathetic play. That you were the true author of the hideous tragedy did not occur to you.'[42]

As the date of his release approached, he began to plan a new life. He hoped that it might include a piece of his past, namely his favourite fur coat. 'It was all over America with me, it was at all my first nights it knows me perfectly, and I really want it,' he told his friend Robbie Ross on 1 April 1897.[43] Fifteen years to the day, on 1 April 1882, Wilde had been in San Francisco happily drinking tea among the Chinese.[44]

Now, he requested that the Home Secretary make discreet arrange-ments for his release, because he wished to 'avoid the notoriety and annoyance of newspaper interviews and descriptions on the occa-sion.'[45] The interviews he had once sought, he now dreaded. Once upon a time, American showmen had persuaded him there was no such thing as bad publicity. No longer. He dreaded the English, French, and American papers that were already angling for release-day inter-views. A few months later, the scandal-hungry *New York Journal* offered him £1,000 for an interview.[46] He refused.

Despite making several enquiries about his American fur coat, it was proving difficult to find. Had it been pawned or sold?, he wondered.[47] Either way, he wanted to know. He was 'anxious to trace it, and if possible get it back.' Eventually, a note from his brother's wife arrived. She enclosed a box of his shirts and some of his play manuscripts. Because she and

Willie needed money, she explained, they had been forced to take smaller rooms and sell a few things. And the beloved fur coat that had carried Oscar across two continents? Willie had pawned it.[48] The fur coat had vanished, like the celebrated career it had mantled.

On 19 May 1897, Wilde was released from jail (see Plate 46). He sailed directly to France on the night boat. On the other side of the Channel, he began a new life. By now he was a stout, grey-haired man who relied on friends to give him the clothes and neckties he wore.[49] He felt like people expected him to starve to death or 'blow my brains out in a Naples urinal,' he told his publisher.[50] Under the name Sebastian Melmoth, he haunted cafés looking like a down at heel imitation of the glamorous dandy he had once been. In Paris he sported a gorgeous blue suit even though it was too tight because, he told Robert Ross, 'people who repent in sackcloth are dreary, but those who repent in a suit by Doré... are worthy of Paradise.'[51] A dandy to the end, he lived like Mrs Erlynne, the unrepentant sinner exiled from England in her beautiful dress in the finale of *Lady Windermere's Fan*.

During the summer, he briefly saw Douglas again, and in autumn 1897 they met in Italy. When she heard about this, Constance was outraged. In their document of separation, she and Oscar had agreed that he was not to keep bad company if he wished her to continue paying him an allowance. Reuniting with Douglas was, she thought, the action 'of a madman who has not even enough imagination to see how trifles affect children, of unselfishness enough to care for the welfare of his wife.'[52] Douglas saw things very differently. With characteristic irresponsibility, he squarely laid the blame on Constance's shoulders. 'As to his wife, he married her solely for love and if she had treated him properly and stuck to him after he had been in prison, as a really good wife would have done, he would have gone on loving her to the end of his life.'[53] Constance's heart stopped on 7 April 1898. She was laid to rest in the foothills of Genoa. Vyvyan, 12, and Cyril, 13, were notified by their schools and put in the care of a guardian named Adrian Hope.[54]

It was not just his family from which Wilde became detached, but, increasingly, his own existence. It became almost impossible for him to publish, even in the United States. 'It seems to me that the withdrawal of my name is essential in America as elsewhere,' he realized.[55] 'I see it is my *name* that terrifies.'

As though watching a curious social drama unfold, he became a spectator of his own condition. In the theatre of his mind, he was no longer the hero of his life story. Instead, Public Opinion was the dogged, vengeful main character driving the drama. 'What astonishes and interests me about my present position is that the moment the world's forces begin to persecute anyone they *never leave off*,' he told Robert Ross.[56] 'This seems to me a historical fact, as well as an interesting psychological problem. To leave off persecution is to admit that one has been wrong, and the world will never do that.'

By mid-November 1900 he had been bedridden for almost two months with doctors and nurses at his side. He was in acute physical pain. His nights were sleepless. Morphine no longer worked, and now only chloral and opium gave him any relief. Around this time, when Robert Ross visited him, Wilde was hysterical. He cried openly.[57] As his life was ending, he was wracked with worries about blackmailing, betrayal, money, and loneliness. He rambled non-stop when friends visited. In one of the last letters he was able to write, he was particularly concerned about who would control the stage rights to his plays in the United States. In his final days, distress got the better of him, and he asked a friend to see to some of his affairs.

'I don't know what you are doing about America,' Wilde wrote from the Hotel d'Alsace in Paris.[58] Wilde wanted to ensure his works would outlive him. The American theatre magnate Charles Frohman was the person Wilde had in mind to help him. Once upon a time, in 1882, Frohman had managed Callender's Consolidated Spectacular Colored Minstrels' hit show, *Utterly Too Too's, or Parodies on Oscar Wilde*. Now he was one of the most important men in theatre on both sides of the Atlantic. In the course of his career, he introduced over 600 new plays to the public. Throughout the 1890s, he transitioned from peddling Wildean replicas to producing the real thing: Charles and his brother, Daniel, produced more authorized productions of Wilde's plays than anyone else. The Frohmans had done *Lady Windermere's Fan* in 1893, *The Importance of Being Earnest* and *An Ideal Husband* in 1895.[59] By the turn of the century, Frohman could afford to stage the kinds of plays that a less daring producer would have shunned.[60] Wilde knew he might risk producing the works of a stigmatized playwright whose name still couldn't be spoken in polite circles.

Wilde was near the end and tired of fighting. He appeared to be revisiting the compromises that had made his early career. 'Do try and get [Charles] Frohman' to buy the American stage rights, he wrote in his penultimate letter, on 12 November 1900.[61] 'He, as you know, I suppose, is the head of the Theatrical Syndicate, the trust that owns all

the big theatres in the great towns. If one is not in with the trust one
has to play in little theatres... You will understand how serious the
matter is.' Two years later, Frohman would be responsible for sponsor-
ing the revival of *The Importance of Being Earnest*, a production in which
the actors were lined up like minstrels (see Plate 47).[62]

Wilde died two weeks after writing that letter, on the afternoon of
30 November 1900. He was 46 years old.

We are all in the gutter,
but some of us are
looking at the stars.

– Lady Windermere's Fan

Epilogue

The Private View

Wilde's body was buried in a plain oak coffin in Bagneux, on the margins of Paris. It was the perfect place to be forgotten. By then, he was notorious, and about as far from fame as he could get. His few remaining friends chose a plain stone marker and a discreet Latin quotation from the Book of Job. If anyone happened to stumble on his grave, they would read a forbidding epitaph. 'To my words they dare add nothing, and my speech dropped upon them.' The inscription seemed to say that there was nothing more to say.

A decade later, in 1905, Wilde's literary executor, Robert Ross, published an expurgated version of *De Profundis*. The prison letter's poignancy caused a sensation, even though it was drastically abridged to half of the original manuscript and all the references to Lord Alfred Douglas had been cut. Thanks to Ross, Wilde's rehabilitation had begun.

In the early years of the twentieth century, it took guts to put on Wilde's plays, let alone speak up for him and defend his honour. What was remembered about him was his spectacular nosedive in 1895 and the splash it had made across newspapers on both sides of the Atlantic. By 1907, the editors of *The Writings of Oscar Wilde: His Life with a Critical Estimate of his Writings* felt that they could restore Wilde's name by reframing his life. Instead of focusing on the trial that overshadowed it, they deliberately emphasized his literary accomplishments.[1] At the dawn of the twentieth century, they wrote, 'Oscar Wilde is once more on trial, but it is a trial whose result can involve no disgrace, but which may—surely will—bring him a radiant wreath of fame.'

Colonel Morse, Wilde's shady ex-tour manager, was asked to contribute two chapters detailing his early career as a lecturer. Morse had moved on from showmanship, and now he worked in sanitation, a business he described as 'getting rid of the "sins of the people." '[2] By the turn of the century, he was one of America's top solid-waste management engineers. As a leading member of the American Public Health Association, he had spent the last years improving furnaces, testing designs, and trying to get consistent results regardless of the character and class of the waste to be destroyed. 'Garbage is not an exact science,' he concluded.[3] Morse's numerous reports included titles like *The Methods of Collection, and the Disposal of Waste and Garbage by Cremation*.[4] 'Public sentiment is in the line of destroying dangerous and offensive matter by the quickest and most effective method,' he announced in one of his papers. His views on garbage were gospel.

To his mind, there were essentially two ways to deal with the sins of the people: one was to scrub trash up and sell it, and the other was to make it disappear. To Morse, much of what people thought of as waste was actually valuable material that could profitably be collected, cleaned, and resold. Whatever was left afterwards could be transferred to incinerators and burned to produce electric power to light up entire cities.[5] He had discovered how to monetize rubbish, and so everyman's trash became his treasure.

When Morse agreed to contribute to *The Writings of Oscar Wilde*, he took the same approach to negative public opinion that he took to rubbish. The book's editors thought Morse well placed to 'throw illuminating sidelights upon the character and personality of Oscar Wilde,' and so he penned a redemptive account of the American tour.[6] He polished up the best bits and wiped away the rest. He cleaned up his star's tarnished story in an effort to improve the public's opinion of him.

From the heap of information at his disposal, Morse hand-picked the first lecture in New York City. But instead of giving the facts about it, he presented the event as another trial—one that went Wilde's way. 'This trial,' Morse began, referring to the Chickering Hall debut on 9 January 1882, 'before a critical, supercilious, almost hostile audience, defined his place as a public speaker, and there was never afterwards a question as to the man's position and power over his hearers.'[7] Morse claimed that Wilde had mastered the crowd, almost casting a spell over them. By the end of it 'his audience was captured.' According to Morse, it had settled the question of Wilde's talent once and for all.

It was highly unusual for a novice to triumph so brilliantly over adversity, Morse insisted, but Wilde was a natural at the podium. 'In a somewhat extended experience in business relations with public speakers of the first rank of America and England, there is no instance in the writer's judgment of so severe a trial or a more complete and convincing success than was made by Mr. Wilde at his first appearance before an American audience.' According to Morse's version, before the 1895 trial that had unmade Wilde, there had been an earlier one in 1882 that made him. That was only partly true: the twelve months of the American tour had been a trial of sorts, but Wilde's metamorphosis hadn't happened overnight. In Morse's sanitized version, however, he alleged that that miraculous first lecture had set the tone for the next twelve months of the tour. Faced with the public's 'misapprehension' or the 'biased' press, Morse attested that Wilde was a gifted novice who handled it all like a seasoned professional. The tour itself, he said, 'was a trial that would have taxed the powers of an older, more experienced and mature man to the uttermost limit of his strength.'[8]

In the end, the aesthete's American tour was nothing short of revolutionary, Morse insisted. 'The facts remain,' he concluded, 'that the direct result of the lectures, writings, interviews, and talks of this young man...left its imprint upon the national life.' Wilde's aesthetic mission made its mark on the United States, Colonel Morse maintained, claiming that its admirable legacy was 'a better and higher national culture.'

By 1909, Wilde's acolytes had gathered sufficient funds to have his remains moved to Père Lachaise Cemetery, in the centre of Paris. Robert Ross and Wilde's son, Vyvyan, presided over the transfer.[9] When the undertaker asked whether Ross wished to inscribe something more than Wilde's name on the coffin, Ross winced and cried out, '*Oh, ma foi, non! Assez d'inscriptions!*' Three years later, a hulking white monument to Wilde's memory was commissioned. Fashioned to look like a sphinx, Jacob Epstein's unusual sculpture towers above the other tombstones, and its bulky beauty makes it a fitting commemoration of Wilde's own bulky body. So, too, is the excerpt from *The Ballad of Reading Gaol* that was chiselled into it, like a tattoo marking him for his difference:

> And alien tears will fill for him
>   Pity's long-broken urn,
> For his mourners will be outcast men,
>   And outcasts always mourn.[10]

As though in fulfilment of this prophecy, Wilde's tomb became a beacon for aliens, for those who have been ostracized, exiled, and cast aside. Mourners now come from far and wide to leave tears, red lipstick kisses, and Sharpie scrawls on his grave. And yet when his friends Ellen Terry and Walford Graham Robertson visited Epstein's studio, the monument's seriousness made Robertson laugh out loud. How ironic that all the lightness Wilde had in life should be 'weighed down by all the gigantic symbols of eternity' in his afterlife, he thought.[11] Why should his friend the comic genius have all the laughter and fun squashed out of him by 'a ponderous crag of stone'? In his memoirs, Robertson said it was as preposterous as watching a mouse being crushed by a mountain. Yet he gloomily recognized that commemoration of the dead necessarily entailed a certain deformation of the life. 'The nimble-witted Irishman' had 'been evolved [into] a sinister figure, half sinner, half saint, unrecognisable to anyone who had known him, a creation of pure fiction, wholly foreign and mythical.'

And so Wilde's public afterlife was to be as fantastic as his real one. By the end of the twentieth century, the Wilde myth had grown to such giant proportions that it overshadowed the man. Homosexuality was decriminalized in England in 1967. Northern Ireland and Scotland followed suit in 1982. In 1987, when Richard Ellmann published his magnificent biography, he claimed Wilde belonged 'to our world more than to Victoria's.'[12] About a decade later, the *New Yorker* critic Adam Gopnick surveyed the flowering of books, plays, and films about Wilde by David Hare, Stephen Fry, and Moisés Kaufman. 'Our turn-of-the-century Wilde is not just a gay martyr but a postmodern one,' he concluded.[13] A kitschy myth had arisen—but would it last? 'His queerness,' Gopnik predicted in 1998, 'will surely diminish as the world becomes more easily reconciled to its own incorrigible queerness.'[14]

Today, Wilde's sainthood is secure. He has become gay history's Christ figure. The relics of his martyrdom have become attractions, sites of pilgrimage. The butter yellow door to Reading Gaol's cell C.3.3 has been unmoored from its hinges and put on exhibition at Tate Britain in London. The key to the cell recently fetched £15,000 at a Sotheby's auction. Reading Prison itself has been used as a stage for sold-out readings of *De Profundis* by celebrities and admirers like Patti Smith, Steve McQueen, Ralph Fiennes, Ben Wishaw, Neil Bartlett, and Colm Tóibín. Close by, a street has been christened Oscar Wilde Road.

In 2017, Wilde may have been among 50,000 gay men posthumously pardoned by the Ministry of Justice for sexual acts that are no longer illegal. His works, which were once said to have a corrupting influence on youth, are taught in schools around the globe.

Magdalen College, which refused to house his archive once upon a time, now proudly lists him among its most famous alumni. His student digs at Oxford have been transformed into a space where willowy college students sometimes practise yoga. From the wall, he watches them from an enormous 1882 Sarony portrait surrounded by a heavy gilt frame. Lit with spotlights, his star power is brighter than ever. He looks like he is having the time of his life.

When I had almost finished writing this book, I realized there was one last picture of Wilde that I needed to see up close: William Powell Frith's *The Private View, 1881* (see Plate 48). It was painted in England around the same time that the artists at Currier and Ives's in the United States were making the poster that started me on this journey. While Currier and Ives were portraying a blackface Oscar in 'THE AESTHETIC CRAZE' and asking 'What's de matter wid de Nigga?,' Frith, one of the most popular painters of the Victorian era, was portraying Wilde surrounded by England's most important men and women. It was a strange paradox. How could Wilde have been a nobody and a celebrity at the same time?, I wondered.

On a sunny London afternoon, the Royal Academy's Senior Curator ushered me toward a gallery that is usually closed to the public. We were walking up the same stairs Wilde himself had once set foot upon, when I started thinking about *The Picture of Dorian Gray*. In the last chapter, Dorian creeps upstairs, unlocks the door to the room in which his hideous portrait is hidden, takes one last look at 'this mirror of his soul,' and slashes it with a knife.[15] 'A new life! That was what he wanted,' Wilde wrote. By stabbing the picture, Dorian believes he is destroying the evidence that his life was not as it seemed. The novel doesn't grant Dorian his last wishes, however. When his servants break into the room, they find their master's portrait intact. There he stands, on the wall, looking as handsome as ever. Beneath the picture, they discover a loathsome, gnarled corpse which they don't recognize. Only later, by closely examining the dead man's rings, do they identify him as Dorian Gray. The novel's haunting finale reveals the paradox at the heart of his life.

What launched this biography was Currier and Ives's ugly 1882 portrait of Wilde. As my research progressed, I realized that it was actually a kind of grim, truth-telling portrait. In other words, it was Wilde's personal 'picture of Dorian Gray,' and it hinted at his life's untold story.

When we reached the top of the Royal Academy's staircase, the Curator unlocked the door, and we entered the dimly lit gallery and beheld the counterpart to Currier and Ives's cheap lithograph caricature—W. P. Frith's *The Private View, 1881*. It was a large oil painting that had been exhibited with all the usual pomp and circumstance at the Royal Academy in 1883, when Wilde returned from America. As I drew closer to Frith's grand, panoramic group portrait, I could see leading Victorian scientists, politicians, two Prime Ministers (Gladstone and Disraeli), novelists (Mrs Braddon, Anthony Trollope), the actor-manager Henry Irving, the journalist George Augustus Sala, the poet Robert Browning, and the painter John Everett Millais. The occasion was the Royal Academy's 1881 Summer Exhibition, but for Frith the scene was an excuse to paint a crowd-pleasing picture and to feed the public's fascination with the famous.

Zooming in on the right side of Frith's enormous gallery of faces, I finally made out the young Oscar in his velvet and fur. Towering a little above the crowd, he was holding forth to an attentive swarm of ladies. Some men looked at him vaguely with expressions ranging from polite curiosity to disdain. With a few exceptions, they were older and much more accomplished than Wilde then was. That was the snide joke Frith had tucked into the painting. The point of setting a young Irishman amid such distinguished company was to mock how alien he was to it, to show him as a pretentious social climber who appeared to be above it all when, in fact, he was the least important person there.

Knowing now how much he had struggled to gain the position he craved and how far he had been from established in 1881, I could see Frith's painting as the cruel taunt it was. It was a public shaming: a picture of the Establishment mocking someone so inexperienced, so boldly ambitious, so Irish. In his memoir, Frith made the attack against Wilde explicit, saying that he 'planned a group, consisting of a well-known apostle of the beautiful, with a herd of eager worshipers surrounding him.' *The Private View, 1881* was intended to satirize 'the folly of listening to self-elected critics in matters of taste.'[16]

The gag wasn't lost on Victorian viewers, who commended Frith for his portrait 'of all sorts of celebrities, great and very little.'[17] It proved so popular that a protective railing had to be installed in front of it to control the crowds.[18] Wilde resented Frith's slight. In an 1890 essay titled 'The Critic as Artist,' he attacked the painter's 1887 autobiography, writing that 'modern memoirs are generally written by people who...have never done anything worth remembering.'[19] As for paintings of the nineteenth century's best and brightest, they, too, are subject to the cruel vicissitudes of forgetfulness. Indeed, to twenty-first-century eyes, it's obvious that Wilde now enjoys greater status and celebrity than anyone else in the painting. Like a stale Victorian joke, Frith's gibe would be totally lost on today's viewers.

The distinguished life that Wilde claimed had been his destiny was an invention. 'Youth! There is nothing like youth,' he wrote in 1892, when he had reached middle age.[20] 'Youth is the Lord of Life. Youth has a kingdom waiting for it.' He was right. His early life was adventurous, dramatic, and extraordinary. It made him into the greatest celebrity of his age, the most celebrated wit the nineteenth century would see. But he was also wrong: he was never a lord, and no kingdom awaited him. As a young man he had had neither aristocratic assurances nor genius's gleaming guarantees; even conventional professional prospects had eluded him. Eccentricity was no promise of success. And yet he believed in himself, and believed in his aesthetic mission. 'I urge you all not to become discouraged because ridicule is thrown upon those who have the boldness to run counter to popular prejudice,' he told Americans in his 1882 lectures.[21]

THROUGHOUT THE WORLD, IN ALL TIMES AND IN ALL AGES, THERE HAVE BEEN THOSE WHO HAVE HAD THE COURAGE TO ADVOCATE OPINIONS THAT WERE FOR THE TIME ABHORRED BY THE PUBLIC. BUT IF THOSE WHO HOLD THOSE OPINIONS HAVE THE COURAGE TO MAINTAIN AND DEFEND THEM, IT IS ABSOLUTELY CERTAIN THAT IN THE END THE TRUTH WILL PREVAIL.

Today, Wilde is having the last laugh. The twenty-first-century Oscar is enshrined among the Greats of English literature, recognized as an

inspired thinker ahead of his time. His afterlife has given him the legitimacy that life itself denied him. His story is intertwined with the history of Anglo-American society as it grappled with massive waves of
immigration, nationalist movements, racial and ethnic conflicts, political upheavals, new media technologies, and a sensation-hungry press.
For better or worse, it was a time that resembles our own in many ways.

As I left the Royal Academy that day and joined the crowds walking
along Piccadilly, Wilde felt closer. He was a martyr, but he was also a
man. The truth behind the legend is that he was a paradox through and
through—which is to say, real, broken, flawed, and human. For all the
ways in which he was exceptional and unique, he did not escape the
prejudices that dominated his age. Indeed, the same genius and free
spirit that made him special also made him vulnerable. His whiteness,
his manhood, and his class did not protect him. By turns victim and
accomplice, some of his attitudes may look like artefacts of Victoria's
time to us now. Though the era's prejudices were visited upon him,
he also visited them upon others. He was made by Victoria's world
and fought its civil wars, but he was wounded by them, too. Like a
survivor, Wilde comes to us now to bear witness. He challenges us to
hear his testimony and heed it. He will always be with us—daring,
fresh, timeless.

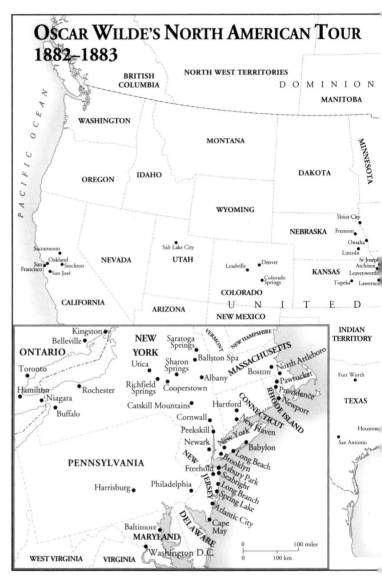

Map of Oscar Wilde's North American Tour, 1882–1883.

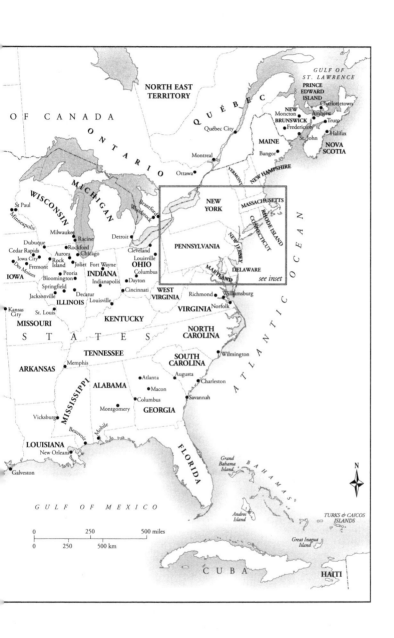

NORTH EAST
TERRITORY
OF CANADA

QUÉBEC

GULF OF
ST. LAWRENCE

PRINCE
EDWARD
ISLAND

Charlottetown

NEW
BRUNSWICK

Moncton
Amherst
Truro

Québec City

Fredericton

Halifax

MAINE

St. John

NOVA
SCOTIA

Montreal

Bangor

Ottawa

ONTARIO

VERMONT

NEW HAMPSHIRE

WISCONSIN

MICHIGAN

St Paul

Minneapolis

Brantford
Woodstock

NEW
YORK

MASSACHUSETTS

RHODE ISLAND

CONNECTICUT

Milwaukee

Racine

Detroit

NEW JERSEY

Dubuque

Rockford

Cleveland

PENNSYLVANIA

Cedar Rapids

Aurora

Chicago

Louisville

DELAWARE

Iowa City

Rock

Joliet

Fort Wayne

Columbus

see inset

Des Moines

Island

OHIO

IOWA

Fremont

Peoria

Dayton

MARYLAND

Bloomington

Indianapolis

Cincinnati

Springfield

Decatur

WEST
VIRGINIA

Richmond

Williamsburg

Jacksonville

ILLINOIS

Louisville

VIRGINIA

Norfolk

Kansas
City

St. Louis

KENTUCKY

MISSOURI

NORTH
CAROLINA

STATES

TENNESSEE

ARKANSAS

Memphis

SOUTH
CAROLINA

Wilmington

MISSISSIPPI

ALABAMA

Atlanta

Augusta

Macon

Charleston

Montgomery

Columbus

Savannah

Vicksburg

GEORGIA

LOUISIANA

Beauvoir

Mobile

New Orleans

Galveston

FLORIDA

GULF OF MEXICO

Grand
Bahama
Island

BAHAMAS

ATLANTIC OCEAN

N

Andros
Island

TURKS & CAICOS
ISLANDS

0   250   500 miles
0   250   500 km

Great Inagua
Island

CUBA

HAITI

Appendix

The Mystery of Wilde's Black Valet

The mystery of Wilde's black valet remains unsolved. In his 1987 biography of Wilde, Richard Ellmann called the man Traquair. This later turned out to be a mistranscription of a theatre manager's name, W. M. Traguier. Regardless, Traquair has been in circulation for nearly three decades and still gets repeated. In 2003, Louis Edwards made Traquair the hero of his novel, *Oscar Wilde Discovers America*. Edwards claims that he based his fiction on a newspaper article from Sioux City in Richard Ellmann's papers at the University of Tulsa's McFarlin Library, but McFarlin Librarians were not able to find this article. That's a shame because the Sioux City article supposedly 'provides one of the few substantive physical descriptions of the valet that I could uncover ("young," "likely-looking," "intelligent face," and "light mixed liver").' There have been a few other suggestions about the valet's identity, but none of them are conclusive. Some say he was called 'John' (too common a name to trace). Kevin O'Brien claims his name was Stephen Davenport but this has been impossible to verify. When I contacted O'Brien, he was unable to provide accurate sources. Yet the mystery of Stephen Davenport may not end there. As I later discovered, there was indeed a 'Stephen' in Wilde's life who hasn't yet been accounted for.

Wilde probably had more than one African American servant throughout his tour. As I pursued these anonymous men through archives, databases, and documents, they led the way like outriding torchbearers illuminating vast unsuspected territories. The trail of clues they dropped point to hidden aspects of Wilde's life that have never made it into his biography. Perhaps the most intriguing hint came

from examining Colonel Morse's accounts, now held in the New York
Public Library. Morse's ledger records each orange Wilde ate in the
United States, the cigarettes he smoked, the wine he drank, the laundry he had washed. Studying these accounts felt like going through a
star's rubbish—the archival equivalent of dumpster diving.

When I examined them, I noticed a curious pattern. The name
'Stephen' and, sometimes, 'Stephens' crops up four times. In an otherwise meticulous inventory of private detail written in magnificently
tidy penmanship, it's odd that this name is spelled inconsistently. It
looks as if Colonel Morse thought Stephen didn't matter much.
Whoever this Stephen was, he was not being paid very much either.
He earned $1.35 on 23 February 1882 in Cincinnati, $0.50 a month
later at Sioux City, another $0.50 in Iowa City, then $3.35 in Kansas
City. So Stephen earned less than $6 for three months' work, a paltry
sum considering Wilde occasionally spent that amount on one evening's worth of wine.

Who would be paid so poorly? Who would be catalogued alongside
consumables? A black servant, that's who. Only a few years earlier,
before the Civil War, it would have been common practice to treat him
like a chattel in accounts. Back then, slaves held 'no higher place in the
records of that grand old Commonwealth than is held by a horse and
ox,' as the abolitionist Frederick Douglass put it. Could this 'Stephen'
be 'Stephen Davenport,' Kevin O'Brien's unverifiable valet?

It's such a tantalizing lead. So I've followed it. Discovering Colonel
Morse's Stephen made me wonder whether he could be the same man
whose voice was silenced in all those American newspapers featuring
Wilde. Sure enough, scouring Canadian and American newspapers, census reports, and genealogical data revealed several Stephen Davenports.
Among them one candidate looks very likely. This Stephen was born
in Virginia in 1856, possibly enslaved. By the age of 15, he was a student
at the Hampton Normal and Agricultural Institute, which was established to educate African Americans after the Civil War. Some Hampton
students became performers in Frohman's company. Stephen's parents
passed away within a month of each other in the summer of 1879. If
he met Wilde in 1882, he would have been 26 and might have needed
to support his young siblings. He could read and write, which would
have been an asset. Late in life, he ended up in Manhattan where he still
listed his occupation as valet. So far, it has been impossible to know

whether this Stephen Davenport worked for Wilde. Perhaps one day we'll be able to confirm the identity of Wilde's African American servants. It's a mystery worth solving. Their stories deserve to be told.

See Richard Ellmann, *Oscar Wilde* (London: Hamish Hamilton, 1987), 177; Hofer and Scharnhorst, *Oscar Wilde in America: The Interviews*, 8. Lewis and Smith, *Oscar Wilde Discovers America, 1882*, 204; Kevin O'Brien, *Oscar Wilde in Canada: An Apostle for the Arts* (Toronto: Personal Library, 1982), 52; Morse, 'Oscar Wilde's American Lecture Tour: W. F. Morse's Statement of Accounts'; Douglass, qtd. in Robert S. Levine, *The Lives of Frederick Douglass* (Cambridge, MA: Harvard University Press, 2016), 147.

Notes

PROLOGUE. WHAT'S THE MATTER WITH OSCAR WILDE?

1. 'Salesladies: A Memorable Scene,' *New York Tribune* 3 March 1882, 4.
2. Andrew Gyory, 'Appendix: The Chinese Exclusion Act,' in *Closing the Gate: Race, Politics, and the Chinese Exclusion Act* (Chapel Hill: University of North Carolina Press, 1998).
3. United States Congress, '1882 Immigration Act, 22 Stat. 214,' in *US Statutes at Large* (Washington, DC: Government Printing Office, 1883).
4. For example, Lord Ronald Sutherland Gower, a possible inspiration for *The Picture of Dorian Gray*'s Lord Henry Wotton, re-edited his reminiscences and his old diaries to reduce and remove references to Wilde.
5. Oscar Wilde, *The Complete Letters of Oscar Wilde*, ed. Merlin Holland and Rupert Hart-Davis (London: Fourth Estate, 2000), 721.

CHAPTER 1. TURNING POINTS

1. Qtd. in 'Our Portrait Gallery: Sir William R. Wilde, M.R.I.A., Surgeon Oculist to the Queen in Ireland,' *Dublin University Magazine* (May 1875), 570.
2. William R. Wilde, *Narrative of a Voyage to Madeira, Teneriffe, and Along the Shores of the Mediterranean Including a Visit to Algiers, Egypt, Palestine, Tyre, Rhodes, Telmessus, Cyprus, and Greece with Observations on the Present State and Prospects of Egypt and Palestine, and on the Climate, Natural History, and Antiquities of the Countries Visited* (Dublin: William Curry, Jun. and Co., 1844), p. vii.
3. Ibid. 407.
4. Ibid. 111.
5. Ibid. 115.
6. 'Our Portrait Gallery: Sir William R. Wilde, M.R.I.A., Surgeon Oculist to the Queen in Ireland,' 575–76.
7. Jane Wilde, 'Genius and Marriage,' in *Robert Ross Memorial Collection* (University College, Oxford, c.1870–1893).
8. Emer O'Sullivan, *The Fall of the House of Wilde: Oscar Wilde and His Family* (London: Bloomsbury, 2016), 9.
9. Merlin Holland, *The Wilde Album* (London: Fourth Estate, 1997), 18.
10. Ibid. 20.
11. Jane Wilde, *Poems* (Dublin: James Duffy, 1864), p. iii.

12. Oscar Wilde, *The Complete Letters of Oscar Wilde*, ed. Merlin Holland and Rupert Hart-Davis (London: Fourth Estate, 2000), 3.

13. Jane Wilde, 'Genius and Marriage.'

14. Qtd. in O'Sullivan, *The Fall of the House of Wilde: Oscar Wilde and His Family*, 64.

15. Jane Wilde, 'The New Era for Women' (13 January 1883), *Robert Ross Memorial Collection* (Box 6. Scrapbook, University College, Oxford), 122.

16. Richard Ellmann, *Oscar Wilde* (London: Hamish Hamilton, 1987); Jane Wilde, 'The New Era for Women.'

17. Qtd. in Robert Secor, 'Aesthetes and Pre-Raphaelites: Oscar Wilde and the Sweetest Violet in England,' *Texas Studies in Literature and Language* 21, no. 3 (1979), 399.

18. Sacvan Bercovitch and Cyrus R. K. Patell, *The Cambridge History of American Literature* (Cambridge: Cambridge University Press, 1994), 80, 82.

19. 'The Hour of Destiny,' *The Nation*, 22 July 1848, qtd. in Ellmann, *Wilde*, 8.

20. Jane Wilde, '"Jacta Alea Est" in *The Nation*,' in *The Life of Oscar Wilde*, ed. Robert Harborough Sherard (New York: Mitchell Kennerley, 1906), 52.

21. R. F. Foster, *Modern Ireland, 1600–1972* (London: Allen Lane, 1988), 313, 15.

22. Ibid. 312.

23. L. W. B. Brockliss, *The University of Oxford: A History*, 1st edn (Oxford: Oxford University Press, 2016), 333.

24. Lloyd Lewis and Henry Justin Smith, *Oscar Wilde Discovers America, 1882* (New York: Harcourt, Brace and Company, 1936), 8–9.

25. E. H. Mikhail, *Oscar Wilde: Interviews and Recollections*, 2 vols. (London: Macmillan, 1979), 1:27.

26. Oscar Wilde, *Letters*, 732.

27. Ibid. 103.

28. G. T. Atkinson, 'Oscar Wilde at Oxford,' *The Cornhill Magazine* (May 1929), 559–64.

29. David Oswald Hunter Blair, *In Victorian Days and Other Papers* (London: Longmans, Green & Co., 1939), 117.

30. Archie Burnett, ed., *The Letters of A. E. Housman* (Oxford Oxford University Press, 2007), 21.

31. The private diary of Lewis Charles Cholmeley also refers to Ruskin's lectures, but for this student the primary attraction was the large number of pretty young ladies who attended them. There is a copy of his diary in the Magdalen College Archive, Oxford.

32. Edward Wakeling, *Lewis Carroll: The Man and His Circle* (London: I. B. Tauris, 2015), 239–40.

33. Hunter Blair, *In Victorian Days and Other Papers*, 117.

34. William Ward, 'Oscar Wilde: An Oxford Reminiscence,' in *Son of Oscar Wilde*, ed. Vyvyan Holland (Oxford: Rupert Hart-Davis, 1954), 250. Years later, Vincent O'Sullivan recalled that Wilde had never lost his exotic outsider's flair, because 'he was too far from the familiar type of the men...there was something 'foreign' about Wilde.' *Aspects of Wilde* (London: Constable, 1936), 78.

35. Hunter Blair, *In Victorian Days and Other Papers*, 117.

36. G. A. Macmillan, letter to his father, 28 March 1877, qtd. in Ellmann, *Wilde*, 68.

37. Atkinson, 'Oscar Wilde at Oxford,' 559–64.

38. Oscar Wilde, 'Chorus of Cloud Maidens,' *The Dublin University Magazine*, 86 (November 1875), 622.

39. *The Annotated Oscar Wilde: Poems, Fiction, Plays, Lectures, Essays, and Letters*, ed. H. Montgomery Hyde (New York: C. N. Potter, 1982), 376.

40. Oscar Wilde, *Letters*, 31.

41. Ibid. 30.

42. Ibid. 29.

43. Ibid. 31.

44. G. W. Kitchin, in a letter to the Vice-Chancellor, 20 April 1881 qtd. in M. G. Brock and M. C. Curthoys, *The History of the University of Oxford*, Vol. 7: *The Nineteenth-Century*. Part 2 (Oxford: Clarendon, 2000), 197.

45. Atkinson, 'Oscar Wilde at Oxford,' 559–64.

46. Between 1823 and 1873, 25% of the Oxford Union Presidents went into politics. Joseph S. Meisel, *Public Speech and the Culture of Public Life in the Age of Gladstone* (New York: Columbia University Press, 2001), 36.

47. Ibid. 22.

48. Oscar Wilde, *Collins Complete Works of Oscar Wilde* (Glasgow: Harper-Collins, 1999), 921.

49. Philip E. Smith II and Michael S. Helfand, eds., *Oscar Wilde's Oxford Notebooks: A Portrait of Mind in the Making* (Oxford: Oxford University Press, 1989), 145.

50. 'Confession Album,' in Holland, *The Wilde Album*, 45.

CHAPTER 2. DO YOU FIND THE WORLD VERY HOLLOW?

1. Francis Robert Benson, *My Memoirs* (London: E. Benn Ltd, 1930).

2. Oscar Wilde, *The Complete Letters of Oscar Wilde*, ed. Merlin Holland and Rupert Hart-Davis (London: Fourth Estate, 2000), 3.

3. Oscar Wilde, 'From Spring Days to Winter,' *Dublin University Magazine*, 87 (January 1876), 47.

4. Vincent O'Sullivan, *Aspects of Wilde* (London: Constable, 1936), 78.

5. Anna Florence Ward, 'Diary' (Magd. MS 618, Magdalen College Archive, Oxford), 16.

6. Ibid. 127.

7. Ibid. 132.

8. Ibid. 136.

9. Arthur Sullivan and W. S. Gilbert, *The Annotated Gilbert and Sullivan*, ed. Ian C. Bradley (Harmondsworth: Penguin, 1984), 143.

10. Ward, 'Diary,' 85-6. The university did not keep records of race at this time. Cole claimed he was the first black African, and this has not been disputed. It is possible there were others before him, however. Half a century earlier, two black West Indian students studied at Oxford, Alexander Heslop (BA, Queen's College, Oxford 1835) and Peter Moncrieffe. Douglas A. Lorimer, *Colour, Class and the Victorians* (Leicester: Leicester University Press, 1978), 216-17.

11. Ray Costello, *Black Liverpool: The Early History of Britain's Oldest Black Community, 1730-1918* (Liverpool: Picton, 2001), 8.

12. Ward, 'Diary,' 46.

13. Ibid. 103.

14. Christopher Fyfe, *A History of Sierra Leone* (Oxford: Oxford University Press, 1962), 406. Costello, *Black Liverpool*, 31.

15. Robin Darwall-Smith, *A History of University College, Oxford* (Oxford: Oxford University Press, 2008), 396.

16. This was a necessary test of their preparation for university-level work because, until 1914, there was no entrance exam at Oxford and colleges could admit whomever they pleased. M. G. Brock and M. C. Curthoys, *The History of the University of Oxford*. Vols. 6-7: *The Nineteenth Century* (Oxford: Clarendon, 2000), 6:356.

17. 'The Encaenia,' *Oxford Chronicle and Berkshire Observer* 29 June 1876. Fyfe, *A History of Sierra Leone*, 406.

18. On the 1876 Slave Circular, see Roland Quinault, 'Gladstone and Slavery,' *The Historical Journal*, 52, no. 2 (June 2009), 379. For Oxford's reaction, see Edward Hutchinson, 'The Fugitive Slave Circulars, or, England the Protector of the Negro Slave,' *Foreign and Commonwealth Office Collection* (1876); Edward Cardwell, 'The Slave Circular: Speeches of Lords Cardwell and Selborne in the House of Lords,' ibid. (7 March 1876).

19. Ward, 'Diary,' 102.

20. Ibid. 108.

21. 'O'Flighty,' *Oxford and Cambridge Undergraduates' Journal* (Oxford), 27 February 1879.

22. Brian Roberts, *The Zulu Kings* (New York: Scribner, 1975), 353, qtd. in Julie F. Codell, 'Victorian Portraits: Re-Tailoring Identities,' *Nineteenth-Century Contexts: An Interdisciplinary Journal*, 34, no. 5 (2012), 505. Codell observes that in British art King Cetewayo was transformed into just about every black Victorian stereotype: from a bare-chested primitive with an animal-tooth necklace, to an Anglo-African and a blackface minstrel. On royal African visitors during the 1880s and 1890s, see David

Olusoga, *Black and British: A Forgotten History* (London: Macmillan, 2016), 413–19.

23. Gretchen Gerzina, *Black England: Life before Emancipation* (London: J. Murray, 1995), 11–13.

24. David Dabydeen, *Hogarth's Blacks: Images of Blacks in Eighteenth Century English Art* (Manchester: Manchester University Press, 1985), 18.

25. Gretchen Gerzina, ed., *Black Victorians/Black Victoriana* (New Brunswick, NJ: Rutgers University Press, 2003), 2, 53–4.

26. As Douglas A. Lorimer points out, censuses 'did enumerate the number, distribution and sex of aliens and colonials in the United Kingdom.' But that doesn't give us anything like the full picture concerning race or ethnicity in Victorian times, and 'therefore, no generalizations about the number of blacks in Britain can be made from these figures.' In the absence of reliable statistics, educated guesstimates have varied hugely: some have put the number of people of colour in nineteenth-century London at 14,000 while others inflate it to 50,000 by including people of African, Asian, and Chinese origin. Lorimer, *Colour, Class and the Victorians*, 213–14. J. Wells, *The Oxford Degree Ceremony* (Oxford: Clarendon Press, 1906), 87.

27. Lorimer, *Colour, Class and the Victorians*, 215. 'Table 23. England and Wales: Number of Natives of Foreign Countries,' in *Census of England and Wales, 1871* (London: Eyre and Spottiswoode), p. li.

28. By 1881, one person in 220 was foreign-born. 'Table 9. Country of Birth of All Foreigners Enumerated in England and Wales,' in *Census of England and Wales, 1881: Ages, Condition as to Marriage, Occupations, and Birth-Places of the People* (London: Eyre and Spottiswoode, 1883), p. xxiv.

29. 'Table 1. Houses and Population of England and Wales as Enumerated in 1881 and 1871,' in *Census of England and Wales, 1881: Area, Houses, and Population: Counties* (London: Eyre and Spottiswoode, 1883), p. v.

30. 'Table 9. Country of Birth of All Foreigners Enumerated in England and Wales,' ibid., p. xxiv.

31. *The Complete Works of Oscar Wilde*, Vol. 1: *Poems and Poems in Prose*, ed. Bobby Fong and Karl Beckson (Oxford: Oxford Univeristy Press, 2000), 27–9. Wilde's poem is modelled on *In Memoriam*, Tennyson's requiem for his beloved friend, Arthur Henry Hallam.

32. Oscar Wilde, *Letters*, 732.

33. Ibid. 20.

CHAPTER 3. ASTONISHING THE DONS

1. Jane Wilde, *Lady Jane Wilde's Letters to Oscar Wilde, 1875–1895*, ed. Karen Tipper (Lewiston, NY: Edwin Mellen Press, 2011), 51.

2. 'This is how it got inserted, and then County papers copied,' Speranza said, revealing how her sons both contributed to creating headlines. Ibid. 52.

3. Henry S. Bunbury, 'Letter to Oscar Wilde' (William Andrews Clark Memorial Library, UCLA, 16 June 1878).

4. 'An Irish Winner of the Newdigate,' *The Irish Monthly* 6 (1878), 630, 33.

5. David Oswald Hunter Blair, *In Victorian Days and Other Papers* (London: Longmans, Green & Co., 1939), 138.

6. Oscar Wilde, *The Complete Letters of Oscar Wilde*, ed. Merlin Holland and Rupert Hart-Davis (London: Fourth Estate, 2000), 26. Wilde's use of 'our' in the phrase 'the greatest work in our literature' indicates that he had already put aside Irish chauvinism and national affiliations when it came to great literature in English. To him, Literature belonged to the commonweal.

   The annotated copy of *Aurora Leigh* that Wilde gave William Ward is now in the British Library. It is possible that Wilde's mother took Aurora's actions literally and applied them to herself for she was known to wear a crown of golden laurels at her London at-homes in the 1880s. Emer O'Sullivan, *The Fall of the House of Wilde: Oscar Wilde and His Family* (London: Bloomsbury, 2016), 254.

7. George Fleming [Julia Constance Fletcher], *Mirage* (Boston: Roberts Bros., 1878), 153.

8. Oscar Wilde, *Letters*, 50.

9. Oscar Wilde, *The Complete Works of Oscar Wilde*, Vol. 1: *Poems and Poems in Prose*, ed. Bobby Fong and Karl Beckson (Oxford: Oxford University Press, 2000), 47.

10. Ibid. 50.

11. Ibid. 53.

12. Hunter Blair, *In Victorian Days and Other Papers*, 137.

13. Ibid. 138.

14. Oscar Wilde, *Letters*, 45, italics added.

15. R. D. Middleton, *Magdalen Studies* (London: Society for Promoting Christian Knowledge, 1936), 274.

16. Oscar Wilde, *The Complete Works of Oscar Wilde*, Vol. 3: *The Picture of Dorian Gray*, ed. Joseph Bristow (Oxford: Oxford University Press, 2005), 170.

17. Oscar Wilde, *The Complete Works of Oscar Wilde*, Vol. 6: *Journalism*, ed. John Stokes and Mark W. Turner, Part I (Oxford: Oxford University Press, 2013), 1:1.

18. Ibid. 1:5.

19. Walter Pater, *Letters of Walter Pater*, ed. Lawrence Evans (Oxford: Clarendon Press, 1970), 24.

20. *The Complete Works of Oscar Wilde*, Vol. 6: *Journalism*, Part I, 1:10.

21. Oscar Wilde, *Letters*, 70.

22. Tipper, *Lady Jane Wilde's Letters to Oscar Wilde, 1875–1895*, 51.

23. Thomas Wentworth Higginson, *Letters and Journals of Thomas Wentworth Higginson, 1846–1906*, ed. Mary Potter Thacher Higginson (Boston: Houghton Mifflin, 1921), 292.

24. Matthew Hofer and Gary Scharnhorst, eds., *Oscar Wilde in America: The Interviews* (Urbana: University of Illinois Press, 2009), 134.

25. Thomas Wentworth Higginson, *Cheerful Yesterdays* (Boston: Houghton, Mifflin and Co., 1898), 277.

26. *Part of a Man's Life* (Boston: Houghton, Mifflin and Co., 1905), 48.

27. Higginson, *Cheerful Yesterdays*, 275–6.

28. 'Letter,' in *Thomas Wentworth Higginson Papers* (Houghton Library, Harvard University, 30 May 1872).

29. *Army Life in a Black Regiment, and Other Writings* (New York: Penguin, 1997), 1.

30. Edward A. Freeman, *Some Impressions of the United States* (London: Longmans, Green & Co., 1883), 152.

31. Ibid. 141. William Richard Wood Stephens, *The Life and Letters of Edward A. Freeman*, 2 vols. (London: Macmillan, 1895), 2:464.

32. Thomas Wentworth Higginson, 'Letter to "Dear Anna",' in *Thomas Wentworth Higginson Papers* (30 October 1881).

33. Higginson, *Cheerful Yesterdays*, 284.

34. Ibid. 278.

35. Mary Potter Thacher Higginson, *Thomas Wentworth Higginson: The Story of His Life* (Port Washington, NY: Kennikat Press, 1971), 326. Higginson, *Cheerful Yesterdays*, 294–5.

36. Higginson, *Cheerful Yesterdays*, 272.

37. *Letters and Journals of Thomas Wentworth Higginson, 1846–1906*, 286.

38. *Army Life in a Black Regiment, and Other Writings*, 23.

39. William Henry Hurlbert, 'Regeneration by Reception,' *The World* 17 February 1882.

40. *Letters and Journals of Thomas Wentworth Higginson, 1846–1906*, 291.

41. 'The Commemoration,' *Jackson's Oxford Journal* Saturday, 29 June 1878. *Letters and Journals of Thomas Wentworth Higginson, 1846–1906*, 291.

42. For Bryce's views on empire and Irish Home Rule, as well as his relationship to Edward A. Freeman, see Christopher Harvie, 'Ideology and Home Rule: James Bryce, A.V. Dicey and Ireland, 1880–1887,' *The English Historical Review* XCI, no. CCCLIX (1976); Duncan Bell, *The Idea of Greater Britain: Empire and the Future of World Order, 1860–1900* (Princeton: Princeton University Press, 2007), 135–6.

43. *The Complete Works of Oscar Wilde*, Vol. 1: *Poems and Poems in Prose*, 46–7.

44. 'The Commemoration.'

45. *Letters and Journals of Thomas Wentworth Higginson, 1846–1906*, 292.

46. 'The Commemoration.'

47. *Letters and Journals of Thomas Wentworth Higginson, 1846–1906*, 292.

48. Cole debated at the Oxford Union on 28 February 1878 (in favour of self-government for India), 16 May (against British imperial federation), and on 31 May (against the abolition of Capital Punishment). He

returned on 30 October 1879 to speak on the subject of the press and governmental paternalism. Oxford Union, *Proceedings of the Oxford Union Society, 1871–1878*, Vol. 2 (Oxford: W. R. Bowden, 1878).

49. Robert I. Rotberg, *Founder: Cecil Rhodes and the Pursuit of Power* (Oxford: Oxford University Press, 1990), 85–6. Christian Frederick Cole, *Reflections on the Zulu War by a Negro, B.A.* (London: Glaisher, 1879), 6.

50. Oxford friends collected money for Cole and helped him find work. Cole's letter of thanks to Herbert Gladstone, then a fellow of Keble College, Oxford is excerpted in Charles Edward Mallet, *Herbert Gladstone: A Memoir* (London: Hutchinson & Co., 1932), 65–6.

51. In the autumn of 1876, another black Sierra Leonean, Joseph Renner Maxwell, went up to Oxford to become a student at Merton College. Like Cole, he debated at the Oxford Union in 1878. It's likely the two met, though neither mentioned it. Class differences between them may have been the decisive factor. Maxwell was the son of a garrison chaplain to British troops and had been brought up in a prominent Creole family. He thought his Oxford experience a positive one. 'I was not once subjected to the slightest ridicule or insult, on account of my colour or race, from any one of my fellow students,' he said, painting an experience quite unlike Cole's. Maxwell experienced racial exclusion in 1879 when he applied to the Colonial Office after having earned a law degree from Oxford. Even such a diploma was not a golden admission ticket, and he found himself shut out of government service. Pamela Roberts, *Black Oxford: The Untold Stories of Oxford University's Black Scholars* (Oxford: Signal Books, 2013), 82.

52. The university had 'a small Scottish, and an even smaller Irish presence from the 1870s.' By the late 1870s, Ireland, Home Rule, India, Africa, and Imperial Federation were regular topics of debate at the Oxford Union. The membership included a number of Irish-sounding names (O'Brien, O'Donoghue, O'Gorman, O'Hanlon, etc.), as well as a few Africans and South-East Asians (for example, Joseph Renner Maxwell and a 'Mr. Ahmed Uddin of Balliol'). L. W. B. Brockliss, *The University of Oxford: A History*, 1st edn (Oxford: Oxford University Press, 2016), 408. Oxford Union, *Proceedings of the Oxford Union Society, 1871–1878*, 2.

53. *The Liberator* 28 May 1858, 86, qtd. in Ethan J. Kytle, *Romantic Reformers and the Antislavery Struggle in the Civil War Era* (New York: Cambridge University Press, 2014), 223.

54. Cole, *Reflections on the Zulu War by a Negro, B.A.*, 7.

55. Ibid. 6.

56. Madan's copy of Cole's book is now in the Beinecke Library, Yale University. 'What Do Men Say About Negroes? Being a Few Remarks on a Passage in "Oxford Days: Or, How Frank Ross Obtained His Degree"' (London: Williams & Co., 1879).

57. Thomas Shrimpton and Son, *1224 Caricatures of Oxford University Life, c.1868–92*, 7 vols. (Oxford, 1866–92), 3:533.

58. Ibid. 3:555.

59. Sir William Wilde had once been caricatured in blackface. See 'A Wilde (K)night in Ireland's Eye' by John Fergus O'Hea, published *c.*1875 by C. Smyth, 57 Dame Street, Dublin. Against the background of a celtic cross, Oscar's father holds out 'A Wilde Essay in Pat-ology.' His skin is darkened, his mouth protuberant, his hair long, and his beard unkempt.

60. Queen Victoria, 'The Diaries of Her Majesty Queen Victoria' (Royal Archives, 1881), 100–2.

61. Jack Haverly, *Negro Minstrels: A Complete Guide to Negro Minstrelsy, Containing Recitations, Jokes, Crossfires, Conundrums, Riddles, Stump Speeches, Ragtime and Sentimental Songs, Etc., Including Hints on Organizing and Successfully Presenting a Performance* (Chicago: Frederick J. Drake & Company, 1902), 5–7.

62. J. H. Haverly, 'J H Haverly Courier,' in *American Minstrel Show Collection, 1823–1947* (Houghton Library, Harvard University), 11.

63. Harry Furniss, *Confessions of a Caricaturist*, 2 vols. (New York: Harper and Brothers Publishers, 1902), 1:66.

64. Wilde's later literary success caused some to look back and magnify his student stardom. In his 1910 history of Oxford, Francis H. Gribble incorrectly claimed that Wilde had been 'a feature—an institution' and that 'probably no undergraduate ever attracted more attention while still an undergraduate, or left a more enduring trail of legend behind him when he went down.' Francis Henry Gribble, *The Romance of the Oxford Colleges* (London: Mills & Boon, 1910), 166–7.

65. The eight-volume *History of the University of Oxford* amply references Cecil Rhodes. Christian Cole is not mentioned by name, although the most recent volume, published in 2000, obliquely notes that 'a few Africans also started to come to Oxford from the 1870s, the two earliest being Creoles from Sierra Leone.' In a similar vein, a 2016 history of the University describes Rhodes as one of Oxford's 'great imperial visionaries' but relegates Cole to a footnote as 'Oxford's first black graduate.' This is incorrect. Although Cole may have been Oxford's first black *African* graduate, there were other black graduates before him. Robin Darwall-Smith's *A History of University College, Oxford*, Christopher Fyfe's *A History of Sierra Leone*, and Pamela Roberts's *Black Oxford* provide some of the most detailed accounts available about Christian Cole but more scholarship will be required to retrieve the full history of Oxford's black students. M. G. Brock and M. C. Curthoys, *The History of the University of Oxford. Vol. 7: The Nineteenth-Century. Part 2* (Oxford: Clarendon, 2000), 714. Brockliss, *The University of Oxford: A History*, 403, 410 n. 37.

66. Rotberg, *Founder: Cecil Rhodes and the Pursuit of Power*, 106.

67. Qtd. in Jeffrey C. Stewart, 'A Black Aesthete at Oxford,' *The Massachusetts Review* 34, no. 3 (1993), 428.

68. Qtd. ibid. 412.

69. Alain Locke, *The Works of Alain Locke*, ed. Charles Molesworth (Oxford: Oxford University Press, 2012), 427.

70. Hunter Blair, *In Victorian Days and Other Papers*, 122.

71. Oscar Wilde, *Letters*, 39–40.

72. Alain Locke described Oxford as having 'a sort of religious dominance over the province of knowledge' that made the right to teach 'a matter of apostolic succession' that was liable to excommunicate those who did not subordinate themselves to the system. *The Works of Alain Locke*, 424.

73. Hunter Blair, *In Victorian Days and Other Papers*, 138.

74. *The Complete Works of Oscar Wilde*, Vol. 1: *Poems and Poems in Prose*, 251.

75. Ibid. 55.

76. The poem is 'Heart's Yearnings,' ibid. 20.

77. Oscar Wilde, *Letters*, 51.

78. *The Complete Works of Oscar Wilde*, Vol. 3: *The Picture of Dorian Gray*, 107.

79. Oscar Wilde, *Collins Complete Works of Oscar Wilde* (Glasgow: HarperCollins, 1999), 1242.

CHAPTER 4. NOT HAVING SET THE WORLD QUITE ON FIRE

1. David Oswald Hunter Blair, *In Victorian Days and Other Papers* (London: Longmans, Green, 1939), 117.

2. Oscar Wilde, *The Complete Letters of Oscar Wilde*, ed. Merlin Holland and Rupert Hart-Davis (London: Fourth Estate, 2000), 71.

3. 'C'est un grand avantage de n'avoir rien fait mais il ne faut pas en abuser.' John Wyse Jackson, ed., *Aristotle at Afternoon Tea: The Rare Oscar Wilde* (London: Fourth Estate, 1991), 17.

4. Jane Wilde, *Lady Jane Wilde's Letters to Oscar Wilde, 1875–1895*, ed. Karen Tipper (Lewiston, NY: Edwin Mellen Press, 2011), 42.

5. Ibid. 43.

6. Richard Ellmann, *Oscar Wilde* (London: Hamish Hamilton, 1987), 83.

7. Jane Wilde, *Lady Jane Wilde's Letters*, 39.

8. Ibid. 53.

9. Ibid. 60.

10. Qtd. in Emer O'Sullivan, *The Fall of the House of Wilde: Oscar Wilde and His Family* (London: Bloomsbury, 2016), 254.

11. Jane Wilde, *Lady Jane Wilde's Letters*, 51.

12. Oscar Wilde, *Letters*, 84.

13. Ibid. 80.

14. Jane Wilde, *Lady Jane Wilde's Letters*, 43.

15. Oscar Wilde, *Letters*, 87, 105.

16. Ibid. 94, 78.

17. Ibid. 86.

18. Ibid. 81, 91.

19. Ibid. 91 n. 5.

20. Ibid. 85.

21. Lillie Langtry, *The Days I Knew* (London: Hutchinson & Co., 1925), 76.

22. Oscar Wilde, *The Complete Works of Oscar Wilde*, Vol. 1: *Poems and Poems in Prose*, ed. Bobby Fong and Karl Beckson (Oxford: Oxford University Press, 2000), 106–7.

23. Wilde to Violet Paget, qtd. in Robert Secor, 'Aesthetes and Pre-Raphaelites: Oscar Wilde and the Sweetest Violet in England,' *Texas Studies in Literature and Language*, 21, no. 3 (1979), 402.

24. William Ward, 'Oscar Wilde: An Oxford Reminiscence,' in *Son of Oscar Wilde*, ed. Vyvyan Holland (Oxford: Rupert Hart-Davis, 1954).

25. Eleanor Fitzsimons, *Wilde's Women* (London: Duckworth Overlook, 2015), 209.

26. Susan R. Hanes, *Wilkie Collins's American Tour, 1873–4* (London: Pickering & Chatto, 2008), 6.

27. Qtd. ibid. 7.

28. Oscar Wilde, *Collins Complete Works of Oscar Wilde* (Glasgow: Harper-Collins, 1999), 686.

29. Oscar Wilde, *Letters*, 98. Wilde was right: the play doesn't read well. But he does have a point about the value of *Vera*, at least from a literary and historical point of view, for it resembles the French Symbolist poets' moody hypnotic style. For nearly a decade, Rimbaud, Verlaine, and Mallarmé had also been privileging indirection and sensuality in their poetry. Some of *Vera* resembles their works. If we zoom forward into the *fin de siècle*, we can see that *Vera* anticipates Wilde's most avant-garde, oblique, and ritualistic play, *Salome*. By then, Smyth-Pigott was still Examiner of Plays and, regarding *Salome* as a dramatic slander on biblical themes, he banned it. But Wilde had grown shrewd. He no longer wrote flattering letters calling Smyth-Pigott a man of 'very brilliant critical powers.' By 1892, Wilde said the Examiner was 'a commonplace official' pandering 'to the vulgarity and hypocrisy of the English people.' Ibid. 98, 531.

30. Ibid. 98–100.

31. Oscar Wilde, *The Complete Works of Oscar Wilde*, Vol. 6: *Journalism*, ed. John Stokes and Mark W. Turner, Part I (Oxford: Oxford University Press, 2013), 79.

32. Oscar Wilde, *Letters*, 100.

33. Like many other Victorian actors, Vezin did not try to demonstrate a character's development. Instead, he took a situational approach. According

to theatre historian Michael Booth, this entailed 'playing each significant dramatic moment for what it was and extracting the maximum
passion and effect from it, plotting his course through the play from
emotional climax to emotional climax.' Michael R. Booth, *Theatre in
the Victorian Age* (Cambridge: Cambridge University Press, 1991), 134.

34. Henry James, 'The London Theaters,' *Scribner's Monthly*, January 1881, 363.
35. Ibid. 369.
36. Michael Newton, '"Nihilists of Castlebar!": Exporting Russian Nihilism
in the 1885 and the Case of Oscar Wilde's *Vera, or the Nihilists*,' in *Russia
in Britain, 1880–1940*, ed. Rebecca Beasley and Philip Ross Bullock
(Oxford: Oxford University Press, 2013), 47, 43.
37. Oscar Wilde, *Letters*, 100.
38. Théophile Gautier, *Mademoiselle De Maupin*, ed. Patricia Duncker,
trans. Helen Constantine (Harmondsworth: Penguin, 1981), 23.
39. James McNeill Whistler, *The Gentle Art of Making Enemies* (New York:
Dover, 1967), 1.
40. Rennell Rodd, *Social and Diplomatic Memories*, 3 vols. (London: Edward
Arnold, 1922), 1:16, italics added.
41. George Du Maurier, 'The Rise and Fall of the Jack Sprats: Ye Aesthetic
Young Geniuses', *Punch* 21 September 1878.
42. Henry James, *Literary Criticism: French Writers, Other European Writers,
the Prefaces to the New York Edition*, ed. Leon Edel and Mark Wilson, Vol. 2
(New York: Library of America, 1984), 908, 939.
43. Qtd. in Linda Merrill, *After Whistler: The Artist and His Influence on
American Painting* (New Haven: Yale University Press, 2003), 24.
44. Felix Moscheles, *In Bohemia with Du Maurier* (New York: Harper,
1897), 125.
45. See 'Nincompoopiana—The Mutual Admiration Society,' *Punch* 14
February 1880, 66. In the late 1870s, Du Maurier created composite
aesthetes by mixing the features of real ones: for instance, in 'A Damper'
(1876), he sketched an opinionated but stuttering 'aesthetic youth' in
knee-breeches called Boniface Brasenose. Although the boy's surname
is an allusion to Pater's Oxford college, his mustachioed face is distinctly Swinburnian. It would be a year before Wilde set foot in the
Grosvenor Gallery and made his first foray into art criticism. Two years
later, in 1878's 'The Rise and Fall of Sprats,' the 'aesthetic young geniuses' still looked nothing like Wilde. It was in 1880 that Du Maurier
phased out the aged, anonymized aesthetes and replaced them with
recognizable personalities, including Wilde.
46. Henry James, 'Du Maurier and London Society,' *Century Illustrated
Monthly Magazine* May 1883.
47. Qtd. in Leonee Ormond, *George Du Maurier* (Pittsburgh: University of
Pittsburgh Press, 1969), 468.

48. The painter went in demanding more than £1,000 in damages for the art critic's sharp-tongued barbs about his *Nocturne in Black and Gold: The Falling Rocket*, but came out with only a nugatory award of one farthing. In *The Gentle Art of Making Enemies*, Whistler called Wilde a plagiarist and false prophet. Years after Whistler's death, his authorized biographers were still pushing this line. 'When Wilde came to London Whistler was the focus of the world,' they wrote, as though to remind their readers that Whistler was the original and best. Elizabeth and Joseph Pennell, *The Life of James McNeill Whistler*, 5th edn (Philadelphia: J. B. Lippincott, 1911), 225.

49. Walter Hamilton, *The Aesthetic Movement in England* (London, 1883), p. vii. In a 1881 sketch the cartoonist depicted the breakdown of Maudle and Postlethwaite who 'fondly flattered themselves that universal fame was theirs at last' when in fact 'they only exist in *Mr. Punch's* vivid imagination.' 'Frustrated Social Ambition,' *Punch* 21 May 1881, 229.

50. Oscar Wilde, *Letters*, 96.

51. *Collins Complete Works of Oscar Wilde*, 209.

52. George Du Maurier, 'Maudle on the Choice of a Profession,' *Punch* 12 February 1881.

53. E. H. Mikhail, *Oscar Wilde: Interviews and Recollections*, 2 vols. (London: Macmillan, 1979), 1:20.

54. Rodd, *Social and Diplomatic Memories*, 1:22–3.

55. Dennis Denisoff, *Aestheticism and Sexual Parody, 1840–1940* (Cambridge: Cambridge University Press, 2001), 83.

56. Mary Warner Blanchard, *Oscar Wilde's America: Counterculture in the Gilded Age* (New Haven: Yale University Press, 1998), 140.

57. Jane Wilde, *Lady Jane Wilde's Letters*, 63.

58. 'The Laws of Dress,' *Burlington Magazine* (May and July 1881), qtd. in Joy Melville, *Mother of Oscar: The Life of Jane Francesca Wilde* (London: Allison & Busby, 1999), 172.

59. James Eli Adams, *A History of Victorian Literature* (Oxford: Blackwell, 2011), 327; Mikhail, *Interviews*, 1:26, 113 n. 2.

60. Francis Cowley Burnand, *The Colonel: Comedy in 3 Acts*, ed. Anton Kirchhofer (Cologne: Pierre Marteau, 2004).

61. G. A. S., 'The Playhouses,' *The Illustrated London News* 12 February 1881, 151. *Punch*, the self-appointed voice of the Philistines, defended the play and said it concluded with 'the triumph of common sense.' '"The Colonel" in a Nut-Shell. A Philistine and Maudle Visit the Prince of Wales's,' *Punch* 19 February 1881, 81.

62. 'Sketches at the Prince of Wales's Theatre,' *The Illustrated London News* 26 March 1881, 302.

63. Elizabeth Aslin, *The Aesthetic Movement: Prelude to Art Nouveau* (London: Elek, 1969), 115–16.

64. Tony Joseph, *The D'Oyly Carte Opera Company 1875–1982: An Unofficial History* (Bristol: Bunthorne, 1994), 64.

65. Oscar Wilde, *Letters*, 110.

66. 'Mr. Oscar Wilde's Poems,' *The Times of India* (New Delhi, India), 26 August 1881, 3.

67. 'The Aesthetes,' *The Critic*, 1, no. 218 (13 August 1881), 101.

68. Qtd. in *The Complete Works of Oscar Wilde*, Vol. 1: *Poems and Poems in Prose*, p. ix.

69. 'Punch's Fancy Portraits. Number 37. Oscar Wilde,' *Punch* 25 June 1881, 298.

70. Queen Victoria, 'Journal Entry' (8 July 1846), *Queen Victoria's Journals* (Princess Beatrice's copies, Vol. 22, Royal Archives), 20.

71. Long before Wilde's time, minstrelsy and sunflowers had become synonymous. This would cause headaches for Wilde. There was already a hint of trials to come when *Punch* put the words to 'The Big Sunflower' in Wilde's mouth to ridicule his growing association with Aestheticism. 'The Big Sunflower' was a time-honoured minstrel song. W. Sheppard of the Original Christy Minstrels made it famous and others sang it for decades afterwards, right up into the early decades of the twentieth century. Performers usually wore a ring of wide yellow petals around their blackened faces to create the sunflower effect. In the 1930 film *Big Boy*, Al Jolson wore the disguise. See Langston Hughes, *Black Magic: A Pictorial History of the Negro in American Entertainment*, ed. Milton Meltzer (Englewood Cliffs, NJ: Prentice-Hall, 1967); William C. Blades, *Negro Poems, Melodies, Plantation Pieces, Camp Meeting Songs, Etc* (Boston: R. G. Badger, 1921), 23; Edward Le Roy Rice, *Monarchs of Minstrelsy: From 'Daddy' Rice to Date* (New York: Kenny, 1911), 186–7, 195; Denes Agay, *Best Loved Songs of the American People* (New York: Doubleday, 1999), 122.

72. *The Complete Works of Oscar Wilde*, Vol. 1: *Poems and Poems in Prose*, 39.

73. 'Oscar Wylde's Poems,' *New York Times* 14 August 1881, 10.

74. Qtd. in Nadia Khomami, 'Literary Success? Don't Give up the Day Job, Advised Oscar Wilde,' *The Daily Telegraph* (London), 19 March 2013.

75. Qtd. in Melville, *Mother of Oscar*, 58.

76. E. Bucalossi, 'The Colonel Waltz' (1881; S.631–2010, Victoria & Albert Museum).

77. Queen Victoria, 'Journal Entry' (4 October 1881), *Queen Victoria's Journals* (Princess Beatrice's copies, Vol. 75, Royal Archives), 73.

78. Aslin, *The Aesthetic Movement: Prelude to Art Nouveau*, 115–16.

79. *Patience* had 170 performances at London's Opera Comique, an artistic theatre lavishly decorated in gold with seats for 862 spectators. By early October, it transferred to the Savoy, D'Oyly Carte's prestigious new theatre. 'I feel sure,' Carte said of the Savoy's Italian Renaissance style and modern electric lights, that it 'will be appreciated by all persons of taste.' Ironically, *Patience*'s satire is directed at 'persons of taste,' i.e. aesthetes. Cyril Rollins and R. John Witts, eds., *The D'Oyly Carte Opera Company in Gilbert and Sullivan Operas: A Record of Productions, 1875–1961*

(London: Michael Joseph, 1962), 1, 23; T. Joseph, *The D'Oyly Carte Opera Company 1875–1982: An Unofficial History*, 78–9.

80. Max Beerbohm, *A Note on 'Patience'* (London: Miles & Company, 1918), 2.

81. Arthur Sullivan and W. S. Gilbert, *The Annotated Gilbert and Sullivan*, ed. Ian C. Bradley (Harmondsworth: Penguin, 1984), 149.

82. Mikhail, *Interviews*, 1:40.

83. Wilde went with Ellen Terry. Norman Page, *An Oscar Wilde Chronology* (London: Macmillan, 1991), 15; Oscar Wilde, *Letters*, 109; Mikhail, *Interviews*, 1:26, 113 n. 2.

84. 'Mr. D'oyley Carte and His Very Numerous Amusement Enterprises,' *Chicago Tribune* (Chicago), 15 January 1882, 9.

85. 'Personalities,' *National Republican* (Washington, DC), 20 June 1881, 2.

86. Mikhail, *Interviews*, 1:252.

87. William F. Morse, 'American Lectures,' in *The Writings of Oscar Wilde: His Life with a Critical Estimate of His Writings* (London: A. R. Keller 1907), 75.

88. Helen Lenoir, 'Letter to Archibald Forbes' (8 January 1885; MS Whistler D130, Glasgow University Library). Wilde would be liable for travelling expenses, hotel bills, and the fees for 'any special acting manager or advance agent' which would be deducted from the profits before he saw a payment. The contract negotiations dragged on throughout the autumn.

89. Oscar Wilde, *Letters*, 123.

90. Rodd, *Social and Diplomatic Memories*, 22–3.

91. 'Notes and Comments. The Sunflower and the Lily,' *Arthur's Home Magazine* March 1882, 211.

92. Mikhail, *Interviews*, 1:40. By mid-December 1881, he was being definitely identified in American books as *Patience*'s Bunthorne. See, for example, *Patience as Seen by Mr Curl Darling and Miss Murry Hill from Ye Orchestra Stalls*, which was published by J. M. Stoddart (soon to become conspicuously associated with Wilde) and illustrated by Charles Kendrick (who would illustrate a fake biography of Wilde, *Ye Soul Agonies in Ye Life of Oscar Wilde*).

CHAPTER 5. COLONEL MORSE'S CAMPAIGN

1. Oscar Wilde, *The Complete Letters of Oscar Wilde*, ed. Merlin Holland and Rupert Hart-Davis (London: Fourth Estate, 2000), 721.

2. Oscar Wilde, *The Complete Works of Oscar Wilde*, Vol. 1: *Poems and Poems in Prose*, ed. Bobby Fong and Karl Beckson (Oxford: Oxford University Press, 2000), 122.

3. Lloyd Lewis and Henry Justin Smith, *Oscar Wilde Discovers America, 1882* (New York: Harcourt, Brace, 1936), 32.

4. Queen Victoria, 'Journal Entry' (31 December 1881), *Queen Victoria's Journals* (Princess Beatrice's copies, Vol. 75, Royal Archives), 165–6.

5. Ibid. 167.

6. Queen Victoria, 'Journal Entry' (6 October 1900), *Queen Victoria's Journals* (Princess Beatrice's copies, Vol. 111, Royal Archives), 50.

7. William King Richardson, 'Letter to Roland Lincoln' (12 June 1881), *William King Richardson Collection, 1859–1951* (Letters to Roland Lincoln, 1880–1884, Am 2006 (23), Houghton Library, Harvard University).

8. Oscar Wilde, *Letters*, 729.

9. This private exchange has passed into myth but, according to John Cooper, the first reference to it was in Arthur Ransome's 1912 *Oscar Wilde: A Critical Study*. On 2 January 1882, at New York harbour, Wilde was hooked to the United States by the SS *Arizona*'s rattling anchor going over the side but passengers were not allowed to disembark until the next day because of quarantine regulations. For a more detailed account of the quotation's origins, see Cooper's website, http://www.oscarwildeinamerica.org/quotations/nothing-to-declare.html

10. William F. Morse, 'American Lectures,' in *The Writings of Oscar Wilde: His Life with a Critical Estimate of His Writings* (London: A. R. Keller 1907), 76.

11. Qtd. in Lewis and Smith, *Oscar Wilde Discovers America, 1882*, 31–2.

12. Oscar Wilde, *Letters*, 115.

13. James M. Hudnut, ed., *The New York Almanac for 1882* (New York: Francis Hart & Co., 1882), 29.

14. *Stoddart's Encyclopaedia Americana*, Vol. 1 (New York: J. M. Stoddart, 1883), 1:767.

15. *Bunthorne Abroad* was a parody of *Patience*, Gilbert and Sullivan's 1882 operetta. John Wilson Bengough, *Bunthorne Abroad or, the Lass That Loved a Pirate* (Toronto: Grip Print, 1883), 19.

16. Oscar Wilde, *Letters*, 124.

17. Ibid. 184.

18. Five months after the London premiere, *Patience* was produced to great acclaim at the Standard Theatre, New York on 22 September 1881. 'Business Manager, Mr. W. F. Morse' was printed on the programmes.

19. William F. Morse, 'The Indian Campaign in Minnesota in 1862,' in *Personal Recollections of the War of the Rebellion*, ed. A. Noel Blakeman (New York: G. P. Putnam's Sons, 1912), 193–4. Later, Morse fought for the Union during the Southern insurrection. Ballantine claims that he contracted ague while in military service. William Ballantine, *The Old World and the New, Being a Continuation of His 'Experiences'* (London: R. Bentley, 1884), 18.

20. Morse described his mission as 'for a period of nearly a year to be responsible for the public appearance of Mr. Wilde before the American and

Canadian public, in the way of preparation for his coming.' His boss was Helen Lenoir, a formidable university-trained Scottish business-woman ten years his junior. D'Oyly Carte called her his 'American brain,' and put her in command of his empire in the United States. W. F. Morse, 'American Lectures,' 73.

21. 'Preparing the Poet for Work,' *New York Tribune* 4 January 1882, Robert Ross Memorial Collection (Box 6. Scrapbook, University College, Oxford).

22. *New York World* 4 May 1882, qtd. in Richard Ellmann, *Oscar Wilde* (London: Hamish Hamilton, 1987), 177.

23. Morse, 'American Lectures,' 77.

24. Lewis and Smith, *Oscar Wilde Discovers America, 1882*, 39.

25. Matthew Hofer and Gary Scharnhorst, eds., *Oscar Wilde in America: The Interviews* (Urbana: University of Illinois Press, 2009), 127.

26. 'Art's Apostle. England's Aesthete at the Photographer's Gallery,' *Evening Star* (Washington, DC), 21 January 1882, 3.

27. Oscar Wilde, *The Complete Works of Oscar Wilde*, Vol. 3: *The Picture of Dorian Gray*, ed. Joseph Bristow (Oxford: Oxford University Press, 2005), 199.

28. 'Art's Apostle. England's Aesthete at the Photographer's Gallery,' 3.

29. 'Sarony and Langtry. A Photographer's Opinion of Her,' *Public Ledger* (Memphis, TN), 5 December 1882, 2.

30. Hofer and Scharnhorst, *Oscar Wilde in America: The Interviews*, 139.

31. Jane Gaines, *Contested Culture: The Image, the Voice, and the Law* (Chapel Hill: University of North Carolina Press, 1991), 52.

32. The 1884 case was *Burrow-Giles Lithographic Company v. Sarony*. Other unauthorized Wilde products included music such as 'Oscar Wilde's Serenade by Oscar Wilde,' published by Brentano Bros of New York in 1882. On the copyright implications of Sarony's photographs of Wilde, see Michael North, 'The Picture of Oscar Wilde,' *PMLA*, 125, no. 1 (2010); Kerry Powell, *Acting Wilde: Victorian Sexuality, Theatre, and Oscar Wilde* (Cambridge: Cambridge University Press, 2009).

33. Qtd. in Gaines, *Contested Culture: The Image, the Voice, and the Law*, 54.

34. *The Complete Works of Oscar Wilde*, Vol. 3: *The Picture of Dorian Gray*, 35.

35. Oscar Wilde, *Letters*, 124.

36. Laura Stedman and George M. Gould, eds., *Life and Letters of Edmund Clarence Stedman*, 2 vols. (New York: Moffat, Yard and Company, 1910), 2:31–2.

37. Oscar Wilde, *Letters*, 135.

38. 'Oscar Wilde Sees Patience,' *New York Herald Tribune*, 6 January 1882.

39. 'Preparing the Poet for Work,' *New York Tribune*.

40. 'Theatrical World,' *Truth* (New York), 8 January 1882.

41. Rennell Rodd, *Social and Diplomatic Memories*, 3 vols. (London: Edward Arnold, 1922), 1:24.

42. Oscar Wilde, *Letters*, 124.

43. Nan Johnson, *Nineteenth-Century Rhetoric in North America* (Carbondale: Southern Illinois University Press, 1991), 8.

44. Susan R. Hanes, *Wilkie Collins's American Tour, 1873–4* (London: Pickering & Chatto, 2008), 6.

45. Ralph Waldo Emerson, *Emerson's Prose and Poetry*, ed. Joel Porte and Saundra Morris (New York: Norton, 2001), 63.

46. Thomas Wentworth Higginson, 'The American Lecture-System,' *Macmillan's Magazine* May 1868, 53.

47. Johnson, *Nineteenth-Century Rhetoric in North America*, 149.

48. See, for example, *Beadle's Dime National Speaker: Embodying Gems of Oratory and Wit, Particularly Adapted to American Schools and Firesides* (New York: Beadle and Co., 1863).

49. Johnson, *Nineteenth-Century Rhetoric in North America*, 237, 228, 9.

50. Qtd. in Hanes, *Wilkie Collins's American Tour, 1873–4*, 7.

51. Oscar Wilde, *Letters*, 118.

52. James McNeill Whistler, 'Letter to Oscar Wilde,' February 1882, in *The Correspondence of James Mcneill Whistler, 1855–1903 Including the Correspondence of Anna Mcneill Whistler, 1855–1880*, ed. Margaret F. MacDonald, Patricia de Montfort, and Nigel Thorp (Glasgow: Glasgow University Library; on-line edition: http://www.whistler.arts.gla.ac.uk/correspondence).

53. Stuart Mason, *Bibliography of Oscar Wilde* (Boston: Longwood, 1977), 488. See also Norbert Kohl and David Henry Wilson, *Oscar Wilde: The Works of a Conformist Rebel* (Cambridge: Cambridge University Press, 1989), 71. Some are typewritten, and Wilde added to them and corrected them by hand.

54. Oscar Wilde, *Aristotle at Afternoon Tea: The Rare Oscar Wilde*, ed. John Wyse Jackson (London: Fourth Estate, 1991), 17.

55. Ibid. 14.

56. Ibid. 15.

57. Ibid. 26.

58. William Morris, *The Collected Letters of William Morris*, ed. Norman Kelvin, 4 vols. (Princeton: Princeton University Press, 1984), 2:38.

59. Oscar Wilde, *Aristotle at Afternoon Tea*, 3.

60. Ibid. 4.

61. Ibid. 19. Wilde's entry for the 1879 Chancellor's Essay Prize at Oxford compared the nineteenth century to Ancient Greece. There were military parallels between the two: fifth-century Athens had seen off Persian invaders and then sought to bolster morale by mythologizing victory and heroism. In the art of the period, the defeated were often represented as effeminate, and the Greek victors as masculine and powerful. Wilde wrote that he admired the 'refined effeminacy' that later Greek statuary had developed
    Although Wilde's analogy between the Hellenic past and the Victorian present was daring and brilliant, the essay's disorganization

diminished it. He didn't win. David Castriota, *Myth, Ethos, and Actuality: Official Art in Fifth-Century B.C. Athens* (Madison: University of Wisconsin Press, 1992), 4–6. Ellmann, *Wilde*, 103.

62. There were other appropriations: for example, he lightly altered Pater's 'desire for a more liberal and comely way of conceiving life' and turned it into the English Renaissance's 'desire for a more gracious and comely way of life.' Walter Pater, *The Renaissance*, ed. Adam Phillips (New York: Oxford University Press, 1986), 2. Oscar Wilde, *Aristotle at Afternoon Tea*, 3.

63. Hofer and Scharnhorst, *Oscar Wilde in America: The Interviews*, 25, 43. Edward Tyas Cook, *The Life of John Ruskin* (London: G. Allen & Company, 1911), 1:83.

64. 'Oscar Wilde's Lecture,' *New York Times*, 10 January 1882, 5.

65. 'Oscar Wilde's Lecture. The Young Apostle of Aestheticism Explaining His Theories of the English Renaissance,' *New York World*, 10 January 1882, 2.

66. Edith Wharton, *The Age of Innocence*, ed. Michael E. Nowlin (Peterborough, Ontario: Broadview, 2002), 64, 67.

67. Morse, 'American Lectures,' 77.

68. Ibid. 78.

69. The Huntington Library has an 88-page incomplete manuscript (HM 465). UCLA's Clark Library has manuscript fragments of the lectures, as well as a 44-page typescript corrected in Wilde's hand.

70. Oscar Wilde, *Aristotle at Afternoon Tea*, 3.

71. 'The Wilde Idiot in New York,' *Washington Post* (Washington, DC), 11 January 1882, 4.

72. 'Mr. D'oyley Carte and His Very Numerous Amusement Enterprises,' *Chicago Tribune* (Chicago), 15 January 1882, 9.

73. 'He began to speak in a voice that might have come from the tomb,' the *New York Times* reported. 'Oscar Wilde's Lecture,' *New York Times* 10 January 1882, 5.

74. Oscar Wilde, *Letters*, 127.

75. Ibid. 126. Compared to his Victorian peers, Wilde held Dickens in low esteem. His art, Wilde said, was limited. 'When he tries to be serious, he only succeeds in being dull, when he aims at truth, he merely reaches platitude.' Wilde respected Dickens's sense of humour and knack for caricature, and admired his ability to create memorable characters. 'None of us would part readily with Micawber and Mrs. Nickleby,' Wilde said. But he despised Dickensian moralizing and labelled his books a 'bacchanalia of benevolence.' For Wilde, Dickens was, above all, a carica-turist whose style was 'slang' and therefore no model for him. Oscar Wilde, *The Complete Works of Oscar Wilde*, Vol. 6: *Journalism*, ed. John Stokes and Mark W. Turner, Part I (Oxford: Oxford University Press, 2013), 137–8.

76. William R. Everdell, 'Monologues of the Mad: Paris Cabaret and Modernist Narrative from Twain to Eliot,' *Studies in American Fiction*, 20, no. 2 (1992), 181.

77. Dickens's first visit was in 1842. Qtd. in Robert McParland, *Charles Dickens's American Audience* (Lanham, MD: Lexington Books, 2010), 177.

78. Qtd. in Philip Collins, ed., *The Public Readings* (Oxford: Clarendon, 1975), p. lix.

79. Hofer and Scharnhorst, *Oscar Wilde in America: The Interviews*, 84.

80. Qtd. in Paul Schlicke, ed., *The Oxford Companion to Charles Dickens* (Oxford: Oxford University Press, 2011), 482.

81. *Atlantic Monthly* February 1878, 239, qtd. in McParland, *Charles Dickens's American Audience*, 170.

82. Everdell, 'Monologues of the Mad: Paris Cabaret and Modernist Narrative from Twain to Eliot,' 183.

83. Robert Douglas-Fairhurst, *Becoming Dickens: The Invention of a Novelist* (Cambridge, MA: Belknap, 2011), 99.

84. Schlicke, *The Oxford Companion to Charles Dickens*, 483. 'Each item had been carefully prepared and intensively rehearsed so that he knew the text by heart, *performed* them rather than read them, and could introduce spontaneous variations in response to the reaction of a particular audience.' Michael Slater, *Charles Dickens* (Oxford: Oxford University Press, 2007), 73.

85. Longfellow, *Letters*, 8 December 1867, qtd. in McParland, *Charles Dickens's American Audience*, 179.

86. Schlicke, *The Oxford Companion to Charles Dickens*, 17.

87. Twain claimed to be unimpressed by Dickens's style. Nevertheless, he conceded that Dickens was responsible for changing Americans' expectations of lecturers. Justin Kaplan, *Mr. Clemens and Mark Twain: A Biography* (New York: Simon and Schuster, 1966), 302.

88. Mark Twain, 'The Approaching Epidemic,' *The Galaxy* (September 1870). By the time Dickens died, Twain had already developed his own successful career as a lecturer. Twain's style was partly modelled on what he had seen in 1867. He was managed by Dickens's business agent, George Dolby. Few of Twain's books paid him better than his lectures. This had also been the case for Dickens and for Thackeray before him. By the 1890s Twain had lucrative engagements as far afield as India, Ceylon, South Africa, Australia, and New Zealand. In three years, he earned $100,000. Everdell, 'Monologues of the Mad: Paris Cabaret and Modernist Narrative from Twain to Eliot,' 183.

89. Qtd. in Hanes, *Wilkie Collins's American Tour, 1873–4*, 43.

90. Collins made £2,500. Ibid. 91.

91. 'Mr. D'Oyley Carte and His Very Numerous Amusement Enterprises,' *Chicago Tribune* 15 January 1882, 9.

92. Edward T. Channing, *Lectures Read to the Seniors in Harvard College* (Boston: Ticknor and Fields, 1856), 70.
93. Jane Wilde, *Lady Jane Wilde's Letters to Oscar Wilde, 1875–1895*, ed. Karen Tipper (Lewiston, NY: Edwin Mellen Press, 2011), 69.
94. 'Oscar Wilde,' *The Nation* 12 January 1882.
95. Hofer and Scharnhorst, *Oscar Wilde in America: The Interviews*, 129.
96. Ibid. 134. For an account of Wilde's powers as a raconteur at the dinner table, see Louise Jopling, *Twenty Years of My Life, 1867 to 1887* (London: John Lane, 1925), 78–80.

CHAPTER 6. OSCAR DEAR

1. Matthew Hofer and Gary Scharnhorst, eds., *Oscar Wilde in America: The Interviews* (Urbana: University of Illinois Press, 2009), 1.
2. Thomas Power O'Connor, 'The New Journalism,' *The New Review*, 1, no. 5 (1889), 423. Joel H. Wiener characterizes New Journalism's methods as 'bold headlines, gossip columns, interviews, sports reporting, pictures.' American journalists started conducting interviews in the 1860s, but their British counterparts were reluctant to adopt the new method. Richard Whiteing, the British correspondent for the *New York World*, said 'interviewing was ever an abomination to me, and I made a firm stand against it as soon as I could.' He devotes a chapter to the technique in his memoir and humorously portrays the difficulties journalists had with it. Joel H. Wiener, *Papers for the Millions: The New Journalism in Britain, 1850s to 1914* (New York: Greenwood, 1988), p. xii. Richard Whiteing, *My Harvest* (New York: Dodd, Mead & Co., 1915), 98.
3. Jane Wilde, *Lady Jane Wilde's Letters to Oscar Wilde, 1875–1895*, ed. Karen Tipper (Lewiston, NY: Edwin Mellen Press, 2011), 75.
4. Ibid. 92.
5. Ibid. 84.
6. Ibid. 92.
7. Mary Watson, 'Oscar Wilde at Home' *San Francisco Examiner*, 9 April 1882, 1, in Hofer and Scharnhorst, *Oscar Wilde in America: The Interviews*, 123. She later published a revised account of her encounter with Wilde in Mary Watson, *People I Have Met* (San Francisco: Francis, Valentine, 1890).

The *New York World* anticipated that women would lionize aesthetes. In a fanciful spoof, a fan visits Queerer, a cynical writer of erotic aesthetic verse modelled on Wilde. She tells him,

> (*Coquettishly*) You know I said I'd come; although it's not
> Quite right to pay a visit at your rooms
> But then a lion's den is not a room.
> A Temple of High Art is always safe.

Hearing this, Queerer demands, 'Embrace me!' upon which, the girl's angry father intervenes, drags his daughter home, and burns Queerer's poems. 'The Aesthetic Boom. Queerer the Utterest!,' *New York World*, 15 January 1882, 2.

8. Hofer and Scharnhorst, *Oscar Wilde in America: The Interviews*, 123.

9. Ibid. 124.

10. Ibid. 126.

11. Ibid. 125.

12. Qtd. in Neil McKenna, *The Secret Life of Oscar Wilde* (London: Arrow, 2004), 12.

13. Qtd. in Robert Secor, 'Aesthetes and Pre-Raphaelites: Oscar Wilde and the Sweetest Violet in England,' *Texas Studies in Literature and Language*, 21, no. 3 (1979), 401.

14. 'My Oscar' by Violet Hunt, qtd. ibid. 403.

15. Oscar Wilde, *The Complete Letters of Oscar Wilde*, ed. Merlin Holland and Rupert Hart-Davis (London: Fourth Estate, 2000), 82.

16. Hunt's diary, qtd. in Secor, 'Aesthetes and Pre-Raphaelites,' 399.

17. Hofer and Scharnhorst, *Oscar Wilde in America: The Interviews*, 34.

18. Charles Kendrick, *Ye Soul Agonies in Ye Life of Oscar Wilde* (New York, 1882), 21.

19. 'Did you read Oscar Wilde's lecture and note his observation about the desirability of having beautiful surroundings?' a high-minded mother asked her daughter. 'If you must know,' came her daughter's reply, an aesthetic young man's arms are 'the most beautiful surroundings in the whole wide world.' 'Short Locals,' *Juniata Sentinel and Republican* (Mifflintown, PA), 8 March 1882, 3.

20. 'The Oscar Wilde Style,' *Daily Globe* (St Paul, MN), 1 July 1882, 6.

21. Oscar Wilde, *The Complete Works of Oscar Wilde*, Vol. 6: *Journalism*, ed. John Stokes and Mark W. Turner, Part I (Oxford: Oxford University Press, 2013), 144.

22. Hofer and Scharnhorst, *Oscar Wilde in America: The Interviews*, 164–5.

23. Qtd. in Lloyd Lewis and Henry Justin Smith, *Oscar Wilde Discovers America, 1882* (New York: Harcourt, Brace, 1936), 65.

24. Hofer and Scharnhorst, *Oscar Wilde in America: The Interviews*, 38.

25. 'Illustration 20—No Title,' *The National Police Gazette*, 39, no. 227 (29 January 1882), 4.

26. Oscar Wilde, *The Complete Works of Oscar Wilde*, Vol. 1: *Poems and Poems in Prose*, ed. Bobby Fong and Karl Beckson (Oxford: Oxford University Press, 2000), 127.

27. 'The Oscar Wilde Style,' *Daily Globe* 1 July 1882, 6.

28. John Ruskin, *Sesame and Lilies*, ed. Deborah Epstein Nord (New Haven: Yale University Press, 2002), 31. 'Suppose you could be put behind a screen in the statesman's cabinet, or the prince's chamber, would you not be glad to listen to their words, though you were forbidden to

advance beyond the screen?' Ruskin wrote in *Sesame and Lilies* (1865). The metaphor seems custom-made to tantalize the curious.

29. *The Complete Works of Oscar Wilde*, Vol. 1: *Poems and Poems in Prose*, 128, 57, 110, 11, 224.

30. Ibid. 261.

31. Ibid. 70. Wilde knew Plato's *Charmides* well. Pater praised the young Charmides as one of Plato's most life-like characters.

32. Ibid. 73.

33. Ibid. 74.

34. Stuart Mason, *Bibliography of Oscar Wilde* (Boston: Longwood, 1977), 317–18.

35. *The Publishers' Weekly*, New York, 30 July 1881, 122, reprinted ibid. 325.

36. For example, George P. Munro's Seaside Library turned out a ten-cent edition that included the text of Wilde's lecture as a bonus.

37. Hofer and Scharnhorst, *Oscar Wilde in America: The Interviews*, 121.

38. James L. W. West III, 'The Chace Act and Anglo-American Literary Relations,' *Studies in Bibliography*, 45 (1992), 303.

39. 'Oscar Dear,' *The Bourbon News* (Millersburg, KY), 28 March 1882, 1.

40. Monroe H. Rosenfeld, *Oscar Dear!* (Cincinnati: F. W. Helmick, 1882).

41. 'Oscar Dear,' 1. The music sold in Cincinnati, Boston, St Louis, Philadelphia, New York, and San Francisco.

42. 'Miscellaneous,' *The Colfax Chronicle* 10 June 1882, 3.

43. Hofer and Scharnhorst, *Oscar Wilde in America: The Interviews*, 135–6.

44. Rosenfeld, *Oscar Dear!*

45. Hofer and Scharnhorst, *Oscar Wilde in America: The Interviews*, 162.

CHAPTER 7. MR WILD OF BORNEO, OR THE PADDY

1. Carl Bock, *The Head Hunters of Borneo: A Narrative of Travel up the Mahakkam and Down the Barito Also, Journeyings in Sumatra*, 2nd edn (London: S. Low, Marston, Searle, & Rivington, 1882), 75–6.

2. Nadja Durbach, *Spectacle of Deformity: Freak Shows and Modern British Culture* (Berkeley: University of California Press, 2010), 31.

3. Michael Epp, ' "Good Bad Stuff": Editing, Advertising, and the Transformation of Genteel Literary Production in the 1890s,' *American Periodicals: A Journal of History & Criticism*, 24, no. 2 (2014), 186–7. Joy Melville, *Mother of Oscar: The Life of Jane Francesca Wilde* (London: Allison & Busby, 1999), 166.

4. John A. Burrison, *Roots of a Region: Southern Folk Culture* (Jackson: University Press of Mississippi, 2007), 211 n. 49.

5. 'Who Oscar Wilde Is,' *National Republican* (Washington, DC), 21 January 1882, 2.

6. 'How Far Is It from This to This?,' *Washington Post* (Washington, DC), 22 January 1882, 4. The image was reprinted in the *St. Louis Post-Dispatch* and in other newspapers, achieving a wide circulation.

7. P. T. Barnum, qtd. in N. Durbach, *Spectacle of Deformity: Freak Shows and Modern British Culture*, 99. Jane R. Goodall, *Performance and Evolution in the Age of Darwin: Out of the Natural Order* (London: Routledge, 2002), 53–7.

8. James W. Cook Jr., 'Of Men, Missing Links, and Nondescripts: The Strange Career of P.T. Barnum's "What Is It?" Exhibition,' in *Freakery: Cultural Spectacles of the Extraordinary Body*, ed. Rosemarie Garland-Thomson (New York: New York University Press, 1996), 140.

9. 'What Can They Be?,' American Museum playbill, September 1860, in Goodall, *Performance and Evolution in the Age of Darwin*, 60. On Barnum and race, see Benjamin Reiss, *The Showman and the Slave: Race, Death, and Memory in Barnum's America* (Cambridge, MA: Harvard University Press, 2001).

10. Bernth Lindfors, 'Introduction,' in *Africans on Stage: Studies in Ethnological Show Business*, ed. Bernth Lindfors (Bloomington, IN: Indiana University Press, 1999), p. viii. See also Goodall, *Performance and Evolution in the Age of Darwin*, 47–80.

11. Gillian Beer, *Forging the Missing Link: Interdisciplinary Stories* (Cambridge: Cambridge University Press, 1992), 19. Charles Lyell used the expression 'missing link' in his 1851 *Elements of Geology*, although the phrase was almost certainly circulating before then.

12. Robert Young, *Colonial Desire: Hybridity in Theory, Culture, and Race* (London: Routledge, 1995), 6, 89.

13. Oscar Wilde, *The Complete Letters of Oscar Wilde*, ed. Merlin Holland and Rupert Hart-Davis (London: Fourth Estate, 2000), 172.

14. Arthur O. Lovejoy, *The Great Chain of Being: A Study of the History of an Idea* (Cambridge, MA: Harvard University Press, 1964).

15. William Dean Howells, 'Life and Letters,' *Harper's Weekly* 25 April 1896, 415.

16. 'Mr. Wilde and Ourselves,' *The Washington Post* 24 January 1882, 2. In June 1882, under the headline 'When Does an Ethiopian become a White Man?' the *Post* covered a little-known case aiming to determine 'where the white man ends and the negro begins.' One lawyer argued it was a matter of blood, while the Chief Justice deemed it 'an aesthetic question.' He was, the lawyer quipped, 'getting Wilde over it!' 'A Great Test Question: When Does an Ethiopian Become a White Man?,' *The Washington Post* (Washington, DC), 2 June 1882, 1. 'Editorial Article 2— No Title,' *The Washington Post* (Washington, DC), 21 January 1882, 2.

17. 'Mr. Wilde and Ourselves,' 2.

18. Cook, 'Of Men, Missing Links, and Nondescripts,' 140.

19. 'Mr. Wilde and Ourselves,' 2.

20. Qtd. in Matthew Hofer and Gary Scharnhorst, eds., *Oscar Wilde in America: The Interviews* (Urbana: University of Illinois Press, 2009), 116.

21. Ibid. 32.

22. John Brannigan, *Race in Modern Irish Literature and Culture* (Edinburgh: Edinburgh University Press, 2009), 89–99.

23. Earnest Hooton, Dupertuis Albert, Clarence Wesley, and Helen Dawson, *The Physical Anthropology of Ireland*, 2 vols. (Cambridge, MA: Peabody Museum of Archaeology and Ethnology, 1955), 1:149.

24. Ibid. 1:171.

25. Philip E. Smith II and Michael S. Helfand, eds., *Oscar Wilde's Oxford Notebooks: A Portrait of Mind in the Making* (Oxford: Oxford University Press, 1989), 214.

26. Oscar Wilde, *The Complete Works of Oscar Wilde*, Vol. 4: *Criticism: Historical Criticism, Intentions, The Soul of Man*, ed. Josephine M. Guy (Oxford: Oxford University Press, 2007), 4.

27. Herbert Spencer, *First Principles*, 2nd edn (London: Williams and Norgate, 1867), 401.

28. *The Complete Works of Oscar Wilde*, Vol. 4: *Criticism: Historical Criticism, Intentions, The Soul of Man*, 177.

29. Ibid. 263.

30. Oscar Wilde, *The Complete Works of Oscar Wilde*, Vol. 3: *The Picture of Dorian Gray*, ed. Joseph Bristow (Oxford: Oxford University Press, 2005), 85.

31. Ibid. 72, 111.

32. Ibid. 72.

33. E. H. Mikhail, *Oscar Wilde: Interviews and Recollections*, 2 vols. (London: Macmillan, 1979), 1:107.

34. Herbert Spencer, 'The Americans: A Conversation and a Speech, with an Addition,' in *The Complete Works of Herbert Spencer* (New York: Appleton, 1892), 481.

35. Herbert Spencer qtd. in David Chalcraft, 'Herbert Spencer's Dangerous Pilgrimage: In America 1882,' in *Transatlantic Voyages and Sociology: The Migration and Development of Ideas*, ed. Cherry Schrecker (Farnham: Ashgate, 2012), 132. In New York, Spencer shocked a banquet given in his honour when he declared that Americans were not 'in general unduly civilized.' Spencer, 'The Americans: A Conversation and a Speech, with an Addition,' 481.

36. Kipling, qtd. in Frederic Lauriston Bullard, *Famous War Correspondents* (Boston: Little, Brown, 1914), 114.

37. Hofer and Scharnhorst, *Oscar Wilde in America: The Interviews*, 36.

38. Wilde declined to publish Forbes's scurrilous letters but the opportunity to retaliate in private may have been too tempting to resist. In *The Picture of Dorian Gray*, Wilde sketched a military man-riddle, 'a most truculent and red-faced old gentleman covered all over with orders and ribbons, and hissing into my ear.' His name? Sir Humpty Dumpty, a 'very successful' nobody who has done battle on the Afghan frontier and led Russian intrigues. Naming a crack-brained character after a

nursery rhyme hero famous for going to pieces is a cunning bit of short-hand. Wilde's deliciously childish portrait knocks the veteran and gives him a great fall. *The Complete Works of Oscar Wilde*, Vol. 3: *The Picture of Dorian Gray*, 9.

39. James McNeill Whistler, *The Correspondence of James McNeill Whistler, 1855–1903*, ed. Margaret F. MacDonald, Patricia de Montfort, and Nigel Thorp (Glasgow: Glasgow University Library; on-line edition: http://www.whistler.arts.gla.ac.uk/correspondence), after April 1881.

40. Oscar Wilde, *Letters*, 135.

41. M. Alison Kibler, 'The Stage Irishwoman,' *Journal of American Ethnic History*, 24, no. 3 (Spring, 2005), 8.

42. Oscar Wilde, *Letters*, 135.

43. Cook, 'Of Men, Missing Links, and Nondescripts,' 150. Bluford Adams, *E Pluribus Barnum: The Great Showman and the Making of U.S. Popular Culture* (Minneapolis, MN: University of Minnesota Press, 1997), 147–63.

44. Boucicault, qtd. in Oscar Wilde, *Letters*, 135.

45. 'Oscar Wilde. He Has Seen Quite Enough of Chicago,' *Chicago Daily Tribune* 15 February 1882, 3.

46. Oscar Wilde, *Letters*, 155.

47. Ibid. 174.

48. William F. Morse, 'Oscar Wilde's American Lecture Tour: W. F. Morse's Statement of Accounts' (1882), George Arents Collection (Arents S 1373, New York Public Library, NY). $30 in 1882 is $718.00 using the Consumer Price Index for 2017. Samuel H. Williamson, 'Seven Ways to Compute the Relative Value of a U.S. Dollar Amount, 1774 to Present,' Measuring Worth.com, http://www.measuringworth.com/uscompare/.

49. Oscar Wilde, *Letters*, 131.

50. 'Oscar Wilde's Little Tribulations,' *Washington Post* (Washington, DC), 19 August 1882, 2.

51. 'Oscar Wilde. He Has Seen Quite Enough of Chicago.'

52. William Edwin Adams, *Our American Cousins: Being Personal Impressions of the People and Institutions of the United States* (London: Walter Scott, 1883), 6.

53. Ibid. 9.

54. Ibid. 348.

55. Charles Fanning, ed., *The Exiles of Erin: Nineteenth-Century Irish-American Fiction* (Notre Dame, IN: University of Notre Dame Press, 1987), 2–3.

56. R. F. Foster, *Modern Ireland, 1600–1972* (London: Allen Lane, 1988), 355–6.

57. Oscar Wilde, *The Complete Works of Oscar Wilde*, Vol. 7: *Journalism*, ed. John Stokes and Mark W. Turner, Part II (Oxford: Oxford University Press, 2013), 203.

58. Foster, *Modern Ireland, 1600–1972*, 358.

59. Owen Dudley Edwards, 'The American Image of Ireland: A Study of Its Early Phases,' *Perspectives in American History*, 4 (1970), 274.

60. Thomas D'Arcy McGee, *Nation* (New York), 10 February 1849, in Fanning, *The Exiles of Erin*, 99.

61. *The Complete Works of Oscar Wilde*, Vol. 7: *Journalism*, Part II, 203.

62. Fanning, *The Exiles of Erin*, 11.

63. The Land League gave direction to escalating peasant unrest over rents and evictions. Widely supported by agrarians and clergy, it promoted self-government and land reform. The landlords were no better than slaveholders before the American Civil War, it argued. William Henry Hurlbert, *Ireland under Coercion: The Diary of an American* (Boston, MA: Houghton, Mifflin and Company, 1888), p. x.

64. Parnell, qtd. in Foster, *Modern Ireland, 1600–1972*, 416.

65. Michael Willem De Nie, *The Eternal Paddy: Irish Identity and the British Press, 1798–1882* (Madison, WI: University of Wisconsin Press, 2004), 213.

66. Throughout the 1880s, Irish-Americans sent money back to Ireland. 'It is a most curious feature of the situation in Ireland,' an American observer wrote, that it is the Irish in America 'who neither sow nor reap in Ireland, pay no taxes there, and bear no burdens, who find the alien oppression most intolerable.' Hurlbert, *Ireland under Coercion*, p. xi.

67. Anne E. Kane, 'Theorizing Meaning Construction in Social Movements: Symbolic Structures and Interpretation During the Irish Land War, 1879–1882,' *Sociological Theory*, 15, no. 3 (1997), 251.

68. 'Who Oscar Wilde Is,' *National Republican* 21 January 1882, 2.

69. *Irish Nation*, qtd. in Davis Coakley, *Oscar Wilde: The Importance of Being Irish* (Dublin: Town House & Country House, 1994), 183.

70. 'The Irish Frankenstein,' *Punch* 20 May 1882.

71. De Nie, *The Eternal Paddy*, 275–6. Foster, *Modern Ireland, 1600–1972*, 408.

72. John J. Appel, 'From Shanties to Lace Curtains: The Irish Image in *Puck*, 1876–1910,' *Comparative Studies in Society and History*, 13, no. 4 (October 1971), 375.

73. Lewis Perry Curtis, *Apes and Angels: The Irishman in Victorian Caricature* (Washington, DC: Smithsonian Institution Press, 1971), 103. Curtis's study considers how Irish radicalism contributed to the simian caricatures that dominated British publications. Foster takes the view that English and American satirical cartoons pertained to religion and class, not to race. R. F. Foster, *Paddy & Mr. Punch: Connections in Irish and English History* (London: Allen Lane, 1993).

74. De Nie notes that 'despite eighty years of political union and exposure to British moral values, the inborn deficiencies of Paddy's Celtic heritage, such as violence and emotionalism, seemed just as prominent in 1882 as they had been in 1798.' De Nie, *The Eternal Paddy*, 276.

75. Qtd. ibid. 256. Likewise, the *Liverpool Journal* decried *Punch*'s influence as a mouthpiece for 'the spirit of society and London,' in a leading article in autumn 1882.

76. 'Preparing the Poet for Work, *New York Tribune*' (4 January 1882), Robert Ross Memorial Collection (Box 6. Scrapbook, University College, Oxford).

77. Michael T. Isenberg, *John L. Sullivan and His America* (Urbana: University of Illinois Press, 1988), 104–5.

78. Oscar Wilde, *Letters*, 185.

79. Newspapers compared the heavyweight to Wilde, describing him as 'two hundred pounds avoirdupois of aesthetic human flesh and bones done up in a mouse-coloured velveteen shooting jacket.' Years later, the boxer John L. Sullivan was brought face to face with a primitive 'missing link' when he fought 'Oofty Goofty,' a well-known San Francisco performer who exhibited himself as the Wild Man of Borneo. Daubed in tar and horsehair, he shouted 'oofty goofty' as he performed, gulped down raw meat, attacked his audiences, and, for a fee, allowed them to hit him with a stick. 'Oofty Goofty' died in 1890 from injuries sustained in the brawl with Sullivan. Hofer and Scharnhorst, *Oscar Wilde in America: The Interviews*, 162.

80. 'The Two Aesthetes,' *Chicago Daily Tribune* 12 February 1882, 4. *Puck* spoofed the meeting in 'Wilde and Sullivan: The Great Fight. The Two Aesthetes Meet near Concord,' *Puck* (New York), 15 February 1882, 3.

81. 'Oscar Wilde. He Has Seen Quite Enough of Chicago.'

82. Oscar Wilde, *Letters*, 175.

83. A. H. Saxon, ed. *Selected Letters of P. T. Barnum* (New York: Columbia University Press, 1983), 226–8.

CHAPTER 8. LIFE IMITATES ART

1. Qtd. in Lloyd Lewis and Henry Justin Smith, *Oscar Wilde Discovers America, 1882* (New York: Harcourt, Brace and Company, 1936), 123.

2. Qtd. in Edmund Clarence Stedman, *Life and Letters of Edmund Clarence Stedman*, ed. Laura Stedman, George M. Gould, and Alice Marsland, 2 vols. (New York: Moffat, Yard and Co., 1910), 2:32.

3. 'Supplement. Our Boston Letter,' *The Morning Star* 11 February 1882.

4. 'Theatrical Attractions Next Week,' *The Harvard Crimson* 28 January 1882.

5. Lewis and Smith, *Oscar Wilde Discovers America, 1882*, 125.

6. 'This Evening's News,' *The Pall Mall Gazette* 2 February 1882.

7. William F. Morse, 'Oscar Wilde's American Lecture Tour: W. F. Morse's Statement of Accounts,' in George Arents Collection (New York Public Library, 1882).

8. Qtd. in Lewis and Smith, *Oscar Wilde Discovers America, 1882*, 128.

9. Matthew Hofer and Gary Scharnhorst, eds., *Oscar Wilde in America: The Interviews* (Urbana: University of Illinois Press, 2009), 62.

10. *The Harvard Crimson 1873–1906*, (Cambridge, MA: The University Press, 1906), 61. Kathryn Allamong Jacob, *King of the Lobby: The Life and Times of Sam Ward, Man-About-Washington in the Gilded Age* (Baltimore: Johns Hopkins University Press, 2010), 144. See also *Harvard University Quinquennial Catalogue of the Officers and Graduates 1636–1930* (Cambridge, MA: Harvard University Press, 1930), 321. In 1882, Harvard had less than a thousand students, so it was a significant proportion of them who felt compelled to attend Wilde's lecture. *Annual Report of the President and Treasurer of Harvard College, 1882–3* (Boston: George H. Ellis, 1882), 45.

11. Letter from Samuel Ward to Oscar Wilde, 9 January 1882, quoted in Michèle Mendelssohn, *Henry James, Oscar Wilde and Aesthetic Culture* (Edinburgh: Edinburgh University Press, 2007), 49. For details of the visit, see Lately Thomas, *Sam Ward: 'King of the Lobby'* (Boston: Houghton, Mifflin Co., 1965), 404.

12. Qtd. in Maude Howe Elliott, *Uncle Sam Ward and His Circle* (New York: Macmillan, 1938), 606.

13. 'Advertising Tricks of Wilde's Agent,' *Washington Post* 13 February 1882.

14. Stefan Collini, *Public Moralists: Political Thought and Intellectual Life in Britain 1850–1930* (Oxford: Clarendon Press, 1991), 30.

15. See James Eli Adams, *A History of Victorian Literature* (Oxford: Blackwell, 2011), 87–8, 118–19. Leslie Butler, *Critical Americans: Victorian Intellectuals and Transatlantic Liberal Reform* (Chapel Hill, NC: University of North Carolina Press, 2007), 22, 274–6.

16. On the history of late nineteenth-century anxieties over American and British gentlemanliness, see Anne M. Windholz, 'An Emigrant and a Gentleman: Imperial Masculinity, British Magazines, and the Colony That Got Away,' *Victorian Studies*, 42, no. 4 (1999).

17. Kate Crombie, 'Aunt Ruth Goes to Hear Oscar Wilde,' *Godey's Lady's Book* (April 1882).

18. 'Harvard Boys Guying Oscar Wilde,' *The Paterson Weekly Press* 2 February 1882.

19. There are discrepancies between the local reports, such as in Lowell, forty miles north of Boston, where the *Daily Courier* sighed with relief that the students hadn't been an embarrassment after all. 'Oscar Wilde's Lectures,' *The Lowell Daily Courier* (Lowell, MA), 2 February 1882.

20. *Waco Daily Examiner*, 25 June 1882, qtd. in Dorothy McLeod MacInerney, William Warren Rogers, and Robert David Ward, 'Oscar Wilde Lectures in Texas, 1882,' *Southwestern Historical Quarterly*, 106, no. 4 (2003), 559.

21. 'Boston Culture at a Discount,' *Sacramento Daily Record-Union* (Sacramento, CA), 3 February 1882.

22. Lewis and Smith, *Oscar Wilde Discovers America, 1882*, 123. For an example of the association between Harvard undergraduates and dandyism, see 'Confessions of a Frivolous Youth' by Carleton Sprague ('81), a satire in which the first-person narrator describes his stockings, 'faultless pumps,' and 'new dress coat from England' and makes conversation about Boston Aestheticism. Carleton Sprague, 'Confessions of a Frivolous Youth,' in *Stories from the Harvard Advocate. Being a Collection of Stories Selected from the Advocate from Its Founding, Eighteen Hundred and Sixty-Six, to the Present Day* (Cambridge, MA: Harvard University, 1896), 31.

23. The front page of the *Yale Daily News* cautioned students not to fall under Wilde's sway as the Harvard sixty had. It would be best if Yale men stayed away from the lecture, the administration recommended, warning that the slightest disrespect would 'receive the censure of the college, the city authorities and faculty.' The Yale administration's authoritarian bluster suggests the magnitude of the reputational risk involved. 'Communication,' *Yale Daily News* 1 February 1882.

24. 'Oscar Wilde in New Haven—a Large Audience Trying to Fathom His Meaning—Advice to Yale Students,' *New York Times* 2 February 1882. In 1882, the men of Yale were more traditional than their Harvard counterparts. They preferred sporting pastimes to culture and art, and favoured the classics (mostly Dickens, Thackeray, and Scott). *Yale Literary Magazine* emphatically stated its opposition to Wilde, saying that the College's real students of culture would refuse to be 'classed with Bunthorne, Wilde & Co.' Joseph Ernest Whitney, 'College Aesthete,' *Yale Literary Magazine*, no. 27 (1882), 235.

25. F. W. Chapman, *The Trowbridge Family, or, Descendants of Thomas Trowbridge, One of the First Settlers of New Haven, CT* (New Haven: Punderson, Crisand & Co., 1872), 23. The servant may have been J. Jackson, a literate, Connecticut-born man who listed himself as a farmworker on the 1870 Census. Several members of the Trowbridge family were students at Yale around this time. The family was associated with H. Trowbridge's Sons, a Barbadian firm that was dissolved in 1891.

26. *Yale Daily News* 30 January 1882; 'Oscar Wilde's American Lecture Tour: W. F. Morse's Statement of Accounts.'

27. Charles Kendrick, *Ye Soul Agonies in Ye Life of Oscar Wilde, Illustr. By C. Kendrick* ([New York], 1882), 21.

28. The illustration was titled *A Symphony in Colour*, a version of Whistler's *Symphony in White* painting. The title *A Symphony in Colour* gestures towards typical minstrel show titles, for example *A Symphony in Black and White*, which was produced a few years later. Wilde publicly praised Whistler in the American press saying, 'he paints symphonies in color,'

and he commended *Symphony in White* as 'the most beautiful picture I ever saw.' *A Symphony in Colour* transforms Wilde into the kind of man that the cultural critic Monica Miller describes as 'a threat to supposed natural aristocracy, [because] he is (hyper) masculine *and* feminine, aggressively heterosexual yet not quite a real man, a vision of an upstanding citizen and an outsider broadcasting his alien status by clothing his dark body in a good suit.' Lansing Industrial Aid Society, *A Symphony in Black and White [Performed by the] Lady Minstrels at Baird's. Wednesday Evening, Feb. 6, 1895* ([n.p.] 1895). Hofer and Scharnhorst, *Oscar Wilde in America: The Interviews*, 145. Monica L. Miller, *Slaves to Fashion: Black Dandyism and the Styling of Black Diasporic Identity* (Durham, NC: Duke University Press, 2009), 11.

29. George M. Marsden, *The Soul of the American University: From Protestant Establishment to Established Nonbelief* (New York: Oxford University Press, 1994), 25.

30. William Graham Sumner, 'What Our Boys Are Reading,' *Scribner's Monthly*, 15 (March 1878), 681.

31. Ibid. 683.

32. Ibid. 681.

33. Ibid. 685.

34. Ibid. 684. Minstrelsy was magnetic to young men, Mark Twain attested in his reminiscences. When the circus came to town, all the boys wanted to be clowns, Twain said. Likewise, 'the first negro minstrel show that came to our section left us all suffering to try that kind of life.' Mark Twain, *Life on the Mississippi* (London: Chatto & Windus, 1883), 41.

35. Sumner, 'Sociology' (1881), qtd. in Mike Hawkins, *Social Darwinism in European and American Thought, 1860–1945: Nature as Model and Nature as Threat* (Cambridge: Cambridge University Press, 1997), 110. Sumner's views are consistent with his position as Herbert Spencer's foremost American disciple.

36. Sumner, 'What Social Classes Owe Each Other' (1883), qtd. ibid. 111.

37. Sumner, 'What Our Boys Are Reading,' 684.

38. Richard Williams, *Hierarchical Structures and Social Value: The Creation of Black and Irish Identities in the United States* (Cambridge: Cambridge University Press, 1990), 2.

39. Richard Hofstadter, *Social Darwinism in American Thought* (Boston: Beacon, 1992), 95.

40. William Graham Sumner, *Folkways: A Study of the Sociological Importance of Usages, Manners, Customs, Mores, and Morals* (Boston: Ginn, 1907), 578, emphasis added.

41. Wilde was no stranger to help. His well-to-do Dublin family had domestics, and he had a servant while he was a student at Oxford.

42. Oscar Wilde, *The Complete Letters of Oscar Wilde*, ed. Merlin Holland and Rupert Hart-Davis (London: Fourth Estate, 2000), 127.

43. Ibid. 175. Howe felt her 'household was thrown into a flutter by the advent of his valet.' Her daughters explained that they felt 'it was one thing to entertain the aesthete, another to put up the gentleman's gentleman.' Laura Elizabeth Howe Richards and Maud Howe Elliott, *Julia Ward Howe, 1819–1910*, 2 vols. (Boston: Houghton Mifflin Company, 1925), 1:72.

44. Hofer and Scharnhorst, *Oscar Wilde in America: The Interviews*, 25.

45. Ibid. 88.

46. Ibid. 162.

47. 'Oscar Wilde Passed Through Richmond, Ind.,' *The Richmond Item* (Richmond, Indiana), 8 May 1882, 1.

48. *Nemaha County Republican* (Sabetha, Kansas), 11 May 1882, 2. 'Oscar Wilde. His Appearance in the City,' *The Leavenworth Times* (Leavenworth, Kansas), 20 April 1882, 4.

49. Hofer and Scharnhorst, *Oscar Wilde in America: The Interviews*, 65.

50. 'Oscar Wilde instructs his valet to keep very dark about the private life of his aesthetic master,' the *New Haven Register* punned, 'as the valet is an American Ethiop he has no difficulty in doing so.' 'Persons and Things,' *New Haven Register* 11 March 1882.

51. Oscar Wilde, *The Complete Works of Oscar Wilde*, Vol. 4: *Criticism: Historical Criticism, Intentions, The Soul of Man*, ed. Josephine M. Guy (Oxford: Oxford University Press, 2007), 90.

52. Ibid. 91.

53. Ibid. 80.

54. Oscar Wilde *Letters*, 386.

55. My phrasing is indebted to chapter 6, 'The Arts of Impression Management,' in Erving Goffman, *The Presentation of Self in Everyday Life* (New York: Doubleday, 1959).

56. University of Rochester, *The University of Rochester, the First Hundred Years* (Rochester, NY: University of Rochester Centennial Committee, 1950), 11. Junior Class of the University of Rochester, 'Intepres '82,' XXIII, no. 1 (April 1881), 48.

57. Martin Brewer Anderson, *The Work and Aims of the University of Rochester. An Address Delivered on Commencement Day, June 28, 1876.* (Rochester, NY: Democrat and Chronicle Print, 1876), 2.

58. 'Martin Brewer Anderson,' Rare Books, Special Collections and Preservation, River Campus Libraries, University of Rochester, http://rbscp.lib.rochester.edu/1243#top. See also 'Martin Brewer Anderson,' *New York Times* 27 February 1980.

59. Rochester, 'Intepres '82,' 44.

60. 'Rochester's Deep Disgrace. Ill-Mannered, Boorish Young Men, Said to Be Students, at Wilde's Lecture,' *Rochester Union and Advertiser* 8 February 1882.

61. 'It Is Pretty Plain,' *Daily Inter Ocean* 9 February 1882.

62. United States Census, 'Peter Craig, Rochester Ward 3, Monroe, New York' (National Archives, Washington, DC, 1850); 'Peter Craig, Rochester Ward 3, Monroe, New York' (National Archives, Washington, DC, 1860); 'Peter Craig, Rochester Ward 3, Monroe, New York' (National Archives, Washington, DC, 1880); 'New York State Board of Charities: Peter Craig,' in *New York Census of Inmates in Almshouses and Poorhouses, 1835–1921* (New York State Archives, Albany, NY, 14 April 1887); 'New York State Board of Charities: Peter Craig,' in *Historical Register of National Homes for Disabled Volunteer Soldiers, 1866–1938* (Records of the Department of Veterans Affairs, National Archives, Washington, DC).

63. Arthur James May, 'The End of an Age,' in *A History of the University of Rochester, 1850–1962*, ed. Lawrence Eliot Klein (Rochester, NY: University of Rochester, 1977).

64. Lewis and Smith, *Oscar Wilde Discovers America, 1882*, 156–60.

65. Levine, *The Lives of Frederick Douglass*, 138, 79.

66. On the politics of optics, see Amy Robinson, 'It Takes One to Know One: Passing and Communities of Common Interest,' *Critical Inquiry*, 20, no. 4 (Summer, 1994), 715–36.

67. Douglass, qtd. in Maurice O. Wallace, 'Framing the Black Soldier,' *Pictures and Progress: Early Photography and the Making of African American Identity* (Durham, NC: Duke University Press, 2012), 253.

68. Douglass, qtd. in Laura Wexler, 'A More Perfect Likeness: Frederick Douglass and the Image of the Nation,' ibid. 21.

69. Hofer and Scharnhorst, *Oscar Wilde in America: The Interviews*, 61–3.

CHAPTER 9. IS IT MANHOOD?

1. Walt Whitman, *Leaves of Grass, 1855 Edition* (Brooklyn, NY: n.p., 1855), 25.

2. Ibid. 78.

3. Ibid. 50.

4. 'The state of society,' Emerson said, 'is one in which the members have suffered amputation from the trunk, and strut about like so many walking monsters,—a good finger, a neck, a stomach, an elbow, but never a man.' Ralph Waldo Emerson, *Emerson's Prose and Poetry*, ed. Joel Porte and Saundra Morris (New York: Norton, 2001), 53.

5. Kenneth M. Price, ed., *Walt Whitman: The Contemporary Reviews* (Cambridge: Cambridge University Press, 1996), 87.

6. Whitman appended Emerson's letter to the 1856 edition of *Leaves of Grass*. Walt Whitman, *Leaves of Grass, 1856 Edition* (Brooklyn, NY: Fowler & Wells, 1856), 356.

7. Gary Schmidgall, *Containing Multitudes: Walt Whitman and the British Literary Tradition* (New York: Oxford University Press, 2014), 280.

8. Walt Whitman, 'Letter to Emma Bouvier Peterson Childs' (18 January 1882), in Walt Whitman, *Daybooks and Notebooks*, ed. William White (New York: New York University Press, 2007), 282.

9. Matthew Hofer and Gary Scharnhorst, eds., *Oscar Wilde in America: The Interviews* (Urbana: University of Illinois Press, 2009), 29.

10. It's unlikely that Whitman would have thought the paternity legitimate, however. Schmidgall, *Containing Multitudes*, 281.

11. Walt Whitman, *The Correspondence, 1876–1885*, ed. Edwin Haviland Miller, 6 vols. (New York: New York University Press, 2007), 3:263.

12. In 1882, Wilde said, 'Lady Wilde bought one of the earliest copies of the poems some sixteen years ago, and was accustomed to read passages from it to him.' This dating makes it likely that the Wildes did not read the expurgated 1868 Rossetti edition, but an earlier American edition, such as one of these:

(1) an imported American *Leaves of Grass* (such as the one the British publishers Wm. Horsell circulated in 1855, or the one Trübner and Co. circulated in 1860);

(2) the legitimate 1860 American edition published by Thayer and Eldridge of Boston;

(3) the 1867 American edition published by W. E. Chapin & Co. of New York (which Rossetti cut down by half to create his 1868 book).

Whitman's works were important to the late nineteenth-century Irish Literary Revival. Edward Dowden, a Trinity College Dublin professor, read Whitman to enthusiastic Dublin audiences. E. H. Mikhail, *Oscar Wilde: Interviews and Recollections*, 2 vols. (London: Macmillan, 1979), 1:47. Edward Whitley, 'Introduction to the British Editions of Leaves of Grass, the Walt Whitman Archive,' Center for Digital Research in the Humanities, University of Nebraska-Lincoln, http://whitmanarchive.org/published/books/other/british/intro.html.

For a detailed analysis of Whitman's influence on Dublin, see chapter 8 of Joann P. Krieg, *Whitman and the Irish* (Des Moines: University of Iowa Press, 2000).

13. Walt Whitman, *Poems, Rossetti Edition*, ed. William Michael Rossetti (John Camden Hotten: London, 1868), 20.

14. Quotation from Walt Whitman, *Leaves of Grass, 1867 Edition* (New York: W. E. Chapin, 1867), 66; see also Walt Whitman, *Leaves of Grass, 1860 Edition* (Boston: Thayer and Eldridge, 1860), 73.

15. Whitman, *The Correspondence*, 2:133. Wilde registered Whitman's protest against the Rossetti edition in an 1889 review. Oscar Wilde, *The Complete Works of Oscar Wilde*, Vol. 7: *Journalism*, Part II, ed. John Stokes and Mark W. Turner (Oxford: Oxford University Press, 2013), 154.

16. Whitman, *Leaves of Grass, 1867 Edition*, 49–50. See also Whitman, *Leaves of Grass, 1860 Edition*, 55.

17. Whitman, *Poems, Rossetti Edition*, 20–1.

18. Ibid. 21–2.

19. Whitman, *Leaves of Grass*, 1867 edition, 38–9. See also Whitman, *Leaves of Grass, 1867 Edition*, 37.

20. Merlin Holland, *The Wilde Album* (London: Fourth Estate, 1997), 20. At Oxford, Wilde talked his way through his Divinity exam by telling the examiners about Whitman, among other things. 'I swaggered horribly, but am really pleased with myself,' he said when he learned he had achieved first-class honours. Oscar Wilde, *The Complete Letters of Oscar Wilde*, ed. Merlin Holland and Rupert Hart-Davis (London: Fourth Estate, 2000), 20.

21. 'With Mr. Oscar Wilde,' *Cincinnati Gazette* (21 February 1882), 10; rpt. in 'Walt Whitman's Æsthetic Den,' *Macon Weekly Telegraph* (2 March 1882), 2, in Gary Scharnhorst, 'Walt Whitman and Oscar Wilde: A Biographical Note,' *Walt Whitman Quarterly Review*, 25, no. 3 (2008), 116.

22. Hofer and Scharnhorst, *Oscar Wilde in America: The Interviews*, 43.

23. Mikhail, *Interviews*, 1:47.

24. The poem was printed in Whitman, *Leaves of Grass, 1867 Edition*, 129. The manuscript is Walt Whitman, 'Are You the New Person Drawn toward Me? To a New Personal Admirer' (1857–9), *Papers of Walt Whitman* (Folder 50–51, Albert H. Small Special Collections Library, University of Virginia).

25. Whitman, *Leaves of Grass, 1860 Edition*, 358–9.

26. Jason Stacy, *Walt Whitman's Multitudes: Labor Reform and Persona in Whitman's Journalism and the First Leaves of Grass, 1840–1855* (New York: Peter Lang, 2008), 69. Schmidgall, *Containing Multitudes*, 282. On Whitman's career as a journalist, see also Henry Seidel Canby, *Walt Whitman, an American: A Study in Biography* (New York: Houghton Mifflin, 1943), 57; Gary Schmidgall, *Walt Whitman: A Gay Life* (New York: Dutton, 1997).

27. 'Oscar Wilde and Whitman,' *Philadelphia Press* 19 January 1882, 8, in Mikhail, *Interviews*, 1:46–7.

28. *The Complete Works of Oscar Wilde*, Vol. 7: *Journalism*, Part II, 154.

29. Qtd. in Richard Ellmann, *Oscar Wilde* (London: Hamish Hamilton, 1987), 163.

30. Qtd. in Schmidgall, *Walt Whitman: A Gay Life*, 403. See also Krieg, *Whitman and the Irish*, 168–70.

31. Whitman deleted thirty-nine poems, inserted seventeen more, and reorganized his materials to produce the 1881 edition of *Leaves of Grass*. It soon had to be withdrawn on the grounds of threatened prosecution for indecency and was banned in Boston. In years to come, it would become the definitive edition of his poems.

32. Thomas Wentworth Higginson, 'Recent Poetry,' *The Nation*, 33, no. 859 (15 December 1881), 476–7.

33. Mikhail, *Interviews*, 1:47.

34. Karl Beckson, ed., *Oscar Wilde: The Critical Heritage* (London: Routledge, 1970), 51.

35. The essay was widely reprinted. An untitled paraphrase was published in the *Sioux County Herald* (Orange City, Iowa), 23 February 1882, 3. Full reprintings of the 'Unmanly Manhood' article included 'Col. Higginson on Clergymen, Webster and Wilde,' *Warren Mail* (Warren, PA), 14 February 1882, 1; 'Higginson on Wilde,' *Indianapolis Journal* (Indianapolis, IN), 25 February 1882, 2.

36. Hofer and Scharnhorst, *Oscar Wilde in America: The Interviews*, 44.

37. Oscar Wilde, *Collins Complete Works of Oscar Wilde* (Glasgow: HarperCollins, 1999), 933.

38. See chapter 5, 'The "New Man" in the Slums,' in Seth Koven, *Slumming: Sexual and Social Politics in Victorian London* (Princeton: Princeton University Press, 2004).

39. Philip E. Smith II and Michael S. Helfand, eds., *Oscar Wilde's Oxford Notebooks: A Portrait of Mind in the Making* (Oxford: Oxford University Press, 1989), 115, 167.

40. Mikhail, *Interviews*, 1:48.

41. Hofer and Scharnhorst, *Oscar Wilde in America: The Interviews*, 44.

42. Lately Thomas, *Sam Ward: 'King of the Lobby'* (Boston: Houghton, Mifflin Co., 1965), 404.

43. Qtd. in Lloyd Lewis and Henry Justin Smith, *Oscar Wilde Discovers America, 1882* (New York: Harcourt, Brace and Company, 1936), 121.

44. Jane Wilde, *Lady Jane Wilde's Letters to Oscar Wilde, 1875–1895*, ed. Karen Tipper (Lewiston, NY: Edwin Mellen Press, 2011), 66.

45. *The Complete Works of Oscar Wilde*, Vol. 7: *Journalism*, Part II, 152.

46. 'As a man he is a precursor of a fresh type. He is a factor in the heroic and spiritual evolution of the human being,' Wilde wrote, sounding as though he was petitioning for Whitman's inclusion in a queer version of Carlyle's *On Heroes, Hero-Worship and the Heroic in History*. Ibid. 155.

47. Oscar Wilde, *Letters*, 145.

48. H. Montgomery Hyde, ed., *The Three Trials of Oscar Wilde* (New York: University Books, 1956), 236.

49. *Farmland Enterprise* (Farmland, IN), 7 June 1895, 4.

50. *Logansport Daily Pharos* (Logansport, IN), 27 May 1895, 2.

51. Oscar Wilde, *Letters*, 129.

52. Ibid. 142.

53. Hurlbert had a personal vendetta against Archibald Forbes. Wilde held Hurlbert at arm's length when he offered to print Forbes's letter. It was

'one of the most filthy and scurrilous things I ever read,' Wilde told his lawyer. Ibid. 135–6.

54. William Henry Hurlbert, 'Letter to Thomas Wentworth Higginson' (3 September 1845), Autograph File, H, 1584–1988 (Houghton Library, Harvard University).

55. Thomas Wentworth Higginson, *Cheerful Yesterdays* (Boston, MA: Houghton, Mifflin and Co, 1898), 107. In his 1861 novel *Cecil Dreeme*, Theodore Winthrop used Hurlbert as a model for an alluring villain who compels a 'strange fascination' from 'old and young.' A young man confesses 'when his eyes are upon me, I feel something stir in my heart.' Qtd. in Daniel W. Crofts, *A Secession Crisis Enigma: William Henry Hurlbert and 'The Diary of a Public Man'* (Baton Rouge: Louisiana State University Press, 2010), 40–1.

56. Crofts, *A Secession Crisis Enigma*, 39.

57. William Henry Hurlbert, 'Regeneration by Reception,' *New York World*, 17 February 1882, 4.

58. Hurlbert's feelings for 'Dear Wentworth' had 'subsided,' he said in the autumn of 1845. Hurlbert wished no longer to give in to the 'imperfect impulse' that had woven 'so inexplicable a pattern' in their life together: 'For all that you have brought me in the past—of wisdom and of love— dear friend—I do most gratefully bless you. As for all the sad experiences which—in our different positions—we have shared—I fervently thank God—that he has made me see the meaning of those things which, being dark, were most painful.' W. H. Hurlbert, 'Letter to Thomas Wentworth Higginson' (Houghton Library, Harvard University).

59. Thomas Wentworth Higginson, 'Letter to William [Hurlbert],' (31 October 1852), *Thomas Wentworth Higginson Papers* (Thomas Wentworth Higginson letters and journals, 1824–1910, MS Am 784, Houghton Library, Harvard University).

60. 'If, after twenty years of non-intercourse, he had written to me to come and nurse him in illness, I should have left all and gone,' Higginson said of Hurlbert. Higginson, *Cheerful Yesterdays*, 110.

61. Maude Howe Elliott, *Uncle Sam Ward and His Circle* (New York: Macmillan, 1938), 620–1.

62. Oscar Wilde, *Letters*, 143.

63. Nathaniel Hawthorne, *The Letters of Hawthorne to William D. Ticknor, 1851–1869*, ed. C. E. Frazer-Clark Jr. (Newark, NJ: Cateret, 1972), 1:78.

64. Oscar Wilde, *Letters*, 143.

65. Ibid. 146.

66. Mikhail, *Interviews*, 1:51.

67. Lloyd Lewis and Henry Justin Smith, *Oscar Wilde Discovers America, 1882* (New York: Harcourt, Brace, 1936), 215.

68. Oscar Wilde, *Letters*, 147.

69. William F. Morse, 'Oscar Wilde's American Lecture Tour: W. F. Morse's Statement of Accounts' (1882), George Arents Collection (Arents S 1373, New York Public Library, NY).

CHAPTER 10. THE WAR OF ART

1. Jane Wilde, *Lady Jane Wilde's Letters to Oscar Wilde, 1875–1895*, ed. Karen Tipper (Lewiston, NY: Edwin Mellen Press, 2011), 70.
2. Merlin Holland, *The Wilde Album* (London: Fourth Estate, 1997), 45.
3. Jane Wilde, *Lady Jane Wilde's Letters to Oscar Wilde, 1875–1895*, 106.
4. See, for example, 'The Best Man' (*The World*, 17 September 1884) and 'The Story of Mrs. Peter Kyne: A Legend of Connemara' (*Vanity Fair*, 16 December 1879). Although signed by Willie, these two stories resemble Oscar's breezy style and sardonic tone. Willie wrote for *Punch* and *The Daily Telegraph*, among others. His influence on his more famous brother's reception remains under-researched.
5. Jane Wilde, *Lady Jane Wilde's Letters to Oscar Wilde, 1875–1895*, 72, 87.
6. Max Beerbohm and William Rothenstein, *Max and Will* (London: J. Murray, 1975), 21.
7. 'Call the book *Rose Leaf and Apple Leaf*, or *Narcissus and Daffodil*,' Wilde instructed Stoddart. Oscar Wilde, *The Complete Letters of Oscar Wilde*, ed. Merlin Holland and Rupert Hart-Davis (London: Fourth Estate, 2000), 167. See also Stuart Mason, *Bibliography of Oscar Wilde* (Boston: Longwood 1977), 185.
8. Rennell Rodd, *Rose Leaf and Apple Leaf. With an Introduction by Oscar Wilde* (Philadelphia: J.M. Stoddart & Co., 1882), 34. 'Heart's brother' alludes to Shelley's *Laon and Cythna*, in which the hero refers to his bosom companion as 'my own heart's brother.' Percy Bysshe Shelley, *The Complete Poetry of Percy Bysshe Shelley*, ed. Donald H. Reiman, Neil Fraistat, and Nora Crook, Vol. 3 (Baltimore: Johns Hopkins University Press, 2012), 158.
9. Oscar Wilde, *Letters*, 140.
10. *Publisher's Weekly* commented on its 'peculiar and original get-up' and *The Aesthetic Movement in England* called it 'a dainty little volume of poems clothed in most exquisite attire.' Qtd. in Mason, *Bibliography of Oscar Wilde*, 182.
11. Wilde toyed with the possibility of giving the cover the Japanese design he had in mind for his own book, but eventually decided against it. Oscar Wilde, *Letters*, 168.
12. Stoddart, qtd. in Mason, *Bibliography of Oscar Wilde*, 184.
13. 'L'envoi (Autograph Manuscript of the Introductory Essay to Rennell Rodd's *Rose Leaf and Apple Leaf*, 1882),' in Elliott Collection (Leeds University Library), 3.
14. Rodd, *Rose Leaf and Apple Leaf. With an Introduction by Oscar Wilde*, 11.

15. 'There is another test of manhood: it lies in action,' Higginson claimed. Karl Beckson, ed., *Oscar Wilde: The Critical Heritage* (London: Routledge, 1970), 51.

16. Rennell Rodd, *Social and Diplomatic Memories*, 3 vols. (London: Edward Arnold, 1922), 1:9.

17. 'University Intelligence,' *Jackson's Oxford Journal*, no. 6640 (Saturday, 19 June 1880).

18. Rodd, *Social and Diplomatic Memories*, 1:12.

19. Ibid. 1:6, 28.

20. Ibid. 1:6.

21. Ibid. 1:12.

22. Ibid. 1:9.

23. Ibid. 1:24.

24. Merlin Holland, ed., *Irish Peacock and Scarlet Marquess: The Real Trial of Oscar Wilde* (New York: HarperCollins, 2003), p. xx.

25. Neil McKenna, *The Secret Life of Oscar Wilde* (London: Arrow, 2004), 14–15, 26, 27.

26. Oscar Wilde, *Letters*, 101.

27. Rodd, *Social and Diplomatic Memories*, 1:25.

28. Ibid. 1:24.

29. Henri Murger, *The Bohemians of the Latin Quarter*, trans. Ellen Marriage and John Selwyn (Philadelphia: University of Pennsylvania Press, 2013), p. xxxii.

30. Rodd, *Rose Leaf and Apple Leaf. With an Introduction by Oscar Wilde*, 21.

31. Oscar Wilde, *Letters*, 103.

32. Rodd, *Social and Diplomatic Memories*, 1:23.

33. Ibid. 1:15–16.

34. Oscar Wilde, *The Complete Works of Oscar Wilde*, Vol. 1: *Poems and Poems in Prose*, ed. Bobby Fong and Karl Beckson (Oxford: Oxford University Press, 2000), 126–7.

35. Iain Ross, *Oscar Wilde and Ancient Greece* (Cambridge: Cambridge University Press, 2013), 75.

36. 'Poems by Oscar Wilde,' *The Nation*, 33, no. 840 (1881), 101.

37. 'Letter to Laura Tennant,' in *Papers of James Rennell Rodd, 1st Baron Rennell* (Bodleian Libraries, Oxford University, after Christmas 1882).

38. Rennell Rodd, *Songs in the South* (London: David Bogue, 1881), 23.

39. Richard Jenkyns, *The Victorians and Ancient Greece* (Oxford: Oxford University Press, 1980), 71, 172.

40. Rodd, *Rose Leaf and Apple Leaf. With an Introduction by Oscar Wilde*, 29.

41. *The Complete Works of Oscar Wilde*, Vol. 1: *Poems and Poems in Prose*, 59–60.

42. 'L'envoi (Autograph Manuscript of the Introductory Essay to Rennell Rodd's *Rose Leaf and Apple Leaf*, 1882),' 76.

43. Oscar Wilde, *Letters*, 140.

44. *New York World* 8 January 1882, 1–5.
45. Rodd, *Rose Leaf and Apple Leaf. With an Introduction by Oscar Wilde*, 14.
46. Ibid. 13.
47. Ibid. 26. As Patricia Clements notes, Pater's idiom tended to dominate Wilde's critical writing from this point on. Patricia Clements, *Baudelaire and the English Tradition* (Princeton: Princeton University Press, 1985), 147–8.
48. 'Oscar Wilde,' *The Nation*, no. 863 (12 January 1882), 28.
49. Thomas Wentworth Higginson, 'The Equation of Fame,' *Current Literature*, 4/4 (1890), 257, qtd. in Oscar Wilde, *The Complete Works of Oscar Wilde*, Vol. 3: *The Picture of Dorian Gray*, ed. Joseph Bristow (Oxford: Oxford University Press, 2005), p. xxxiii.
50. Oscar Wilde, *Letters*, 178.
51. 'Oscar Wilde's Protégé,' *The Critic*, 46 (7 October 1882).
52. Rodd, qtd. in Mason, *Bibliography of Oscar Wilde*, 185.
53. Rodd, *Social and Diplomatic Memories*, 1:23.
54. 'Literary Notes,' *New York Tribune* 25 November 1882.
55. Oscar Wilde, *Letters*, 205.
56. H. Montgomery Hyde, ed., *The Three Trials of Oscar Wilde* (New York: University Books, 1956), 339.
57. Still hewing to the spirit of Rennell Rodd's wishes, it seems, the family executor refused my request for permission to quote from his unpublished letters about the incident with Wilde. Rennell Rodd, 'Letter to Walter Ledger,' in Robert Ross Memorial Collection (University College, Oxford, 14 February 1905).

CHAPTER 11. AIN'T NOTHING LIKE THE REAL THING

1. Matthew Hofer and Gary Scharnhorst, eds., *Oscar Wilde in America: The Interviews* (Urbana: University of Illinois Press, 2009), 141, 54.
2. Ibid. 121.
3. Ibid. 68.
4. Ibid. 135.
5. Ibid. 87.
6. Qtd. in John Davenport Neville, 'Oscar Wilde: An Apostle of Aestheticism in the Old Dominion,' *Virginia Cavalcade*, 28, no. 2 (1978), 68.
7. 'Foreign Intelligence—Mr. Oscar Wilde in America,' *The Derby Mercury* 8 March 1882, italics added.
8. Hofer and Scharnhorst, *Oscar Wilde in America: The Interviews*, 135.
9. Qtd. in Robert C. Toll, *Blacking Up: The Minstrel Show in Nineteenth Century America* (New York: Oxford University Press, 1974), 25.
10. 'Advertising,' *Daily Globe* 11 January 1882.
11. Laurence Senelick, 'Boys and Girls Together: Subcultural Origins of Glamour Drag and Impersonation on the Ninetenth Century Stage,'

in *Crossing the Stage: Controversies on Cross-Dressing*, ed. Lesley Ferris (London: Routledge, 1993), 86. 'Kelly & Leon's Minstrels. Programme,' in American Minstrel Show Collection, 1823–1947 (Houghton Library, Harvard University).

12. F. Cardella, 'Leon Schottisch,' in Robert Cushman Butler Collection of Theatrical Illustrations (Firth, Pond & Co., New York: Manuscripts, Archives, and Special Collections, Washington State University Libraries, 1861). Heather May, 'Middle-Class Morality and Blackwashed Beauties: Francis Leon and the Rise of the Prima Donna in the Post-War Minstrel Show' (PhD thesis, Indiana University, 2007), 220, 32, 25, 27, 38. Annmarie Bean, 'Presenting the Prima Donna: Black Femininity and Performance in 19th Century American Blackface Minstrelsy,' in *Performance Research: On Illusion*, ed. Richard Gough (Psychology Press, 1997), 40.

13. Qtd. in Toll, *Blacking Up*, 142.

14. 'Advertising,' *The Argus* 9 December 1880.

15. The following performances of *Patience Wilde; or Ten Sisters of Oscar* (sometimes under the title *Patience Wiled; or the Sister of Oscar*, or as *The Black Patience*) have been confirmed: 12 January 1882, Opera House (St Paul, MN); 3–4 March 1882, Ford's Theatre (Washington, DC); 20 March–1 April 1882 at the Fourteenth-Street Theatre (New York); 10 April 1882 at the Globe Theatre (Boston, MA); 4 May 1882, Comstock's (Columbus, OH). It is likely there were others.

16. See 'Amusements. Ford's. *The Black Patience*,' *The Evening Critic* 3 March 1882; 'Amusements. Ford's. Minstrels Farewell. Patience in Black,' *The Evening Critic* 4 March 1882; 'Amusements. The Opera House,' *Daily Globe* 12 January 1882. May, 'Middle-Class Morality and Blackwashed Beauties,' 240.

17. George Thatcher, 'Death of Bones and Tambo. George Thatcher Talks of the Decline of Minstrelsy,' in American Minstrel Show Collection, 1823–1947 (Houghton Library, Harvard University, 1882).

18. For example, in May, Leon and Wilde's tour almost overlapped in Columbus, Ohio. The receipts for Wilde's evening lecture on 'The Decorative Arts' totalled $200. The following night, Leon leapt onto the same stage and proved there was still more money to be made with Wilde's name.

19. 'Amusements: Fourteenth Street Theatre,' *New York Times* 21 March 1882.

20. Toll, *Blacking Up*, 142.

21. Kenneth W. Goings, *Mammy and Uncle Mose: Black Collectibles and American Stereotyping* (Bloomington: Indiana University Press, 1994), 43.

22. Some scholars date the European tradition later, pointing to Queen Anne's *Masque of Blacknesse* in the seventeenth century. This lineage forms a pre-history to American minstrelsy. In the 1820s, the actor Charles Matthews

used blackface in Britain and the United States. Robert Nowatzki compares British and American minstrel show programmes and concludes persuasively that 'there is little to distinguish British minstrelsy from the American version in its depictions of black people.' Robert Nowatzki, *Representing African Americans in Transatlantic Abolitionism and Blackface Minstrelsy* (Baton Rouge: Louisiana State University Press, 2010), 72. See also George F. Rehin, 'Harlequin Jim Crow: Continuity and Convergence in Blackface Clowning,' *The Journal of Popular Culture*, IX, no. 3 (1975), 686; Gretchen Gerzina, *Black England: Life before Emancipation* (London: J. Murray, 1995), 69; Michael Paul Rogin, *Blackface, White Noise: Jewish Immigrants in the Hollywood Melting Pot* (Berkeley: University of California Press, 1996), 19, 22; Sarah Meer, *Uncle Tom Mania: Slavery, Minstrelsy, and Transatlantic Culture in the 1850s* (University of Georgia Press, 2005), 150; W.T. Lhamon, *Raising Cain: Blackface Performance from Jim Crow to Hip Hop* (Cambridge, MA: Harvard University Press, 1998), 59.

23. Nowatzki, *Representing African Americans in Transatlantic Abolitionism and Blackface Minstrelsy*, 65.

24. James Weldon Johnson, qtd. in Henry T. Sampson, *Blacks in Blackface: A Source Book on Early Black Musical Shows*, Vol. 1 (Metuchen, NJ: Scarecrow Press, 1980), 4.

25. From the 1840s, the minstrel wench or 'high yaller gal' occasionally played a supporting role as a companion to male minstrel characters. Wenches clumsily mimicked their social superiors by imitating high-class attitudes and manners. After the Civil War, the wench was reborn and was no longer ancillary to her male counterpart. The female impersonator rapidly moved from novelty act to become the star attraction of the minstrel show. The Only Leon, Rollin Howard, Julian Eltinge, and Eugene d'Ameli were the specialty's divas. The popularity of the female impersonator combined with the rise of the burlesque 'leg show,' in the 1860s and 1870s, eroticized minstrel shows. Senelick, 'Boys and Girls Together,' 86. Laurence Senelick, *The Changing Room: Sex, Drag, and Theatre* (London: Routledge, 2000), 299.

26. Houston Baker, Jr. describes the minstrel mask as 'a space of habitation not only for repressed spirits of sexuality, ludic play, id satisfaction, castration anxiety, and a mirror stage of development, but also for that deep-seated denial of the indisputable humanity of inhabitants of and descendants from the continent of Africa.' The female impersonator was 'a model of properly "giddy" femininity' who 'could reassure men that women were in their places while at the same time showing women how to behave without competing with them.' Toll, *Blacking Up*, 144. Houston A. Baker, *Modernism and the Harlem Renaissance* (Chicago: University of Chicago Press, 1987), 17.

27. See chapter 4, 'The Romance of the Real,' in Miles Orvell, *The Real Thing: Imitation and Authenticity in American Culture, 1880–1940* (Chapel Hill: University of North Carolina Press, 1989).

28. 'Dressmaking for Men,' *The National Police Gazette* 25 September 1880.

29. This incident was fictionalized by Molly Elliot Seawell in an 1888 story of stage life.

30. Marybeth Hamilton, '"I'm the Queen of the Bitches": Female Impersonation and Mae West's *Pleasure Man*,' in *Crossing the Stage: Controversies on Cross-Dressing*, ed. Lesley Ferris (London: Routledge, 1993), 107–19, at 110. 'Vying with voluptuous sopranos and svelte ballerinas on their own ground, the minstrel show superimposed on to an unacceptable, because flagrant, heterosexual desire an acceptable, because sublimated homoerotic appeal.' Senelick, *The Changing Room*, 299.

31. Henry James, *Autobiography: A Small Boy and Others, Notes of a Son and Brother, the Middle Years*, ed. Frederick W. Dupee (London: W.H. Allen, 1956), 130, 27, 33. James's memory of the minstrel show contrasts with his lack of interest in Barnum's grotesque human displays. He recalled that the vivid prospect of the minstrel show sustained him as he was made to wait 'in the dusty halls of humbug, amid bottled mermaids, "bearded ladies" and chill dioramas.' The keen anticipation kept him going even as his stomach cried out for a doughnut from the refreshment counter.

It is possible that the bosom that fascinated James belonged to a woman, rather than a cross-dressed man. It may have been Emily Mestayer, a dime museum favourite James had much admired as Eliza, the mulatta in Barnum's controversial version of *Uncle Tom's Cabin*. 'One almost envies,' the mature James concluded in 1913, 'the simple faith of an age beguiled by arts so rude.' James's backward glance at minstrelsy's history in the second half of the nineteenth century shows that the form was already respectable in this period even though, as a mature aesthete, James doubted its artistic merit.

32. Oscar Wilde, *The Complete Letters of Oscar Wilde*, ed. Merlin Holland and Rupert Hart-Davis (London: Fourth Estate, 2000), 127. For different reasons, Abraham Lincoln was also represented in blackface. See Darcy Grimaldo Grigsby, *Enduring Truths: Sojourner's Shadows and Substance* (Chicago: University of Chicago Press, 2015), 6–7.

33. Isaac F. Marcosson and Daniel Frohman, *Charles Frohman: Manager and Man* (London: Bodley Head, 1916), 46.

34. Ibid. 63–4.

35. From December 1881 to March 1882.

36. *Indianapolis People* 24 December 1881. *Indianapolis Journal* 19 December 1881. *Indianapolis Journal* 26 December 1881.

37. ' "Rude Disturbers of the Peace": Haverly's New Mastodon Minstrels at the Park Opera House,' in American Minstrel Show Collection, 1823–1947 (Houghton Library, Harvard University, 17 March 1882).

38. Qtd. in Neville, 'Oscar Wilde: An Apostle of Aestheticism in the Old Dominion,'68; *Junior Outline of History* (London: D. Archer), 1.

39. Jane Wilde, *Lady Jane Wilde's Letters to Oscar Wilde, 1875–1895*, ed. Karen Tipper (Lewiston, NY: Edwin Mellen Press, 2011), 69.

40. Ibid. 71.

41. 'Oscar Wilde Interview,' *The Inter Ocean* 1 March 1882.

42. Oscar Wilde, *Collins Complete Works of Oscar Wilde* (Glasgow: Harper-Collins, 1999), 925.

43. Ibid. 917–18.

44. 'Oscar Wilde: The Second Lecture of the Apostle of Estheticism,' *Chicago Tribune* 12 March 1882.

45. *Collins Complete Works of Oscar Wilde*, 928.

46. Ibid.

47. Ibid. 914.

48. Walter Benjamin, *The Work of Art in the Age of Mechanical Reproduction*, ed. J. A. Underwood (London: Penguin, 2008).

49. Hofer and Scharnhorst, *Oscar Wilde in America: The Interviews*, 143.

50. Ibid. 81.

51. 'Oscar Wilde: The Second Lecture of the Apostle of Estheticism.'

52. Ibid. 181 n. 3.

53. Like Wilde, Jules Barbey d'Aurevilly and Charles Baudelaire insisted the dandy was a man of substance, not merely a superficial, materialist fashion-horse. Jules Barbey d'Aurevilly, *Du Dandysme et de Georges Brummell*, ed. Marie-Christine Natta (Bassac: Plein Chant, 1989); Charles Baudelaire, *The Painter of Modern Life, and Other Essays*, ed. Jonathan Mayne, 2nd edn (London: Phaidon, 1995).

54. Oscar Wilde, *The Importance of Being Earnest and Other Plays*, ed. Peter Raby (Oxford: Oxford University Press, 1995), 132.

55. Oscar Wilde, *Letters*, 586.

56. Toll, *Blacking Up*, 205.

57. 'Is He Busted?,' *Daily Globe* 27 March 1882, 1. 'Haverly's Affairs,' *Salt Lake Herald* 1 April 1882.

58. Marcosson and Frohman, *Charles Frohman*, 50.

59. Ibid. 48.

60. Ibid. 49. Wilde's familiarity with similar tactics for boosting ticket sales dated from around this time. See Oscar Wilde, *Letters*, 203.

61. Marcosson and Frohman, *Charles Frohman*, 53.

62. Ibid. 57. The show's only hiccup was caused by the late entrance of Lillie Langtry and her revealing décolletage. The Mastodons had already begun their 1880 performance when Langtry sauntered into the hall. The effect of her low-cut dress prompted a ripple of murmurs that soon reached the stage. In short order, forty men in blackface stopped, turned, and stared at the beauty.

63. Marcosson and Frohman, *Charles Frohman*, 58.

64. 'Haverly in Trouble,' *The Day* 29 March 1882.
65. Ibid. 75. The African American minstrel troupe had already changed hands many times. A white saloon keeper called Charles Callender bought the Georgia Minstrels from their black owner in 1872 and renamed them Callender's Minstrels. He was bought out by Colonel Jack Haverly, who ran the troupe as Haverly's Colored Minstrels. In 1882, it was sold to Charles Frohman.
66. 'The Minstrels,' *The Salt Lake Herald* 19 April 1882.
67. 'Callender's Minstrels,' *Port Jervis Evening Gazette* 29 December 1882.
68. 'Callender's Colored Minstrels,' *Port Jervis Evening Gazette* 29 December 1882.
69. Toll, *Blacking Up*, 210.
70. It is worth emphasizing the ephemeral nature of these shows, because it explains why they are difficult to track and why we find gaps in the archive. By the 1880s, minstrelsy was such an integral part of the fabric of 19th-century cultural life that it didn't necessarily register as an occasion worth memorializing. Shows constantly evolved, often changing nightly to suit local tastes and to speak to the issues of the day, but these variations were rarely recorded. These performances could be transgressive, political, and shocking, but they could also be seen as simple entertainment—sort of like a *Saturday Night Live* sketch is today. Then, as now, people tended not to document and preserve what was usual, familiar, and plentiful precisely because it was usual, familiar, and plentiful.
71. 'Monumental Theatre: Muldoon's Blunders Combination: "Takeoff on the Oscar Wilde Rage",' *Baltimore American and Commercial Advertiser* 23 February 1882. The following Hyde and Behman's Minstrels performances have been confirmed: 18 February 1882, Fulton Opera House (Lancaster, PA); 20–7 February 1882, Kernan's Monumental Theatre (Baltimore). There were several others billed as 'Muldoon's Picnic' in which a 'Wilde' character may have been introduced.
72. 'Classified Ad 13,' *New York Times* 3 March 1882.
73. 'The San Francisco Minstrels,' *New York Times* 13 December 1881.
74. 'Amusements,' *Truth* 7 January 1882. *Patients, or Bunion Salve's Bride* began running in mid-December 1881, playing to enormous audiences. Charlie Backus, a mimic in drag, was Patience, and the musician Billy Birch was the Bunion Salve of the sketch. 'The San Francisco Minstrels.'
75. Jill Van Nostrand, 'Minstrelsy in Post-Civil War New York, 1865–1870' (PhD thesis, City University of New York, 2005), 214.
76. 'Playbills,' in American Minstrel Show Collection, 1823–1947 (Houghton Library, Harvard University, 1881–91).
77. 'George Thatcher's Great Minstrel Show,' *The Evening Critic* 15 March 1882.
78. George Thatcher, *Talks* (Philadelphia: Penn Publishing Company, 1898), 96–7.

79. 'Advertisement,' *The Evening Critic* 18 March 1882.

80. Today, satirists still succeed by using their targets' unaltered words, as Tina Fey's 2008 *Saturday Night Live* impersonations of American vice presidential nominee Sarah Palin amply demonstrate. On the limits of satire as social protest, see Malcolm Gladwell, 'The Satire Paradox,' *Revisionist History*, season 1, episode 10. http://revisionisthistory.com/episodes/10-the-satire-paradox.

81. 'The Ray,' in American Minstrel Show Collection, 1823–1947 (Houghton Library, Harvard University, 5–9 February 1883). 'Daily Evening Traveller,' in American Minstrel Show Collection, 1823–1947 (Houghton Library, Harvard University, 6 February 1883).

82. 'The Theatres Last Night,' *The Baltimore Sun* 28 March 1882.

83. H. H. Wheeler, ed., *Up-to-Date Minstrel Jokes: A Collection of the Latest and Most Popular Jokes, Talks, Stump-Speeches, Conundrums and Monologues for Amateur Minstrels, Many of Which Have Never Before Appeared in Print; Also, a Special Department of Female Minstrel Jokes, Stump Speeches and Monologues, Arranged Especially for 'Lady Minstrels,' This Being the Only Collection of the Kind Ever Printed* (Boston, MA: Up-To-Date Publishing Co., 1902), 56.

84. 'Stage 'Stump Speakers': An Old-Fashioned Type of Entertainer Who Has Disappeared,' *Washington Post* 17 September 1905.

85. *Standard Stump Speeches and Ethiopian Lectures: A Choice Collection of Stump Speeches and Negro Burlesque: Recitations on All the Principal Topics of the Day as Delivered in All the Great Minstrel Shows Both in America and Europe by Such Artists as Hughey Dougherty, Add Ryman, Sen. Bob Hart* (New York: M. J. Ivers & Co., 1888), 12–13.

86. In addition to the performers of Irish extraction mentioned in this chapter (The Only Leon, Hughey Dougherty, and John T. Kelly), others included Stephen Foster, Dan Emmett, Dan Bryant, Joel Walker Sweeney, and George Christy. Eric Lott, *Love and Theft: Blackface Minstrelsy and the American Working Class* (New York: Oxford University Press, 1993), 95.

87. Stereotypes such as these were often rewarded with cheers even when the audience was primarily Irish, Cedric J. Robinson notes in *Forgeries of Memory and Meaning: Blacks and the Regimes of Race in American Theater and Film before World War Two* (Chapel Hill: University of North Carolina Press, 2007), 32.

88. Richard Williams, *Hierarchical Structures and Social Value: The Creation of Black and Irish Identities in the United States* (Cambridge: Cambridge University Press, 1990), 100. The Irish 'have come to this fair land to escape from the chains of British tyranny; and now, will they, dare they, in their turn become the worst of oppressors?' one indignant American observer asked. Qtd. in William Lloyd Garrison, *The Letters of William Lloyd Garrison*, ed. Walter M. Merrill and Louis Ruchames, Vol. 3 (Cambridge, MA: Harvard University Press, 1973), 56.

89. See Matthew Frye Jacobson, *Whiteness of a Different Color: European Immigrants and the Alchemy of Race* (Cambridge, MA: Harvard University Press, 1998); Noel Ignatiev, *How the Irish Became White*, Routledge Classics (New York: Routledge, 2009), 89.
90. 'Advertisement, George Thatcher's Minstrels,' *The Morning Herald* 27 March 1882. The following performances of 'Oscar Wilde's Lecture' have been confirmed but it is very likely there were others: 20–7 March 1882, Ford's Opera House (Washington, DC); April 1882, Taylor Opera House (Trenton, NJ); 5 May 1882, Opera House (Lancaster, PA); 31 August 1882, Ford's Opera House (Washington, DC); 6 December 1882, The Grand (Chicago); 7 December 1882 (Detroit); 8 December 1882, Opera House (St Paul, MN); 5–12 February 1883, Boston Theatre (Boston, MA); 2 March 1883, Niblo's Garden (New York, NY). 'Playbills Ms Thr 556.' 'Thatcher, Primrose, & West,' in *Robert Harold Brisendine Papers* (Robert W. Woodruff Library, Emory University). The year before Wilde's arrival, Thatcher's announced that *Patients*, 'the Funny Burlesque Opera,' was in preparation.

CHAPTER 12. SON OF SPERANZA

1. 'Ghastly If True,' *Daily Inter Ocean* 8 March 1882.
2. Qtd. in Lloyd Lewis and Henry Justin Smith, *Oscar Wilde Discovers America, 1882* (New York: Harcourt, Brace and Company, 1936), 224.
3. 'St. Patrick,' *Daily Globe* 18 March 1882.
4. Jocelyn Wills, *Boosters, Hustlers, and Speculators: Entrepreneurial Culture and the Rise of Minneapolis and St. Paul, 1849–1883* (St Paul, MN: Minnesota Historical Society Press, 2005), 207.
5. 'Advertisement, Electricity Is Life! American Galvanic Co.,' *Fort Collins Courier* 20 April 1882. See also, for example, 'Advertisement, Dr. Dye's Celebrated Electro Voltaic Belts and Suspenders,' *St. Laundry Democrat* 29 April 1882.
6. 'Times Square Market One Pager,' Times Square District Management Association, http://www.timessquarenyc.org/do-business-here/market-facts/economic-impact/index.aspx.
7. June Drenning Holmquist, ed., *They Chose Minnesota: A Survey of the State's Ethnic Groups* (St Paul: Minnesota Historical Society Press, 1988), 3.
8. Wills, *Boosters, Hustlers, and Speculators*, 190.
9. Philip H. Bagenal, *The American Irish and Their Influence on Irish Politics* (Boston: Roberts Brothers, 1882), 75.
10. Ibid. 76. Anne Regan, 'The Irish,' in *They Chose Minnesota*, ed. Holmquist (St Paul: Minnesota Historical Society Press, 1988), 130.
11. Bagenal, *The American Irish and Their Influence on Irish Politics*, 124.
12. Jane Wilde, *Lady Jane Wilde's Letters to Oscar Wilde, 1875–1895*, ed. Karen Tipper (Lewiston, NY: Edwin Mellen Press, 2011), 68.

13. Jane Wilde, *Ancient Cures, Charms, and Usages of Ireland; Contributions to Irish Lore* (London: Ward and Downey, 1890), 202.

14. 'Oscar Wilde,' *Daily Globe* 18 March 1882.

15. Bagenal, *The American Irish and Their Influence on Irish Politics*, 110.

16. Jane Wilde, '"Jacta Alea Est" in *The Nation*,' in *The Life of Oscar Wilde*, ed. Robert Harborough Sherard (New York: Mitchell Kennerley, 1906), 53.

17. Bernard Henry Becker, *Disturbed Ireland; Being the Letters Written During the Winter of 1880–81* (London: Macmillan, 1881), 29.

18. Oscar Wilde, *The Complete Letters of Oscar Wilde*, ed. Merlin Holland and Rupert Hart-Davis (London: Fourth Estate, 2000), 141.

19. 'In June 1523 Francis I and the Earl of Desmond had negotiated a treaty by which Desmond agreed "to make war, in person and at his own charge against Henry VIII, as soon as the French army should land in Ireland." The object of their attack on Henry was to place Richard de la Pole, the last and strongest of the Yorkist claimants, on the English throne.' William Palmer, *The Problem of Ireland in Tudor Foreign Policy, 1485–1603* (Woodbridge: Boydell, 1994), 37. See also Mary Ann Lyons, *Franco-Irish Relations, 1500–1610: Politics, Migration and Trade* (Woodbridge: Boydell, 2003), 34.

20. 'Saint Patrick: St. Paul Observes the Day in Appropriate Style,' *St. Paul Globe* 18 March 1882. For a long time after the Civil War, scores of cavalry officers retained the long hair they had sported in battle. Lewis and Smith, *Oscar Wilde Discovers America, 1882*, 245.

21. Mary Warner Blanchard, *Oscar Wilde's America: Counterculture in the Gilded Age* (New Haven: Yale University Press, 1998), 7.

22. 'Amusements. The Opera House,' *Daily Globe* 12 January 1882.

23. 'Saint Patrick: St. Paul Observes the Day in Appropriate Style.' *Oscar Wilde Discovers America, 1882*, 225–6.

24. 'Oscar Wilde on Irish Art,' in Robert Ross Memorial Collection (University College, Oxford, March 1882), 81.

25. Oscar Wilde, *Letters*, 155.

26. Lewis and Smith, *Oscar Wilde Discovers America, 1882*, 231.

27. Matthew Hofer and Gary Scharnhorst, eds., *Oscar Wilde in America: The Interviews* (Urbana: University of Illinois Press, 2009), 115. Lois Foster Rodecape, 'Gilding the Sunflower: A Study of Oscar Wilde's Visit to San Francisco,' *California Historical Society Quarterly* 19, no. 2 (1940), 99.

28. Ibid. 99.

29. Qtd. in Lewis and Smith, *Oscar Wilde Discovers America, 1882*, 242. Hofer and Scharnhorst, *Oscar Wilde in America: The Interviews*, 140.

30. Oscar Wilde, *The Importance of Being Earnest and Other Plays*, ed. Peter Raby (Oxford: Oxford University Press, 1995), 204.

31. Oscar Wilde, *Letters*, 153. Joseph Donohue, James Ellis, and Peggy Russo, 'Adelphi Theatre, Calendar for 1880–1881,' https://www.umass.edu/AdelphiTheatreCalendar/m80d.htm#Label002.

32. Oscar Wilde, *Letters*, 173. Wilde's fan is now in the Pitt Rivers Museum, Oxford.
33. Ibid. 153.
34. Hofer and Scharnhorst, *Oscar Wilde in America: The Interviews*, 102. Oscar Wilde, *Letters*, 154.
35. Oscar Wilde, *Letters*, 158.
36. Ibid. 154.
37. Hofer and Scharnhorst, *Oscar Wilde in America: The Interviews*, 146.
38. 'Advertisement, Grand Announcement, Jacoby Brothers,' *Daily Los Angeles Herald* 29 September 1883, 2.
39. Hofner and Scharnhorst, *Oscar Wilde in America: The Interviews*, 101.
40. Oscar Wilde, *The Complete Works of Oscar Wilde*, Vol. 1: *Poems and Poems in Prose*, ed. Bobby Fong and Karl Beckson (Oxford: Oxford University Press, 2000), 149.
41. Hofer and Scharnhorst, *Oscar Wilde in America: The Interviews*, 100–1.
42. Ibid. 104, 101.
43. Hofer and Scharnhorst, *Oscar Wilde in America: The Interviews*, 102–3.
44. *The Complete Works of Oscar Wilde*, Vol. 1: *Poems and Poems in Prose*, 148.
45. Like Wilde's 1880 play *Vera; or, The Nihilists*, this sonnet responded to contemporary terrorist attacks against Czar Alexander II by Russian nihilists. Wilde was critical of the nihilists' utilitarianism and their disregard for aesthetic sophistication. On the alliance between Russian and Fenian politics, see Michael Newton, ' "Nihilists of Castlebar!": Exporting Russian Nihilism in the 1885 and the Case of Oscar Wilde's *Vera, or the Nihilists*,' in *Russia in Britain, 1880–1940*, ed. Rebecca Beasley and Philip Ross Bullock (Oxford: Oxford University Press, 2013).
46. John Garvey and Karen Hanning, *Irish San Francisco* (Charleston, SC: Arcadia Publishing, 2008), 7.
47. Hofer and Scharnhorst, *Oscar Wilde in America: The Interviews*, 102.
48. Oscar Wilde, *Letters*, 158.
49. 'Oscar Wilde's Visit to America,' in Lewis Papers (Bodleian Libraries, Oxford University, 1882).
50. Jane Wilde, *Lady Jane Wilde's Letters*, 65.
51. 'Oscar Wilde and the Irish Nationalists,' *The Daily Astorian* 25 February 1882.
52. Lady Wilde, *The American Irish*, ed. Walter Hamilton, 2nd edn (Dublin: William McGee, 1882), 4.
53. Oscar Wilde, *Letters*, 116.
54. Malcolm Campbell, *Ireland's New Worlds Immigrants, Politics, and Society in the United States and Australia, 1815–1922* (Madison: University of Wisconsin Press, 2008), 129. David Noel Doyle, 'The Remaking of Irish America, 1845–1880,' in *Making the Irish American: History and*

Heritage of the Irish in the United States, ed. Joseph Lee and Marion R. Casey (New York: New York University Press, 2006), 214.

55. Ely M. Janis, *A Greater Ireland: The Land League and Transatlantic Nationalism in Gilded Age America* (Madison, WI: University of Wisconsin Press, 2015), 62.

56. Davitt was imprisoned in England from February 1881 to May 1882. Parnell was imprisoned in Ireland until May 1882.

57. 'A Home Ruler: Oscar Wilde Has Some Well-Settled Opinions on the Irish Question,' *St. Louis Globe-Democrat* 27 February 1882. In other interviews, Wilde repeatedly praised the Irish National Land League for its work in abolishing landlordism. Hofer and Scharnhorst, *Oscar Wilde in America: The Interviews*, 115.

58. Michael Willem De Nie, *The Eternal Paddy: Irish Identity and the British Press, 1798–1882* (Madison, WI: University of Wisconsin Press, 2004), 216.

59. R. F. Foster, *Modern Ireland, 1600–1972* (London: Allen Lan, 1988), 313, 15.

60. In 1876, when the editor of *The Irish Monthly* objected to Wilde's use of the phrase 'our English land' in his poem, 'The Grave of Keats,' Wilde agreed to change the words. 'I am sorry you object to the words "*our* English Land,"' he replied. 'It is a noble privilege to count oneself of the same race as Keats or Shakespeare. However I have changed it. I would not shock the feelings of your readers for anything.' Oscar Wilde, *Letters*, 53. *The Complete Works of Oscar Wilde*, Vol. 1: *Poems and Poems in Prose*, 36.

61. 'Timely Old World Topics,' *New York Times* 11 June 1882.

62. Jane Wilde, '"Jacta Alea Est" in *The Nation*,' 55.

63. Hofer and Scharnhorst, *Oscar Wilde in America: The Interviews*, 103.

64. Nicholas Frankel, *Oscar Wilde's Decorated Books* (Ann Arbor, MI: University of Michigan Press, 2000), 45.

65. Oscar Wilde, *The Annotated Oscar Wilde: Poems, Fiction, Plays, Lectures, Essays, and Letters*, ed. H. Montgomery Hyde (New York: C. N. Potter, 1982), 374. *Irish Poets and Poetry of the Nineteenth Century: A Lecture Delivered in Platt's Hall, San Francisco on Wednesday, April 5, 1882*, ed. Robert D. Pepper (San Francisco: Book Club of California, 1972), 374.

66. *The Annotated Oscar Wilde: Poems, Fiction, Plays, Lectures, Essays, and Letters*, 376.

67. Ibid. 378.

68. Ibid. 374.

69. *The Sentinel* review qtd. in Joy Melville, *Mother of Oscar: The Life of Jane Francesca Wilde* (London: Allison & Busby, 1999), 141.

70. William Smith O'Brien was one of the leaders of the abortive Irish revolution of 1848, 'an incoherent conspiracy followed by a rising inescapably connected with a "cabbage patch" in Tipperary.' Foster, *Modern Ireland, 1600–1972*, 316.

71. Roy Morris Jr., *Declaring His Genius: Oscar Wilde in North America* (Cambridge, MA: Harvard University Press, 2013), 127.
72. Wilde, *The Annotated Oscar Wilde: Poems, Fiction, Plays, Lectures, Essays, and Letters*, 374.
73. Ibid. 378. 'Courage' was reprinted earlier in the tour. Commentators said it was hard to believe that the son of the patriot who had written these lines 'could find no better mission than to don the motley cap.' In Dublin, he would be pelted with rotten eggs for his betrayal, they said. 'Who Oscar Wilde Is,' *National Republican* 21 January 1882.
74. Oscar Wilde, *Letters*, 182.
75. *Philadelphia Press* 9 May 1882, qtd. in Melville, *Mother of Oscar*, 169.
76. Hofer and Scharnhorst, *Oscar Wilde in America: The Interviews*, 103.
77. Jane Wilde, *Lady Jane Wilde's Letters*, 65.
78. Ibid. 74.
79. Qtd. in Melville, *Mother of Oscar*.

CHAPTER 13. UNDERGROUND MEN

1. Stephen C. Massett, *Drifting About, or What Jeems Pipes of Pipesville Saw-and-Did: An Autobiography* (New York: Carleton, 1863), 243–4.
2. 'Anticipation of Oscar Wilde,' *Leavenworth Times* (Leavenworth, KS), 16 April 1882, 3.
3. 'Oscar Dear,' *The Leadville Daily Herald* (Leadville, CO), 14 April 1882, 4.
4. 'The Globe,' *The Leadville Daily Herald* (Leadville, CO), 12 April 1882, 2.
5. Matthew Hofer and Gary Scharnhorst, eds., *Oscar Wilde in America: The Interviews* (Urbana: University of Illinois Press, 2009), 128, italics added.
6. 'Mr. Wilde's presentation,' *Denver Times,* 12 April 1882, p. 4, qtd. ibid. 181.
7. 'The Outlook,' *The Leadville Daily Herald* (Leadville, CO), 11 April 1882, 2.
8. 'Advertisement, an Address by Oscar Wilde: Subject: "Art Decoration!",' *The Leadville Daily Herald* (Leadville, CO), 11 April 1882, 4.
9. 'Oscar Dear,' 4.
10. 'Oscar Wilde's Lecture in Denver,' *Fort Collins Courier* (Fort Collins, CO), 20 April 1882, 4.
11. The young male students in Wilde's East Coast audiences tended to have slighter builds than the workmen who came to his Colorado lectures. The typical University of Rochester student averaged five feet nine in height and 145 pounds in weight. The measurements for Yale students were similar. University of Rochester, *The University of Rochester, the First Hundred Years* (Rochester, NY: University of Rochester Centennial Committee, 1950), chapter 10, 'The End of an Age.' 'Yale Class Statistics' 1882, Charles Locke Scudder, 'Scrapbook of Yale Memorabilia of Charles

Locke Scudder, Class of 1882' (Manuscripts and Archives, Sterling Library, Yale University), 10.

12. Hofer and Scharnhorst, *Oscar Wilde in America: The Interviews*, 139. 'Oscar Wilde's Lecture in Denver,' *Fort Collins Courier* 20 April 1882, 4.

13. Oscar Wilde, *Collins Complete Works of Oscar Wilde* (Glasgow: Harper-Collins, 1999), 931.

14. 'Oscar Wilde's Lecture in Denver,' 4.

15. Hofer and Scharnhorst, *Oscar Wilde in America: The Interviews*, 63.

16. 'Oscar Wilde's Lecture in Denver,' 4.

17. Oscar Wilde, *The Complete Works of Oscar Wilde*, Vol. 3: *The Picture of Dorian Gray*, ed. Joseph Bristow (Oxford: Oxford University Press, 2005), 238.

18. 'Oscar Dear,' 4.

19. *Collins Complete Works of Oscar Wilde*, 940. Geoffrey Dibb, *Oscar Wilde: A Vagabond with a Mission* (London: Oscar Wilde Society, 2013), 45, 83.

20. *Collins Complete Works of Oscar Wilde*, 940, italics added.

21. Hofer and Scharnhorst, *Oscar Wilde in America: The Interviews*, 137.

22. Oscar Wilde, *The Complete Letters of Oscar Wilde*, ed. Merlin Holland and Rupert Hart-Davis (London: Fourth Estate, 2000), 160.

23. According to Colonel Morse, Wilde saw his tour as synonymous with 'his study of American people under different aspects and surroundings.' William F. Morse, 'American Lectures,' in *The Writings of Oscar Wilde: His Life with a Critical Estimate of His Writings* (London: A. R. Keller, 1907), 90.

24. John Ruskin, *Modern Painters*, ed. E. T. Cook and Alexander Wedderburn, Vol. 3 of *The Works of John Ruskin* (London: George Allen, 1903–12), 333.

25. Hofer and Scharnhorst, *Oscar Wilde in America: The Interviews*, 137.

26. Oscar Wilde, *The Complete Works of Oscar Wilde*, Vol. 6: *Journalism*, ed. John Stokes and Mark W. Turner, Part I (Oxford: Oxford University Press, 2013), 133.

27. Ibid. 144.

28. Oscar Wilde, *The Importance of Being Earnest and Other Plays*, ed. Peter Raby (Oxford: Oxford University Press, 1995), 45.

29. *The Complete Works of Oscar Wilde*, Vol. 6: *Journalism*, Part I, 143.

30. From 1867 to 1886, the number of divorces in the United States rose from 9,937 to 25,535. Cathy N. Davidson, Linda Wagner-Martin, and Elizabeth Ammons, eds., *A Companion to Women's Writing in the United States* (New York: Oxford University Press, 1995), 956.

31. *The Complete Works of Oscar Wilde*, Vol. 6: *Journalism*, Part I, 143.

32. *Collins Complete Works of Oscar Wilde*, 925.

33. Matthew Arnold, *Culture and Anarchy*, ed. Samuel Lipman (New Haven: Yale University Press, 1994), 35.

34. *Collins Complete Works of Oscar Wilde*, 925.

35. *The Complete Works of Oscar Wilde*, Vol. 6: *Journalism*, Part I, 143.

36. Henry James, *Collected Travel Writings: Great Britain and America*, Vol. 1 (New York: Library of America, 1993), 638.
37. Maude Howe Elliott, *Three Generations* (Boston: Little, Brown, 1923), 150.
38. *Denver Times*, qtd. in Lloyd Lewis and Henry Justin Smith, *Oscar Wilde Discovers America, 1882* (New York: Harcourt, Brace, 1936), 308.
39. Ibid. 306.
40. Oscar Wilde, *Letters*, 162.
41. Qtd. in Lewis and Smith, *Oscar Wilde Discovers America, 1882*, 316.
42. *Collins Complete Works of Oscar Wilde*, 925.
43. Qtd. in Lewis and Smith, *Oscar Wilde Discovers America, 1882*, 317.
44. Oscar Wilde, *Letters*, 162, 164.
45. Hofer and Scharnhorst, *Oscar Wilde in America: The Interviews*, 140.
46. Ibid. 146.
47. *Collins Complete Works of Oscar Wilde*, 940.
48. Ibid. 932.
49. Ibid. 924.
50. Oscar Wilde, *Letters*, 161.
51. Ibid. 154. By the time Wilde met Leadville's miners, he had already encountered many other American workers like them. Earlier in the tour, he gushed to Mrs Beere about meeting miners who were almost as realistic as those he had read about in his favourite Bret Harte Wild West romances.

CHAPTER 14. GOING SOUTH

1. Oscar Wilde, *The Complete Letters of Oscar Wilde*, ed. Merlin Holland and Rupert Hart-Davis (London: Fourth Estate, 2000), 176.
2. United States Census, 'Peter Tracy, Memphis City, Ward 3, Shelby, TN' (1900), (microfilm T623, National Archives, Washington, DC). United States Census, 'Peter Tracy, Memphis, Shelby, TN' (1880), (microfilm T9, roll 1279, National Archives, Washington, DC). 'General Notes,' *The Weekly Democratic Statesman* (Austin, TX), 29 June 1882, 3.
3. 'Oscar Wilde—the Career of the Prophet of Aestheticism,' *The Atlanta Constitution* (Atlanta, GA), 2 July 1882, 2.
4. David R. Roediger, *The Wages of Whiteness: Race and the Making of the American Working Class* (London: Verso, 1991), 133–4.
5. Bronwen Walter, *Outsiders Inside: Whiteness, Place, and Irish Women* (New York: Routledge, 2000), 66. Eric Lott, *Love and Theft: Blackface Minstrelsy and the American Working Class* (New York: Oxford University Press, 1993), 71, 95. See also Noel Ignatiev, *How the Irish Became White* (New York: Routledge, 2009), 34–61.
6. D. R. Roediger, *The Wages of Whiteness: Race and the Making of the American Working Class*, 149.
7. 'City Items,' *The Macon Telegraph and Messenger* (Macon, GA), 5 July 1882, 4; Matthew Hofer and Gary Scharnhorst, eds., *Oscar Wilde in America: The Interviews* (Urbana: University of Illinois Press, 2009), 162.

8. Ashley Phosphate Company of Charleston, *The Aesthetic Darkey,* 1883. Aestheticism's promise of social mobility generated a backlash. One example of the way it mocked black social aspiration was through jokes printed alongside the news, such as reports that there were 'a couple of would-be darkies on our streets to-night, artistically arrayed; Sambo and Pete, apostles of Oscar Wilde, we anticipate.' 'Neighborhood News,' *The Northern Pacific Farmer* (Wadena, MN), 9 March 1882, 1.

9. 'Oscar Wilde. A Visit to the Apostle of Modern Art. The Negro, the Indian and the Sunflower His Theme,' *Daily Picayune* (New Orleans), 17 June 1882, 3. See also Mary Warner Blanchard, *Oscar Wilde's America: Counterculture in the Gilded Age* (New Haven: Yale University Press, 1998), 19, 250 n. 50; Lloyd Lewis and Henry Justin Smith, *Oscar Wilde Discovers America, 1882* (New York: Harcourt, Brace, 1936), 362.

10. Hofer and Scharnhorst, *Oscar Wilde in America: The Interviews,* 157.

11. *Northern Tribune* (Cheboygan, MI), 15 July 1882, 3. 'Hints for the Household,' *Douglas Independent* (Roseburg, OR), 5 August 1882. Many others reprinted the item including the *Detroit Free Press, Boston Post, Turners Falls Reporter* (MA).

12. *Omaha Herald* (Omaha, NE), 2 July 1882, 2.

13. 'The Herald,' *The Leadville Daily Herald* (Leadville, CO), 28 June 1882, 2.

14. Qtd. in David Margolick, *Strange Fruit: Billie Holliday, Café Society and an Early Cry for Civil Rights* (Edinburgh: Canongate Books, 2013).

15. Ashraf Rushdy, *American Lynching* (New Haven: Yale University Press, 2012), 15.

16. Ibid. 92–3.

17. This was in 1892, at the high point. August Meier, *Negro Thought in America, 1880–1915: Racial Ideologies in the Age of Booker T. Washington* (Ann Arbor: University of Michigan Press, 1963), 20.

18. Michael J. Pfeifer, *Rough Justice: Lynching and American Society, 1874–1947* (Urbana: University of Illinois Press, 2004), 162.

19. Exceptionally, 'Mealy Howard' gets a mention in Gilles Vandal, *Rethinking Southern Violence: Homicides in Post-Civil War Louisiana, 1866–1884* (Columbus, OH: Ohio State University Press, 2000), 108.

20. Frederick Stephen Ellis, *St. Tammany Parish: L'autre Côté Du Lac* (Gretna, LA: Pelican, 1998), 166. Dan Ellis, 'Slidell, Louisiana—Camellia City: History Sketch of Slidell: Slidell—the Building of a Railroad—the Building of a City,' http://slidell.danellis.net/slidell_101.htm.

21. Sam Hyde, 'History of St. Tammany Parish,' Southeastern Channel, http://www2.stpgov.org/pdf/aboutsttammany_history.pdf.

22. 'New Orleans. Terrible Outrage and Lynching,' *Galveston Weekly News* (Galveston, TX), 22 June 1882, 3.

23. United States Census, 'Milan Howard, Buster, Darlington, SC' (1870; microfilm M593_1493, National Archives, Washington, DC), 382A-

117, 382B–118. Milan Howard appears on the 1870 US Census but he and his brother, Mingo Jr., are absent from the 1880 Census. Mingo Jr. turns up on later censuses.

24. Mary Anne Hamblen, *Darlington County* (Charleston, SC: Arcadia, 2008), 7.

25. Pfeifer, *Rough Justice*, 162.

26. 'New Orleans. Terrible Outrage and Lynching,' 3; 'Served Him Right,' *The Evening Critic* (Washington, DC), 15 June 1882, 1.

27. Ibid. 'Hung for Rape by Judge Lynch,' *St. Tammany Farmer* (Covington, LA), 24 June 1882, 3.

28. 'New Orleans. Terrible Outrage and Lynching,' 3.

29. Rushdy, *American Lynching*, 72.

30. Ibid. 78.

31. Ibid. 75.

32. Jacqueline Goldsby, *A Spectacular Secret: Lynching in American Life and Literature* (Chicago: University of Chicago Press, 2006), 20.

33. Qtd. in Rushdy, *American Lynching*, 75.

34. Winthrop Sheldon, 'Shall Lynching be Suppressed, and How,' *Arena*, 36 (September 1906), 227, qtd. in Goldsby, *A Spectacular Secret*, 20.

35. The rape victim has never been identified. 'New Orleans. Terrible Outrage and Lynching,' 3.

36. 'Served Him Right,' 1.

37. William W. Rogers and Robert David Ward, 'Aesthetic Messenger: Oscar Wilde Lectures in Memphis, 1882,' *Tennessee Historical Quarterly*, 63, no. 4 (2004), 262.

38. 'Homicide at Vicksburg,' *Daily Picayune* (New Orleans), 15 June 1882, 2.

39. Lewis and Smith, *Oscar Wilde Discovers America, 1882*, 359.

40. *St. Tammany Farmer* (Covington, LA), 17 June 1882, 2.

41. 'New Orleans. Terrible Outrage and Lynching,' 3. The report is dated 'New Orleans, June 12.' For a similar account, see also *Lake Charles Commercial* (Lake Charles, LA), 1 July 1882, 2.

42. 'Random Notes,' *Evening Bulletin* (San Francisco), 29 June 1882, 1. *The Sedalia Weekly Bazoo* (Sedalia, MO), 27 June 1882, 4. This account also ran in California, Colorado, Massachusetts, Michigan, Missouri, New Jersey, Ohio, and Washington. See also *The Highland Weekly News* (Hillsborough, OH), 12 July 1882; 'Odds and Ends,' *Seattle Daily Post-Intelligencer* (Seattle), 16 September 1882.

43. 'Mixed Facts and Fancies. Odds and Ends of News, Gossip and Scandal from All Sources,' *National Police Gazette* 8 July 1882, 15.

44. Martin Gusman, 'Report of the Justice of the Peace of the 9th Ward and Acting Coroner' (16 June 1882), *Clerk of Court's Collections* (St. Tammany Parish Archive, Covington, LA). Since Milan was never given a criminal trial, it's impossible to know exactly what transpired between him and the woman, or if anything happened at all. The only story we have,

then, is the story of an outraged white mob and street justice. The vigil-antes who murdered him ensured that his side of the story would never be heard. The news reports that stick to the facts are thin, for example, 'Dans le voisinage de Bonfouca, paroisse Tammany, le juge *lynch* dis-posa sommairement d'un certain individu de couleur nommé Milan Howard, qui avait outragé une femme blanche.' (In the neighborhood of Bonfouca, Tammany Parish, Judge Lynch summarily disposed of a certain colored individual named Milan Howard who had outraged a white woman.) *Le Meridional: Journal Officiel de la Paroisse Vermillon* (Abbeville, LA), 1 July 1882, 1.

45. The 'colored citizens' of St. Tammany held a meeting to protest. 'We Have Received the Proceedings,' *St. Tammany Farmer* (Covington, LA), 1 July 1882, 3.

46. Ellis, *St. Tammany Parish: L'autre Côté Du Lac*, 166. *Poor's Manual of the Railroads of the United States, 24th Annual Number* (New York: H. V. & H. W. Poor, 1895), 754. Bonfouca was on the Bogue Chitto Branch of the East Louisiana RR, later GM&O, two miles west of Slidell. The company was chartered in 1887, so the references to the bridge from which Howard was hanged was a road bridge, there being no railroads there in 1882. Wilde travelled from Vicksburg to New Orleans, but the direct rail line between those two cities was not complete until 1890. The obvious and most direct route was from Vicksburg to Jackson, MI (over the Alabama & Vicksburg RR) and then by Illinois Central from Jackson to New Orleans. Both of these rail routes were in place by the opening of the Civil War in 1860 and were heavily patronized lines. Because we know that Wilde stopped in Grenada, MI (where he was offered a bouquet by a Native American) we can be certain that he trav-elled on the Illinois Central Railroad (ICRR) for the north–south por-tions of his journey. The 1893 *Official Guide to the Railways* shows three daily trains in each direction on the ICRR between Jackson and New Orleans. None of these routes comes anywhere near Bonfouca, LA, so the presence there by a through train passenger, Oscar Wilde or anyone else, is impossible.

47. Even though the Bonfouca incident was a hoax, historians still discuss it as though it actually took place. See, for instance, Kieran Quinlan, *Strange Kin: Ireland and the American South* (Baton Rouge: Louisiana State University Press, 2005), 73; Eileen Knott, William Warren Rogers, and Robert David Ward, 'Oscar Wilde in Vicksburg, at Beauvoir, and Other Southern Stops,' *Journal of Mississippi History*, 59, no. 3 (1997); Mary Louise Ellis, 'Improbable Visitor: Oscar Wilde in Alabama, 1882,' *Alabama Review*, 39, no. 4 (1986).

48. *Truth* (New York), 7 July 1882, 2.

49. In 1882, William Edwin Adams visited the United States; his travelogue describes the resemblances he saw between the North's relationship to the

secessionist South and Britain's relationship to Ireland. William Edwin Adams, *Our American Cousins: Being Personal Impressions of the People and Institutions of the United States* (London: Walter Scott, 1883), 349–50.

50. Edward A. Freeman, *Some Impressions of the United States* (London: Longmans, Green & Co., 1883), 141.

51. Ibid. 138.

52. Qtd. in Vincent John Cheng, *Inauthentic: The Anxiety over Culture and Identity* (New Brunswick, NJ: Rutgers University Press, 2004), 30.

53. Qtd. in Neville Wallace Hoad, 'Wild(e) Men and Savages: The Homosexual and the Primitive in Darwin, Wilde and Freud' (PhD dissertation, Columbia University, 1998), 137.

54. John Beddoe, qtd. in Cheng, *Inauthentic*, 31.

55. Freeman, *Some Impressions of the United States*, 262.

56. 'Review of *Some Impressions of the United States* by Edward A. Freeman,' *Oxford Magazine*, (18 April 1883).

57. 'Oscar Wilde: A Visit to the Apostle of Modern Art: The Negro, the Indian and the Sunflower His Theme,' *Daily Picayune* (New Orleans), 16 June 1882.

58. There are two official documents pertaining to the inquest:

> (1) a one-page report from the Justice of the Peace of the 9th Ward and Acting Coroner, Martin J. Gusman, regarding the body of 'Amilia Houerd' dated 'Bonfouca, June 16th, 1882.' It describes how 'a yellow man, aged about 24 or 25 years of age, came to his death by hanging by the neck and sundry gun done in his body by parties unknown.'
>
> (2) a transcription of the report in the Clerk of Court's Inquest Book where the name of the deceased is 'Amelia Howard.'

M. Gusman, 'Report of the Justice of the Peace of the 9th Ward and Acting Coroner' (St. Tammany Parish Archive, Covington, LA). 'A. Howard,' ibid. (Clerk of Court's Inquest Book A), 25.

59. 'The Herald,' *The Leadville Daily Herald* 28 June 1882, 2.

60. 'It Is Stated That While in Louisiana Oscar Wilde Was a Guest at a Lynching,' *Galveston Daily News* (Houston, TX), 8 July 1882, 2.

61. Rumours about Wilde's uncle Elgee circulated in Southern newspapers (but rarely Northern ones) before he arrived in the United States and throughout the tour; see, for example: *Daily Picayune* (New Orleans), 20 August 1881, 2; 'Oscar Wilde a Nephew of Judge Elgee,' *Daily Picayune* (New Orleans), 11 January 1882, 2; 'Editorial Notes,' *Brenham Weekly Banner* (Brenham, TX), 2 February 1882, 1.

CHAPTER 15. THE CONFEDERATE

1. Eleanor Fitzsimons, *Wilde's Women* (London: Duckworth Overlook, 2015), 19.

2. 'John K. Elgee' *1820–1874, Index to Passenger Arrivals, Atlantic and Gulf Ports* (United States Department of the Treasury, Bureau of Customs).

3. United States Census, 'Slave Schedule, Rapides Parish, Louisiana,' (1850, National Archives, Washington, DC).

4. Daniel A. Gleason, ed., *Memorial of the Harvard College Class of 1856* (Boston: G. H. Ellis, 1906), 86. Helen P. Trimpi, *Crimson Confederates: Harvard Men Who Fought for the South* (Knoxville: University of Tennessee Press, 2010), 66.

5. 'Burning of Alexandria, Louisiana,' *Galveston Weekly News* (Galveston, TX), 21 September 1864, 2. United States Census, 'Free Inhabitants in Town of Alexandria, Rapides Parish, LA: John K. Elgee' (1860, National Archives, Washington, DC). 'Large Investment,' *Sugar Planter* (Port Allen, LA), 24 March 1860, 2. Michael Wayne, *The Reshaping of Plantation Society: The Natchez District, 1860–1880* (Baton Rouge, LA: Louisiana State University Press, 1983), 66.

6. 'Our New Orleans Correspondence,' *New York Times* 16 April 1864.

7. Thomas P. Kettell, *History of the Great Rebellion* (Hartford, CT: L. Stebbins, 1866), 40.

8. Charles B. Dew, 'The Long Lost Returns: The Candidates and Their Totals in Louisiana's Secession Election,' *Louisiana History: The Journal of the Louisiana Historical Association*, 10, no. 4 (1969), 366.

9. 'The Flag of Louisiana,' *The Louisiana Democrat* (Alexandria, LA), 5 August 1891, 2.

10. 'Louisiana State Convention,' *New Orleans Daily Crescent* (New Orleans), 12 February 1861, 1.

11. Nancy Isenberg, *White Trash: The 400-Year Untold History of Class in America* (New York: Viking, 2016), 161–9.

12. Gleason, *Memorial of the Harvard College Class of 1856*, 86.

13. 'Death of J. K. Elgee,' *Shreveport News* (Shreveport, LA), 25 October 1864, 2.

14. 'Our New Orleans Correspondence,' *New York Times* 16 April 1864.

15. Trimpi, *Crimson Confederates*, 67. In Dublin, Speranza dressed in black to mourn her brother and nephew.

16. Wayne, *The Reshaping of Plantation Society*, 66.

17. 'Oscar Wilde,' *The Louisiana Democrat* (Alexandria, LA), 21 June 1882, 2.

18. Jane Wilde, *Lady Jane Wilde's Letters to Oscar Wilde, 1875–1895*, ed. Karen Tipper (Lewiston, NY: Edwin Mellen Press, 2011), 80–1.

19. Ibid. 83.

20. Ibid. 78.

21. Fitzsimons, *Wilde's Women*, 18.

22. Jane Wilde, *Lady Jane Wilde's Letters*, 81, 83.

23. Jane Francesca Wilde, *Social Studies* (London: Ward & Downey, 1893), 170–1.

24. Nominally, Greater Britain referred to Britain's 'imperial possessions on a global scale.' Inspired by Charles Wentworth Dilke's *Greater Britain*

(1868) and, later, John Robert Seeley's *The Expansion of England* (1883), it was a state of mind as well as a political philosophy. British imperialism justified its dominance of Asian and African colonies as a manifestation of 'racial and cultural superiority.' It claimed that Britain had a right to dominate these countries because the British were better than its indigenous peoples. As it evolved, Greater Britain went a step further by introducing a pigmentocratic shading into its argument. It produced a colonial pecking order that created qualitative racial gradations among Britain's imperial possessions. John Wolffe, *God and Greater Britain: Religion and National Life in Britain and Ireland 1843–1945* (London: Routledge, 1994), p. x. Duncan Bell, *The Idea of Greater Britain: Empire and the Future of World Order, 1860–1900* (Princeton: Princeton University Press, 2007), 8.

25. David Powell, *Nationhood and Identity: The British State since 1800* (London: I. B. Tauris, 2002), 105.

26. William Edwin Adams, *Our American Cousins: Being Personal Impressions of the People and Institutions of the United States* (London: Walter Scott, 1883), 349–50.

27. David T. Gleeson, *The Green and the Gray: The Irish in the Confederate States of America* (Chapel Hill: University of North Carolina Press, 2013), 118.

28. Ibid. 196.

29. 'The Last Conquest of Ireland (Perhaps),' qtd. in Stephen Howe, *Ireland and Empire: Colonial Legacies in Irish History and Culture* (Oxford: Oxford University Press, 2000), 44–5. Sinn Fein founder Arthur Griffith similarly refused to 'hold the negro his peer in right.' Mitchel and Griffith preferred 'an aristocratic conception of Irish liberty akin to that of the Greek, Roman and American slaveholders.' R. P. Davis, *Arthur Griffith and Non-Violent Sinn Fein* (Dublin: Anvil Books, 1974), 107, 109.

30. Oscar Wilde, 'The Irish Poets of 48,' in *The Annotated Oscar Wilde*, ed. H. Montgomery Hyde (New York: C. N. Potter, 1982), 375.

31. Matthew Hofer and Gary Scharnhorst, eds., *Oscar Wilde in America: The Interviews* (Urbana: University of Illinois Press, 2009), 157.

32. Qtd. in Eileen Knott, William Warren Rogers, and Robert David Ward, 'Oscar Wilde in Vicksburg, at Beauvoir, and Other Southern Stops,' *Journal of Mississippi History*, 59, no. 3 (1997), 203.

33. Sacvan Bercovitch and Cyrus R. K. Patell, *The Cambridge History of American Literature* (Cambridge: Cambridge University Press, 1994), 80, 82. Varina Davis, *Jefferson Davis, Ex-President of the Confederate States of America, a Memoir by His Wife*, 2 vols. (New York: Belford, 1890), 1:11. The Davises were invited to visit Wilde's parents in Dublin in 1870 but they declined. Joan E. Cashin, *First Lady of the Confederacy Varina Davis's Civil War* (Cambridge, MA: Belknap, 2006), 199.

34. Qtd. in Knott, Rogers, and Ward, 'Oscar Wilde in Vicksburg,' 203.

35. Hofer and Scharnhorst, *Oscar Wilde in America: The Interviews*, 157.

36. David Williams, *Rich Man's War: Class, Caste, and Confederate Defeat in the Lower Chattahoochee Valley* (Athens, GA: University of Georgia Press, 1998), 195.

37. Hofer and Scharnhorst, *Oscar Wilde in America: The Interviews*, 157.

38. Emily Virginia Mason, *The Southern Poems of the War* (Baltimore: John Murphy & Co., 1878), 484, 20. Lee Meriwether interviewed Wilde in Memphis and saw the volume in his hotel room. In 1895, the book was included in the auction of Wilde's effects. Knott, Rogers, and Ward, 'Oscar Wilde in Vicksburg,' 203. A. N. L. Munby, 'Oscar Wilde,' in *Sale Catalogues of Libraries of Eminent Persons* (London: Mansell Publishing, 1971), 381.

39. Hofer and Scharnhorst, *Oscar Wilde in America: The Interviews*, 159–60.

40. Heath Hardage Lee, *Winnie Davis: Daughter of the Lost Cause* (Lincoln, NE: Potomac Books, 2014), 74.

41. Charles Fanning, ed., *The Exiles of Erin: Nineteenth-Century Irish-American Fiction* (Notre Dame, IN: University of Notre Dame Press, 1987), 3.

42. Knott, Rogers, and Ward, 'Oscar Wilde in Vicksburg,' 204.

43. William C. Davis, *The Cause Lost: Myths and Realities of the Confederacy* (Lawrence, KS: University Press of Kansas, 1966), 175.

44. Hofer and Scharnhorst, *Oscar Wilde in America: The Interviews*, 159–60.

45. *Macon Telegram and Messenger* (Macon, GA), 6 June 1882, qtd. in William W. Rogers and Robert David Ward, 'Aesthetic Messenger: Oscar Wilde Lectures in Memphis, 1882,' *Tennessee Historical Quarterly*, 63, no. 4 (2004), 262.

46. 'Oscar Wilde and His Negro Valet,' *New York Times* 9 July 1882, 2. For an extended discussion about the identity of Wilde's valet, see the Appendix.

47. 'Oscar Wilde Hung,' *The Leadville Daily Herald* (Leadville, CO), 19 April 1882, 4. In August, Wilde was hung in effigy in Spring Lake, New Jersey. Described as 'a funny scene on the beach,' the life-sized doll had flowing hair like Wilde's, and was dressed in knee-breeches and a corset with a huge sunflower pinned to it. To great applause, it was run up to the top of the flagpole. *Daily Evening Bulletin* (San Francisco), 31 August 1882, 3. *Harper's Weekly* reported on an African American woman lynched with 'a large sunflower pinned on her dress' and wondered 'whether the favor shown to the sunflower by this negro woman will make that flower unpopular.' The magazine's chilling answer was that the sunflower would remain fashionable because it had already 'withstood the test of even Oscar Wilde's ostentatious preference.' 'Waifs and Strays,' *Harper's Weekly* 3 November 1883, 695.

CHAPTER 16. SUCCESS IS A SCIENCE

1. Walter Hamilton, *The Aesthetic Movement in England* (London, 1882), 100–9.
2. Jane Wilde, *Lady Jane Wilde's Letters to Oscar Wilde, 1875–1895*, ed. Karen Tipper (Lewiston, NY: Edwin Mellen Press, 2011), 76.
3. Ibid. 78.
4. Qtd. in Geoffrey Dibb, *Oscar Wilde: A Vagabond with a Mission* (London: Oscar Wilde Society, 2013), 16.
5. Jane Wilde, *Lady Jane Wilde's Letters*, 78.
6. Franny Moyle, *Constance: The Tragic and Scandalous Life of Mrs Oscar Wilde* (London: John Murray, 2011), 64.
7. Jane Wilde, *Lady Jane Wilde's Letters*, 75.
8. Moyle, *Constance*, 56–8, 31.
9. Jane Wilde, *Lady Jane Wilde's Letters*, 91.
10. Moyle, *Constance*, 77.
11. Oscar Wilde, *The Complete Letters of Oscar Wilde*, ed. Merlin Holland and Rupert Hart-Davis (London: Fourth Estate, 2000), 221–2.
12. Moyle, *Constance*, 76–7.
13. Oscar Wilde, *Letters*, 224; Moyle, *Constance*, 87.
14. Moyle, *Constance*, 83.
15. Oscar Wilde, *Letters*, 224; Moyle, *Constance*, 87.
16. Dibb, *Oscar Wilde: A Vagabond with a Mission*, 45, 83–5.
17. Oscar Wilde, *Letters*, 297. Wilde hoped *Woman's World* would become 'the recommended organ for the expression of women's opinions on all subjects of literature, art and modern life, and yet it should be a magazine that men could read with pleasure, and consider it a privilege to contribute to.'
18. Oscar Wilde, *The Complete Works of Oscar Wilde*, Vol. 7: *Journalism*, ed. John Stokes and Mark W. Turner, Part II (Oxford: Oxford University Press, 2013), 211.
19. 'Lady Wilde in the *Kentish Mercury*' (2 September 1892), Robert Ross Memorial Collection, (Box 6. Scrapbook, University College, Oxford).
20. Oscar Wilde, *Letters*, 303; Moyle, *Constance*, 110–11, 130.
21. Vyvyan Holland, ed., *Son of Oscar Wilde* (Oxford: Rupert Hart-Davis, 1954), 52–4.
22. Ibid. 200.
23. Anya Clayworth, '*The Woman's World*: Oscar Wilde as Editor,' *Victorian Periodicals Review*, 30, no. 2 (1997), 86–7.
24. Oscar Wilde, *The Complete Works of Oscar Wilde*, Vol. 6: *Journalism*, ed. John Stokes and Mark W. Turner, Part I (Oxford: Oxford University Press, 2013), 131–2.
25. Oscar Wilde, *Letters*, 303.
26. Ibid. 297.

27. *The Complete Works of Oscar Wilde,* Vol. 7: *Journalism,* Part II, 9.
28. Arthur Fish, 'Oscar Wilde as Editor,' *Harper's Weekly,* 58 (1913), 18.
29. Clayworth, '*The Woman's World*: Oscar Wilde as Editor,' 97.
30. Arthur Conan Doyle, *Memories and Adventures* (Cambridge: Cambridge University Press, 2012), 78–9.
31. Karl Beckson, ed., *Oscar Wilde: The Critical Heritage* (London: Routledge, 1970), 72. Merlin Holland, ed., *Irish Peacock and Scarlet Marquess: The Real Trial of Oscar Wilde* (New York: HarperCollins, 2003), 141.
32. Beckson, *Oscar Wilde: The Critical Heritage,* 72.
33. Oscar Wilde, *The Complete Works of Oscar Wilde,* Vol. 3: *The Picture of Dorian Gray,* ed. Joseph Bristow (Oxford: Oxford University Press, 2005), 168.
34. Qtd. in Moyle, *Constance,* 201.
35. Wilde met Edward Shelley in October 1892, when John Lane introduced them and they had 'a long talk about literature.' Holland, *The Real Trial of Oscar Wilde,* 227.
36. Ibid. 135. Wilde described Edward Shelley as a sort of Dorian figure, a 'gentleman' with 'an intellectual face' and 'a very interesting personality.' He had 'a great deal of cultivation and a great desire for culture.' Giving Shelley his novel about an older man's corrupting influence over a younger man could hardly have been a more symbolic gesture. Ibid. 141, 134, 228.
37. Ibid. 323.
38. Oscar Wilde, *Letters,* 204.
39. Oscar Wilde, *The Importance of Being Earnest and Other Plays,* ed. Peter Raby (Oxford: Oxford University Press, 1995), 44.
40. W. Graham Robertson and Johnston Forbes-Robertson, *Time Was: The Reminiscences of W. Graham Robertson* (London: Hamish Hamilton, 1931), 135.
41. *The Sheffield and Rotherham Independent* (Sheffield, England), 5 March 1892, 5; 'Fun's Tip-Topical Touches,' *Fun* (London) 16 March 1892, 107.
42. Oscar Wilde, *Letters,* 617.
43. 'Current Carols; or, Ditties in Doselets up to Date,' *Fun* (London), 16 March 1892, 114.
44. 'The Man About Town,' *The County Gentleman: Sporting Gazette, Agricultural Journal* (London), 5 March 1892, 298.
45. 'Our Ladies' Column,' *The Wrexham Advertiser, and North Wales News* (Wrexham, Wales), 5 March 1892, 2.
46. 'Theater Program for *The Idler* by C. Haddon Chambers' (26 February 1892) (London Playbills, St. James's Theatre, John Johnson Collection).
47. 'The Blue Gardenia (a Colourable Imitation),' *Punch, or the London Charivari* (London), 20 October 1884, 185.
48. Qtd. in Richard Ellmann, *Oscar Wilde* (London: Hamish Hamilton, 1987), 346.

49. Aristophanes, *Clouds, Women at the Thesmophoria, Frogs: A Verse Translation, with Introduction and Notes*, trans. Stephen Halliwell (Oxford: Oxford University Press, 2015), 42.

50. Holland, *The Real Trial of Oscar Wilde*, 230.

51. Jane Wilde, *Lady Jane Wilde's Letters*, 135.

52. In a letter to the editor of the *St. James's Gazette*, published on 27 February 1892, Wilde described how 'after the play was over, and the author, cigarette in hand, had delivered a delightful and immortal speech, I had the pleasure of entertaining at supper a small number of personal friends.' Oscar Wilde, *Letters*, 521.

53. Holland, *The Real Trial of Oscar Wilde*, 230.

54. Laura Elizabeth Howe Richards and Maud Howe Elliott, *Julia Ward Howe, 1819–1910*, 2 vols. (Boston: Houghton Mifflin, 1925), 2:167.

55. The *Journal* was the American Woman Suffrage Association's unofficial magazine.

56. Beckson, *Oscar Wilde: The Critical Heritage*, 51.

57. Samuel Ward, 'The Aesthetic. Sam Ward to Oscar Wilde,' *New York World* 4 January 1882, 11.

58. Beckson, *Oscar Wilde: The Critical Heritage*, 51. Higginson's opinion on women who entertained Wilde was widely reprinted and commentators generally took his side. 'We acknowledge a shiver when we hear a presumably pure woman speak familiarly the name of Oscar Wilde,' was a fairly typical response. 'Julia Ward Howe and Oscar Wilde,' *Warren Sheaf* (Warren, MN), 16 March 1882, 3. See also 'Fireside Chit-Chat,' *Mower County Transcript* (Lansing, MN), 22 February 1882, 4.

59. Richards and Elliott, *Julia Ward Howe, 1819–1910*, 1:362. Colonel Higginson had once been an ally to Mrs Howe, which must have made his rebuke all the more galling. Her daughters credited him with encouraging their mother to make her first public speech. During the Civil War, Mrs Howe was so frightened by the prospect of addressing the Army of the Potomac that she ran away from the stage. She was cowering in a camp tent when Higginson appeared and emboldened her to rise to the occasion and display her 'gift of ready speech and pure diction' on stage. Ibid. 1:366.

60. Qtd. in Elaine Showalter, *The Civil Wars of Julia Ward Howe: A Biography* (New York: Simon & Schuster, 2016), 207.

61. Maude Howe Elliott, *Three Generations* (Boston: Little, Brown, 1923), 147, 206.

62. Maude Howe Elliott, *Uncle Sam Ward and His Circle* (New York: Macmillan, 1938), 602.

63. Oscar Wilde, *Letters*, 176.

64. Ibid. 175.

65. Richards and Elliott, *Julia Ward Howe, 1819–1910*, 2:168.

66. Oscar Wilde, *The Importance of Being Earnest and Other Plays*, 8.

67. Ibid. 11–12.

68. Richards and Elliott, *Julia Ward Howe, 1819–1910*, 2:168.

69. Oscar Wilde, *Letters*, 1081.

70. 'Oscar Wilde's New Play,' *New York Times*, 28 February 1892, 13. For an example of the grudging appreciation *Lady Windermere's Fan* garnered, see 'Oscar Wilde's Comedy,' *The Spectator*, 69, no. 3361 (26 November 1892).

71. Charles Brookfield and James M. Glover, 'The Poet and the Puppets,' in *Victorian Theatrical Burlesques*, ed. Richard W. Schoch (Aldershot: Ashgate, 2003), 232–3.

72. Ibid. 239.

73. E. H. Mikhail, *Oscar Wilde: Interviews and Recollections*, 2 vols. (London: Macmillan, 1979), 1:190, 188.

74. Oscar Wilde, *Letters*, 532, 531. Glover's autobiography offers a dubious account according to which he and Brookfield read the play aloud to Wilde, whose only objection was that his name was used in one of the play's songs. James M. Glover, *Jimmy Glover, His Book* (London: Methuen, 1911), 20.

75. Oscar Wilde, *Letters*, 531.

76. *The Theatre*, 1 June 1892, qtd. in Brookfield and Glover, 'The Poet and the Puppets,' 213.

77. 'Garden Theatre: *The Poet and the Puppets* and *His Wedding Day*,' *New York Times* 4 April 1893, 4.

78. 'Advertisement for *The Poet and the Puppets*,' *New York Times*, 16 April 1893, 7.

79. Nestor, 'Slashes and Puffs,' *Fun*, 55, no. 1412 (1 June 1892), 226.

80. John Corbin, 'Topics of the Drama,' *New York Times*, 8 March 1903, 25.

81. 'Manager Frohman Home Again,' *New York Times*, 23 June 1892, 9.

82. Kim Marra and Robert A. Schanke, *Staging Desire: Queer Readings of American Theater History* (Ann Arbor: University of Michigan Press, 2002), 39.

83. 'Manager Frohman Home Again,' 9.

84. Isaac F. Marcosson and Daniel Frohman, *Charles Frohman: Manager and Man* (London: Bodley Head, 1916), 423.

CHAPTER 17. YOU HAVE MADE YOUR NAME

1. 'At the Play,' *The Observer* 23 April 1893, 6. Josephine M. Guy and Ian Small, *Oscar Wilde's Profession: Writing and the Culture Industry in the Late Nineteenth Century* (Oxford: Oxford University Press, 2000), 116.

2. Oscar Wilde, *The Complete Letters of Oscar Wilde*, ed. Merlin Holland and Rupert Hart-Davis (London: Fourth Estate, 2000), 204.

3. Ibid. 535.

4. Sos Eltis, *Acts of Desire: Women and Sex on Stage, 1800–1930* (Oxford: Oxford University Press, 2013), 114.

5. Oscar Wilde, *The Importance of Being Earnest and Other Plays*, ed. Peter Raby (Oxford: Oxford University Press, 1995), 13.

6. Ibid. 132.

7. Baudelaire, qtd. in Rhonda K. Garelick, *Rising Star: Dandyism, Gender, and Performance in the Fin De Siècle* (Princeton: Princeton University Press, 1998), 28–9. The Wildean dandy is a trickster. He (or she) is polite society's hermaphrodite—he can be This and That, X and Y. He can walk a class line, as well as use his clothes to inhabit the boundary between conventional order (his perfect necktie) and chaos (the nature-defying green carnation he wears in his buttonhole). He is a polyvalent figure and a skilful negotiator of race, sexuality, and class identities, as Monica Miller and Ellen Crowell have noted. Ellen Crowell, *The Dandy in Irish and American Southern Fiction: Aristocratic Drag* (Edinburgh: Edinburgh University Press, 2007). Monica L. Miller, *Slaves to Fashion: Black Dandyism and the Styling of Black Diasporic Identity* (Durham, NC: Duke University Press, 2009).

8. Newman I. White, *American Negro Folk-Songs* (Cambridge, MA: Harvard University Press, 1928), 445. For a detailed analysis of Dandy Jim as a stereotype of black masculinity, see William J. Mahar, *Behind the Burnt Cork Mask: Early Blackface Minstrelsy and Antebellum American Popular Culture* (Urbana: University of Illinois Press, 1999), 209 ff.

9. Qtd. in Eric Lott, *Love and Theft: Blackface Minstrelsy and the American Working Class* (New York: Oxford University Press, 1993), 26. Annemarie Bean, James Vernon Hatch, and Brooks McNamara, eds., *Inside the Minstrel Mask: Readings in Nineteenth-Century Blackface Minstrelsy* (Hanover, NH: Wesleyan University Press, 1996), 258.

10. Stephen Collins Foster, *Stephen Foster & Co.: Lyrics of America's First Great Popular Songs*, ed. Ken Emerson (New York: Library of America, 2010), 30, 32. On Zip Coon as urban dandy, see Dale Cockrell, *Demons of Disorder: Early Blackface Minstrels and Their World* (Cambridge: Cambridge University Press, 1997), 93; Kenneth W. Goings, *Mammy and Uncle Mose: Black Collectibles and American Stereotyping* (Bloomington: Indiana University Press, 1994), 43.

11. Max Beerbohm, ed., *Herbert Beerbohm Tree: Some Memories of Him and of His Art* (London: Hutchinson & Co., 1920), 77.

12. Oscar Wilde, *Letters*, 540.

13. Ibid. 539.

14. Ibid. 538.

15. Oscar Wilde, *The Importance of Being Earnest and Other Plays*, 133. Lord Illingworth is kin with Wilde's other well-tailored rakes and smooth-talking swells including *The Picture of Dorian Gray*'s Lord Henry (who believes 'the one charm of marriage is that it makes a life of deception absolutely necessary for both parties') and Dorian (who throws over Sybil Vane in a fit of pique when her performances cease to please him). Ibid. 171.

16. Franny Moyle, *Constance: The Tragic and Scandalous Life of Mrs Oscar Wilde* (London: John Murray, 2011), 224.

17. Robert Smythe Hichens, *The Green Carnation* (New York: Appleton, 1894), 13, 17, 21.

18. 'Two Decadent Guys: A Colour Study in Green Carnations,' *Punch*, 10 November 1894, 225.

19. Moyle, *Constance*, 250–1.

20. Jack Haverly, *Negro Minstrels: A Complete Guide to Negro Minstrelsy, Containing Recitations, Jokes, Crossfires, Conundrums, Riddles, Stump Speeches, Ragtime and Sentimental Songs, Etc., Including Hints on Organizing and Successfully Presenting a Performance* (Chicago: Frederick J. Drake & Company, 1902), 11, 43.

21. Oscar Wilde, *The Importance of Being Earnest and Other Plays*, 113, 131.

22. Ibid. 103–5.

23. 'A Work of—Some Importance,' *Punch*, 6 May 1893, 213.

24. 'Judy's Diary,' *Judy: or The London Serio-Comic Journal*, 7 June 1893, 269.

25. P.J.M., 'Manchester Theatres: Oscar Wilde at Rusholme,' *Manchester Guardian*, 16 June 1931, 11.

26. William Archer, *The Old Drama and the New: An Essay in Re-Valuation* (London: W. Heinemann, 1923), 303–4.

27. Oscar Wilde, *The Complete Works of Oscar Wilde*, Vol. 7: *Journalism*, ed. John Stokes and Mark W. Turner, Part II (Oxford: Oxford University Press, 2013), 158.

28. Ibid. 53.

29. On the relationship between food and class, see Peter Raby, 'Wilde, and How to Be Modern: Or, Bags of Red Gold,' in *Wilde Writings: Contextual Conditions*, ed. Joseph Bristow (Toronto: University of Toronto Press, 2003), 147–62.

30. 'Our Captious Critic,' *The Illustrated Sporting and Dramatic News*, 26 January 1895, 742.

31. Saidiya V. Hartman, *Scenes of Subjection: Terror, Slavery, and Self-Making in Nineteenth-Century America* (New York: Oxford University Press, 1997), 27. 'The *minstrel mask*,' Houston Baker, Jr. explains, 'is a space of habitation not only for repressed spirits of sexuality, ludic play, id satisfaction, castration anxiety, and a mirror stage of development, but also for that deep-seated denial of the indisputable humanity of inhabitants of and descendants from the continent of Africa.' Houston A. Baker, *Modernism and the Harlem Renaissance* (Chicago: University of Chicago Press, 1987), 17. See also David Krasner, *Resistance, Parody, and Double Consciousness in African American Theatre, 1895–1910* (New York: St. Martin's Press, 1997); Marvin McAllister, *Whiting Up: Whiteface Minstrels and Stage Europeans in African American Performance* (Chapel Hill: University of North Carolina Press, 2011); Matthew Frye Jacobson, *Whiteness of a Different Color: European Immigrants and the Alchemy of Race* (Cambridge, MA: Harvard University Press, 1998); W. T. Lhamon, *Raising Cain:*

Blackface Performance from Jim Crow to Hip Hop (Cambridge, MA: Harvard University Press, 1998).

32. Marvin McAllister, *White People Do Not Know How To Behave at Entertainments Designed for Ladies and Gentlemen of Colour: William Brown's African and American Theater* (Chapel Hill, NC: University of North Carolina Press, 2003), 15.

33. Oscar Wilde, *The Complete Works of Oscar Wilde*, Vol. 4: *Criticism: Historical Criticism, Intentions, The Soul of Man*, ed. Josephine M. Guy (Oxford: Oxford University Press, 2007), 107.

34. Ibid. 187.

35. Ibid. 228.

36. Archer, *The Old Drama and the New: An Essay in Re-Valuation*, 303–4.

37. Karl Beckson, ed., *Oscar Wilde: The Critical Heritage* (London: Routledge, 1970), 157. On Wilde's radical use of melodrama to expose conservative attitudes, see Sos Eltis, *Revising Wilde: Society and Subversion in the Plays of Oscar Wilde* (Oxford: Clarendon, 1996); Katherine Worth, *Oscar Wilde* (London: Macmillan, 1983).

38. 'Oscar Wilde's Comedy,' *The Spectator*, 69, no. 3361 (26 November 1892).

39. 'Public Amusements,' *The Irish Times*, 6 November 1893, 6.

40. Beckson, *Oscar Wilde: The Critical Heritage*, 144.

41. Jane Wilde, *Lady Jane Wilde's Letters to Oscar Wilde, 1875–1895*, ed. Karen Tipper (Lewiston, NY: Edwin Mellen Press, 2011), 145.

CHAPTER 18. BY THE THROAT

1. A. N. Wilson, *The Victorians* (London: Hutchinson, 2002), 524.

2. The *Oxford English Dictionary* states that 'Wildean' was first mentioned in 1924, but Minnesota's *New Ulm Review* had already referred to it three decades earlier, on 11 October 1893, 4. 'Wildese' was also current by the 1890s.

3. *Truth* 21 February 1895, qtd. in Karl Beckson, ed., *Oscar Wilde: The Critical Heritage* (London: Routledge, 1970), 192.

4. Gustave Le Bon, *The Crowd: A Study of the Popular Mind* (Mineola, NY: Dover, 2001), 61, 64–5, ix, italics added.

5. Oscar Wilde, *The Complete Letters of Oscar Wilde*, ed. Merlin Holland and Rupert Hart-Davis (London: Fourth Estate, 2000), 632.

6. Ibid. 634.

7. Ibid. 690.

8. Ibid. 75.

9. Merlin Holland, ed., *Irish Peacock and Scarlet Marquess: The Real Trial of Oscar Wilde* (New York: HarperCollins, 2003), 277.

10. Ibid. 270.

11. Ibid., xxxviii, 302.

12. Ibid. 45–6.

13. Holman Hunt, qtd. in Vyvyan Holland, *Son of Oscar Wilde* (London: Rupert Hart-Davis, 1954), 204.

14. William James, *The Correspondence of William James*, ed. Ignas K. Skrupskelis and Elizabeth M. Berkeley, 10 vols. (Charlottesville: University Press of Virginia, 1993), 8:359.

15. Louise Jopling, *Twenty Years of My Life, 1867 to 1887* (London: John Lane, 1925), 82.

16. Holland, *Son of Oscar Wilde*, 60–1.

17. 'The Wilde Case,' *Morning Post* (London), 25 April 1895, 2.

18. Franny Moyle, *Constance: The Tragic and Scandalous Life of Mrs Oscar Wilde* (London: John Murray, 2011), 273, 284.

19. Holland, *Son of Oscar Wilde*, 61.

20. Ibid. 52.

21. Oscar Wilde, *Letters*, 657.

22. Ibid. 658.

23. Ibid. 803.

24. Ibid. 757.

25. Constance Holland to Otho Lloyd, 21 February 1896, qtd. in Moyle, *Constance*, 288.

26. Oscar Wilde, *Letters*, 668.

27. Ibid. 673, 682. A soft-hearted soul with a schoolgirl's prim penmanship, Harold Frederic was a strapping six-footer with a vice-like handshake and the voice of a foghorn. Though not a single drop of Irish blood flowed through his veins, when he came to Ireland he was legendary for being 'more Irish than the Irish.' Wilde met Frederic in 1890s Paris. Arthur Warren, 'Harold Frederic,' *New York Times* 23 October 1898, 19; Richard Ellmann, *Oscar Wilde* (London: Hamish Hamilton, 1987), 331 n., 574 n. 29.

28. Harold Frederic, *The Damnation of Theron Ware, or, Illumination* (New York: Penguin, 1986), 49.

29. Oscar Wilde, *Letters*, 790.

30. Chris Healy, *Confessions of a Journalist* (London: Chatto & Windus, 1904), 133.

31. In correspondence with his publisher, however, Wilde wrote, 'I am describing a general scene with general types.' Oscar Wilde, *Letters*, 983.

32. Oscar Wilde, *The Complete Works of Oscar Wilde*, Vol. 1: *Poems and Poems in Prose*, ed. Bobby Fong and Karl Beckson (Oxford: Oxford University Press, 2000), 200.

33. Ibid. 207.

34. Healy, *Confessions of a Journalist*, 132–3.

35. Oscar Wilde, *Letters*, 986.

36. 'I believe they all wear red,' he wrote to Leonard Smithers in 1897 while worrying about the accuracy of the uniform's colours. One

reader took him to task for his failure to document the colour of the hanged soldier's coat accurately. Hesketh Pearson, *The Life of Oscar Wilde* (London: Methuen, 1946), 350.

37. Oscar Wilde, *Letters*, 976, 926.
38. Elisabeth Marbury, *My Crystal Ball: Reminiscences* (London: Hurst & Blackett, 1924), 94, 97.
39. Oscar Wilde, *Letters*, 981. Stuart Mason, *Bibliography of Oscar Wilde* (Boston: Longwood, 1977), 412–13.
40. Ibid. 408.
41. Oscar Wilde, *Letters*, 996.
42. Ibid. 710.
43. Ibid. 785.
44. Asked to comment on the city's scenery, he had called it 'Italy without its art.' Ellmann, *Wilde*, 185.
45. Oscar Wilde, *Letters*, 803.
46. Ibid. 937. Mason, *Bibliography of Oscar Wilde*, 416.
47. Oscar Wilde, *Letters*, 785.
48. Qtd. in Joy Melville, *Mother of Oscar: The Life of Jane Francesca Wilde* (London: Allison & Busby, 1999), 277.
49. Oscar Wilde, *Letters*, 808–9.
50. Ibid. 996.
51. Ibid. 1081.
52. Qtd. in Moyle, *Constance*, 311.
53. Alfred Douglas, *Without Apology* (London: M. Secker, 1938), 99.
54. Moyle, *Constance*, 324.
55. Oscar Wilde, *Letters*, 1011.
56. Ibid. 993.
57. Ibid. 1214.
58. Ibid. 1205.
59. Isaac F. Marcosson and Daniel Frohman, *Charles Frohman: Manager and Man* (London: Bodley Head, 1916), 423.
60. John Corbin, 'Topics of the Drama,' *New York Times*, 8 March 1903, 25.
61. Oscar Wilde, *Letters*, 1205.
62. Ibid. Josephine M. Guy and Ian Small, *Oscar Wilde's Profession: Writing and the Culture Industry in the Late Nineteenth Century* (Oxford: Oxford University Press, 2000), 110, 128, 208. Kim Marra, *Strange Duets: Impresarios and Actresses in the American Theatre, 1865–1914* (Iowa City: University of Iowa Press, 2006), 89.

EPILOGUE. THE PRIVATE VIEW

1. Oscar Wilde, *The Writings of Oscar Wilde: His Life with a Critical Estimate of His Writings*, Vol. 15 (London: A. R. Keller, 1907), 274–96.
2. William F. Morse, 'The Disposal of the Garbage and Waste of the World's Columbian Exposition,' *Public Health Papers and Reports*, 19 (1893), 54.

3. William F. Morse, 'The Destruction of Town Waste by Fire,' *Journal of the Massachusetts Associated Boards of Health*, 2, no. 4 (November 1892), 5.

4. William F. Morse, *The Methods of Collection, and the Disposal of Waste and Garbage by Cremation* (New York: Engle Sanitary and Cremation Co., 1892). See also, among others, William F. Morse, 'The Sanitary Disposal of Municipal and Institutional Waste by Cremation.' *Public Health Papers and Reports*, 29 (1903), 134–40.

5. Morse, 'The Disposal of the Garbage and Waste of the World's Columbian Exposition,' 60. Morse, 'The Destruction of Town Waste by Fire,' 13.

6. William F. Morse, 'American Lectures,' in *The Writings of Oscar Wilde: His Life with a Critical Estimate of His Writings* (London: A. R. Keller 1907), 72.

7. Ibid. 78–9.

8. Ibid. 93–4. According to Morse's sanitized history, he and Wilde worked harmoniously throughout the tour and 'there was no cause for complaint or heart-burning on either side.'

9. Vyvyan Beresford Holland, *Son of Oscar Wilde* (London: Rupert Hart-Davis, 1954), 196–7.

10. Oscar Wilde, *The Complete Works of Oscar Wilde*, Vol. 1: *Poems and Poems in Prose*, ed. Bobby Fong and Karl Beckson (Oxford: Oxford University Press, 2000), 212.

11. W. Graham Robertson and Johnston Forbes-Robertson, *Time Was: The Reminiscences of W. Graham Robertson* (London: Hamish Hamilton, 1931), 138.

12. Richard Ellmann, *Oscar Wilde* (London: Hamish Hamilton, 1987), 553.

13. Adam Gopnick, 'The Invention of Oscar Wilde,' *The New Yorker* 18 May 1998, 78.

14. Ibid. 88.

15. Oscar Wilde, *The Complete Works of Oscar Wilde*, Vol. 3: *The Picture of Dorian Gray*, ed. Joseph Bristow (Oxford: Oxford University Press, 2005), 355–6.

16. William Powell Frith, *My Autobiography and Reminiscences*, 2 vols. (London: Richard Bentley & Son, 1887), 2:256.

17. 'The Picture Galleries,' *The Saturday Review of Politics, Literature, Science, and Art*, 5 May 1883, 566.

18. Frith, *My Autobiography and Reminiscences*, 2:335.

19. Oscar Wilde, *The Complete Works of Oscar Wilde*, Vol. 4: *Criticism: Historical Criticism, Intentions, The Soul of Man*, ed. Josephine M. Guy (Oxford: Oxford University Press, 2007), 124. In a draft of the essay now held at the British Library, Wilde mentions Frith by name, but perhaps thinking better of it, he marked the passage for deletion.

20. Oscar Wilde, *The Importance of Being Earnest and Other Plays*, ed. Peter Raby (Oxford: Oxford University Press, 1995), 131.

21. Oscar Wilde, *Collins Complete Works of Oscar Wilde* (Glasgow: HarperCollins, 1999), 925.

Acknowledgements

It is a truth rarely acknowledged that research involves reaching out. It takes supportive family, friends, colleagues, librarians, and archivists. It also helps to have an Internet village of digitizers and scholars, research funding to trawl archives for treasures, and—above all—time to write, edit, rethink, and rewrite. It was my great blessing to enjoy all of this, and I am deeply grateful to those who contributed, through acts of kindness great and small, to the making of this book.

My first debts are to Peter Robinson at Rogers, Coleridge and White and Jacqueline Norton at Oxford University Press for believing in this project from the start. OUP's Eleanor Collins and Emma Slaughter skilfully and patiently helped me make it a reality.

For research funding and fellowships, my profound thanks to the Leverhulme Trust; the University of Utah Tanner Humanities Centre; the British Library Eccles Centre for American Studies; the Manuscript, Archives and Rare Book Library at Emory University; the Beinecke Library at Yale University; the John Fell Fund; the Oxford University English Faculty; Mansfield College, Oxford. Without these generous benefactions, this book would not exist.

I am indebted to the librarians, archivists, and curators who opened up their collections and shared their knowledge: Elizabeth Adams (University College, Oxford), Colin Harris (Special Collections, Bodleian Libraries), Robin Darwall-Smith (Magdalen College, Oxford), the late Beth M. Howse (John Hope and Aurelia E. Franklin Library, Fisk University), Ida E. Jones (Moorland Spingarn Research Center, Howard University), Cornelia S. King (The Library Company of Philadelphia), Jennifer Schaffner and Bruce Whiteman (William Andrews Clark Memorial Library, UCLA), Katherine Fox and Christine Riggle (Special Collections, Harvard Business School), James Capobianco (Houghton Library, Harvard), Becky Filner and Kyle R. Triplett (New York Public Library), Helen Valentine (Royal Academy of Arts).

Merlin Holland proved exceptionally generous with his inside knowledge of Wilde's world. For their assistance in tracing Wilde's Louisiana railroad route, I want to give a special shout out to Ralph W. Hawkins (http://www.hawkinsrails.net), Louis Saillard, Samuel Hyde (Center for Southeast Louisiana Studies), and Robin Perkins (St. Tammany Parish Court).

My research benefited from access to numerous private and public digital resources. I want to thank two exceptional archives that yielded some of the most significant material for my study: the Internet Archive, a non-profit online library that makes millions of books accessible to all, and Chronicling America, a public database of US newspapers created by the National Endowment for the Humanities and the Library of Congress.

I would like to thank the kind colleagues and wonderful friends who read draft chapters and made suggestions: Faith Binckes, Emily Coit, Daniel Crewe, Sos Eltis, Jacqueline Goldsby, Michael Gorra, Alexandra Harris, Marti Leimbach, Kate McLoughlin, Matthew Potolsky, Rebecca Roach, Vincent Sherry, and Helen Small. Two heroic editors—Adrian Poole and my father—gave the manuscript their undivided attention and critiqued it with honesty and compassion. Dorothy McCarthy provided eagle-eyed copy-editing. My gratitude to all these readers knows no bounds.

Many people helped me along the way by offering guidance and good cheer. My heartfelt thanks goes out to all of them, especially to Hilton Als, Joyce Arregui, Laura Ashe, Alex and Tooda Attwood, Ros Ballaster, Celeste-Marie Bernier, Donald 'Field' Brown, Stephen Blundell, Rachel Calder, Sarah Churchwell, Georgia Cohen, Susanna Cohen, Robin Crawford, Daniel Crofts, Margaret de Vaux, Eileen Myles, Robert Douglas-Fairhurst, Simone Dubois, Merve Emre, Sarah, Jason and Gail Emsley, Denis Flannery, Eric Foner, Geoff Fox, Jonathan Freedman, Julian Gewirtz, Lyndall Gordon, Terry Greenwood, Andrew Higgins, John Hood, Hal Jones, Caroline Jowett, Helena Kennedy, Victoria and Joe Klein, Hermione Lee, Christopher Looby, Eric Lott, Laura Marcus, Heather May, Derek McCormack, Jamie McCrone, Jim McCue, Victoria McGuinness, Rebecca N. Mitchell, Katie Murphy, Nikki Mihalopoulous, Lisa Miller, Eileen Myles, Emily Nacol, Nadine, Dirk, Johanna, Lena, and Selma Neumayer, Supha Prawatto-Mandel, Peter Raby, Claudia Rothermere, Lucinda Rumsey, Carol Sanger, Michael Seeney, Jay Sexton, Kirsten Shepherd-Barr, Elaine Showalter, Tom Spasic, Isa Tozzi, Anne Vial, Elisabeth Wadge, Errollyn Wallen, Alun Ward, and Machilu Zimba. *The Making of Oscar Wilde* is dedicated with love to my family because they have always made the impossible feel possible.

Permissions and Picture Credits

The publisher and the author would like to thank the following for permission to quote from copyrighted materials:

Her Majesty Queen Elizabeth II and the Royal Archives, Windsor Castle; Merlin Holland; HarperCollins Publishers Ltd; Houghton Library, Harvard University; University of Illinois Press; Edwin Mellen Press; William Andrews Clark Memorial Library, University of California, Los Angeles.

PICTURE CREDITS

1. The William Andrews Clark Memorial Library, University of California, Los Angeles
2. Merlin Holland Image Collection
3. Merlin Holland Image Collection
4. Merlin Holland Image Collection
5. Merlin Holland Image Collection
6. Merlin Holland Image Collection
7. Merlin Holland Image Collection
8. Merlin Holland Image Collection
9. The Bodleian Library University of Oxford, G.A. Oxon 4° 414 (v.3), p. 533
10. Houghton Library, Harvard University, MS Thr 556 (33)
11. Harry Ransom Center, The University of Texas at Austin
12. Pictorial Press Ltd/Alamy Stock Photo
13. National Library of Australia, CDC-10615454
14. Lester S. Levy Collection of Sheet Music, Sheridan Libraries, Johns Hopkins University
15. Merlin Holland Image Collection
16. Merlin Holland Image Collection
17. Merlin Holland Image Collection
18. Merlin Holland Image Collection
19. Merlin Holland Image Collection

20. Lester S. Levy Collection of Sheet Music, Sheridan Libraries, Johns Hopkins University
21. Merlin Holland Image Collection
22. *Washington Post*, 22 January 1882, p. 4
23. New York Historical Society/Bridgeman Images
24. National Library of Australia, CDC-10615455
25. Library of Congress, Prints and Photographs Division
26. Merlin Holland Image Collection
27. Merlin Holland Image Collection
28. Merlin Holland Image Collection
29. Granger Historical Picture Archive/Alamy Stock Photo
30. Michael Seeney Collection
31. Harvard Theatre Collection, HTC Photographs 1.640, Houghton Library, Harvard University
32. Houghton Library, Harvard University, MS Thr 556 (430)
33. Museum of the City of New York, USA/Bridgeman Images
34. Houghton Library, Harvard University, MS Thr 556 (25)
35. Houghton Library, Harvard University, MS Thr 556 (52)
36. Houghton Library, Harvard University, US 102.9.2
37. Merlin Holland Image Collection
38. Michael Seeney Collection
39. Michael Seeney Collection
40. Merlin Holland Image Collection
41. Merlin Holland Image Collection
42. Merlin Holland Image Collection
43. Houghton Library, Harvard University, MS Thr 556 (430)
44. National Library of Australia, CDC-10615456
45. Michael Seeney Collection
46. Newspapers.com
47. Museum of the City of New York, USA/Bridgeman Images
48. The Pope Family Trust

Index